THE ENCYCLOPEDIA OF
TAPAS

THE ENCYCLOPEDIA OF
TAPAS

400 SMALL PLATES
FOR ALL OCCASIONS

CIDER MILL
PRESS

BOOK
PUBLISHERS

The Encyclopedia of Tapas

● 13-Digit ISBN: 978-1-64643-343-8 ● 10-Digit ISBN: 1-64643-343-2 ● This book may be ordered by mail from the publisher. Please include $5.99 for postage and handling. Please support your local bookseller first! ● Books published by Cider Mill Press Book Publishers are available at special discounts for bulk purchases in the United States by corporations, institutions, and other organizations. For more information, please contact the publisher. ● Cider Mill Press Book Publishers ● "Where good books are ready for press" ● 501 Nelson Place ● Nashville, Tennessee 37214 ● cidermillpress.com ● Typography: Hansief, Freight Sans, Freight Serif ● Image credits: Pages 28, 31, 38, 59, 63, 64, 79, 82, 96, 104–105, 114–115, 122–123, 125, 145, 146, 154, 157, 161, 180–181, 196–197, 201, 204–205, 214–215, 222, 237, 242, 253, 254, 257, 264, 272, 278, 306–307, 311, 324, 328–329, 331, 336–337, 343, 344, 347, 348, 353, 366, 372, 393, 400, 412–413, 415, 426–427, 433, 438–439, 445, 446, 450–451, 454–455, 457, 458, 461, 467, 477, 480–481, 482, 499, 502, 505, 508, 517, 518, and 544–545 courtesy of Cider Mill Press. All other images used under official license from Shutterstock ● Printed in China ● 23 24 25 26 27 TYC 5 4 3 2 1

CONTENTS

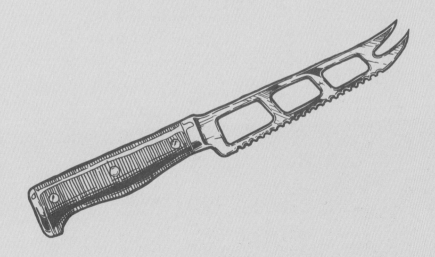

INTRODUCTION

When you order a drink at any bar in Spain, the response from the bartender will always be the same: "Do you want a snack to go along with it?" Essentially, that's what a tapa is, a snack to pair with a beverage.

Tapa means "cover" in Spanish, and it developed into an epithet for snacks due to an ancient custom. Legend holds that taverns and inns used to cover beer and wine glasses with a piece of bread or a slice of ham to prevent flies or dust from entering the glass. What began as bread, cheese, and/or ham then evolved into more elaborate preparations, and eventually into larger portions that can function as everything from an appetizer to an entree.

These evolutions helped turn tapas into a global phenomenon, and also provided them with a new sobriquet: small plates. This surge into the spotlight was powered by innovative chefs who saw that these smaller spaces allowed for tremendous experimentation, enabling dishes that were more daring in terms of taste and texture—since, if someone happened to find it unpleasant, it was only a few bites that would be pushed aside rather than a whole dish—and

opened up a world of ingredients, including some costly and/or rare items that would be unthinkable of executing at the scale of an entree. When this approach is done correctly, the results can be nothing short of astounding. As anyone who has eaten at The French Laundry or Manresa can attest, a steady stream of small plates issued over the course of 2 to 3 hours has the potential to be the meal of a lifetime.

The prospect of offering a series of small bites is not only appealing for the chef, but also the customer. First, it eliminates the very real anxiety over making the wrong choice. Second, this style of eating is in line with the way our favorite evenings with family and friends tend to unfold, those moments where the combination of conversation, food, and drink keep shaping an occasion in surprising and delightful ways. At these times, we do not want to be weighed down by formality and ponderous dishes. Instead, we want something small, light, and delicious that can be consumed without sapping any of the energy and excitement present.

Obviously, a meal composed of tapas has massive upside. But, believe it or not, there is a downside, one that has given them something of a bad reputation in certain corners. The presence of this grey cloud is due to the less-capable chefs who have come to rely too heavily upon them, interested more in profit margin or Instagram opportunities than on satisfying their customers. This development has caused a number of diners to walk away from a table with their wallets lighter than ever, but without the satisfaction one would expect from such expenditures.

This book intends to take the small plate back from these misguided few and put all of its considerable potential in your hands.

We start with that category of foods that were likely the very first tapas ever served—breads, flatbreads, and crackers. These offerings remain a crucial piece of any encounter with small plates—simple and delicious enough that they need nothing else, but which become heavenly when paired with a nice wedge of cheese, some cold cuts and/or cured meats, and a flavorful spread. This latter item, along with dips and sauces, make up the next chapter. Of course, they will have to be prepared along with some other dish, but they are a wonderful spot for odds and ends and herbs plucked fresh from the garden, and also have the advantage of being ready in a flash.

That simple start leads into the chapters containing the more substantial (and thus more modern) preparations, those centered around meat, seafood, and vegetables, and pulled from cuisines all over the world. We recommend mixing and matching the recipes in these sections liberally in order to experience the exhilarating and intoxicating atmosphere that a spread composed entirely of tapas can create.

Finally, there is a chapter devoted to the decadent—recipes featuring cheese, nuts, and confections—since they are welcome at most every occasion, and can be counted on to conclude an evening on a pleasant note.

All of that, gathered in one place. No more flipping incessantly through food blogs, websites, and your shelves of cookbooks—the next time you're looking to dazzle a crowd, or take the edge off with something quick and comforting the following day, pick up this book, and remember: it's the little things that count.

BREADS, FLATBREADS, CRACKERS & CHIPS

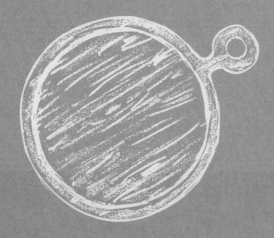

Challah

YIELD: 1 LOAF | **ACTIVE TIME:** 1 HOUR | **TOTAL TIME:** 5 HOURS

1½ CUPS LUKEWARM WATER (90ºF)

1 TABLESPOON PLUS 2 TEASPOONS ACTIVE DRY YEAST

4 EGGS, 1 BEATEN

¼ CUP EXTRA-VIRGIN OLIVE OIL

7 CUPS BREAD FLOUR, PLUS MORE AS NEEDED

¼ CUP SUGAR

1½ TABLESPOONS KOSHER SALT

1. Place the water and yeast in the work bowl of a stand mixer and gently whisk to combine. Let the mixture sit until it starts to foam, about 10 minutes.

2. Fit the mixer with the dough hook, add the 3 unbeaten eggs, oil, flour, sugar, and salt to the work bowl, and work the mixture on low until it comes together as a dough, about 2 minutes.

3. Raise the speed to medium and knead until the dough becomes elastic and starts to pull away from the side of the bowl, about 6 minutes.

4. Cover the mixing bowl with a kitchen towel, place it in a naturally warm spot, and let the dough rise until it has doubled in size.

5. Place the dough on a flour-dusted work surface and punch it down. Divide the dough into four pieces that are each 12.7 oz. Shape the pieces into ovals, cover with linen towels, and let them rest for 15 to 30 minutes.

6. Preheat the oven to 350ºF. Line a baking sheet with parchment paper.

7. Using the palms of your hands, gently roll the dough into strands that are about 2 feet long.

8. Take the strands and fan them out so that one end of each of them is touching. Press down on the ends where they are touching. Take the right-most strand (Strand 1) and cross it over to the left so that it is horizontal. Take the left-most strand (Strand 2) and cross it over to the right so that it is horizontal.

9. Move Strand 1 between the two strands that have yet to move. Move the strand to the right of Strand 1 to the left so that it is horizontal. This will be known as Strand 3.

10. Move Strand 2 between Strand 1 and Strand 4. Move Strand 4 to the right so that it is horizontal.

11. Repeat moving the horizontal strands to the middle and replacing them with the opposite, outer strands until the entire loaf is braided. Pinch the ends of the loaf together and tuck them under the bread.

12. Brush the dough with the beaten egg. If you want to top the bread with poppy seeds, sesame seeds, or herbs, now is the time to sprinkle them over the top.

13. Place the bread in the oven and bake it until golden brown, about 30 minutes. The cooked challah should have an internal temperature of 210ºF.

14. Remove the challah from the oven, place it on a wire rack, and let it cool completely before enjoying.

Sourdough Starter

YIELD: 2 CUPS | **ACTIVE TIME:** 2 HOURS | **TOTAL TIME:** 2 WEEKS

1 CUP WATER, AT ROOM
TEMPERATURE, PLUS MORE
DAILY

2 CUPS ALL-PURPOSE
FLOUR, PLUS MORE DAILY

1. Place the water and flour in a large jar (the jar should be at least 1 quart). Combine the ingredients by hand, cover the jar, and let it stand in a sunny spot at room temperature for 24 hours.

2. Place 1 cup of the starter in a bowl, add 1 cup water and 2 cups all-purpose flour, and stir until thoroughly combined. Discard the remainder of the starter. Place the new mixture back in the jar and let it sit at room temperature for 24 hours. Repeat this process every day until you notice bubbles forming in the starter. This should take approximately 2 weeks.

3. Once the starter begins to bubble, it can be used in recipes. The starter can be stored at room temperature or in the refrigerator. If the starter is kept at room temperature it must be fed once a day; if the starter is refrigerated it can be fed every 3 days. The starter can be frozen for up to a month without feeding.

4. To feed the starter, place 1 cup of the starter in a bowl, add 1 cup flour and 1 cup water, and work the mixture with your hands until combined. Discard the remainder of the starter. It is recommended that you feed the starter 6 to 8 hours before making bread.

Sourdough Bread

YIELD: 1 LOAF | **ACTIVE TIME:** 1 HOUR AND 30 MINUTES | **TOTAL TIME:** 24 HOURS

1 CUP WATER, AT ROOM TEMPERATURE

3⅓ CUPS BREAD FLOUR, PLUS MORE AS NEEDED

⅓ CUP WHOLE WHEAT FLOUR

1 CUP SOURDOUGH STARTER (SEE OPPOSITE PAGE)

2 TEASPOONS KOSHER SALT

1. Place the water and flours in the work bowl of a stand mixer fitted with the dough hook and work the mixture at low speed for 6 minutes. Remove the bowl from the mixer and cover it with plastic wrap. Let the dough sit at room temperature for 1 hour to allow the dough to autolyse.

2. Place the work bowl back on the mixer and add the starter and salt. Knead the mixture at low speed until the dough starts to come together, about 2 minutes. Increase the speed to medium and knead until the dough is elastic and pulls away from the side of the bowl.

3. Dust a 9-inch banneton (proofing basket) with flour. Shape the dough into a ball and place it in the proofing basket, seam side down. Cover the bread with plastic wrap and let it sit on the counter for 2 hours.

4. Place the basket in the refrigerator and let it rest overnight.

5. Preheat the oven to 450°F and place a baking stone on a rack positioned in the middle.

6. Dust a peel with flour and gently turn the bread onto the peel so that the seam is facing up.

7. With a very sharp knife, carefully score the dough just off center. Make sure the knife is at a 45-degree angle to the dough.

8. Gently slide the sourdough onto the baking stone. Spray the oven with 5 spritzes of water and bake the bread for 20 minutes.

9. Open the oven, spray the oven with 5 more spritzes, and bake until the crust is golden brown, about 20 minutes. The internal temperature of the bread should be at minimum 210°F. Remove the bread from the oven, place it on a wire rack, and let it cool completely before slicing.

Sourdough Bread
SEE PAGE 17

Brioche

YIELD: 2 LOAVES | **ACTIVE TIME:** 45 MINUTES | **TOTAL TIME:** 4 HOURS

FOR THE SPONGE

½ CUP MILK, WARMED

4½ TEASPOONS ACTIVE DRY YEAST

2 TABLESPOONS HONEY

4 OZ. BREAD FLOUR

FOR THE DOUGH

5 EGGS, 1 BEATEN

2 OZ. SUGAR

1 LB. BREAD FLOUR

2 TEASPOONS KOSHER SALT

4 OZ. UNSALTED BUTTER, SOFTENED

1. To prepare the sponge, place all the ingredients in the work bowl of a stand mixer. Cover with plastic wrap and let the mixture sit until it starts to bubble, about 30 minutes.

2. To begin preparations for the dough, add the 4 unbeaten eggs to the sponge and whisk until incorporated.

3. Add the sugar, flour, and salt, fit the mixer with the dough hook, and knead the mixture on low speed for 5 minutes.

4. Over the course of 2 minutes, add the butter a little at a time with the mixer running. When all of the butter has been added, knead the mixture on low for 5 minutes.

5. Raise the speed to medium and knead the dough until it begins to pull away from the side of the work bowl, about 6 minutes. Cover the bowl with a kitchen towel, place the dough in a naturally warm spot, and let it rise until it has doubled in size, about 1 hour.

6. Preheat the oven to 350ºF. Coat two 8 x 4–inch loaf pans with nonstick cooking spray.

7. Divide the dough into two equal pieces and flatten each one into a rectangle the width of a loaf pan. Tuck in the sides to form the dough into loaf shapes and place one in each pan, seam side down.

8. Cover the pans with plastic wrap and let the dough rise until it has crested over the tops of the pans.

9. Brush the loaves with the beaten egg, place them in the oven, and bake until golden brown, 35 to 45 minutes. The loaves should reach an internal temperature of 200ºF.

10. Remove them from the oven, place the pans on a wire rack, and let them cool before enjoying.

Black Sesame Sourdough Bread

YIELD: 1 LOAF | **ACTIVE TIME:** 1 HOUR AND 30 MINUTES | **TOTAL TIME:** 24 HOURS

1 CUP WATER, AT ROOM TEMPERATURE

3⅓ CUPS BREAD FLOUR, PLUS MORE AS NEEDED

⅓ CUP WHOLE WHEAT FLOUR

½ CUP BLACK TAHINI PASTE

1 CUP SOURDOUGH STARTER (SEE PAGE 16)

2 TEASPOONS KOSHER SALT

1 CUP BLACK SESAME SEEDS

1. Place the water and flours in the work bowl of a stand mixer fitted with the dough hook and work the mixture at low speed for 6 minutes. Remove the bowl from the mixer and cover it with plastic wrap. Let the dough sit at room temperature for 1 hour to allow the dough to autolyse.

2. Place the work bowl back on the mixer and add the black tahini paste, starter, and salt. Knead the mixture at low speed until the dough starts to come together, about 2 minutes. Increase the speed to medium and knead until the dough is elastic and pulls away from the side of the bowl.

3. Place the sesame seeds on a plate. Shape the dough into a ball and spray the seam side with water. Roll the top of the dough in the sesame seeds until coated.

4. Dust a 9-inch banneton (proofing basket) with flour. Place the dough in the proofing basket, seeded side down. Cover the bread with plastic wrap and let it sit on the counter for 2 hours.

5. Place the basket in the refrigerator and let it rest overnight.

6. Preheat the oven to 450°F and place a baking stone on a rack positioned in the middle.

7. Dust a peel with flour and gently turn the bread onto the peel so that the seeded side is facing up.

8. With a very sharp knife, carefully score the dough just off center. Make sure the knife is at a 45-degree angle to the dough.

9. Gently slide the sourdough onto the baking stone. Spray the oven with 5 spritzes of water and bake the bread for 20 minutes.

10. Open the oven, spray the oven with 5 more spritzes, and bake until the crust is golden brown, about 20 minutes. The internal temperature of the bread should be at minimum 210°F. Remove the bread from the oven, place it on a wire rack, and let it cool completely before slicing.

Focaccia

YIELD: 18 x 13–INCH FOCACCIA | **ACTIVE TIME:** 45 MINUTES | **TOTAL TIME:** 4 HOURS

FOR THE POOLISH

3¼ CUPS WATER

2 TABLESPOONS ACTIVE DRY YEAST

½ CUP SUGAR

½ CUP PLUS 2 TABLESPOONS EXTRA-VIRGIN OLIVE OIL

FOR THE DOUGH

28 OZ. BREAD FLOUR

20 OZ. ALL-PURPOSE FLOUR

2 TABLESPOONS FINELY CHOPPED FRESH ROSEMARY

1 TABLESPOON FINELY CHOPPED FRESH THYME

2 TABLESPOONS FINELY CHOPPED FRESH BASIL

3 TABLESPOONS KOSHER SALT

1½ TEASPOONS BLACK PEPPER

1½ CUPS EXTRA-VIRGIN OLIVE OIL, PLUS MORE AS NEEDED

1 CUP FRESHLY SHAVED PARMESAN CHEESE

1. To prepare the poolish, place all the ingredients in a mixing bowl and whisk to combine. Cover the bowl with a linen towel and let it sit at room temperature for 30 minutes.

2. To begin preparations for the dough, place the poolish in the work bowl of a stand mixer fitted with the dough hook. Add all the remaining ingredients, except for the olive oil and Parmesan, and work the mixture on low for 1 minute. Raise the speed to medium and knead the mixture until it comes together as a smooth dough, about 5 minutes. Cover the bowl with a linen towel and let the dough rise until it has doubled in size.

3. Preheat the oven to 350ºF.

4. Coat an 18 x 13–inch baking sheet with olive oil and place the dough on the pan. Use your fingers to gradually stretch the dough until it fills the entire pan and is as even as possible. If the dough is difficult to stretch, let it rest for 10 minutes before resuming.

5. Cover the dough with plastic wrap and let it rise at room temperature until it has doubled in size.

6. Use your fingertips to gently press down on the dough and make dimples all over it. The dimples should go about halfway down. Drizzle about 1 cup of olive oil over the focaccia and sprinkle the Parmesan on top.

7. Place the focaccia in the oven and bake until it is a light golden brown, 20 to 30 minutes.

8. Remove the focaccia from the oven and brush it generously with olive oil. Let it cool slightly before slicing and serving.

Popovers

YIELD: 12 POPOVERS | **ACTIVE TIME:** 15 MINUTES | **TOTAL TIME:** 35 MINUTES

1½ CUPS MILK

3 EGGS

6.3 OZ. ALL-PURPOSE FLOUR

½ TEASPOON FINE SEA SALT

2 TABLESPOONS UNSALTED BUTTER, MELTED

1. Preheat the oven to 450°F. Place the milk and eggs in a bowl and whisk until you cannot see any sign of the egg yolk. Whisk briskly, until the mixture is nice and foamy. This will help the dough rise.

2. Whisk in the flour and salt, making sure there are no large lumps. Stir in the melted butter.

3. Coat a popover pan with nonstick cooking spray. Place it in the oven for 2 minutes right before you are going to add the batter. After 2 minutes, fill the cups up three-quarters of the way with the batter.

4. Place the pan in the oven and bake for 20 minutes. Reduce the temperature to 350°F and bake for another 20 minutes, checking to make sure the popovers don't get too brown on top. If they begin to get too dark, place your pan on a baking sheet and move it to a lower rack in the oven.

5. Remove the popovers from the oven, immediately turn them out of the pan, and enjoy.

Corn Tortillas

YIELD: 32 TORTILLAS | **ACTIVE TIME:** 30 MINUTES | **TOTAL TIME:** 30 MINUTES

1 LB. MASA HARINA

1½ TABLESPOONS KOSHER SALT

3 CUPS WARM FILTERED WATER, PLUS MORE AS NEEDED

1. In the work bowl of stand mixer fitted with the paddle attachment, combine the masa harina and salt. With the mixer on low speed, slowly begin to add the water. The mixture should come together as a soft, smooth dough. You want the masa to be moist enough so that when a small ball of it is pressed flat in your hands the edges do not crack. Also, the masa should not stick to your hands when you peel it off your palm.

2. Let the masa rest for 10 minutes and check the hydration again. You may need to add more water, depending on environmental conditions.

3. Warm a cast-iron skillet over high heat. Portion the masa into 1-ounce balls and cover them with a damp linen towel.

4. Line a tortilla press with two 8-inch circles of plastic. You can use a grocery store bag, a resealable bag, or even a standard kitchen trash bag as a source for the plastic. Place a ball of masa in the center of one circle and gently push down on it with the palm of one hand to flatten it. Place the other plastic circle on top and then close the tortilla press, applying firm, even pressure to flatten the masa into a round tortilla.

5. Open the tortilla press and remove the top layer of plastic. Carefully pick up the tortilla and remove the bottom piece of plastic.

6. Gently lay the tortilla flat in the pan, taking care to not wrinkle it. Cook for 15 to 30 seconds, until the edges begin to lift up slightly. Turn the tortilla over and let it cook for 30 to 45 seconds before turning it over one last time. If the hydration of the masa was correct and the heat is high enough, the tortilla should puff up and inflate. Remove the tortilla from the pan and store in a tortilla warmer lined with a linen towel. Repeat until all of the prepared masa has been made into tortillas.

Steamed Buns

YIELD: 12 BUNS | **ACTIVE TIME:** 20 MINUTES | **TOTAL TIME:** 1 HOUR AND 30 MINUTES

1 TEASPOON ACTIVE DRY YEAST

3 TABLESPOONS WATER, AT ROOM TEMPERATURE

1 CUP BREAD FLOUR, PLUS MORE AS NEEDED

4 TEASPOONS SUGAR

2 TEASPOONS NONFAT DRY MILK POWDER

1 TEASPOON KOSHER SALT

1/8 TEASPOON BAKING POWDER

1/8 TEASPOON BAKING SODA

4 TEASPOONS VEGETABLE SHORTENING, PLUS MORE AS NEEDED

1. Place the yeast and water in the work bowl of a stand mixer fitted with the dough hook, gently stir the mixture, and let it sit until it becomes foamy, about 10 minutes.

2. Add the remaining ingredients to the work bowl and knead the mixture on low speed until it comes together as a smooth dough, about 10 minutes. Cover the bowl with a kitchen towel and let the dough rise in a naturally warm spot until it has doubled in size, about 45 minutes.

3. Place the dough on a flour-dusted work surface and cut it into 12 pieces. Roll them into balls, cover them with plastic wrap, and let them rise for 30 minutes.

4. Cut a dozen 4-inch squares of parchment paper. Roll each ball into a 4-inch oval. Grease a chopstick with shortening, gently press the chopstick into the middle of each oval, and fold the dough over the chopstick to create a bun. Place each bun on a square of parchment paper and let them rest for 30 minutes. To cook the buns, follow the instructions on page 228.

Coques

YIELD: 2 FLATBREADS | **ACTIVE TIME:** 45 MINUTES | **TOTAL TIME:** 24 HOURS

FOR THE DOUGH

½ CUP BREAD FLOUR, PLUS MORE AS NEEDED

1 CUP WHOLE WHEAT FLOUR

2 TEASPOONS SUGAR

½ TEASPOON INSTANT YEAST

½ CUP PLUS 2 TABLESPOONS WARM WATER (105°F)

1 TABLESPOON EXTRA-VIRGIN OLIVE OIL, PLUS MORE AS NEEDED

1 TEASPOON FINE SEA SALT

FOR THE TOPPING

¼ CUP EXTRA-VIRGIN OLIVE OIL

1 RED ONION, HALVED AND SLICED THIN

1¼ CUPS THINLY SLICED ROASTED RED PEPPERS

1 TABLESPOON SUGAR

1 TEASPOON DRIED OREGANO

2 GARLIC CLOVES, MINCED

PINCH OF RED PEPPER FLAKES

1 TABLESPOON SHERRY VINEGAR

⅓ CUP PINE NUTS

SALT AND PEPPER, TO TASTE

¼ CUP FRESH CHOPPED PARSLEY, FOR GARNISH

1. To begin preparations for the dough, place all of the ingredients in the work bowl of a stand mixer fitted with the dough hook and work the mixture on low until it comes together as a smooth dough. Increase the speed to medium and work the dough until it no longer sticks to the side of the bowl.

2. Coat a bowl with olive oil. Dust a work surface with bread flour. Place the dough on the work surface and knead it for 30 seconds. Form the dough into a ball and place it, seam side down, in the bowl. Cover the bowl with plastic wrap and place it in the refrigerator to chill overnight.

3. To begin preparations for the topping, place 2 tablespoons of the olive oil in a skillet and warm it over medium heat. Add the onion, peppers, and sugar and cook, stirring occasionally, until the onion and peppers are golden brown, about 10 minutes. Add the oregano, garlic, and red pepper flakes and cook, stirring continually, for 1 minute. Stir in the vinegar and pine nuts, season the mixture with salt and pepper, and remove the pan from heat. Let the mixture cool.

4. Remove the dough from the refrigerator and let it sit at room temperature for 1 hour.

5. Preheat the oven to 450°F. Line two baking sheets with parchment paper. Divide the dough in half and place it on a flour-dusted work surface. Roll them out into 12 x 4–inch rectangles. Brush the coques with olive oil and prick them all over with a fork.

6. Place the coques on the baking sheets, place them in the oven, and bake for 6 minutes. Remove the coques from the oven, brush them with the remaining olive oil, and distribute the pepper-and-onion mixture over the top.

7. Return the coques to the oven and bake until the pine nuts and edges are golden brown, about 10 minutes, rotating the pans halfway through. Remove the coques from the oven and let them cool for 5 minutes. Garnish with the parsley and enjoy.

Pides

YIELD: 4 PIDES | **ACTIVE TIME:** 45 MINUTES | **TOTAL TIME:** 1 HOUR AND 30 MINUTES

FOR THE DOUGH

2 CUPS PLUS 2 TABLESPOONS BREAD FLOUR, PLUS MORE AS NEEDED

1 TEASPOON SUGAR

¼ TEASPOON INSTANT YEAST

⅔ CUP PLUS 2 TABLESPOONS WARM WATER (105°F)

1 TEASPOON FINE SEA SALT

2 TEASPOONS EXTRA-VIRGIN OLIVE OIL, PLUS MORE AS NEEDED

FOR THE FILLING

¼ CUP EXTRA-VIRGIN OLIVE OIL

4 CUPS DICED EGGPLANT (¼-INCH CUBES)

2 TABLESPOONS WHITE WINE

1 ONION, CHOPPED

½ RED BELL PEPPER, DICED

2 GARLIC CLOVES, MINCED

⅛ TEASPOON RED PEPPER FLAKES

½ TEASPOON PAPRIKA

1 (28 OZ.) CAN OF WHOLE PEELED SAN MARZANO TOMATOES, DRAINED

SALT AND PEPPER, TO TASTE

1 CUP CRUMBLED FETA CHEESE

1 TEASPOON MALDON SEA SALT

FRESH MINT, CHOPPED, FOR GARNISH

1. To begin preparations for the dough, place all of the ingredients in the work bowl of a stand mixer fitted with the dough hook attachment and work the mixture on low until it comes together as a smooth dough. Increase the speed to medium and work the dough until it no longer sticks to the side of the bowl.

2. Coat a bowl with olive oil. Place the dough on a flour-dusted work surface and knead it for 2 minutes. Form the dough into a ball and place it, seam side down, in the greased bowl. Cover the bowl with a linen towel and let the dough rise in a naturally warm spot until it has doubled in size, about 1 hour.

3. To begin preparations for the filling, place 2 tablespoons of the olive oil in a large saucepan and warm it over medium heat. Add the eggplant and cook, stirring occasionally, until it has browned and is soft, about 5 minutes. Stir in the wine, remove the pan from heat, and set the eggplant aside.

4. Place 1 tablespoon of the olive oil in a clean large saucepan and warm it over medium heat. Add the onion and pepper and cook, stirring occasionally, until they have softened, about 5 minutes. Add the garlic, red pepper flakes, and paprika and cook, stirring continually, for 1 minute.

5. Add the tomatoes and bring the mixture to a boil. Reduce the heat and simmer the mixture until the tomatoes start to collapse, about 10 minutes, mashing the tomatoes with a wooden spoon as they cook.

6. Stir in the eggplant and cook until warmed through. Season the mixture with salt and pepper, remove the pan from heat, and let the mixture cool.

7. Preheat the oven to 450°F. Line two baking sheets with parchment paper. Cut four 12 x 4–inch strips of parchment paper. Divide the dough into four pieces and place each one on a piece of parchment paper. Roll out the dough until each piece extends ½ inch over the strips of parchment on all sides.

8. Spread the eggplant mixture over the pieces of dough, leaving a 1 inch border on the sides. Sprinkle the crumbled feta over the eggplant mixture and brush the border of dough with some of the remaining olive oil.

9. Fold each side toward the center, leaving about a 1 inch of the filling exposed. Pinch the bottoms of the pides to secure them, brush the dough with some of the remaining olive oil, and sprinkle the Maldon sea salt over the top.

10. Place the pides in the oven and bake until the edges are crispy and golden brown, about 12 minutes. Remove the pides from the oven and let them cool slightly before enjoying.

Lavash

YIELD: 10 SERVINGS | **ACTIVE TIME:** 30 MINUTES | **TOTAL TIME:** 2 HOURS

FOR THE LAVASH

7 TABLESPOONS WARM WATER (105°F)

7 TABLESPOONS MILK, WARMED

2 TEASPOONS EXTRA-VIRGIN OLIVE OIL, PLUS MORE AS NEEDED

¼ TEASPOON SUGAR

½ TEASPOON FINE SEA SALT

1½ TEASPOONS ACTIVE DRY YEAST

1¾ CUPS ALL-PURPOSE FLOUR, PLUS MORE AS NEEDED FOR THE TOPPING

FOR THE TOPPING

1 TABLESPOON EXTRA-VIRGIN OLIVE OIL

2 CUPS CHOPPED EGGPLANT

½ RED BELL PEPPER, SLICED THIN

2 GARLIC CLOVES, MINCED

1 TABLESPOON TOMATO PASTE

½ TEASPOON RED PEPPER FLAKES

2 CUPS ARUGULA

½ CUP GREEN OLIVES, PITS REMOVED AND SLICED THIN

SALT AND PEPPER, TO TASTE

½ CUP FRESHLY GRATED PARMESAN CHEESE

1. To begin preparations for the lavash, place all of the ingredients in the work bowl of a stand mixer fitted with the dough hook and mix on low speed until the mixture comes together as a dough. Raise the speed to medium and work the dough for about 10 minutes, until it no longer sticks to the side of the work bowl.

2. Remove the dough from the work bowl and place it on a flour-dusted work surface. Knead the dough by hand for 2 minutes. Coat a bowl with olive oil and place the dough in it, seam side down. Cover the dough with plastic wrap and let it sit in a naturally warm spot until it has doubled in size, about 1 hour.

3. Line a baking sheet with parchment paper. Divide the dough into 10 pieces, shape each one into a ball, and place the balls on the baking sheet. Cover the dough with a linen towel and let it rest for 10 minutes.

4. Warm a cast-iron skillet over medium-high heat. Working with one ball of dough at a time, place the dough on a flour-dusted work surface and roll it out into a 6-inch circle. Place the dough in the dry skillet, reduce the heat to medium, and cook until it starts to bubble and brown around the edge, about 2 minutes. Turn the lavash over and cook for another minute. Remove the cooked lavash from the pan, place them on a wire rack, and let them cool.

5. Preheat the oven to 450°F. To begin preparations for the topping, warm a large cast-iron skillet over medium heat. Add the olive oil and eggplant and cook, stirring occasionally, until the eggplant starts to collapse, about 5 minutes. Add the bell pepper and cook, stirring occasionally, for another 5 minutes.

6. Add the garlic, tomato paste, and red pepper flakes and cook, stirring continually, for 1 minute. Add the arugula and cook, stirring frequently, until it has wilted, about 2 minutes. Remove the pan from heat and fold in the olives. Season the mixture with salt and pepper and spread it over the lavash, leaving a ½ inch border around the edge.

Beet Chips

YIELD: 8 SERVINGS | **ACTIVE TIME:** 30 MINUTES | **TOTAL TIME:** 1 HOUR

4 CUPS CANOLA OIL

3 BEETS, RINSED WELL AND DRIED

SALT AND PEPPER, TO TASTE

1. Place the canola oil in a Dutch oven and warm it to 375°F. Line a baking sheet with paper towels and set a wire rack in it.

2. Cut the root end from the beets and use a mandoline to cut the beets into ⅛-inch-thick slices.

3. Working in batches to avoid crowding the pot, gently slip the beets into the hot oil and fry until they are browned and stop bubbling and sizzling, 3 to 4 minutes. Remove the chips with a slotted spoon, place them on the baking sheet, season them with salt and pepper, and let them cool—they will crisp up as they do. Serve once all of the beets have been fried.

Blueberry Scones

YIELD: 10 SCONES | **ACTIVE TIME:** 20 MINUTES | **TOTAL TIME:** 2 HOURS AND 30 MINUTES

1½ CUPS UNSALTED BUTTER

4½ CUPS ALL-PURPOSE FLOUR

¾ CUP SUGAR, PLUS MORE FOR TOPPING

2 TABLESPOONS BAKING POWDER

1 TEASPOON FINE SEA SALT

1 CUP FROZEN BLUEBERRIES

1½ CUPS COLD HEAVY WHIPPING CREAM, PLUS MORE AS NEEDED

1. Cut the butter into ½-inch cubes and chill it in the freezer for 45 minutes.

2. Place the flour, sugar, baking powder, and salt in a large bowl and whisk to combine.

3. Add the butter and work the mixture with your hands until it comes together in pea-sized clumps. Add the blueberries and toss until evenly distributed. Slowly drizzle in the cream and work the mixture until it is a smooth dough.

4. Pat the dough into a ¾-inch mound. Using a 3-inch ring cutter, cut scones out of the dough. Gently work any leftover dough back together and continue to cut scones until the dough runs out. Place the scones on a parchment-lined baking sheet and freeze them for 1 hour.

5. Preheat the oven to 375°F. Remove the scones from the freezer and brush their tops with heavy cream. Sprinkle sugar over the scones and place them in the oven. Bake until the scones are golden brown, 18 to 25 minutes. Remove them from the oven and let the scones cool briefly before enjoying.

Purple Potato Chips

YIELD: 6 SERVINGS | **ACTIVE TIME:** 5 MINUTES | **TOTAL TIME:** 20 MINUTES

3 LARGE PURPLE POTATOES, SLICED THIN

¼ CUP EXTRA-VIRGIN OLIVE OIL

2 TEASPOONS FINE SEA SALT

1. Preheat the oven to 400°F.

2. Place the potatoes, olive oil, and salt in a bowl and toss until the potatoes are evenly coated. Place the potatoes on a baking sheet in a single layer. Bake for 12 to 15 minutes, until crispy.

3. Remove from the oven and serve warm or store in an airtight container, where they will keep for up to 1 week.

Goat Cheese, Date & Pistachio Focaccia

YIELD: 8 SERVINGS | **ACTIVE TIME:** 10 MINUTES | **TOTAL TIME:** 20 MINUTES

FOCACCIA (SEE PAGE 22)

1 CUP WHIPPED GOAT CHEESE

¼ CUP CHOPPED DATES

¼ CUP PISTACHIOS, CHOPPED

POMEGRANATE MOLASSES, TO TASTE

1. Preheat the oven to 375ºF. Cut the Focaccia into squares, place them on a baking sheet, and place them in the oven. Toast until golden brown, 6 to 8 minutes.

2. Remove the toasted focaccia from the oven, spread the goat cheese over the top, and sprinkle the dates and pistachios over the goat cheese. Drizzle pomegranate molasses over the pieces of toasted focaccia and enjoy.

Avocado Toast

YIELD: 4 TO 6 SERVINGS | **ACTIVE TIME:** 15 MINUTES | **TOTAL TIME:** 15 MINUTES

¼ CUP CANNED CORN, DRAINED

4 TO 6 SLICES OF SOURDOUGH BREAD (SEE PAGE 17)

FLESH FROM 2 AVOCADOS, MASHED

CREMA OR SOUR CREAM, TO TASTE

FRESH CILANTRO, CHOPPED, FOR GARNISH

1. Warm a large cast-iron skillet over medium heat. Place the corn in the dry skillet and cook, stirring occasionally, until the corn is lightly charred, 6 to 10 minutes. Remove the pan from heat.

2. Place the slices of bread in a toaster and toast them until golden brown.

3. Spread the mashed avocado over the slices of toasted bread. Top each slice with a dollop of crema and the charred corn, and garnish with cilantro.

Short Rib & Rye Toast

YIELD: 4 TO 6 SERVINGS | **ACTIVE TIME:** 30 MINUTES | **TOTAL TIME:** 3 HOURS AND 30 MINUTES

1 LB. BEEF SHORT RIBS

SALT AND PEPPER, TO TASTE

2 TABLESPOONS CANOLA OIL

1 SMALL YELLOW ONION, CHOPPED

1 CARROT, PEELED AND CHOPPED

1 CELERY STALK, CHOPPED

2 GARLIC CLOVES, CRUSHED

1 TEASPOON DRIED THYME

½ CUP RED WINE

2 CUPS BEEF STOCK (SEE PAGE 553)

4 TO 6 SLICES OF MARBLE RYE BREAD

HORSERADISH CREAM (SEE PAGE 126), FOR SERVING

1. Season the short ribs with salt and pepper and let them sit at room temperature for 1 hour.

2. Place the canola oil in a Dutch oven and warm it over medium-high heat. Add the short ribs to the pot and sear until they are browned all over, turning them as they cook. Remove the short ribs from the pot and set them aside.

3. Add the onion, carrot, celery, garlic, and thyme to the pot and cook, stirring frequently, until the vegetables have softened and are starting to caramelize, about 8 minutes.

4. Deglaze the pot with the red wine, scraping up any browned bits from the bottom. Return the short ribs to the pot and add the stock. Reduce the heat to medium-low, cover the Dutch oven, and braise the ribs until they are so tender that they start to fall apart, about 2½ hours.

5. Remove the short ribs from the pot and shred the meat with a fork. Place the bread in a toaster and toast until golden brown.

6. Top the slices of toasted bread with the short ribs. Top each portion with some of the Horseradish Cream and enjoy.

Grits Bread

YIELD: 1 LOAF | **ACTIVE TIME:** 4 HOURS | **TOTAL TIME:** 20 HOURS

FOR THE DOUGH

⅔ CUP GRITS, RINSED

17 OZ. WATER

4 OZ. UNSALTED BUTTER

1½ TABLESPOONS KOSHER SALT, PLUS MORE TO TASTE

2½ CUPS BUTTERMILK

18.2 OZ. BREAD FLOUR

3¾ OZ. WHOLE WHEAT FLOUR

FOR THE SOAKER

2¾ CUPS CORNMEAL

1¾ CUPS BUTTERMILK

FOR THE LEVAIN

½ CUP COLD WATER

½ CUP WHOLE WHEAT FLOUR

1. About 12 hours before you plan to start mixing, begin preparations for the dough. Place the grits and water in a medium saucepan and let the mixture sit at room temperature.

2. About 8 hours prior to mixing, prepare the soaker. Combine the ingredients in a mixing bowl, cover the bowl, and let it sit at room temperature.

3. Prepare the levain right after preparing the soaker. Combine the ingredients in a mixing bowl, cover the bowl, and let it sit at room temperature.

4. About 2 hours prior to mixing, bring the grits and water to a boil. Reduce the heat so that the grits simmer and cook, gently stirring occasionally, until the grits are tender. Stir in the butter, season the grits with salt to taste, remove the pan from heat, and let the grits cool.

5. Place 1¾ cups of the cooked grits, the soaker, the levain, the buttermilk, salt, and flours in the work bowl of a stand mixer fitted with the dough hook and work the mixture on low until it comes together as a rough, shaggy dough.

6. Cover the bowl with plastic wrap and place it in a naturally warm location. Let the dough rise for 4 hours, folding all of the sides of the dough into the center every 45 minutes.

7. Coat an 8 x 4-inch loaf pan with nonstick cooking spray and transfer the dough into it. Cover the dough with a linen towel and let it rise in a naturally warm spot until it is about ½ inch from the lip of the pan.

8. Preheat the oven to 450°F. Place a small baking sheet on the bottom rack of the oven.

9. Fill the baking sheet with water. Place the loaf pan on the top rack of the oven and bake until the top is a deep golden brown, about 1 hour. Remove the bread from the oven, place the pan on a wire rack, and let it cool completely before enjoying.

Tequeño

YIELD: 8 SERVINGS | **ACTIVE TIME:** 2 HOURS | **TOTAL TIME:** 16 HOURS

4 LARGE EGGS

¾ CUP PLUS ½ CUP WATER

2⅔ OZ. SUGAR

2 TABLESPOONS HONEY

1⅔ CUPS ALL-PURPOSE FLOUR

1 TEASPOON BAKING SODA

½ TEASPOON FINE SEA SALT

CANOLA OIL, AS NEEDED

7 OZ. PLANTAINS, CHOPPED

2 TEASPOONS CINNAMON, PLUS MORE FOR DUSTING

1. Place the eggs, ¾ cup of water, the sugar, and honey in a mixing bowl and stir to combine. Gradually add the flour, baking soda, and salt and stir until the mixture comes together as a smooth dough. Form the dough into a ball, coat a bowl lightly with canola oil, and place the dough in it. Cover the bowl with plastic wrap and let it rest in the refrigerator overnight.

2. Place the plantains, remaining water, and cinnamon in a saucepan and simmer over medium-low heat until the plantains are tender, about 15 minutes. Remove the pan from heat and let the mixture cool for 1½ hours. After 1½ hours, mash the plantains, place them in a piping bag fitted with a fine tip, and set it aside.

3. Remove the dough from the refrigerator and cut it into 20 pieces. Form the pieces into seamless balls, place them on a piece of parchment paper, and let them rest for 30 minutes.

4. Add canola oil to a Dutch oven until it is about 2 inches deep and warm it to 375ºF. Poke holes into the balls of dough and pipe some of the mashed plantains into each one.

5. Working in batches to avoid crowding the pot, gently slip the balls of dough into the hot oil and cook until they are golden brown all over, turning them as necessary. Transfer the fried bread to a paper towel–lined plate and let them drain.

6. Dust the fried bread with cinnamon and enjoy.

Sfincione Palermitano

YIELD: 1 LARGE FOCACCIA | **ACTIVE TIME:** 1 HOUR | **TOTAL TIME:** 4 HOURS AND 30 MINUTES

2½ TEASPOONS ACTIVE DRY YEAST OR 2 TEASPOONS INSTANT YEAST

22½ OZ. WATER

19¾ OZ. BREAD FLOUR, PLUS MORE AS NEEDED

8.4 OZ. FINE SEMOLINA FLOUR

1 TABLESPOON TABLE SALT, PLUS MORE TO TASTE

2 TABLESPOONS PLUS 2 TEASPOONS EXTRA-VIRGIN OLIVE OIL

2 ONIONS, SLICED

22.9 OZ. CRUSHED TOMATOES, WITH THEIR LIQUID

12 ANCHOVIES IN OLIVE OIL, DRAINED AND TORN

BLACK PEPPER, TO TASTE

1 LB. CACIOCAVALLO CHEESE, TWO-THIRDS CUBED, ONE-THIRD GRATED

FRESH OREGANO, CHOPPED, TO TASTE

BREAD CRUMBS, TO TASTE

1. If using active dry yeast, warm 3½ tablespoons of the water until it is about 105°F. Add the water and the yeast to a bowl and gently stir. Let the mixture sit until it is foamy, 5 to 10 minutes. Instant yeast does not need to be proofed.

2. In a large bowl, combine the flours, yeast, and water until the mixture comes together as a dough. If kneading by hand, transfer the dough to a flour-dusted work surface. Work the dough until it is compact, smooth, and elastic.

3. Add the salt and work the dough until it is developed, elastic, and extensible, about 5 minutes. Form the dough into a ball, place it in a bowl, and cover the bowl with a damp linen towel. Let it rest at room temperature until it has doubled in size, about 2 hours.

4. Coat the bottom of a skillet with olive oil and warm it over medium-low heat. When the oil starts to shimmer, add the onions and cook, stirring frequently, until they are starting to brown, about 12 minutes. Add the tomatoes and three of the anchovies, cover the skillet, reduce the heat, and simmer until the flavor is to your liking, 20 to 30 minutes. Season with salt and pepper and let cool completely.

5. Coat an 18 x 13–inch baking pan with olive oil, place the dough on the pan, and gently stretch it until it covers the entire pan. Cover the dough with plastic wrap and let it rest for 1 hour.

6. Preheat the oven to 430°F. Top the focaccia with the cubed caciocavallo and the remaining anchovies and press down on them until they are embedded in the dough. Cover with the tomato sauce, generously sprinkle oregano over the sauce, and drizzle olive oil over everything. Sprinkle the grated caciocavallo and a generous handful of bread crumbs over the focaccia.

7. Place it in the oven and bake for 20 minutes. Lower the temperature to 180°F and bake for another 15 to 20 minutes, until the focaccia is golden brown, both on the edges and on the bottom.

8. Remove the focaccia from the oven and let it cool slightly before serving.

Sesame Loaf

YIELD: 1 LOAF | **ACTIVE TIME:** 20 MINUTES | **TOTAL TIME:** 3 HOURS AND 50 MINUTES

1½ TEASPOONS ACTIVE DRY YEAST

9.3 OZ. WATER

11.8 OZ. BREAD FLOUR, PLUS MORE AS NEEDED

2.1 OZ. WHOLE WHEAT FLOUR

1½ TABLESPOONS EXTRA-VIRGIN OLIVE OIL

1½ TEASPOONS FINE SEA SALT

¼ CUP SESAME SEEDS

1. Combine the yeast and water in a bowl and gently stir to combine. Let the mixture sit until it starts to foam, about 10 minutes.

2. Place all of the ingredients, except for the salt and sesame seeds, in the work bowl of a stand mixer fitted with the dough hook and work the mixture at low speed until it comes together as a smooth dough. Add the salt, raise the speed to medium, and knead the dough until it is elastic and extensible. Place the dough in a clean mixing bowl, cover it with plastic wrap, and let it rest until it has doubled in size, about 1½ hours.

3. Spread the sesame seeds over the bottom of a loaf pan or oblong banneton and spray them with water. Invert the dough onto a flour-dusted work surface and shape it into a round. Gently fold the round to shape it into an oval. Place the loaf, seam side up, on top of the sesame seeds. Cover the loaf with a kitchen towel and let it rest until it has nearly doubled in size, 1 to 1½ hours.

4. Preheat the oven to 480°F. Place a baking stone or a baking sheet on the middle rack of the oven as it warms. Place another baking sheet on the bottom of the oven. Have a ½ cup of water ready to toss in this bottom sheet to create steam.

5. Invert the loaf onto a flat baking sheet or peel covered with parchment paper. Score the loaf with a sharp knife or scissors and load it onto the hot baking sheet or baking stone. Place the water in the baking sheet on the lower rack.

6. Reduce the oven's temperature immediately to 430°F and bake the bread for 15 minutes, then lower the temperature to 390°F and bake the bread until it is golden brown, 15 to 20 minutes.

7. Remove the bread from the oven and let it cool on a wire rack before slicing.

Chocolate & Hazelnut Sourdough Bread

YIELD: 1 LOAF | **ACTIVE TIME:** 30 MINUTES | **TOTAL TIME:** 5 HOURS AND 30 MINUTES

⅔ CUP BLANCHED HAZELNUTS

8½ OZ. WATER, AT ROOM TEMPERATURE

4.2 OZ. SOURDOUGH STARTER (SEE PAGE 16)

13.7 OZ. BREAD FLOUR, PLUS MORE AS NEEDED

1½ TEASPOONS FINE SEA SALT

3 TABLESPOONS UNSWEETENED COCOA POWDER

1. Preheat the oven to 390°F. Place the hazelnuts on a baking sheet, place them in the oven, and roast until lightly browned and fragrant, about 10 minutes. Remove the hazelnuts from the oven and let them cool completely.

2. Combine the water and starter. Add the flour and work the mixture by hand or with a stand mixer for a minutes until it just comes together as a dough. Let the dough rest for 20 minutes.

3. Add the salt and cocoa powder and work the dough until it is elastic, about 5 minutes. Add the hazelnuts and knead to incorporate.

4. Place the dough in a clean bowl, cover it with plastic wrap, and let it rest until it has increased to 1½ times its original size, about 2 to 2½ hours. Make a series of folds during the first hour.

5. Transfer the dough to a floured surface and shape it into a round. Place the round in a banneton (proofing basket) or a bowl lined with a flour-dusted kitchen towel. Cover the proofing basket with a kitchen towel and let the dough sit at room temperature for 1½ to 2 hours.

6. Meanwhile, preheat the oven to 520°F. Place a baking stone or a baking sheet on the middle rack of the oven as it warms. Place another baking sheet on the bottom of the oven. Have a ½ cup of water ready to toss in this bottom sheet to create steam.

7. Invert the dough onto a flour-dusted peel and score it. Place it on the hot baking sheet or baking stone and add the water to the sheet on the lower rack.

8. Reduce the oven's temperature immediately to 460°F and bake for 10 minutes, then lower the temperature to 430°F and bake the bread until it is golden brown, 20 to 25 minutes. The bread is ready when the loaf feels lighter when lifted and makes a hollow sound when tapped.

9. Remove the bread from the oven and let it cool on a wire rack before slicing.

Arepas

YIELD: 6 AREPAS | **ACTIVE TIME:** 20 MINUTES | **TOTAL TIME:** 50 MINUTES

21.1 OZ. AREPA FLOUR
(PRECOOKED CORNMEAL)

13.4 OZ. WARM WATER
(105°F)

1 TEASPOON FINE SEA SALT

1. Place all of the ingredients in the work bowl of a stand mixer fitted with the dough hook and work the mixture until it comes together as a smooth dough. Cover the work bowl with plastic wrap and let the dough rest at room temperature for 30 minutes.

2. Place the dough on a parchment-lined work surface and roll it out into a ⅘-inch-thick rectangle. Cut 6 rounds out of the dough and then trim the rounds so that they are as close as possible to perfect circles.

3. Preheat the oven to 400°F. Warm a cast-iron skillet over medium-high heat. Coat the skillet with nonstick cooking spray and add the arepas, working in batches to avoid crowding the pan. Cook until they are cooked through and browned on each side, 3 to 4 minutes each side.

4. If the insides of the arepas feel too soft for your liking, place them in the oven and bake for 10 minutes.

Poori

YIELD: 18 POORI | **ACTIVE TIME:** 30 MINUTES | **TOTAL TIME:** 50 MINUTES

6.3 OZ. ULTRA-FINE WHOLE WHEAT FLOUR

4 TEASPOONS CANOLA OIL

2.6 OZ. WATER

⅓ TEASPOON FINE SEA SALT

1. Combine all of the ingredients in the work bowl of a stand mixer fitted with the dough hook and knead the mixture until it comes together as a stiff dough. Form the dough into a round, place it in a bowl, and cover it with plastic wrap. Let the dough rest for 15 minutes.

2. Line a baking sheet with paper towels. Divide the dough into 18 pieces and shape them into rounds.

3. Add canola oil to a Dutch oven until it is about 2 inches deep and warm it to 350°F.

4. Roll a couple of the rounds into disks that are about ⅓ inch thick. Gently slip them into the oil and fry until puffy and golden brown, 4 to 5 minutes. Transfer the cooked poori to the baking sheet lined with paper towels. Repeat with the remaining pieces of dough.

Naan

YIELD: 8 NAAN | **ACTIVE TIME:** 30 MINUTES | **TOTAL TIME:** 3 HOURS

1 TEASPOON ACTIVE DRY YEAST

4 OZ. WARM WATER (105ºF)

11.6 OZ. ALL-PURPOSE FLOUR

½ CUP PLAIN YOGURT

3 TABLESPOONS CANOLA OIL

UNSALTED BUTTER, MELTED, FOR TOPPING

1. Combine the yeast and the water, gently stir, and let the mixture rest for 10 minutes.

2. Place the yeast mixture and the remaining ingredients, except for the melted butter, in the work bowl of a stand mixer fitted with the paddle attachment and work the mixture until it comes together as a smooth dough, about 10 minutes. Cover the work bowl with plastic wrap and let the dough rest in a naturally warm spot until it has doubled in size, about 1 hour.

3. Line a baking sheet with plastic wrap. Place the dough on a flour-dusted work surface, divide it into 8 pieces, and shape them into rounds. Place the rounds on the baking sheet, cover them with plastic wrap, and let them rest for 30 minutes.

4. Warm a cast-iron skillet over medium-high heat. Coat the skillet with nonstick cooking spray, flatten one of the rounds, and place it in the pan. Cook until it is browned and bubbly on both sides, 2 to 3 minutes per side.

5. Remove the cooked naan from the pan, brush it with the melted butter, and let it cool on wire rack. Repeat with the remaining pieces of dough.

Naan
SEE PAGE 47

Roti

10.6 OZ. FINELY GROUND
WHOLE WHEAT FLOUR

1 TABLESPOON PLUS 1
TEASPOON VEGETABLE OIL

1 TEASPOON SALT

1 CUP WATER

1. Combine all of the ingredients, except ¼ cup of the water, in the work bowl of a stand mixer fitted with the dough hook. Knead the mixture, checking it regularly, until it comes together as a soft, but not sticky, dough. Add the rest of the water, if needed, and a little at a time. Form the dough into a round, place it in a bowl, and cover it with plastic wrap. Let the dough rest for 1 hour.

2. Transfer the dough to a flour-dusted work surface, divide it into 15 pieces, and shape them into rounds.

3. Warm a cast-iron skillet over medium-high heat. Coat the skillet with nonstick cooking spray, flatten one of the rounds into a thin disk, and place it in the pan. Cook until it is browned and bubbly on both sides, gently pressing down on the surface as it cooks, about 30 seconds per side.

4. Remove the cooked roti from the pan, transfer it to a plate, and cover it loosely with aluminum foil. Repeat with the remaining pieces of dough.

Tunnbröd

YIELD: 12 TUNNBRÖD | **ACTIVE TIME:** 30 MINUTES | **TOTAL TIME:** 2 HOURS AND 30 MINUTES

1½ CUPS MILK

2½ TEASPOONS ACTIVE DRY YEAST

9½ OZ. ALL-PURPOSE FLOUR

3½ OZ. GRAHAM FLOUR

2.8 OZ. RYE FLOUR

1¾ OZ. LIGHT MOLASSES

1 TEASPOON FENNEL SEEDS, CRUSHED

2 OZ. UNSALTED BUTTER

1 TEASPOON FINE SEA SALT

1. Warm the milk to 105°F. Stir the yeast into the milk and let the mixture rest for 5 minutes.

2. Combine the yeast mixture with the flours, molasses, and crushed seeds in the work bowl of a stand mixer fitted with the dough hook. Knead the mixture, checking it regularly, until it comes together as a shaggy dough. Add the butter in pieces and knead until it has all been incorporated. Add the salt and knead until it has been incorporated and the dough is smooth. Form the dough into a round, place it in a bowl, and cover it with plastic wrap. Let the dough rest until it has doubled in size, about 1½ hours.

3. Transfer the dough to a flour-dusted work surface, divide it into 12 pieces, and shape them into rounds. Place the rounds on a piece of parchment paper, cover them with a kitchen towel, and let them rest for 1 hour.

4. Place one round on a flour-dusted work surface and roll it out into a ¼-inch-thick disk. Use a fork to poke some holes in the disk, making sure not to poke all the way through.

5. Warm a cast-iron skillet over medium-high heat. Coat the skillet with nonstick cooking spray, place the disk in the pan, and cook until it is puffy and browned on both sides, about 3 minutes per side. Repeat Steps 3 and 4 with the remaining pieces of dough.

Knäckebröd

YIELD: 12 KNÄCKEBRÖD | **ACTIVE TIME:** 50 MINUTES | **TOTAL TIME:** 2 HOURS AND 30 MINUTES

1¾ TEASPOONS ACTIVE DRY YEAST

10.6 OZ. WARM WATER (105°F)

1 TABLESPOON CARAWAY SEEDS

1¾ OZ. LIGHT RYE FLOUR

10.6 OZ. BREAD FLOUR

2.1 OZ. ALL-PURPOSE FLOUR

1 CUP MIXED SEEDS (SESAME, SUNFLOWER, ETC.)

1½ TEASPOONS FINE SEA SALT

1. Combine the yeast, water, and caraway seeds in the work bowl of a stand mixer and let the mixture rest for 10 minutes.

2. Add all the other ingredients, adding the salt at the very end of the mixing process, and knead the mixture on low speed until it comes together as a smooth dough. Form the dough into a round, place it in a bowl, and cover it with plastic wrap. Let the dough rest until it has doubled in size, about 1½ hours.

3. Transfer the dough to a flour-dusted work surface and roll it into a log. Cut the log into 12 pieces and shape them into rounds. Place the rounds on a piece of parchment paper, cover them with a kitchen towel, and let them rest for 1 hour.

4. Place one round on a flour-dusted work surface and roll it out until it is as thin as possible, making sure not to tear the dough. Use a fork to poke some holes in the disk, making sure not to poke all the way through. Repeat with the remaining rounds and cover them with plastic wrap.

5. Preheat the oven to its highest temperature and place a baking stone or baking sheet on the middle rack. Place a few rounds at a time on the baking sheet and bake until they are browned and crispy, about 10 minutes. Repeat with the remaining rounds, making sure to keep those that have not yet been baked covered with plastic wrap.

Schüttelbrot

YIELD: 8 SCHÜTTELBROT | **ACTIVE TIME:** 40 MINUTES | **TOTAL TIME:** 2 HOURS AND 30 MINUTES

2½ TEASPOONS ACTIVE DRY YEAST

1½ CUPS WATER

12.9 OZ. MEDIUM RYE FLOUR

5.3 OZ. ALL-PURPOSE FLOUR

1 TEASPOON CARAWAY SEEDS

1 TEASPOON FENNEL SEEDS

1½ TEASPOONS FINE SEA SALT

1 TEASPOON SUGAR

1¾ OZ. BUTTERMILK

1. Combine the yeast and water in the work bowl of a stand mixer and let the mixture rest for 10 minutes.

2. Add all the other ingredients, adding the salt at the very end of the mixing process, and knead the mixture on low speed until it comes together as a smooth dough. Form the dough into a round, place it in a bowl, and cover it with plastic wrap. Let the dough rest for 40 minutes.

3. Transfer the dough to a flour-dusted work surface and roll it into a log. Cut the log into 8 pieces and shape them into rounds. Place the rounds on a piece of parchment paper, cover them with a kitchen towel, and let them rest for 1 hour.

4. Place one round on a flour-dusted work surface and roll it out until it is ¼ inch thick. Repeat with the remaining rounds, cover them with plastic wrap, and let them rest for 20 minutes.

5. Preheat the oven to 410°F and place a baking stone or baking sheet on the middle rack. Place a few rounds at a time on the baking sheet and bake until they are lightly browned, about 20 minutes. Repeat with the remaining rounds, making sure to keep those that have not yet been baked covered with plastic wrap.

Feta & Herb Quickbread

YIELD: 1 LOAF | **ACTIVE TIME:** 10 MINUTES | **TOTAL TIME:** 1 HOUR

½ CUP FINELY CHOPPED
FRESH BASIL

½ CUP FINELY CHOPPED
FRESH CHIVES

UNSALTED BUTTER, AS
NEEDED

2 TABLESPOONS SESAME
SEEDS

1¼ CUPS ALL-
PURPOSE FLOUR

1 TABLESPOON BAKING
POWDER

3 LARGE ORGANIC EGGS

¼ CUP EXTRA-VIRGIN OLIVE
OIL

½ CUP PLUS 2
TABLESPOONS PLAIN
YOGURT

½ TEASPOON FINE SEA SALT

½ TEASPOON BLACK PEPPER

7 OZ. FETA CHEESE

1. Preheat the oven to 350°F. Combine the basil and chives in a small bowl and set the mixture aside. Coat a 9 x 5-inch loaf pan with butter and sprinkle half of the sesame seeds onto the bottom and sides, shaking the pan to coat.

2. Combine the flour and baking powder in a bowl. In a separate bowl, whisk together the eggs, oil, yogurt, salt, and pepper. Stir in the feta and the herb mixture. Fold the flour mixture into the egg mixture. Be careful not to overmix the batter—it is fine if a few lumps remain.

3. Pour the batter into the prepared pan. Level the surface with a spatula and sprinkle the remaining sesame seeds on top. Bake until the top is golden and a knife inserted into the center comes out clean, 40 to 50 minutes.

4. Remove the bread from the oven and let it cool in the pan for a few minutes. Run a knife around the edges of the pan to loosen the bread and then transfer it to a wire rack. Let the bread cool completely before enjoying.

Vegetarian Musakhan

YIELD: 4 FLATBREADS | **ACTIVE TIME:** 30 MINUTES | **TOTAL TIME:** 2 HOURS

FOR THE DOUGH

1 CUP BREAD FLOUR, PLUS MORE AS NEEDED

½ CUP WHOLE WHEAT FLOUR

2 TEASPOONS HONEY

½ TEASPOON INSTANT YEAST

¾ CUP WARM WATER (105°F)

1 TABLESPOON EXTRA-VIRGIN OLIVE OIL, PLUS MORE AS NEEDED

1 TEASPOON FINE SEA SALT

FOR THE TOPPING

5 TABLESPOONS EXTRA-VIRGIN OLIVE OIL

½ LB. PORTOBELLO MUSHROOMS, SLICED

1 CUP CHOPPED ONIONS

1 CARROT, PEELED AND GRATED

2 TABLESPOONS CHOPPED FRESH OREGANO

2 GARLIC CLOVES, MINCED

¾ TEASPOON SUMAC

⅛ TEASPOON CINNAMON

⅛ TEASPOON CARDAMOM

PINCH OF FRESHLY GRATED NUTMEG

PINCH OF SAFFRON

2 TEASPOONS LIGHT BROWN SUGAR

SALT AND PEPPER, TO TASTE

¼ CUP PINE NUTS

1. To begin preparations for the dough, place all of the ingredients in the work bowl of a stand mixer fitted with the dough hook and work the mixture on low until it comes together as a dough. Increase the speed to medium and work the dough until it no longer sticks to the side of the bowl, about 10 minutes.

2. Coat a bowl with olive oil. Place the dough on a bread flour–dusted work surface and knead it for 2 minutes. Form the dough into a ball and place it, seam side down, in the bowl. Cover the bowl with a linen towel and let the dough rise in a naturally warm spot until it has doubled in size, about 1 hour.

3. To begin preparations for the topping, place 1 tablespoon of the olive oil in a large skillet and warm it over medium heat. Add the mushrooms and sear them until browned, about 5 minutes. Turn them over and sear until browned on that side, about 5 minutes. Transfer the mushrooms to a paper towel–lined plate.

4. Place 1 tablespoon of the olive oil in the skillet and warm it over medium heat. Add the onions and cook, stirring occasionally, until they have softened, about 5 minutes. Add the carrot and cook, stirring occasionally, for 2 minutes. Add the oregano, garlic, sumac, cinnamon, cardamom, nutmeg, and saffron and cook, stirring continually, for 1 minute. Stir in the brown sugar, season the mixture with salt and pepper, and remove the pan from heat. Let the mixture cool.

5. Place the mixture in a food processor, add the remaining olive oil, and blitz until smooth. Preheat the oven to 400°F and position a baking stone on a rack in the middle. Divide the dough into four pieces, place them on a flour-dusted work surface, and roll each one into a 10 x 4–inch rectangle. Spread the puree over each musakhan, leaving a ½-inch crust. Sprinkle the pine nuts and mushrooms over the puree.

6. Using a flour-dusted peel or the back of a baking sheet, slide the musakhan onto the baking stone one at a time. Bake until the crust is golden brown, about 10 minutes. Remove the musakhan from the oven and let them cool slightly before enjoying.

Lavash Crackers

YIELD: 4 SERVINGS | **ACTIVE TIME:** 45 MINUTES | **TOTAL TIME:** 2 HOURS AND 30 MINUTES

½ CUP SEMOLINA FLOUR

6 TABLESPOONS WHOLE WHEAT FLOUR

½ CUP PLUS 2 TABLESPOONS ALL-PURPOSE FLOUR, PLUS MORE AS NEEDED

1 TEASPOON FINE SEA SALT

3 TABLESPOONS EXTRA-VIRGIN OLIVE OIL

1 TEASPOON INSTANT YEAST

½ CUP WARM WATER (105°F)

1 TABLESPOON ZA'ATAR

1 TABLESPOON TOASTED SESAME SEEDS

1 TABLESPOON POPPY SEEDS

1. Place the flours, ½ teaspoon of the salt, 2 tablespoons of the olive oil, the yeast, and water in the work bowl of a mixer fitted with the dough hook and work the mixture on low until it comes together as a dough. Increase the speed to medium and work the dough until it no longer sticks to the side of the work bowl, about 10 minutes.

2. Cover the bowl with a linen towel and let the dough rise in a naturally warm place until it has doubled in size, about 1 hour.

3. Line two baking sheets with parchment paper. Dust a work surface with all-purpose flour. Divide the dough into two pieces, place one piece on the work surface, and roll it out into a rectangle that is about ⅛ inch thick. Place the rolled-out dough on one of the baking sheets and repeat with the other ball of dough. Don't be overly concerned with the shape of the dough, a rustic look is what we are looking for in these crackers.

4. Brush the pieces of dough with the remaining olive oil. Sprinkle the remaining salt over them.

5. Place the za'atar, sesame seeds, and poppy seeds in a bowl and stir to combine. Sprinkle the mixture over the dough and press down gently to help the mixture adhere. Place the dough in a naturally warm place and let it rest for 30 minutes.

6. Preheat the oven to 425°F. Place the baking sheets in the oven and bake until the crackers are a deep golden brown, about 15 minutes. Remove the crackers from the oven and let them cool.

7. Break the crackers into pieces and enjoy.

Socca

YIELD: 4 TO 6 SERVINGS | **ACTIVE TIME:** 30 MINUTES | **TOTAL TIME:** 1 HOUR

7 TABLESPOONS EXTRA-VIRGIN OLIVE OIL

3 SMALL ONIONS, CHOPPED

1½ CUPS CHICKPEA FLOUR

½ TEASPOON KOSHER SALT, PLUS MORE TO TASTE

1 TEASPOON TURMERIC

1½ CUPS WATER

PEPPER, TO TASTE

2 TABLESPOONS CHOPPED FRESH CHIVES

TZATZIKI (SEE PAGE 152), FOR SERVING

1. Place 1 tablespoon of the olive oil in a small cast-iron skillet and warm it over medium-high heat. Add the onions, reduce the heat to low, and cook, stirring occasionally, until the onions are caramelized, about 30 minutes. Transfer the onions to a bowl and let them cool.

2. Place the chickpea flour, salt, and turmeric in a mixing bowl and whisk to combine. While whisking, slowly drizzle in 2 tablespoons of the olive oil. When the mixture comes together as a smooth batter, season it with salt and pepper.

3. Warm the cast-iron pan over medium-high heat. Add 1 tablespoon of the olive oil and then add ⅓ cup of the batter, tilting the pan to make sure the batter is evenly distributed. Reduce the heat to medium and cook until the batter starts to firm up, about 2 minutes.

4. Sprinkle some of the caramelized onions over the socca and cook until the edges are golden brown, 2 to 4 minutes. Flip the socca over and cook until golden brown and cooked through, about 2 minutes.

5. Gently remove the socca from the pan and repeat Steps 3 and 4 until all of the batter and caramelized onions have been used.

6. When all of the socca have been made, serve with Tzatziki.

Blue Pea Flower Sourdough Bread

YIELD: 1 LOAF | **ACTIVE TIME:** 1 HOUR AND 30 MINUTES | **TOTAL TIME:** 24 HOURS

1 CUP WATER, AT ROOM TEMPERATURE

3⅓ CUPS BREAD FLOUR, PLUS MORE AS NEEDED

⅓ CUP WHOLE WHEAT FLOUR

¼ CUP BLUE PEA FLOWER POWDER

1 CUP SOURDOUGH STARTER (SEE PAGE 16)

2 TEASPOONS KOSHER SALT

1. Place the water, flours, and blue pea flower powder in the work bowl of a stand mixer fitted with the dough hook and work the mixture at low speed for 6 minutes. Remove the bowl from the mixer and cover it with plastic wrap. Let the dough sit at room temperature for 1 hour to allow the dough to autolyse.

2. Place the work bowl back on the mixer and add the starter and salt. Knead the mixture at low speed until the dough starts to come together, about 2 minutes. Increase the speed to medium and knead until the dough is elastic and pulls away from the side of the bowl.

3. Shape the dough into a ball and spray the seam side with water. Dust a 9-inch banneton (proofing basket) with flour. Place the dough in the proofing basket, seam side down. Cover the bread with plastic wrap and let it sit on the counter for 2 hours.

4. Place the basket in the refrigerator and let it rest overnight.

5. Preheat the oven to 450°F and place a baking stone on a rack positioned in the middle.

6. Dust a peel with flour and gently turn the bread onto the peel so that the seam is facing up.

7. With a very sharp knife, carefully score the dough just off center. Make sure the knife is at a 45-degree angle to the dough.

8. Gently slide the sourdough onto the baking stone. Spray the oven with 5 spritzes of water and bake the bread for 20 minutes.

9. Open the oven, spray the oven with 5 more spritzes, and bake until the crust is golden brown, about 20 minutes. The internal temperature of the bread should be at minimum 210°F.

Baguettes

YIELD: 2 BAGUETTES | **ACTIVE TIME:** 1 HOUR AND 30 MINUTES | **TOTAL TIME:** 24 HOURS

5 OZ. WATER

11½ OZ. BREAD FLOUR, PLUS MORE AS NEEDED

½ OZ. WHOLE WHEAT FLOUR

1 TEASPOON SUGAR

1 CUP SOURDOUGH STARTER (SEE PAGE 16)

1 TABLESPOON KOSHER SALT

1. Place the water, flours, and sugar in the work bowl of a stand mixer fitted with the dough hook and work the mixture at low speed for 6 minutes. Remove the bowl from the mixer and cover it with plastic wrap. Let the dough sit at room temperature for 1 hour to allow the dough to autolyse.

2. Place the work bowl back on the mixer and add the starter and salt. Knead the mixture at low speed until the dough starts to come together, about 2 minutes. Increase the speed to medium and knead until the dough is elastic and pulls away from the side of the bowl.

3. Shape the dough into a ball and spray the seam side with water. Dust a 9-inch Banneton (proofing basket) with flour. Place the dough in the proofing basket, seam side down. Cover the bread with plastic wrap and let it sit on the counter for 2 hours.

4. Place the dough on a flour-dusted work surface, divide it in half, and shape each piece into a ball. Cover the dough with a moist linen towel and let it sit on the counter for 15 minutes.

5. Punch down the pieces of dough until they are rough ovals. Working with one piece at a time, take the side closest to you and roll it away from you. Starting halfway up, fold in the corners and roll the dough into a rough baguette shape.

6. Place both hands over one piece of dough. Gently roll the dough while moving your hands back and forth over it and gently pressing down until it is about 16 inches long. Repeat with the other piece of dough.

7. Place the baguettes on a baguette pan, cover with plastic wrap, and chill them in the refrigerator overnight.

8. Remove the baguettes from the refrigerator, place the pan in a naturally warm spot, and let it sit for 2 hours.

9. Preheat the oven to 450°F.

10. Using a very sharp knife, cut four slits at a 45-degree angle along the length of each baguette.

11. Place the baguettes in the oven, spray the oven with 5 spritzes of water, and bake until the baguettes are a deep golden brown, 20 to 30 minutes.

12. Remove the baguettes from the oven, place them on a wire rack, and let them cool slightly before slicing.

Ciabatta

YIELD: 1 LOAF | **ACTIVE TIME:** 1 HOUR | **TOTAL TIME:** 24 HOURS

FOR THE POOLISH
7½ OZ. LUKEWARM WATER (90ºF)
¼ TEASPOON ACTIVE DRY YEAST
2¼ CUPS ALL-PURPOSE FLOUR

FOR THE DOUGH
¾ CUP WATER
¾ TEASPOON ACTIVE DRY YEAST
2 TEASPOONS HONEY
12½ OZ. BREAD FLOUR, PLUS MORE AS NEEDED
2¼ TEASPOONS KOSHER SALT

1. To prepare the poolish, place all the ingredients in a mixing bowl and whisk to combine. Cover the bowl with a linen towel and let it sit at room temperature overnight.

2. To begin preparations for the dough, place the poolish in the work bowl of a stand mixer fitted with the dough hook. Add the water, yeast, and honey and whisk to combine. Add the flour and work the mixture on low for 1 minute. Raise the speed to medium and knead the mixture for 5 minutes. Turn off the mixer and let it rest for 5 minutes.

3. Add the salt and knead the mixture on low for 1 minute. Raise the speed to medium and knead the dough until it is very well developed and starts to pull away from the side of the work bowl, about 8 minutes.

4. Spray a 13 x 9–inch baking pan with nonstick cooking spray. Place the dough in the pan, cover it with plastic wrap, and let it rise for 45 minutes.

5. Take one end of the dough and fold a third of it over the center of the dough. Take the other end of the dough and fold over this third. Turn the pan 90 degrees and gently flip the dough over so that the fresh fold is facing down. Cover the pan and let it rise for 45 minutes. After 45 minutes, repeat the folding and resting process twice more.

6. Line a baking sheet with parchment paper. Place the dough on a flour-dusted work surface and repeat the folding process used in Step 5. Place the dough on the baking sheet and let it rise for 45 minutes.

7. Preheat the oven to 400ºF.

8. Place the bread in the oven and spray the oven generously with water to increase the humidity in the oven. Bake for 10 minutes, open the oven, and generously spray it with water again. Bake for another 10 minutes, open the oven, and spray it generously with water one last time.

9. Close the oven and let the ciabatta bake until golden brown and crispy, about 20 minutes. The internal temperature should be 210ºF.

10. Remove the ciabatta from the oven, place it on a wire rack, and let it cool before enjoying.

Harvest Loaf

YIELD: 1 LOAF | **ACTIVE TIME:** 45 MINUTES | **TOTAL TIME:** 4 HOURS

6 OZ. LUKEWARM WATER (90°F)

1 TABLESPOON ACTIVE DRY YEAST

2 EGGS, 1 BEATEN

1 EGG YOLK

1 OZ. EXTRA-VIRGIN OLIVE OIL

1 OZ. SUGAR

15 OZ. BREAD FLOUR, PLUS MORE AS NEEDED

1 TEASPOON GROUND CLOVES

1 TABLESPOON CINNAMON

1 CUP DRIED CRANBERRIES

½ CUP PUMPKIN SEEDS, TOASTED

2 TEASPOONS KOSHER SALT

1. Place the water in the work bowl of a stand mixer. Sprinkle the yeast over the water, gently whisk, and let the mixture sit for 10 minutes.

2. Add the unbeaten egg, egg yolk, olive oil, and sugar and fit the mixer with the dough hook. Add the flour, cloves, cinnamon, cranberries, pumpkin seeds, and salt and work the mixture on low speed until it just starts to come together as a dough, about 1 minute.

3. Raise the speed to medium and work the dough until it comes away clean from the side of the work bowl and is elastic, about 6 minutes.

4. Spray a mixing bowl with nonstick cooking spray. Transfer the dough to a flour-dusted work surface and knead it until it is extensible. Shape the dough into a ball, place it in the bowl, and cover the bowl with a kitchen towel. Place the dough in a naturally warm spot and let it rise until doubled in size, 1 to 2 hours.

5. Preheat the oven to 350°F. Spray an 8 x 4–inch loaf pan with nonstick cooking spray.

6. Place the dough on a flour-dusted work surface and roll it into a tight round. Tuck the ends in toward the center and place the dough in the loaf pan, seam side down. Cover the dough with plastic wrap, place it in a naturally warm spot, and let it rise until doubled in size.

7. Brush the dough with the beaten egg. Using a very sharp knife, cut a seam that runs the length of the bread on top. Place the dough in the oven and bake the bread until it is golden brown, 35 to 45 minutes. The internal temperature of the bread should be 200°F.

8. Remove the bread from the oven, place it on a cooling rack, and let it cool completely before slicing.

Fougasse

YIELD: 1 LOAF | **ACTIVE TIME:** 30 MINUTES | **TOTAL TIME:** 3 HOURS

9 OZ. WATER

2½ TEASPOONS ACTIVE DRY YEAST

3 TABLESPOONS EXTRA-VIRGIN OLIVE OIL, PLUS MORE AS NEEDED

15 OZ. BREAD FLOUR, PLUS MORE AS NEEDED

1 TABLESPOON PLUS 1 TEASPOON DRIED BASIL

2 GARLIC CLOVES, MINCED

1 TABLESPOON KOSHER SALT

¼ CUP FRESHLY SHAVED PARMESAN CHEESE

1. In the work bowl of a stand mixer fitted with the paddle attachment, add the water and yeast, gently whisk to combine, and let the mixture sit for 10 minutes.

2. Add the oil, flour, basil, garlic, and salt and work the mixture on low for 1 minute. Raise the speed to medium and work the mixture until it comes together as a smooth dough, about 5 minutes.

3. Remove the dough from the work bowl, place it on a flour-dusted work surface, and knead it until it is elastic. Shape the dough into a ball, return it to the work bowl, and cover it with plastic wrap. Place the dough in a naturally warm spot and let it rise until it has doubled in size.

4. Turn the dough out onto a flour-dusted surface. Lightly flour the top of the dough. Using a rolling pin, roll the dough out by starting in the middle of the dough and rolling toward you until it is an approximately 10 x 6–inch oval.

5. Preheat the oven to 350ºF. Coat an 18 x 13–inch baking sheet with olive oil. Carefully place the dough in the center of the pan.

6. Using a pizza cutter, cut a lengthwise line in the center of the oval, leaving an inch uncut at each end so that the dough remains one piece. Make three small, angled slices to the left of the center cut. Do the same to the right of the center cut.

7. The bread should resemble a leaf. Lightly brush the dough with olive oil, cover the pan with plastic wrap, and let it rise until it has doubled in size.

8. Preheat the oven to 350ºF.

9. Sprinkle the Parmesan over the bread, place it in the oven, and bake until it is golden brown, 20 to 30 minutes.

10. Remove the fougasse from the oven and brush it with more olive oil. Transfer it to a wire rack and let it cool completely before enjoying.

Bulkie Rolls

YIELD: 8 ROLLS | **ACTIVE TIME:** 45 MINUTES | **TOTAL TIME:** 4 HOURS

6 OZ. WATER

1½ TEASPOONS ACTIVE DRY YEAST

2 EGGS, 1 BEATEN

1 EGG YOLK

1 OZ. EXTRA-VIRGIN OLIVE OIL

1 OZ. SUGAR

15 OZ. BREAD FLOUR, PLUS MORE AS NEEDED

1 TEASPOON KOSHER SALT

1. Place the water, yeast, unbeaten egg, egg yolk, olive oil, and sugar in the work bowl of a stand mixer fitted with the dough hook and whisk to combine. Add the flour and salt and knead on low for 1 minute. Raise the speed to medium and knead the mixture until it comes together as a smooth dough and begins to pull away from the side of the work bowl, 6 to 8 minutes.

2. Coat a mixing bowl with nonstick cooking spray. Remove the dough from the work bowl, place it on a flour-dusted work surface, and shape it into a ball. Place the dough in the bowl, cover it with plastic wrap, place it in a naturally warm spot, and let it rise until doubled in size.

3. Line an 18 x 13–inch baking sheet with parchment paper. Place the dough on a flour-dusted work surface and divide it into 3.5-oz. portions. Roll the portions into tight balls. Place the balls on the pan, cover the pan with plastic wrap, and place it in a naturally warm spot. Let them rise until they have doubled in size.

4. Preheat the oven to 350ºF.

5. Brush the balls with the beaten egg. Using a sharp knife, score an X on top of each ball.

6. Place the pan in the oven and bake until the rolls are golden brown, 20 to 25 minutes. The internal temperature of the rolls should be 190ºF.

7. Remove from the oven, transfer the rolls to a wire rack, and let them cool completely before enjoying.

Brown Bread

YIELD: 1 LOAF | **ACTIVE TIME:** 15 MINUTES | **TOTAL TIME:** 1 HOUR

11 OZ. MILK

½ CUP MOLASSES

2 TABLESPOONS LIGHT BROWN SUGAR

5 OZ. ALL-PURPOSE FLOUR

2½ OZ. CORNMEAL

5 OZ. WHOLE WHEAT FLOUR

2 TEASPOONS BAKING POWDER

¾ TEASPOON BAKING SODA

5 OZ. RAISINS

1. Preheat the oven to 350ºF. Coat an 8 x 4–inch loaf pan with nonstick cooking spray.

2. In the work bowl of a stand mixer fitted with the paddle attachment, combine the milk and molasses. Add the remaining ingredients and beat until the mixture comes together as a smooth batter, about 2 minutes.

3. Pour the batter into the loaf pan, place it in the oven, and bake until a cake tester inserted into the center comes out clean, 45 minutes to 1 hour.

4. Remove the bread from the oven and let the bread cool slightly. Remove it from the pan, place it on a cooling rack, and let it cool slightly before serving.

Pāo de Queijo

YIELD: 12 BUNS | **ACTIVE TIME:** 20 MINUTES | **TOTAL TIME:** 45 MINUTES

9 OZ. TAPIOCA STARCH

1 CUP MILK

4 OZ. UNSALTED BUTTER

1 TEASPOON KOSHER SALT

2 EGGS

1½ CUPS GRATED PARMESAN CHEESE

1. Preheat the oven to 350ºF. Line an 18 x 13–inch baking sheet with parchment paper. Place the tapioca starch in the work bowl of a stand mixer fitted with the paddle attachment.

2. Place the milk, butter, and salt in a small saucepan and warm over medium heat until the butter has melted and the mixture is simmering.

3. Turn the mixer on low and slowly pour the milk mixture into the work bowl. Raise the speed to medium and work the mixture until it has cooled considerably.

4. Add the eggs one at a time and knead to incorporate. Add the grated Parmesan and knead the mixture until incorporated.

5. Scoop 2-oz. portions of the dough onto the pan, making sure to leave enough space between them.

6. Place the pan in the oven and bake until the rolls are puffy and light golden brown, 15 to 20 minutes.

7. Remove from the oven and enjoy immediately.

Crostini

YIELD: 6 SERVINGS | **ACTIVE TIME:** 15 MINUTES | **TOTAL TIME:** 30 MINUTES

1 BAGUETTE (SEE PAGE 66), SLICED

2 TABLESPOONS EXTRA-VIRGIN OLIVE OIL, PLUS MORE TO TASTE

SALT AND PEPPER, TO TASTE

1. Preheat the oven to 400°F. Brush the slices of baguette with the olive oil and place them on a baking sheet. Place in the oven and bake for 12 to 15 minutes, turning the slices over halfway through. When the slices are crispy and golden brown on both sides, remove the pan from the oven.

2. Top the crostini as desired, drizzle olive oil over them, and season with salt and pepper.

Note: There are limitless ways you can utilize these crostini. Those pictured feature ricotta and fresh peas, but you can top them with anything you like, or just serve them on the side and let people top them as they please.

Grissini Sticks

YIELD: 24 STICKS | **ACTIVE TIME:** 30 MINUTES | **TOTAL TIME:** 3 HOURS

4½ OZ. MILK

1 OZ. WATER

2 TEASPOONS ACTIVE DRY YEAST

1 OZ. UNSALTED BUTTER, MELTED

9 OZ. ALL-PURPOSE FLOUR, PLUS MORE AS NEEDED

2 TEASPOONS KOSHER SALT, PLUS MORE TO TASTE

1 TABLESPOON DRIED OREGANO

EXTRA-VIRGIN OLIVE OIL, AS NEEDED

1. Place the milk, water, and yeast in the work bowl of a stand mixer fitted with the dough hook, gently stir to combine, and let the mixture sit until it starts to foam, about 10 minutes.

2. Add the butter, flour, salt, and oregano and knead on low for 1 minute. Raise the speed to medium and knead the mixture until it comes together as a smooth dough and begins to pull away from the side of the work bowl, about 5 minutes.

3. Coat a mixing bowl with nonstick cooking spray. Remove the dough from the work bowl, place it on a flour-dusted work surface, and shape it into a ball. Place the dough in the bowl, cover it with plastic wrap, place it in a naturally warm spot, and let it rise until doubled in size.

4. Preheat the oven to 400°F.

5. Line two baking sheets with parchment paper. Place the dough on a flour-dusted work surface and divide it in half. Roll each piece out until it is ¼ inch thick and cut them into ⅛-inch-wide ribbons.

6. Place the ribbons on the baking sheets, brush them with olive oil, and sprinkle salt over them. Place them in the oven and bake until golden brown, 10 to 15 minutes.

7. Remove from the oven and let the grissini sticks cool slightly before enjoying.

Toast Points

YIELD: 4 SERVINGS | **ACTIVE TIME:** 5 MINUTES | **TOTAL TIME:** 25 MINUTES

6 SLICES OF BREAD

EXTRA-VIRGIN OLIVE OIL, TO TASTE

SALT AND PEPPER, TO TASTE

1. Preheat the oven to 350°F. Remove the crusts from the slices of bread and use a rolling pin to roll the slices flat.

2. Cut each slice into triangles, drizzle olive oil over them, and season with salt and pepper. Place them on a baking sheet, place it in the oven, and toast until they are crispy, about 6 minutes. Remove them from the oven and let them cool slightly before serving.

Thyme & Asiago Crackers

YIELD: 15 CRACKERS | **ACTIVE TIME:** 10 MINUTES | **TOTAL TIME:** 1 HOUR

½ CUP UNSALTED BUTTER

1 CUP FRESHLY GRATED ASIAGO CHEESE

ZEST OF 1 LEMON

2 TABLESPOONS CHOPPED FRESH THYME

1¼ CUPS ALL-PURPOSE FLOUR, PLUS MORE AS NEEDED

½ TEASPOON KOSHER SALT

¼ TEASPOON BLACK PEPPER

1. Place all the ingredients in a food processor and pulse until the mixture comes together as a dough.

2. Place the dough on a flour-dusted work surface and roll it into a 2-inch log. Cover the dough tightly with plastic wrap and chill it in the refrigerator for 30 minutes.

3. Preheat the oven to 350°F and line two baking sheets with parchment paper. Remove the dough from the refrigerator, cut it into ½-inch-thick slices, and place them on the baking sheets.

4. Place the crackers in the oven and bake until the crackers are golden brown, about 12 minutes. Remove from the oven and let the crackers cool before serving.

Fett'unta

YIELD: 4 SERVINGS | **ACTIVE TIME:** 10 MINUTES | **TOTAL TIME:** 30 MINUTES

4 SLICES FROM LOAF OF CRUSTY BREAD (EACH SLICE SHOULD BE 1½ INCHES THICK)

¾ CUP QUALITY EXTRA-VIRGIN OLIVE OIL, PLUS MORE AS NEEDED

1 GARLIC CLOVE

MALDON SEA SALT, TO TASTE

1. Preheat your gas or charcoal grill to high heat (500°F). Brush both sides of the bread generously with olive oil.

2. Place the bread on the grill and cook until crisp and browned on both sides, about 2 minutes per side.

3. Remove from heat, rub the garlic clove over one side of each piece, and pour 3 tablespoons of oil over each one. Sprinkle salt generously over the top and serve.

Whole Wheat Crackers

YIELD: 40 CRACKERS | **ACTIVE TIME:** 20 MINUTES | **TOTAL TIME:** 45 MINUTES

5½ OZ. WHOLE WHEAT
FLOUR, PLUS MORE AS
NEEDED

1 OZ. SUGAR

½ TEASPOON KOSHER SALT

4 TABLESPOONS UNSALTED
BUTTER, CHILLED AND
CUBED

2 OZ. WATER

EXTRA-VIRGIN OLIVE OIL, AS
NEEDED

MALDON SEA SALT, FOR
TOPPING

1. Preheat the oven to 400°F. Line an 18 x 13–inch baking sheet with parchment paper. Place the flour, sugar, kosher salt, and butter in a food processor and pulse until combined and the butter has been reduced to pea-sized pieces.

2. While the food processor is running, add the water and blitz until incorporated.

3. Tip the mixture onto a lightly floured work surface and knead it until it comes together as a soft, smooth dough. Place the dough in a small bowl, cover it with plastic wrap, and let it rest for 10 minutes.

4. Place the dough on a flour-dusted work surface and divide it in half. Roll each half until it is ⅛ inch thick, brush it with olive oil, and cut it into 2-inch squares. Place them on the pan and sprinkle sea salt over them.

5. Place the pan in the oven and bake until the crackers are crispy and lightly golden brown, 8 to 10 minutes. Remove from the oven and let the crackers cool on the pan before enjoying.

Yogurt & Buckwheat Crackers

YIELD: 30 CRACKERS | **ACTIVE TIME:** 15 MINUTES | **TOTAL TIME:** 1 HOUR AND 30 MINUTES

1½ CUPS BUCKWHEAT FLOUR

1 TEASPOON KOSHER SALT

½ CUP PLAIN YOGURT

½ CUP UNSALTED BUTTER, SOFTENED, PLUS MORE AS NEEDED

MALDON SEA SALT, TO TASTE

1. Place the flour, kosher salt, yogurt, and butter in a mixing bowl and work the mixture until it comes together as a dough.

2. Place the dough between two sheets of parchment paper and roll it out to about ¼ inch thick. Chill the dough in the refrigerator for 30 minutes.

3. Preheat the oven to 450ºF and line two baking sheets with parchment paper. Place some butter in a skillet, melt it over medium heat, and set it aside.

4. Cut the dough into the desired shapes and place the crackers on the baking sheets. Brush each cracker with some of the melted butter and sprinkle the Maldon sea salt over them.

5. Place them in the oven and bake until crisp, about 12 minutes. Remove from the oven and let the crackers cool completely before serving.

Chia Seed Crackers

YIELD: 30 CRACKERS | **ACTIVE TIME:** 20 MINUTES | **TOTAL TIME:** 2 HOURS

9 TABLESPOONS CHIA SEEDS

5 TABLESPOONS WATER

½ CUP ALMOND FLOUR

½ TEASPOON KOSHER SALT

¼ TEASPOON BLACK PEPPER

1. Use a spice grinder or a mortar and pestle to grind 1 tablespoon of the chia seeds into a powder. Transfer the powder to a bowl and add 3 tablespoons of the water. Gently stir to combine and let the mixture rest for 10 minutes.

2. Add the remaining chia seeds and water along with the almond flour, salt, and pepper. Fold until the mixture comes together as a dough, place it between two sheets of parchment paper, and roll out until it is approximately ¼ inch thick. Chill the dough in the refrigerator for 30 minutes.

3. Preheat the oven to 350ºF and line two baking sheets with parchment paper. Cut the dough into the desired shapes and place them on the baking sheets.

4. Place them in the oven and bake until the crackers are golden brown, about 20 minutes. Remove from the oven and let the crackers cool completely before serving.

Pecan & Blue Cheese Crackers

YIELD: 30 CRACKERS | **ACTIVE TIME:** 20 MINUTES | **TOTAL TIME:** 24 HOURS

¾ CUP PECANS

¾ CUP ALL-PURPOSE FLOUR

4 TABLESPOONS UNSALTED BUTTER, FROZEN AND GRATED

3 OZ. BLUE CHEESE

1 TABLESPOON FRESH THYME, CHOPPED

1 TEASPOON KOSHER SALT

1. Place all the ingredients in a food processor and pulse until the mixture comes together as a dough.

2. Place the dough between two sheets of parchment paper and roll it out until it is about ¼ inch thick. Place the dough in the refrigerator and chill for 24 hours.

3. Preheat the oven to 350ºF and line two baking sheets with parchment paper. Cut the dough into the desired shapes, place them on the baking sheets, and bake in the oven until crispy, about 15 minutes. Remove from the oven and let cool before serving.

Candied Ritz Crackers

YIELD: 4 SERVINGS | **ACTIVE TIME:** 10 MINUTES | **TOTAL TIME:** 40 MINUTES

10 TABLESPOONS
UNSALTED BUTTER

1½ TABLESPOONS BROWN
SUGAR

6 OZ. RITZ CRACKERS

2 TEASPOONS KOSHER SALT

1 TEASPOON GARLIC
POWDER

1 TEASPOON ONION
POWDER

¼ TEASPOON BLACK PEPPER

¼ TEASPOON RED PEPPER
FLAKES

1 TEASPOON OLD BAY
SEASONING

1. Preheat the oven to 350°F and line two baking sheets with parchment paper. Place the butter and brown sugar in a saucepan and melt over medium heat, stirring to combine.

2. Place the crackers in a large mixing bowl, pour the butter mixture over them, and gently stir to combine, taking care not to break the crackers.

3. Place the crackers on the baking sheets and sprinkle a bit of the remaining ingredients over each one. Place the sheets in the oven and bake until the glaze has hardened, about 12 minutes. Remove and let cool completely before serving.

Chocolate Cherry Crackers

YIELD: 30 CRACKERS | **ACTIVE TIME:** 15 MINUTES | **TOTAL TIME:** 1 HOUR AND 30 MINUTES

½ CUP ALL-PURPOSE FLOUR

½ CUP WHEAT FLOUR

¼ CUP BROWN SUGAR

¼ CUP COCOA POWDER

½ TEASPOON FINE SEA SALT

8 TABLESPOONS UNSALTED BUTTER, COLD AND CUBED

3 TABLESPOONS WHOLE MILK

½ CUP DRIED CHERRIES

⅓ CUP SUNFLOWER SEEDS

1. Place all the ingredients in a food processor and pulse until the mixture comes together as a dough.

2. Place the dough between two sheets of parchment paper and roll out until it is ¼ inch thick. Place the dough in the refrigerator and chill for 45 minutes.

3. Preheat the oven to 350ºF and line two baking sheets with parchment paper. Cut the dough into the desired shapes, place them on the baking sheets, and bake in the oven until crispy, about 12 minutes. Remove and let cool completely before serving.

Rum & Caramelized Banana Bread

YIELD: 1 LOAF | **ACTIVE TIME:** 30 MINUTES | **TOTAL TIME:** 2 HOURS

2 CUPS ALL-PURPOSE FLOUR

1 TEASPOON BAKING SODA

¼ TEASPOON CINNAMON

¼ TEASPOON ALLSPICE

½ TEASPOON KOSHER SALT

4 TABLESPOONS UNSALTED BUTTER, SOFTENED

3½ RIPE BANANAS, PEELED AND SLICED

4 OZ. LIGHT BROWN SUGAR

2 TABLESPOONS SPICED RUM

6 OZ. SUGAR

½ CUP EXTRA-VIRGIN OLIVE OIL

2 EGGS

1½ TEASPOONS PURE VANILLA EXTRACT

2 TABLESPOONS CRÈME FRAÎCHE

1. Preheat the oven to 350ºF. Coat an 8 x 4–inch loaf pan with nonstick cooking spray.

2. Place the flour, baking soda, cinnamon, allspice, and salt in a mixing bowl and whisk to combine. Set aside.

3. Place the butter in a large skillet and melt it over medium heat. Add the bananas and brown sugar and cook until the bananas start to brown, about 3 minutes. Remove the pan from heat, stir in the rum, and let the mixture steep for 30 minutes.

4. In the work bowl of a stand mixer fitted with the paddle attachment, cream the caramelized banana mixture, sugar, olive oil, eggs, and vanilla on medium for 5 minutes. Add the dry mixture, reduce the speed to low, and beat until the mixture comes together as a smooth batter. Add the crème fraîche and beat to incorporate.

5. Pour the batter into the prepared loaf pan, place it in the oven, and bake until a cake tester inserted into the center of the banana bread loaf comes out clean, 60 to 70 minutes. Remove the pan from the oven and place it on a wire rack to cool completely.

English Muffins

YIELD: 8 MUFFINS | **ACTIVE TIME:** 30 MINUTES | **TOTAL TIME:** 3 HOURS

7 OZ. WATER

1 TEASPOON ACTIVE DRY YEAST

4½ TEASPOONS UNSALTED BUTTER, SOFTENED

1 TABLESPOON SUGAR

1 EGG

10 OZ. BREAD FLOUR, PLUS MORE AS NEEDED

1 TEASPOON KOSHER SALT

SEMOLINA FLOUR, AS NEEDED

1. Place the water and yeast in the work bowl of a stand mixer fitted with the dough hook, gently stir to combine, and let the mixture sit until it starts to foam, about 10 minutes.

2. Add the butter, sugar, egg, bread flour, and salt and knead on low for 1 minute. Raise the speed to medium and knead the mixture until it comes together as a smooth dough and begins to pull away from the side of the work bowl, about 5 minutes.

3. Coat a mixing bowl with nonstick cooking spray. Remove the dough from the work bowl, place it on a flour-dusted work surface, and shape it into a ball. Place the dough in the bowl, cover it with plastic wrap, place it in a naturally warm spot, and let it rise until doubled in size.

4. Line an 18 x 13–inch baking sheet with parchment paper.

5. Place the dough on a flour-dusted work surface and divide it into 2½-oz. portions. Flatten each ball into 3½-inch circle and place them on the pan. Cover with plastic wrap, place the muffins in a naturally warm spot, and let them rest for 30 minutes.

6. Warm a stovetop griddle over low heat and lightly sprinkle semolina on the griddle. Place the muffins on the griddle and cook until golden brown on both sides, 12 to 20 minutes. The internal temperature of the muffins should be 190ºF. If the muffins browned too quickly and are not cooked through in the center, bake them in a 350ºF oven for 5 to 10 minutes.

7. Let the muffins cool before slicing and enjoying.

Soft Pretzels

YIELD: 4 SERVINGS | **ACTIVE TIME:** 45 MINUTES | **TOTAL TIME:** 2 HOURS

½ CUP WARM WATER (105ºF)

2 TABLESPOONS BROWN SUGAR

¼ TEASPOON INSTANT YEAST

6 TABLESPOONS UNSALTED BUTTER, MELTED

2½ TEASPOONS FINE SEA SALT

4½ CUPS ALL-PURPOSE FLOUR

⅓ CUP BAKING SODA

1 EGG

1 TABLESPOON WATER, AT ROOM TEMPERATURE

COARSE SEA SALT, TO TASTE

1. In the work bowl of a stand mixer fitted with the dough hook, combine the warm water, brown sugar, yeast, and melted butter and knead on low for 5 minutes.

2. Add the fine sea salt and flour, raise the speed to medium, and knead for another 4 minutes. Coat a large mixing bowl with nonstick cooking spray, transfer the dough to the bowl, and cover it with plastic wrap. Let the dough rest at room temperature until it has doubled in size, about 1 hour.

3. Cut the dough into ½-inch-thick ropes. Cut the ropes into bite-size pieces or twist them into traditional pretzel shapes.

4. Preheat the oven to 425ºF. Line two baking sheets with parchment paper and coat with nonstick cooking spray. Bring water to a boil in a medium saucepan. Gradually add the baking soda and gently stir to combine.

5. Place the pretzels in the water and poach them briefly—30 seconds for bites, 1 minute for traditional pretzels. Carefully remove the pretzels with a slotted spoon and transfer them to the baking sheets.

6. Place the egg and room-temperature water in a small bowl, beat to combine, and brush the egg wash over the pretzels. Sprinkle the coarse sea salt over the pretzels and bake them in the oven until golden brown, about 15 minutes. Remove from the oven and briefly let cool before serving.

Saltines

YIELD: 30 CRACKERS | **ACTIVE TIME:** 30 MINUTES | **TOTAL TIME:** 2 HOURS

12½ OZ. WATER, AT ROOM TEMPERATURE

1 TABLESPOON ACTIVE DRY YEAST

½ CUP EXTRA-VIRGIN OLIVE OIL

2 LBS. BREAD FLOUR, PLUS MORE AS NEEDED

1 TABLESPOON KOSHER SALT

MALDON SEA SALT, FOR TOPPING

1. Place the water and yeast in the work bowl of a stand mixer, gently stir, and let the mixture sit until it starts to foam, about 10 minutes.

2. Add the olive oil to the work bowl and beat the mixture on medium for 1 minute. Add the flour and kosher salt and beat the mixture until it comes together as a soft dough. Cover the dough in plastic wrap and chill it in the refrigerator for at least 1 hour.

3. Preheat the oven to 350°F. Line a 26 x 18–inch baking sheet with parchment paper.

4. Place the dough on a flour-dusted work surface and roll it out to ⅛ inch thick. Cut the dough into 2-inch squares, transfer them to the baking sheet, and use a fork to poke holes in each one. Sprinkle the sea salt over the crackers.

5. Place the crackers in the oven and bake them until the edges are golden brown, 12 to 15 minutes.

6. Remove the crackers from the oven, place the pan on a wire rack, and let them cool completely.

Honey Cornbread

YIELD: 12 SERVINGS | **ACTIVE TIME:** 20 MINUTES | **TOTAL TIME:** 1 HOUR

½ CUP HONEY

¾ LB. UNSALTED BUTTER, SOFTENED

1 LB. ALL-PURPOSE FLOUR

½ LB. CORNMEAL

1 TABLESPOON PLUS 1 TEASPOON BAKING POWDER

1 TABLESPOON KOSHER SALT

7 OZ. SUGAR

4 EGGS

2 CUPS MILK

1. Preheat the oven to 350°F. Coat a large cast-iron skillet with nonstick cooking spray.

2. Place the honey and 4 oz. of the butter in a small saucepan and warm over medium heat until the butter has melted. Whisk to combine and set the mixture aside.

3. Place the flour, cornmeal, baking powder, and salt in a mixing bowl and whisk to combine. Set the mixture aside.

4. In the work bowl of a stand mixer fitted with the paddle attachment, cream the remaining butter and the sugar on medium until light and fluffy, about 5 minutes. Add the eggs and beat until incorporated. Add the dry mixture, reduce the speed to low, and beat until the mixture comes together as a smooth batter. Gradually add the milk and beat until incorporated.

5. Pour the batter into the cast-iron skillet, place the pan in the oven, and bake until a cake tester inserted into the center of the cornbread comes out clean, 25 to 30 minutes.

6. Remove from the oven and place the pan on a wire rack. Brush the cornbread with the honey butter and enjoy it warm.

Honey Cornbread
SEE PAGE 91

Stout Gingerbread

YIELD: 1 LOAF | **ACTIVE TIME:** 15 MINUTES | **TOTAL TIME:** 1 HOUR AND 30 MINUTES

10 OZ. ALL-PURPOSE FLOUR

1½ TEASPOONS BAKING POWDER

2 TABLESPOONS GROUND GINGER

½ TEASPOON CINNAMON

½ TEASPOON GROUND CLOVES

¼ TEASPOON FRESHLY GRATED NUTMEG

¼ TEASPOON KOSHER SALT

1 CUP MOLASSES

1 CUP STOUT

1½ TEASPOONS BAKING SODA

3 EGGS

4 OZ. SUGAR

4 OZ. DARK BROWN SUGAR

¾ CUP CANOLA OIL

1. Preheat the oven to 350ºF. Coat an 8 x 4–inch loaf pan with nonstick cooking spray.

2. Place the flour, baking powder, ginger, cinnamon, cloves, nutmeg, and salt in a mixing bowl and whisk to combine. Set it aside.

3. Combine the molasses and stout in a small saucepan and bring it to a simmer over medium heat. Remove the pan from heat and whisk in the baking soda. Set the mixture aside.

4. In the work bowl of a stand mixer fitted with the paddle attachment, beat the eggs, sugar, brown sugar, and canola oil on medium until light and fluffy, about 5 minutes. Add the molasses mixture, beat until incorporated, and then add the dry mixture. Reduce the speed to low and beat until the mixture comes together as a smooth batter.

5. Pour the batter into the prepared loaf pan, place it in the oven, and bake until a cake tester inserted into the center of the loaf comes out clean, 50 to 60 minutes.

6. Remove the pan from the oven and place it on a wire rack to cool completely before serving.

Bagel Chips

YIELD: 4 SERVINGS | **ACTIVE TIME:** 10 MINUTES | **TOTAL TIME:** 25 MINUTES

3 EVERYTHING BAGELS (SEE PAGE 107), SLICED THIN

1. Preheat the oven to 350ºF.

2. Place the bagel slices on baking sheets and toast them in the oven until they are crispy and golden brown, about 8 minutes. Remove from the oven and let the chips cool slightly before enjoying.

Wonton Chips

YIELD: 4 TO 6 SERVINGS | **ACTIVE TIME:** 10 MINUTES | **TOTAL TIME:** 25 MINUTES

CANOLA OIL, AS NEEDED

12 WONTON WRAPPERS (SEE PAGE 560), CUT INTO WEDGES

SALT, TO TASTE

1. Add canola oil to a Dutch oven until it is about 1 inch deep and warm it to 350ºF.

2. Add the wrappers and fry, turning them frequently, until they are crispy and golden brown, 3 to 5 minutes.

3. Transfer the fried wonton wrappers to a paper towel–lined plate, season them with salt, and enjoy.

Nori Crackers

YIELD: 30 CRACKERS | **ACTIVE TIME:** 30 MINUTES | **TOTAL TIME:** 45 MINUTES

1 EGG

1 TABLESPOON WATER

3 SPRING ROLL WRAPPERS

3 SHEETS OF NORI

6 TABLESPOONS SESAME SEEDS

4 CUPS CANOLA OIL

SALT, TO TASTE

1. Combine the egg and water and brush the spring roll wrappers with the egg wash. Place a sheet of nori on top of each wrapper and brush the nori with the egg wash. Sprinkle the sesame seeds on top and let them sit for 10 minutes.

2. Place the oil in a Dutch oven and warm it to 300°F over medium heat. Cut each sheet into nine squares, place them in the oil, and fry until browned and crispy, about 5 minutes. Transfer to a paper towel–lined plate, season with salt, and enjoy.

Focaccia Barese

YIELD: 2 SMALL FOCACCIA | **ACTIVE TIME:** 40 MINUTES | **TOTAL TIME:** 4 HOURS

1 TEASPOON INSTANT YEAST OR 1⅓ TEASPOONS ACTIVE DRY YEAST

14 OZ. WATER

14 OZ. BREAD FLOUR, PLUS MORE AS NEEDED

7 OZ. SEMOLINA FLOUR

1 POTATO, BOILED, PEELED, AND MASHED

2½ TEASPOONS TABLE SALT, PLUS MORE TO TASTE

EXTRA-VIRGIN OLIVE OIL, AS NEEDED

2 VERY RIPE TOMATOES, CHOPPED

GREEN OLIVES, PITTED AND CHOPPED, TO TASTE

FRESH OREGANO, FINELY CHOPPED, TO TASTE

1. If using active dry yeast, warm 3½ tablespoons of the water until it is about 90°F. Add the water and the yeast to a bowl and gently stir. Let the mixture sit until it starts to foam.

2. In a large bowl, combine the flours, potato, yeast, and water. Work the mixture until it just holds together as a rough dough. Transfer the dough to a flour-dusted work surface and knead it until it is compact, smooth, and elastic.

3. Add the salt and knead until the dough is developed, elastic, and extensible, about 5 minutes. Form the dough into a ball and place it in an airtight container that has been coated with olive oil. Let the dough rest at room temperature until it has doubled in size, about 2 hours.

4. Generously grease two 10-inch cast-iron skillets or round cake pans with olive oil. Place the dough on a flour-dusted work surface and divide it into two pieces. Place the dough in the pans and spread it to the edge of each one, making sure not to press down too hard and deflate the focaccia. Let the focaccia rest at room temperature for another hour.

5. Preheat the oven to its maximum temperature and position a rack in the center. Top the focaccia with the tomatoes, olives, and oregano, season it with salt, and drizzle olive oil over the top. Place the pans directly on the bottom of the oven and bake for 10 minutes.

6. Transfer the pans to the middle rack and bake until the edges of the focaccia look brown and crunchy, 5 to 7 more minutes. Remove and let cool lightly before serving.

Paratha

YIELD: 8 SERVINGS | **ACTIVE TIME:** 30 MINUTES | **TOTAL TIME:** 1 HOUR

2 CUPS PASTRY FLOUR, PLUS MORE AS NEEDED

1 CUP WHOLE WHEAT FLOUR

¼ TEASPOON KOSHER SALT

1 CUP WARM WATER (105°F)

5 TABLESPOONS EXTRA-VIRGIN OLIVE OIL, PLUS MORE AS NEEDED

5 TABLESPOONS GHEE OR MELTED UNSALTED BUTTER

1. Place the flours and salt in the work bowl of a stand mixer fitted with the paddle attachment. With the mixer running on low, slowly add the warm water. Mix until incorporated and then slowly add the olive oil. When the oil has been incorporated, place the dough on a lightly floured work surface and knead until it is quite smooth, about 8 minutes.

2. Divide the dough into 8 small balls and dust them with flour. Use your hands to roll each ball into a long rope, and then coil each rope into a large disk. Use a rolling pin to flatten the disks until they are no more than ¼ inch thick. Lightly brush each disk with a small amount of olive oil.

3. Place a cast-iron skillet over very high heat for about 4 minutes. Brush the surface with some of the ghee or melted butter and place a disk of the dough on the surface. Cook until it is blistered and brown, about 1 minute. Turn the paratha over and cook the other side. Transfer the cooked paratha to a plate and repeat with the remaining pieces of dough. Serve warm or at room temperature.

Pita Bread

YIELD: 8 PITAS | **ACTIVE TIME:** 1 HOUR | **TOTAL TIME:** 3 HOURS

1 CUP LUKEWARM WATER (90°F)

1 TABLESPOON ACTIVE DRY YEAST

1 TABLESPOON SUGAR

1¾ CUPS ALL-PURPOSE FLOUR, PLUS MORE AS NEEDED

1 CUP WHOLE WHEAT FLOUR

1 TABLESPOON KOSHER SALT

1. In a large mixing bowl, combine the water, yeast, and sugar. Let the mixture sit until it starts to foam, about 15 minutes.

2. Add the flours and salt and work the mixture until it comes together as a smooth dough. Cover the bowl with a linen towel and let it rise for about 15 minutes.

3. Preheat the oven to 500°F and place a baking stone on the floor of the oven.

4. Divide the dough into 8 pieces and form them into balls. Place the balls on a flour-dusted work surface, press them down, and roll them until they are about ¼ inch thick.

5. Working with one pita at a time, place the pita on the baking stone and bake until it is puffy and brown, about 8 minutes. Remove from the oven and serve warm or at room temperature.

Cheese Twists

YIELD: 12 SERVINGS | **ACTIVE TIME:** 15 MINUTES | **TOTAL TIME:** 30 MINUTES

2 SHEETS OF FROZEN PUFF PASTRY, THAWED

ALL-PURPOSE FLOUR, AS NEEDED

½ CUP GRATED FONTINA CHEESE

½ CUP GRATED PARMESAN CHEESE

1 TEASPOON FINELY CHOPPED FRESH THYME

1 TEASPOON BLACK PEPPER

1 EGG, BEATEN

1. Preheat the oven to 375°F and line a baking sheet with parchment paper. Place the sheets of puff pastry on a flour-dusted surface and roll them out until the sheets are approximately 10 x 12–inch rectangles.

2. Place the cheeses, thyme, and pepper in a mixing bowl and stir to combine.

3. Lightly brush the tops of the pastry sheets with the egg. Sprinkle the cheese mixture over them and gently press down so it adheres to the pastry. Cut the sheets into ¼-inch-wide strips and twist them.

4. Place the twists on the baking sheet, place in the oven, and bake for 12 to 15 minutes, until the twists are golden brown and puffy. Turn the twists over and bake for another 2 to 3 minutes. Remove from the oven and let the twists cool on a wire rack before serving.

Pita Bread
SEE PAGE 102

Laffa

YIELD: 8 LAFFA | **ACTIVE TIME:** 30 MINUTES | **TOTAL TIME:** 1 HOUR AND 30 MINUTES

1½ CUPS WARM WATER (ABOUT 95°F), PLUS MORE AS NEEDED

2½ TEASPOONS ACTIVE DRY YEAST

2 TEASPOONS SUGAR

2 CUPS ALL-PURPOSE FLOUR, PLUS MORE AS NEEDED

2 CUPS BREAD FLOUR

1 TEASPOON FINE SEA SALT

2 TABLESPOONS EXTRA-VIRGIN OLIVE OIL

1. In a mixing bowl, combine the water, yeast, and sugar, gently stir, and let the mixture stand until it starts to foam, 5 to 10 minutes.

2. Combine the flours and salt in the work bowl of a stand mixer fitted with the dough hook. Work the mixture on low until thoroughly combined.

3. Add the yeast mixture, another ½ cup water, and the olive oil to the work bowl and work the mixture on low until it comes together as a ball of dough and pulls away from the side of the work bowl.

4. Add another ½ cup water and continue to mix until it has been incorporated. The dough should feel tacky when slapped with a clean hand, but it should not be sticky. If it is too sticky, incorporate more flour, a tablespoon at a time.

4. Cover the dough with plastic wrap and let it rise at room temperature until it has doubled in size, about 1 hour.

5. Place a baking stone on a rack in the upper third of the oven and preheat it to 500°F.

6. Form the dough into 8 baseball-sized rounds and place them on a parchment-lined baking sheet. Cover with a linen towel and let the rounds rise until they are the size of softballs.

7. Place the balls on a flour-dusted work surface and roll them as thin as possible.

8. When the dough is rolled out and the baking stone is hot, carefully drape one laffa over your hand and then quickly lay the stretched laffa onto the baking stone, quickly pulling any wrinkles flat. Repeat with the remaining laffa.

9. Bake the laffa until puffy and cooked through, about 1 minute. Remove from the oven and enjoy immediately.

Everything Bagels

YIELD: 6 BAGELS | **ACTIVE TIME:** 1 HOUR | **TOTAL TIME:** 6 HOURS

FOR THE DOUGH

6 OZ. WATER

¼ CUP HONEY

1 EGG WHITE

1 TABLESPOON CANOLA OIL

2 TEASPOONS ACTIVE DRY YEAST

1½ OZ. SUGAR

19 OZ. BREAD FLOUR, PLUS MORE AS NEEDED

1½ TEASPOONS KOSHER SALT

1 EGG, BEATEN

FOR THE BATH

12 CUPS WATER

½ CUP HONEY

FOR THE EVERYTHING SEASONING

2 TABLESPOONS POPPY SEEDS

1 TABLESPOON FENNEL SEEDS

1 TABLESPOON ONION FLAKES

1 TABLESPOON GARLIC FLAKES

2 TABLESPOONS SESAME SEEDS

1. To begin preparations for the dough, place the water, honey, egg white, and canola oil in the work bowl of a stand mixer fitted with the dough hook and whisk to combine. Add the yeast, sugar, flour, and salt and work the mixture for 1 minute on low. Raise the speed to medium and knead the mixture until it comes together as a smooth dough and pulls away from the side of the work bowl, about 10 minutes.

2. Place the dough on a flour-dusted work surface and shape it into a ball. Return the dough to the work bowl, cover it with plastic wrap, and let the dough rise at room temperature until it has doubled in size.

3. Divide the dough into six 5-oz. pieces and form each one into a ball.

4. Coat an 18 x 13–inch baking sheet with nonstick cooking spray. Place the pieces of dough on the pan, cover them with plastic wrap, and let them rise until they have doubled in size.

5. Using your fingers, make a small hole in the centers of the balls of dough. Place both of your index fingers in the holes and, working in a rotating motion, slowly stretch the pieces of dough into 4-inch-wide bagels. Place the bagels on the baking sheet, cover them with plastic wrap, and let them sit for 30 minutes.

6. Preheat the oven to 350°F. To prepare the bath, place the ingredients in a wide saucepan and bring to a boil.

7. Gently place the bagels in the boiling water and poach them on each side for 30 seconds.

8. Place the bagels back on the baking sheet.

9. To prepare the everything seasoning, place all the ingredients in a mixing bowl and stir to combine.

10. Brush the bagels with the egg and sprinkle the seasoning mixture over them.

11. Place the bagels in the oven and bake until they are a deep golden brown, 20 to 25 minutes.

12. Remove the pan from the oven, place the bagels on a cooling rack, and let them cool before enjoying.

Sourdough Crackers

YIELD: 40 TO 80 CRACKERS | **ACTIVE TIME:** 30 MINUTES | **TOTAL TIME:** 2 HOURS

1 CUP SOURDOUGH STARTER (SEE PAGE 16)

1 CUP ALL-PURPOSE FLOUR, PLUS MORE AS NEEDED

½ TEASPOON FINE SEA SALT

4 TABLESPOONS UNSALTED BUTTER, SOFTENED

EXTRA-VIRGIN OLIVE OIL, AS NEEDED

MALDON SEA SALT, TO TASTE

1. Place the starter, flour, salt, and butter in a mixing bowl and work the mixture until it comes together as a smooth dough.

2. Divide the dough in half and form each piece into a rectangle. Cover the dough in plastic wrap and chill in the refrigerator until it is firm, about 1 hour.

3. Preheat the oven to 350°F. Dust a piece of parchment paper and a rolling pin with flour. Place one piece of dough on the parchment and roll it until it is about ¹⁄₁₆ inch thick.

4. Transfer the parchment, with the dough on it, to a baking sheet. Brush the dough with some olive oil and sprinkle the Maldon sea salt over the top.

5. Cut the crackers to the desired size and shape and prick each cracker with a fork. Repeat with the remaining piece of dough.

6. Place the crackers in the oven and bake until crispy and golden brown, 20 to 25 minutes, rotating the baking sheets halfway through.

7. Remove the crackers from the oven, place the baking sheets on wire racks, and let the crackers cool completely before enjoying.

Note: Incorporate 2 to 3 tablespoons of herbs or seeds into the dough, and don't be afraid to experiment.

SAUCES, DIPS & SPREADS

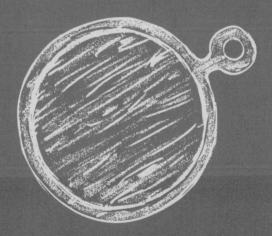

Pea & Parmesan Dip

YIELD: 2 CUPS | **ACTIVE TIME:** 10 MINUTES | **TOTAL TIME:** 20 MINUTES

SALT AND PEPPER, TO TASTE

3 CUPS PEAS

1 CUP WATER

3 TABLESPOONS PINE NUTS

1 CUP FRESHLY GRATED PARMESAN CHEESE

1 GARLIC CLOVE, MINCED

½ CUP FRESH MINT, CHIFFONADE

1. Bring water to a boil in a large saucepan. Add salt and the peas and cook until the peas are bright green and warmed through, about 2 minutes.

2. Transfer half of the peas to a food processor. Add the water, pine nuts, Parmesan, and garlic and blitz until pureed.

3. Place the puree in a serving dish, add the remaining peas and the mint, and fold to incorporate. Season the dip with salt and pepper and chill in the refrigerator until ready to serve.

Hummus

YIELD: 20 SERVINGS | **ACTIVE TIME:** 1 HOUR | **TOTAL TIME:** 24 HOURS

2 LBS. DRIED CHICKPEAS

1 TABLESPOON BAKING SODA

12 CUPS ROOM-TEMPERATURE WATER

12 CUPS VEGETABLE STOCK (SEE PAGE 552)

1 CUP TAHINI PASTE

2 TABLESPOONS ZA'ATAR

2 TABLESPOONS SUMAC

2 TABLESPOONS CUMIN

2 TABLESPOONS KOSHER SALT

2 TABLESPOONS BLACK PEPPER

2 GARLIC CLOVES, GRATED

½ BUNCH OF FRESH CILANTRO, CHOPPED

1 CUP EXTRA-VIRGIN OLIVE OIL

1 CUP SESAME OIL

1 CUP ICE WATER

½ CUP FRESH LEMON JUICE

1. Place the chickpeas, baking soda, and water in a large saucepan, stir, and cover. Let the chickpeas soak overnight at room temperature.

2. Drain the chickpeas and rinse them. Place them in a large saucepan, add the stock, and bring to a steady simmer. Cook until the chickpeas are quite tender, about 1 hour.

3. In a blender or food processor, combine all of the remaining ingredients and puree until achieving a perfectly smooth, creamy sauce; the ice water is the key to getting the correct consistency.

4. Add the warm, drained chickpeas to the tahini mixture and blend until the hummus is perfectly smooth and not at all grainy, occasionally stopping to scrape down the sides of the bowl. This blending process may take 3 minutes; remain patient and keep going until the mixture is very creamy and fluffy, adding water as necessary to get the right consistency.

5. Taste, adjust the seasoning as necessary, and enjoy.

Gochujang & Scallion Sauce

YIELD: 2 CUPS | **ACTIVE TIME:** 25 MINUTES | **TOTAL TIME:** 40 MINUTES

CANOLA OIL, AS NEEDED

½ CUP GARLIC CLOVES

2-INCH PIECE OF FRESH
GINGER, PEELED AND
CHOPPED

5 SCALLIONS, TRIMMED AND
FINELY DICED, WHITE AND
GREEN PARTS SEPARATED

½ CUP BROWN SUGAR

3 TABLESPOONS
GOCHUJANG PASTE

1 CUP SOY SAUCE

1 TABLESPOON GINGER
JUICE

1. Add canola oil to a Dutch oven until it is about 1 inch deep and warm it to 300ºF.

2. Gently slip the garlic into the hot oil and fry until it is golden brown, 2 to 3 minutes. Remove the garlic with a slotted spoon and transfer it to a paper towel–lined plate to drain.

3. Add the ginger to the hot oil and fry until it is golden brown, 2 to 3 minutes. Remove the ginger with a slotted spoon and transfer it to the paper towel–lined plate to drain.

4. Add 1 tablespoon of the hot oil to medium saucepan and warm it over medium-low heat. Add the scallion whites and cook, stirring occasionally, until they are very tender, about 15 minutes.

5. Stir in the brown sugar and cook until it is about to caramelize. Add the gochujang and stir until well combined.

6. Stir in the soy sauce and ginger juice and bring the sauce to a gentle simmer. Cook for 5 minutes, stirring frequently.

7. Remove the pan from heat, stir the fried garlic, fried ginger, and scallion greens into the sauce, and let it cool to room temperature before serving.

Hummus
SEE PAGE 112

Tahini & Yogurt Sauce

YIELD: 1 CUP | **ACTIVE TIME:** 5 MINUTES | **TOTAL TIME:** 5 MINUTES

¾ CUP FULL-FAT GREEK
YOGURT

1 GARLIC CLOVE, MINCED

2 TABLESPOONS TAHINI
PASTE

JUICE OF 1 LEMON

½ TEASPOON CUMIN

SALT AND PEPPER, TO TASTE

1 TABLESPOON BLACK
SESAME SEEDS

1 TABLESPOON EXTRA-
VIRGIN OLIVE OIL

1. Place the yogurt, garlic, tahini, lemon juice, and cumin in a small bowl and whisk to combine.

2. Season the sauce with salt and pepper, add the sesame seeds and olive oil, and whisk until incorporated. Use immediately or store in the refrigerator until needed.

Peanut Sauce

YIELD: 1 CUP | **ACTIVE TIME:** 10 MINUTES | **TOTAL TIME:** 10 MINUTES

2 GARLIC CLOVES, MINCED

2 SHALLOTS, MINCED

2 TABLESPOONS AVOCADO OIL

½ CUP COCONUT MILK

¼ CUP CREAMY PEANUT BUTTER

1 TABLESPOON TAMARIND PASTE

1½ TABLESPOONS KECAP MANIS

2 TEASPOONS FISH SAUCE

2 TEASPOONS FRESH LIME JUICE

2 TEASPOONS SWEET CHILI DIPPING SAUCE (SEE BELOW)

1. Using a mortar and pestle, grind the garlic and shallots into a paste.

2. Place the paste and the avocado oil in a small saucepan and warm the mixture over low heat, stirring frequently, for 2 minutes.

3. Stir in the remaining ingredients and cook until the sauce starts to bubble. Remove the pan from heat, taste the sauce, and adjust the seasoning as necessary. Use immediately or store in the refrigerator.

Sweet Chili Dipping Sauce

YIELD: 1½ CUPS | **ACTIVE TIME:** 10 MINUTES | **TOTAL TIME:** 10 MINUTES

3 RED BIRD'S EYE CHILI PEPPERS, STEMS REMOVED

4 GARLIC CLOVES

⅓ CUP WHITE VINEGAR

½ CUP SUGAR

1 TEASPOON KOSHER SALT

1 CUP PLUS 2 TABLESPOONS WATER

1 TABLESPOON CORNSTARCH

1. Place the chilies, garlic, vinegar, sugar, salt, and 1 cup of the water in a blender and blend until the mixture is a chunky puree.

2. Place the puree in a small saucepan and bring it to a boil over medium-high heat. Reduce the heat and simmer, stirring frequently, until the garlic is tender, about 3 minutes.

3. Place the cornstarch and remaining water in a small bowl and stir until well combined. Stir the slurry into the sauce and simmer until the sauce has thickened, about 1 minute.

4. Remove the pan from heat and let the sauce cool before using or storing in the refrigerator.

Pot Sticker Dipping Sauce

YIELD: ½ CUP | **ACTIVE TIME:** 5 MINUTES | **TOTAL TIME:** 5 MINUTES

2 TABLESPOONS SOY SAUCE

1 TABLESPOON SAMBAL OELEK

1 TABLESPOON WHITE WINE VINEGAR

1 TABLESPOON CHINKIANG VINEGAR

1 TABLESPOON SUGAR

2 GARLIC CLOVES, MINCED

1 TABLESPOON MINCED SCALLION

1 TABLESPOON CHOPPED FRESH CILANTRO

1 TEASPOON SESAME OIL

1 TEASPOON CHILI OIL

1. Place all of the ingredients in a bowl and stir until well combined. Let the sauce marinate for 30 minutes before using or storing.

Pineapple & Plum Dipping Sauce

YIELD: 1 CUP | **ACTIVE TIME:** 5 MINUTES | **TOTAL TIME:** 5 MINUTES

⅔ CUP PINEAPPLE JUICE

¼ CUP PLUM SAUCE

2 TABLESPOONS SWEET CHILI DIPPING SAUCE (SEE OPPOSITE PAGE)

1. Place all of the ingredients in a bowl and stir until well combined. Use immediately or store in the refrigerator.

Guacamole

YIELD: 4 SERVINGS | **ACTIVE TIME:** 15 MINUTES | **TOTAL TIME:** 25 MINUTES

1 LARGE TOMATO, FINELY DICED

2 SERRANO CHILE PEPPERS, STEMS AND SEEDS REMOVED, FINELY DICED

½ ONION, FINELY DICED

1 GARLIC CLOVE, MASHED

4 LARGE AVOCADOS, PITTED AND DICED

6 TABLESPOONS FRESH LIME JUICE

SALT, TO TASTE

½ CUP FRESH CILANTRO, CHOPPED

1. Combine the tomato, chiles, and onion in a bowl. Place the garlic clove in a separate bowl.

2. Add the avocados to the bowl containing the garlic and stir until well combined. Stir in the lime juice and season with salt.

3. Add the tomato mixture and stir until it has been incorporated. Add the cilantro and stir to combine. Taste and adjust the seasoning as necessary.

Sweet Corn & Pepita Guacamole

YIELD: 4 SERVINGS | **ACTIVE TIME:** 15 MINUTES | **TOTAL TIME:** 30 MINUTES

1 EAR OF YELLOW CORN, WITH HUSK ON

1 OZ. PUMPKIN SEEDS

1 OZ. POMEGRANATE SEEDS

FLESH OF 3 AVOCADOS

½ RED ONION, CHOPPED

½ CUP FRESH CILANTRO, CHOPPED

1 TEASPOON FRESH LIME JUICE

SALT AND PEPPER, TO TASTE

1. Preheat a gas or charcoal grill to medium-high heat (about 450ºF). Place the corn on the grill and cook until it is charred all over and the kernels have softened enough that there is considerable give in them.

2. Remove the corn from the grill and let it cool. When cool enough to handle, husk the corn and cut off the kernels.

3. Combine the corn, pumpkin seeds, and pomegranate seeds in a small bowl. Place the avocados in a separate bowl and mash until it is just slightly chunky. Stir in the corn mixture, onion, cilantro, and lime juice, season the mixture with salt and pepper, and work the mixture until the guacamole is the desired texture.

Salsa de Chiltomate

YIELD: 1½ CUPS | **ACTIVE TIME:** 20 MINUTES | **TOTAL TIME:** 1 HOUR

8½ OZ. ROMA TOMATOES, HALVED

2 HABANERO CHILE PEPPERS

1 SMALL WHITE ONION, QUARTERED

4 GARLIC CLOVES, UNPEELED

2 TABLESPOONS EXTRA-VIRGIN OLIVE OIL

SALT, TO TASTE

JUICE OF 1 LIME

1. Preheat the oven to 450°F. Line a baking sheet with parchment paper, place the tomatoes, chiles, onion, and garlic on it, and place it in the oven.

2. Roast until the vegetables are charred all over, checking every 5 minutes or so and removing them as they become ready.

3. Peel the garlic cloves, remove the stem and seeds from the habaneros (gloves are strongly recommended while handling habaneros), and place the roasted vegetables in a blender. Puree until smooth.

4. Place the olive oil in a medium saucepan and warm it over medium-high heat. Carefully pour the puree into the pan, reduce the heat, and simmer until it has reduced slightly and the flavor is to your liking, 15 to 20 minutes.

5. Season with salt, stir in the lime juice, and let the salsa cool. Taste, adjust the seasoning as necessary, and enjoy.

Salsa Borracha

YIELD: 1½ CUPS | **ACTIVE TIME:** 20 MINUTES | **TOTAL TIME:** 30 MINUTES

½ LB. TOMATILLOS, HUSKED AND RINSED

1 SMALL WHITE ONION

5 GARLIC CLOVES, UNPEELED

2 TABLESPOONS LARD

3 PASILLA CHILE PEPPERS, STEMS AND SEEDS REMOVED

2 CHIPOTLE MORITA CHILE PEPPERS, STEMS AND SEEDS REMOVED

3½ OZ. MEXICAN LAGER

1 TEASPOON MEZCAL OR TEQUILA

1 TEASPOON MAGGI SEASONING SAUCE

SALT, TO TASTE

1. Warm a cast-iron skillet over medium-high heat. Add the tomatillos, onion, and garlic and toast until charred all over, turning them as needed. Remove the vegetables from the pan and let them cool. When cool enough to handle, peel the garlic cloves and place the mixture in a blender.

2. Place half of the lard in the skillet and warm it over medium heat. Add the chiles and fry until fragrant and pliable. Place the chiles in the blender.

3. Add the beer, mezcal, and Maggi and puree until smooth.

4. Place the remaining lard in a saucepan and warm it over medium heat. Add the puree and fry it for 5 minutes. Season the salsa with salt and let it cool before enjoying.

Sweet Corn & Pepita Guacamole
SEE PAGE 120

Salsa Verde

YIELD: 1½ CUPS | **ACTIVE TIME:** 20 MINUTES | **TOTAL TIME:** 30 MINUTES

1 LB. TOMATILLOS, HUSKED AND RINSED

5 GARLIC CLOVES, UNPEELED

1 SMALL WHITE ONION, QUARTERED

10 SERRANO CHILE PEPPERS

2 BUNCHES OF FRESH CILANTRO

SALT, TO TASTE

1. Warm a cast-iron skillet over high heat. Place the tomatillos, garlic, onion, and chiles in the pan and cook until charred all over, turning them occasionally.

2. Remove the vegetables from the pan and let them cool slightly.

3. Peel the garlic cloves and remove the stems and seeds from the chiles. Place the charred vegetables in a blender, add the cilantro, and puree until smooth.

4. Season the salsa with salt and enjoy.

Horseradish Cream

YIELD: 1 CUP | **ACTIVE TIME:** 5 MINUTES | **TOTAL TIME:** 5 MINUTES

2 TABLESPOONS GRATED FRESH HORSERADISH

2 TEASPOONS WHITE WINE VINEGAR

½ TEASPOON DIJON MUSTARD

1 CUP HEAVY CREAM

SALT AND PEPPER, TO TASTE

1. Combine the horseradish, vinegar, mustard, and ¼ cup of the cream in a mixing bowl.

2. Lightly whip the remaining cream and then fold this into the horseradish mixture. Season to taste and refrigerate until ready to serve.

Habanero Honey

YIELD: 1 CUP | **ACTIVE TIME:** 10 MINUTES | **TOTAL TIME:** 2 HOURS

4 HABANERO CHILE PEPPERS, PIERCED

1 CUP HONEY

1. Place the chile peppers and honey in a saucepan and bring to a very gentle simmer over medium-low heat. Reduce heat to lowest possible setting and cook for 1 hour.

2. Remove the saucepan from heat and let the mixture infuse for another hour.

3. Remove the peppers. Transfer the honey to a container, cover, and chill in the refrigerator until ready to serve.

Peanut Hoisin Dipping Sauce

YIELD: 1 CUP | **ACTIVE TIME:** 15 MINUTES | **TOTAL TIME:** 30 MINUTES

CANOLA OIL, AS NEEDED

¼ CUP PEANUTS

¼ CUP HOISIN SAUCE (SEE BELOW)

¼ CUP RICE VINEGAR

2 TABLESPOONS SUGAR

2 TABLESPOONS SOY SAUCE

2 TABLESPOONS SWEET CHILI DIPPING SAUCE (SEE PAGE 118)

1. Add canola oil to a small cast-iron skillet until it is about 1 inch deep and warm it to 350ºF.

2. Add the peanuts to the warm oil and fry until they are golden brown, 3 to 4 minutes. Transfer the fried peanuts to a paper towel–lined plate to drain and cool. When they are cool enough to handle, chop the peanuts and set them aside.

3. Place the remaining ingredients in a bowl and stir to combine. Top the sauce with the peanuts and use immediately or store in the refrigerator.

Hoisin Sauce

YIELD: ½ CUP | **ACTIVE TIME:** 5 MINUTES | **TOTAL TIME:** 5 MINUTES

2 TABLESPOONS AVOCADO OIL

4 GARLIC CLOVES, MINCED

¼ CUP SOY SAUCE

3 TABLESPOONS HONEY

2 TABLESPOONS WHITE VINEGAR

2 TABLESPOONS TAHINI

2 TEASPOONS SRIRACHA

1. Place the avocado oil in a saucepan and warm it over medium heat. Add the garlic and cook, stirring continually, for 1 minute.

2. Stir in the soy sauce, honey, vinegar, tahini, and sriracha and cook until the sauce is smooth, about 5 minutes. Remove the pan from heat and let the sauce cool before using or storing in the refrigerator.

Chili Garlic Sauce

YIELD: 1 CUP | **ACTIVE TIME:** 15 MINUTES | **TOTAL TIME:** 30 MINUTES

1 CUP CHOPPED FRESNO
CHILE PEPPERS

8 GARLIC CLOVES, CHOPPED

¼ CUP WHITE VINEGAR

2 TABLESPOONS SUGAR

1 TEASPOON KOSHER SALT,
PLUS MORE TO TASTE

BLACK PEPPER, TO TASTE

1. Place the chiles, garlic, and vinegar in a small saucepan and bring to a simmer over medium heat, stirring occasionally. Cook for 10 minutes.

2. Transfer the mixture to a blender and puree until smooth.

3. Strain the puree through a fine sieve into a clean saucepan. Add the sugar and salt and bring the sauce to a simmer. Season the sauce with salt and pepper, remove the pan from heat, and let the sauce cool completely before using or storing.

Thai Chili Jam

YIELD: 2 CUPS | **ACTIVE TIME:** 45 MINUTES | **TOTAL TIME:** 1 HOUR AND 30 MINUTES

8 DRIED THAI CHILI PEPPERS, STEMS AND SEEDS REMOVED

1½ CUPS CANOLA OIL, PLUS MORE AS NEEDED

1 CUP THINLY SLICED GARLIC

4 SHALLOTS, SLICED THIN

¼ CUP DRIED SHRIMP

1 TABLESPOON SHRIMP PASTE

3 TABLESPOONS SEEDLESS TAMARIND PASTE

3 CUPS BOILING WATER

⅓ CUP COCONUT OR PALM SUGAR

2 TABLESPOONS FISH SAUCE

1 TEASPOON KOSHER SALT

1. Place the chilies in a dry skillet and toast them over medium heat for 5 to 8 minutes, making sure not to burn them. Transfer the toasted chiles to a plate.

2. Add 1 cup of the canola oil and the garlic to the hot skillet and fry the garlic until it is light brown and crispy, about 6 minutes. Use a slotted spoon to transfer the garlic to a paper towel–lined plate.

3. Add the shallots and dried shrimp and fry until lightly golden brown, about 4 minutes. Transfer the mixture to the paper towel–lined plate.

4. Place the chiles, garlic, shallots, dried shrimp, and shrimp paste in a food processor and blitz until the mixture is a thick paste. Set the mixture aside.

5. Break the tamarind paste into chunks, place them in a bowl, and cover with the boiling water. Cover the bowl and let the tamarind steep for 30 minutes.

6. Using your hands or a masher, break the tamarind down further. Let the tamarind steep for another 15 minutes.

7. Strain the mixture through a fine mesh sieve and scrape the pulp from the underside of the sieve into the bowl. Discard the stringy material, stir the juice and pulp until combined, and set the tamarind water aside.

8. Place the paste, sugar, ⅓ cup of the tamarind water, fish sauce, and salt in a clean saucepan and cook over medium heat, stirring occasionally, until the mixture is jammy, 15 to 20 minutes.

9. Transfer the jam to a mason jar and let it cool. To can this jam, see page 396. You can also store this jam in the refrigerator, where it will keep for up to 1 month.

Raspberry Jam

YIELD: 2 CUPS | **ACTIVE TIME:** 30 MINUTES | **TOTAL TIME:** 3 HOURS

1 LB. FRESH RASPBERRIES

1 LB. SUGAR

ZEST AND JUICE OF 1 LEMON

1. Place the ingredients in a large saucepan fitted with a candy thermometer and cook it over medium-high heat until the mixture is 220°F. Stir the jam occasionally as it cooks.

2. Pour the jam into jars and let it cool completely. To can this jam, see page 396. If not, cover the jars and store the jam in the refrigerator, where it will keep for up to 1 month.

Salata Mechouia

YIELD: 6 SERVINGS | **ACTIVE TIME:** 1 HOUR AND 15 MINUTES | **TOTAL TIME:** 3 HOURS AND 15 MINUTES

1 JALAPEÑO CHILE PEPPER

6 LARGE PLUM TOMATOES

3 GREEN BELL PEPPERS

2 GARLIC CLOVES, UNPEELED

1 TEASPOON KOSHER SALT

¼ TEASPOON BLACK PEPPER

¼ CUP FRESH LEMON JUICE

3 TABLESPOONS EXTRA-VIRGIN OLIVE OIL

PITA BREAD (SEE PAGE 102), FOR SERVING

1. Preheat the oven to 375°F. Use a knife to poke a small slit in the jalapeño.

2. Place the tomatoes, bell peppers, jalapeño, and garlic on an aluminum foil–lined baking sheet. Place it in the oven and roast until the vegetables are well browned and just tender, about 30 minutes for the garlic and 1 hour for the peppers and tomatoes.

3. Remove the vegetables from the oven. Place the garlic cloves on a plate and let them cool. Place the other roasted vegetables in a large bowl and cover it with plastic wrap. Let them rest for about 15 minutes.

4. Peel the garlic cloves and set them aside. Remove the charred skins from the other vegetables, place the vegetables in a colander, and let them drain.

5. Using a fork, mash the roasted garlic.

6. Transfer the drained vegetables to a cutting board. Remove the seeds from the bell peppers and the jalapeño. Finely chop all of the vegetables and place them in a mixing bowl. Add the mashed garlic, salt, pepper, lemon juice, and olive oil and stir until well combined.

7. Enjoy immediately with Pita Bread.

Chicken Liver Mousse

YIELD: 6 SERVINGS | **ACTIVE TIME:** 30 MINUTES | **TOTAL TIME:** 3 HOURS AND 30 MINUTES

1 TABLESPOON UNSALTED BUTTER

½ LB. CHICKEN LIVER, CHOPPED

2 TABLESPOONS CHOPPED WHITE ONION

1 TEASPOON KOSHER SALT

1 TEASPOON BLACK PEPPER

2 TABLESPOONS BALSAMIC VINEGAR

3 OZ. HEAVY CREAM

CRACKERS OR GRILLED BREAD, FOR SERVING

1. Place the butter in a large skillet and melt it over medium-high heat. When the butter begins to foam, add the liver, onion, salt, and pepper and cook, stirring frequently, until the liver is no longer pink, about 8 minutes.

2. Transfer the mixture to a food processor and puree. With the food processor running, slowly add the balsamic vinegar. When all of the vinegar has been incorporated, slowly add the cream and puree until smooth.

3. Transfer the mixture to a container, place it in the refrigerator, and chill, uncovered, for 1 hour.

4. Cover the mousse and refrigerate for another 2 hours, or until the mousse is set.

5. Serve with crackers or grilled bread.

Nuoc Cham

YIELD: 1 CUP | **ACTIVE TIME:** 10 MINUTES | **TOTAL TIME:** 10 MINUTES

¼ CUP FISH SAUCE

⅓ CUP WATER

2 TABLESPOONS SUGAR

¼ CUP FRESH LIME JUICE

1 GARLIC CLOVE, MINCED

2 BIRD'S EYE CHILIES, STEMS AND SEEDS REMOVED, SLICED THIN

1 TABLESPOON CHILI GARLIC SAUCE (SEE PAGE 128)

1. Place all of the ingredients in a mixing bowl and stir until the sugar has dissolved and the mixture is well combined.

2. Taste, adjust the seasoning as necessary, and use as desired.

Sweet Potato & Tahini Dip

YIELD: 1 CUP | **ACTIVE TIME:** 15 MINUTES | **TOTAL TIME:** 1 HOUR

EXTRA-VIRGIN OLIVE OIL, AS NEEDED

1 SWEET POTATO, HALVED

1 YELLOW ONION, QUARTERED

2 LARGE GARLIC CLOVES

¼ CUP TAHINI PASTE

1 TEASPOON FRESH LEMON JUICE

½ TEASPOON KOSHER SALT

2 TABLESPOONS HONEY

½ TEASPOON ANCHO CHILE POWDER

1 TABLESPOON MINCED PISTACHIOS, FOR GARNISH

1. Preheat the oven to 400°F and coat a baking sheet with olive oil. Place the sweet potato, cut side down, and the onion on the baking sheet. Place the garlic in a small piece of aluminum foil, sprinkle a few drops of oil on them, wrap them up, and place on the baking sheet.

2. Place the baking sheet in the oven and roast for approximately 20 minutes, then remove the garlic. Roast the sweet potato and onion until the sweet potato is very tender, another 10 minutes or so. Remove from the oven and let cool.

3. Scoop the sweet potato's flesh into a food processor. Add the roasted onion, garlic, tahini, lemon juice, and salt. Pulse until the mixture is a smooth paste. Taste and adjust the seasoning as necessary.

4. Place the honey in a very small pot and warm it over low heat. Add the ancho chile powder, remove the pan from heat, and let it sit for a few minutes.

5. Place the puree in a shallow bowl and make a well in the center. Pour some of the spiced honey in the well, garnish with the pistachios, and enjoy.

Okonomiyaki Sauce

YIELD: ½ CUP | **ACTIVE TIME:** 5 MINUTES | **TOTAL TIME:** 5 MINUTES

3 TABLESPOONS WORCESTERSHIRE SAUCE

3½ TABLESPOONS KETCHUP

2 TABLESPOONS OYSTER SAUCE

1½ TABLESPOONS LIGHT BROWN SUGAR

1. Place all of the ingredients in a bowl and whisk until the brown sugar has dissolved and the mixture is well combined.

2. Use immediately or store in the refrigerator.

Red Pepper Feta & Ricotta

YIELD: 1½ CUPS | **ACTIVE TIME:** 5 MINUTES | **TOTAL TIME:** 5 MINUTES

4 OZ. FETA CHEESE

2 OZ. RICOTTA CHEESE

1 CUP CHOPPED ROASTED RED PEPPERS

¼ CUP EXTRA-VIRGIN OLIVE OIL, PLUS MORE FOR GARNISH

1 TABLESPOON FRESH LEMON JUICE

ZA'ATAR SEASONING, FOR GARNISH

FRESH CHIVES, CHOPPED, FOR GARNISH

SESAME SEEDS, TOASTED, FOR GARNISH

1. Place all of the ingredients, except for the garnishes, in a food processor and blitz until pureed.

2. Garnish with za'atar, chives, sesame seeds, and additional olive oil and enjoy.

Garlic Butter

YIELD: 1¼ CUPS | **ACTIVE TIME:** 5 MINUTES | **TOTAL TIME:** 5 MINUTES

1 CUP UNSALTED BUTTER, SOFTENED

1½ TEASPOONS FRESH LEMON JUICE

2 GARLIC CLOVES, MINCED

3 TABLESPOONS CHOPPED FRESH PARSLEY

SALT AND PEPPER, TO TASTE

1. Place the butter in a bowl and whisk it until it is fluffy, about 2 minutes.

2. Add the remaining ingredients, whisk to combine, and either use immediately or store in the refrigerator.

Chipotle & Bourbon Queso

YIELD: 8 SERVINGS | **ACTIVE TIME:** 20 MINUTES | **TOTAL TIME:** 20 MINUTES

¼ CUP BOURBON

1½ TABLESPOONS CORNSTARCH

1 CUP MILK

2 CUPS SHREDDED CHEDDAR CHEESE

2 TABLESPOONS PUREED CHIPOTLES IN ADOBO

1 TABLESPOON CHOPPED FRESH CILANTRO

TORTILLA CHIPS, FOR SERVING

1. Place the bourbon and cornstarch in a small bowl and whisk to combine. Set the mixture aside.

2. Place the milk in a large saucepan and bring it to a simmer over medium heat. Gradually add the cheddar cheese, whisking until the cheese has melted and the mixture is smooth.

3. Stir in the bourbon mixture and the pureed chipotles. Cook, whisking continually, until the mixture has thickened slightly, 1 to 2 minutes.

4. Transfer the queso dip to a serving bowl, top it with the cilantro, and serve with tortilla chips.

Caramelized Spring Onion Dip

YIELD: 8 SERVINGS | **ACTIVE TIME:** 30 MINUTES | **TOTAL TIME:** 1 HOUR AND 30 MINUTES

3 LBS. SPRING ONIONS, RINSED WELL AND PATTED DRY

2 TABLESPOONS UNSALTED BUTTER

2 CUPS MAYONNAISE

1 CUP SOUR CREAM

1 CUP FULL-FAT GREEK YOGURT

ZEST AND JUICE OF 2 LEMONS

1 TEASPOON KOSHER SALT

½ TEASPOON BLACK PEPPER

¼ TEASPOON ONION POWDER

¼ TEASPOON GARLIC POWDER

1. Slice the spring onions thin from the top of the green part to the bottom of the white bulb. Place the butter in a large skillet and melt it over medium heat. Add the spring onions and reduce the heat to low. Cook the spring onions, stirring every few minutes, until they are golden brown, 10 to 12 minutes.

2. Remove the onions from the pan, place them in a large mixing bowl, and chill them in the refrigerator until completely cool.

3. Remove the spring onions from the refrigerator, add the remaining ingredients to the bowl, and stir to combine. Cover the bowl with plastic wrap and chill the dip in the refrigerator for at least 1 hour. If time allows, chill the dip in the refrigerator overnight.

Apricot & Chile Jam

YIELD: 8 CUPS | **ACTIVE TIME:** 20 MINUTES | **TOTAL TIME:** 1 HOUR AND 30 MINUTES

2 LBS. APRICOTS, HALVED, PITTED, AND CHOPPED

ZEST AND JUICE OF 1 LEMON

2 LBS. SUGAR

1 CUP WATER

3 RED CHILE PEPPERS, SEEDS REMOVED, MINCED

1 TABLESPOON UNSALTED BUTTER

1. Place all the ingredients, except for the butter, in a saucepan and bring to a gentle boil over medium heat, stirring to help the sugar dissolve. Boil the mixture for about 5 minutes.

2. Reduce the heat and simmer for 15 minutes, stirring frequently. If you prefer a smoother jam, mash the mixture with a wooden spoon as it cooks.

3. When the jam has formed a thin skin, remove the pan from the heat. Add the butter and stir to disperse any froth. Let cool for 15 minutes. To can this jam, see page 396. If you are not interested in canning it, let the jam cool completely before storing in the refrigerator.

Green Tomato Jam

YIELD: 2 CUPS | **ACTIVE TIME:** 35 MINUTES | **TOTAL TIME:** 5 TO 7 HOURS

¾ LB. GREEN TOMATOES, DICED

¼ LARGE ONION, DICED

½-INCH PIECE OF FRESH GINGER, PEELED AND MINCED

2 GARLIC CLOVES, CHOPPED

1 TEASPOON MUSTARD SEEDS

1 TEASPOON CUMIN

1 TEASPOON CORIANDER

2 TEASPOONS KOSHER SALT

½ CUP HONEY OR MAPLE SYRUP

1 CUP APPLE CIDER VINEGAR

1 CUP RAISINS

1. Place all the ingredients in a large saucepan and bring to a boil. Reduce the heat so that the mixture simmers and cook, stirring occasionally, until the onions and tomatoes are tender and the juices have thickened, 20 to 30 minutes. If a smoother jam is desired, mash the mixture with a wooden spoon as it simmers.

2. Remove the pan from heat. To can this jam, see page 396. If you are not interested in canning it, let cool completely before storing it in the refrigerator.

Blueberry & Basil Jam

YIELD: 3½ CUPS | **ACTIVE TIME:** 10 MINUTES | **TOTAL TIME:** 1 HOUR AND 30 MINUTES

3 QUARTS OF FRESH
BLUEBERRIES

LEAVES FROM 1 BUNCH OF
BASIL, FINELY CHOPPED

2 TEASPOONS FRESH
LEMON JUICE

2 CUPS SUGAR

½ CUP WATER

1. Place all the ingredients in a large saucepan and bring to a boil, while stirring frequently, over medium-high heat.

2. Once the mixture has come to a boil, reduce the heat so that it simmers and cook, stirring frequently, until the mixture has reduced by half and is starting to thicken, about 1 hour. Remove from heat and let it thicken and set as it cools. If the jam is still too thin after 1 hour, continue to simmer until it is the desired consistency.

3. To can this jam, see page 396. If you are not interested in canning it, let cool completely before storing it in the refrigerator.

Mostarda

YIELD: 1 CUP | **ACTIVE TIME:** 5 MINUTES | **TOTAL TIME:** 15 MINUTES

4 OZ. DRIED APRICOTS,
CHOPPED

¼ CUP CHOPPED DRIED
CHERRIES

1 SHALLOT, MINCED

1½ TEASPOONS MINCED
CRYSTALLIZED GINGER

½ CUP DRY WHITE WINE

3 TABLESPOONS WHITE
WINE VINEGAR

3 TABLESPOONS WATER

3 TABLESPOONS SUGAR

1 TEASPOON MUSTARD
POWDER

1 TEASPOON DIJON
MUSTARD

1 TABLESPOON UNSALTED
BUTTER

1. Place the apricots, cherries, shallot, ginger, wine, vinegar, water, and sugar in a saucepan and bring to a boil over medium-high heat. Cover, reduce the heat to medium, and cook until all the liquid has been absorbed and the fruit is soft, about 10 minutes.

2. Uncover the pot and stir in the mustard powder, mustard, and butter. Simmer until the mixture is jam-like, 2 to 3 minutes. Remove from heat and let cool slightly before serving. The mostarda will keep in the refrigerator for up to 1 week.

Cultured Butter

YIELD: 2 CUPS | **ACTIVE TIME:** 10 MINUTES | **TOTAL TIME:** 2 DAYS

4 CUPS HIGH-QUALITY HEAVY CREAM

½ CUP WHOLE MILK YOGURT

½ TEASPOON KOSHER SALT

1. Place the heavy cream and yogurt in a jar. Seal it and shake vigorously to combine.

2. Open the jar, cover it with cheesecloth, and secure it with a rubber band or kitchen twine.

3. Place the mixture away from direct sunlight and let it sit at room temperature for 36 hours.

4. After 36 hours, seal the jar and place it in the refrigerator for 4 to 6 hours.

5. Remove the mixture from the refrigerator and pour it into the work bowl of a stand mixer fitted with the whisk attachment. Add the salt and whip on high, covering with a towel to prevent spilling, until the butter separates from the buttermilk. Reserve the buttermilk for another preparation.

6. Transfer the butter to a piece of cheesecloth and squeeze out any excess liquid. Wash the butter under ice-cold water and store in an airtight container. It will keep in the refrigerator for approximately 3 months.

Pork Pâté

YIELD: 10 TO 12 SERVINGS | **ACTIVE TIME:** 20 MINUTES | **TOTAL TIME:** 24 HOURS

3- TO 5-LB. BONE-IN PORK SHOULDER

3 ONIONS, SLICED

2 TEASPOONS GROUND CLOVES

1 TABLESPOON KOSHER SALT, PLUS MORE TO TASTE

4 BAY LEAVES

2 TEASPOONS BLACK PEPPER, PLUS MORE TO TASTE

1 TEASPOON FRESHLY GRATED NUTMEG

1. Preheat the oven to 300°F. Place all the ingredients in a Dutch oven and stir to combine. Cover, place in the oven, and braise until the pork falls apart at the touch of a fork, about 3 to 4 hours.

2. Remove from the oven, discard the bay leaves, and transfer the pork shoulder to a plate. When the pork shoulder has cooled slightly, shred it with a fork.

3. Place the shredded pork and ½ cup of the cooking liquid in a blender. Puree until it forms a paste, adding more cooking liquid as needed to achieve the desired consistency.

4. Season with salt and pepper, transfer the paste to a large jar, and then pour the remaining cooking liquid over it. Cover the jar and store it in the refrigerator overnight before serving.

Tequila Cheese Dip

YIELD: 4 SERVINGS | **ACTIVE TIME:** 10 MINUTES | **TOTAL TIME:** 25 MINUTES

6 OZ. OAXACA CHEESE, CUBED

½ PLUM TOMATO, DICED

¼ WHITE ONION, DICED

2 TABLESPOONS DICED GREEN CHILE PEPPERS

2 TABLESPOONS SUGAR

¼ CUP FRESH LIME JUICE

1 TEASPOON CHILI POWDER

1 OZ. TEQUILA

1. Preheat the oven to 350°F. Place the cheese, tomato, onion, and chiles in a small cast-iron skillet and stir to combine. Set the mixture aside.

2. Combine the sugar, lime juice, and chili powder in a small saucepan and cook over medium heat, stirring to dissolve the sugar, until the mixture is syrupy.

3. Drizzle the syrup over the cheese mixture, place it in the oven, and bake until the cheese has melted and is golden brown on top, about 15 minutes.

4. Remove the pan from the oven, pour the tequila over the mixture, and use a long match or a wand lighter to ignite it. Bring the flaming skillet to the table and enjoy once the flames have gone out.

Cilantro Pesto

YIELD: 1½ CUPS | **ACTIVE TIME:** 5 MINUTES | **TOTAL TIME:** 5 MINUTES

1 CUP FRESH CILANTRO

1 GARLIC CLOVE

¼ CUP ROASTED AND SHELLED SUNFLOWER SEEDS

¼ CUP SHREDDED QUESO ENCHILADO

¼ CUP EXTRA-VIRGIN OLIVE OIL

1 TEASPOON FRESH LEMON JUICE

SALT AND PEPPER, TO TASTE

1. Place all of the ingredients in a food processor and blitz until emulsified and smooth. Chill in the refrigerator until ready to serve.

Balsamic Ranch

YIELD: 2 CUPS | **ACTIVE TIME:** 5 MINUTES | **TOTAL TIME:** 5 MINUTES

½ CUP MAYONNAISE

½ CUP SOUR CREAM

½ CUP BUTTERMILK

3 TABLESPOONS BALSAMIC VINEGAR

¼ TEASPOON ONION POWDER

½ TEASPOON GARLIC POWDER

2 TEASPOONS CHOPPED FRESH PARSLEY

1. Place all the ingredients in a mixing bowl and whisk until the mixture is thoroughly combined.

2. Taste, adjust the seasoning as necessary, and refrigerate until ready to serve.

Smoked Egg Aioli

YIELD: 1 CUP | **ACTIVE TIME:** 20 MINUTES | **TOTAL TIME:** 45 MINUTES

2 EGG YOLKS

½ CUP WOOD CHIPS

1 TABLESPOON WHITE VINEGAR

1 TEASPOON KOSHER SALT

1 CUP AVOCADO OIL

1. Place the yolks in a metal bowl and set the bowl in a roasting pan.

2. Place the wood chips in a cast-iron skillet and warm them over high heat. Remove the pan from heat, light the wood chips on fire, and place the skillet in the roasting pan beside the bowl. Cover the roasting pan with aluminum foil and allow the smoke to flavor the yolks for 20 minutes.

3. Place the yolks and vinegar in a bowl, gently break the yolks, and let the mixture sit for 5 minutes.

4. Add the salt to the egg yolk mixture. Slowly drizzle the oil into the mixture while beating it with an electric mixer or immersion blender until it is thick and creamy. Use immediately or store in the refrigerator.

Roasted Garlic Aioli

YIELD: 2 SERVINGS | **ACTIVE TIME:** 10 MINUTES | **TOTAL TIME:** 40 MINUTES

1 HEAD OF GARLIC

½ CUP EXTRA-VIRGIN OLIVE OIL, PLUS MORE AS NEEDED

SALT AND PEPPER, TO TASTE

1 EGG YOLK

1 TEASPOON FRESH LEMON JUICE

1. Preheat the oven to 350ºF. Cut off the top ½ inch of the head of garlic. Place the remainder in a piece of aluminum foil, drizzle olive oil over it, and season it with salt.

2. Place the garlic in the oven and roast until the garlic cloves have softened and are caramelized, about 30 minutes. Remove from the oven, remove the cloves from the head of garlic, and place them in a mixing bowl.

3. Add the egg yolk and lemon juice and whisk to combine. While whisking continually, add the olive oil in a slow stream. When all the oil has been emulsified, season the aioli with salt and pepper and serve.

Sriracha & Honey Mayonnaise

YIELD: ½ CUP | **ACTIVE TIME:** 5 MINUTES | **TOTAL TIME:** 15 MINUTES

½ CUP MAYONNAISE

2 TABLESPOONS HONEY

1 TABLESPOON SRIRACHA

1. Place all of the ingredients in a small bowl and stir until thoroughly combined.

2. Chill the mayonnaise in the refrigerator for 10 minutes before serving.

Tzatziki

YIELD: 2 CUPS | **ACTIVE TIME:** 5 MINUTES | **TOTAL TIME:** 1 HOUR AND 5 MINUTES

1 CUP PLAIN FULL-FAT YOGURT

¾ CUP DESEEDED AND MINCED CUCUMBER

1 GARLIC CLOVE, MINCED

JUICE FROM 1 LEMON WEDGE

SALT AND WHITE PEPPER, TO TASTE

FRESH DILL, FINELY CHOPPED, TO TASTE

1. Place the yogurt, cucumber, garlic, and lemon juice in a mixing bowl and stir to combine. Taste and season with salt and pepper. Stir in the dill.

2. Place in the refrigerator and chill for 1 hour before serving.

Sultana & Mango Chutney

YIELD: 1 CUP | **ACTIVE TIME:** 10 MINUTES | **TOTAL TIME:** 20 MINUTES

1½ TABLESPOONS EXTRA-VIRGIN OLIVE OIL

½ RED ONION, DICED

½ TEASPOON RED PEPPER FLAKES

½ TEASPOON CURRY POWDER

½ TEASPOON GRATED FRESH GINGER

1 GARLIC CLOVE, MINCED

⅓ CUP RED WINE VINEGAR

½ CUP MANGO JAM

¼ CUP SULTANAS (GOLDEN RAISINS)

⅓ CUP WATER

1. Place the olive oil in a large skillet and warm it over medium heat. When the oil starts to shimmer, add the onion, red pepper flakes, and curry powder and cook, stirring frequently, until the onion starts to soften, about 3 minutes.

2. Stir in the ginger and garlic, cook for 1 minute, and then add the remaining ingredients. Bring to a simmer and cook until the mixture has reduced. Transfer to a serving dish and serve warm or at room temperature.

Crab Dip

YIELD: 4 SERVINGS | **ACTIVE TIME:** 15 MINUTES | **TOTAL TIME:** 50 MINUTES

1 TABLESPOON UNSALTED BUTTER

½ SHALLOT, MINCED

¼ CUP PANKO

SALT, TO TASTE

1½ TEASPOONS DRY VERMOUTH

5 OZ. CREAM CHEESE, SOFTENED

¼ CUP CRÈME FRAÎCHE

¼ CUP MAYONNAISE

1 TABLESPOON DIJON MUSTARD

¼ CUP CHOPPED FRESH CHIVES

½ LB. LUMP CRABMEAT

½ TEASPOON CAYENNE PEPPER

½ TEASPOON OLD BAY SEASONING

1. Preheat the oven to 350ºF. Place the butter in a skillet and melt it over medium heat. Add the shallot and cook, stirring frequently, until it has softened, about 4 minutes.

2. Stir in the panko and cook until golden brown, 2 to 4 minutes. Remove the pan from heat.

3. Combine the panko mixture and the remaining ingredients in a mixing bowl and then transfer the mixture to a ramekin or a crock. Place the dip in the oven and bake until golden brown on top, about 35 minutes. Remove from the oven and serve immediately.

Italian Dipping Oil

YIELD: 1½ CUPS | **ACTIVE TIME:** 5 MINUTES | **TOTAL TIME:** 5 MINUTES

1 TABLESPOON BLACK PEPPER

2 TABLESPOONS HERBES DE PROVENCE

1 TABLESPOON DRIED THYME

1 TABLESPOON DRIED MINT

1 TABLESPOON DRIED OREGANO

1 TABLESPOON GARLIC POWDER

3 GARLIC CLOVES, MINCED

1 TEASPOON KOSHER SALT

1 TEASPOON RED PEPPER FLAKES

1 CUP EXTRA-VIRGIN OLIVE OIL

¼ CUP BALSAMIC VINEGAR

1. Combine all the ingredients, except for the balsamic vinegar, in a mixing bowl and let the mixture sit at room temperature until ready to serve.

2. Stir in the balsamic vinegar right before serving.

Raspberry & Chia Jam

YIELD: 2 CUPS | **ACTIVE TIME:** 20 MINUTES | **TOTAL TIME:** 1 HOUR AND 30 MINUTES

2 CUPS RASPBERRIES

2 TABLESPOONS WATER

1 TABLESPOON FRESH
LEMON JUICE

3 TABLESPOONS CHIA
SEEDS

3 TABLESPOONS HONEY

1. Place the raspberries and water in a saucepan and cook the mixture over medium heat for 2 minutes.

2. Stir in the remaining ingredients and cook until the mixture has thickened and acquired a jammy consistency. Remove from heat and let the jam cool completely. To can this jam, see page 396. You can also store the jam in the refrigerator, where it will keep for up to 1 month.

Cranberry Relish

YIELD: 2 CUPS | **ACTIVE TIME:** 5 MINUTES | **TOTAL TIME:** 1 HOUR

¾ LB. CRANBERRIES

1 GRANNY SMITH APPLE,
CORED AND DICED

SEGMENTS OF ½ ORANGE

1 CUP SUGAR

1. Place the cranberries in a food processor and pulse for 1 minute. Add the apple and orange and pulse until combined. Add the sugar and pulse until incorporated.

2. Transfer the mixture to a bowl and let it macerate for at least 1 hour before serving.

Orange Marmalade

YIELD: 2 CUPS | **ACTIVE TIME:** 30 MINUTES | **TOTAL TIME:** 4 HOURS

2 ORANGES, SLICED

2 LEMONS, SLICED

4 CUPS WATER

4 CUPS SUGAR

1. Place the ingredients in a large saucepan fitted with a candy thermometer. Cook over medium-low heat, stirring occasionally, until the mixture reaches 220ºF, about 2 hours.

2. Pour the marmalade into a mason jar and let it cool completely before serving.

Roasted Artichoke & Spinach Dip

YIELD: 1 CUP | **ACTIVE TIME:** 5 MINUTES | **TOTAL TIME:** 15 MINUTES

¾ LB. ARTICHOKE HEARTS, QUARTERED

4 GARLIC CLOVES, UNPEELED

2 CUPS BABY SPINACH

2 TABLESPOONS APPLE CIDER VINEGAR

¼ TEASPOON KOSHER SALT

¼ CUP EXTRA-VIRGIN OLIVE OIL

PINCH OF ONION POWDER (OPTIONAL)

1. Preheat the oven's broiler to high. Place the artichoke hearts and garlic on a baking sheet and broil, turning them occasionally, until browned all over, about 10 minutes. Remove them from the oven and let cool. When cool enough to handle, peel the garlic cloves.

2. Place the artichoke hearts and garlic in a food processor, add the remaining ingredients, and blitz until the spread has the desired texture.

Beer Cheese Dip

YIELD: 4 SERVINGS | **ACTIVE TIME:** 20 MINUTES | **TOTAL TIME:** 20 MINUTES

2 TABLESPOONS UNSALTED BUTTER

1½ TEASPOONS ALL-PURPOSE FLOUR

¾ CUP BROWN ALE

1 TABLESPOON WORCESTERSHIRE SAUCE

½ TEASPOON MUSTARD POWDER

PINCH OF CAYENNE PEPPER

1½ CUPS GRATED CHEDDAR CHEESE

SALT AND PEPPER, TO TASTE

1. Place the butter in a saucepan and melt it over medium heat. Add the flour and cook, stirring constantly, until the mixture starts to brown, about 2 minutes.

2. Deglaze the pan with the brown ale and Worcestershire sauce, scraping up any browned bits from the bottom.

3. Add the remaining ingredients, cook until the cheese has melted, and serve immediately.

Pesto

YIELD: 2 CUPS | **ACTIVE TIME:** 10 MINUTES | **TOTAL TIME:** 10 MINUTES

2 CUPS PACKED FRESH BASIL LEAVES

1 CUP PACKED FRESH BABY SPINACH

2 CUPS FRESHLY GRATED PARMESAN CHEESE

¼ CUP PINE NUTS

1 GARLIC CLOVE

2 TEASPOONS FRESH LEMON JUICE

SALT AND PEPPER, TO TASTE

½ CUP EXTRA-VIRGIN OLIVE OIL

1. Place all the ingredients, except for the olive oil, in a food processor and pulse until pureed.

2. Transfer the puree to a mixing bowl. While whisking, add the olive oil in a slow stream until it is emulsified. Serve immediately or store in the refrigerator.

White Bean & Rosemary Spread

YIELD: 2 CUPS | **ACTIVE TIME:** 5 MINUTES | **TOTAL TIME:** 35 MINUTES

1 (14 OZ.) CAN OF CANNELLINI BEANS, DRAINED AND RINSED

2 TABLESPOONS EXTRA-VIRGIN OLIVE OIL

2 TEASPOONS BALSAMIC VINEGAR

2 GARLIC CLOVES, MINCED

1 TABLESPOON CHOPPED FRESH ROSEMARY

½ CELERY STALK, PEELED AND MINCED

SALT AND PEPPER, TO TASTE

2 PINCHES OF RED PEPPER FLAKES

1. Place half of the beans in a bowl and mash them until they are smooth.

2. Add the rest of the beans, the olive oil, vinegar, garlic, rosemary, and celery and stir to combine.

3. Season the dip with salt, pepper, and red pepper flakes and cover the bowl with plastic wrap. Let the dip sit so that the flavors combine for about 30 minutes before serving.

Roasted Pumpkin Dip

YIELD: 6 TO 8 SERVINGS | **ACTIVE TIME:** 5 MINUTES | **TOTAL TIME:** 35 MINUTES

1 (3 LB.) SUGAR PUMPKIN, HALVED, SEEDS REMOVED

5 TABLESPOONS EXTRA-VIRGIN OLIVE OIL

2 TEASPOONS KOSHER SALT

1 TEASPOON BLACK PEPPER

1 TEASPOON FRESH THYME

¼ TEASPOON FRESHLY GRATED NUTMEG

¼ CUP FRESHLY GRATED PARMESAN CHEESE

1 TABLESPOON FRESH LEMON JUICE

1 TABLESPOON FULL-FAT GREEK YOGURT

1. Preheat the oven to 425ºF. Place the pumpkin, cut side up, on a parchment-lined baking sheet and brush it with 1 tablespoon of the olive oil. Sprinkle half of the salt over the pumpkin, place it in the oven, and roast for 25 to 30 minutes, until the flesh is tender. Remove from the oven and let the pumpkin cool.

2. When the pumpkin is cool enough to handle, scrape the flesh into a food processor. Add the remaining ingredients and puree until smooth. Taste, adjust the seasoning as necessary, and enjoy.

Coconut & Cilantro Chutney

YIELD: 6 SERVINGS | **ACTIVE TIME:** 5 MINUTES | **TOTAL TIME:** 5 MINUTES

1 BUNCH OF FRESH CILANTRO

¼ CUP GRATED FRESH COCONUT

15 FRESH MINT LEAVES

1 TABLESPOON MINCED CHILE PEPPER

1 GARLIC CLOVE

1 TEASPOON GRATED GINGER

1 PLUM TOMATO, CHOPPED

1 TABLESPOON FRESH LEMON JUICE

WATER, AS NEEDED

SALT, TO TASTE

1. Place all the ingredients, except for the water and salt, in a food processor and puree until smooth, adding water as needed to get the desired consistency.

2. Taste, season with salt, and chill in the refrigerator until ready to serve.

Pesto
SEE PAGE 162

Green Goddess Dip

YIELD: 6 CUPS | **ACTIVE TIME:** 5 MINUTES | **TOTAL TIME:** 5 MINUTES

1½ CUPS MAYONNAISE

2 CUPS SOUR CREAM

1 TABLESPOON CHOPPED FRESH PARSLEY

1 TABLESPOON CHOPPED FRESH TARRAGON

1 TABLESPOON CHOPPED FRESH CHIVES

1 TABLESPOON CHOPPED FRESH BASIL

1 TABLESPOON RED WINE VINEGAR

1 TABLESPOON SUGAR

1 TEASPOON GARLIC POWDER

1 TABLESPOON WORCESTERSHIRE SAUCE

SALT AND PEPPER, TO TASTE

6 OZ. BLUE CHEESE

1. Place all the ingredients, except for the blue cheese, in a food processor and blitz until pureed.

2. Add the blue cheese and pulse a few times, making sure to maintain a chunky texture. Store the dip in the refrigerator until ready to serve.

Mignonette Sauce

YIELD: ½ CUP | **ACTIVE TIME:** 5 MINUTES | **TOTAL TIME:** 5 MINUTES

½ CUP RED WINE VINEGAR

1½ TABLESPOONS MINCED SHALLOT

½ TEASPOON FRESHLY CRACKED BLACK PEPPER

1. Place the ingredients in a bowl, stir to combine, and chill in the refrigerator for 1 hour before serving.

Smoked Potato Puree

YIELD: 8 SERVINGS | **ACTIVE TIME:** 15 MINUTES | **TOTAL TIME:** 1 HOUR AND 15 MINUTES

½ CUP WOOD CHIPS

2 SWEET POTATOES, PEELED AND CHOPPED

1 YUKON GOLD POTATO, PEELED AND CHOPPED

2 TEASPOONS KOSHER SALT, PLUS MORE TO TASTE

½ CUP HEAVY CREAM

2 TABLESPOONS UNSALTED BUTTER

1. Preheat the oven to 250ºF. Place the wood chips in a cast-iron skillet and place the pan over high heat. When the wood chips start to smoke, place the skillet in a deep roasting pan. Set the sweet potatoes and potato in the roasting pan (not in the skillet) and cover the roasting pan with aluminum foil. Place in the oven for 30 minutes.

2. While the potatoes are smoking in the oven, bring water to a boil in a large saucepan. Remove the potatoes from the oven, salt the boiling water, and add the potatoes. Cook until they are fork-tender, 20 to 25 minutes. Drain, place the potatoes in a mixing bowl, and add the remaining ingredients. Mash until smooth, season with salt, and serve immediately.

Beet Relish

YIELD: 8 SERVINGS | **ACTIVE TIME:** 15 MINUTES | **TOTAL TIME:** 1 HOUR

4 RED BEETS, TRIMMED AND RINSED WELL

1 LARGE SHALLOT, MINCED

2 TEASPOONS WHITE WINE VINEGAR

SALT AND PEPPER, TO TASTE

1 TABLESPOON RED WINE VINEGAR

2 TABLESPOONS EXTRA-VIRGIN OLIVE OIL

1. Preheat the oven to 400°F. Place the beets in a baking dish, add a splash of water, cover the dish with aluminum foil, and place it in the oven. Roast the beets until they are so tender that a knife easily goes to the center when poked, 45 minutes to 1 hour. Remove from the oven, remove the foil, and let the beets cool.

2. While the beets are in the oven, place the shallot and white wine vinegar in a mixing bowl, season the mixture with salt, and stir to combine. Let the mixture marinate.

3. Peel the beets, dice them, and place them in a mixing bowl. Add the remaining ingredients and the shallot mixture, season to taste, and serve.

Beet Relish
SEE PAGE 171

Tabbouleh

YIELD: 4 CUPS | **ACTIVE TIME:** 15 MINUTES | **TOTAL TIME:** 45 MINUTES

½ CUP BULGUR WHEAT

1½ CUPS BOILING WATER

½ TEASPOON KOSHER SALT, PLUS MORE TO TASTE

½ CUP FRESH LEMON JUICE

2 CUPS FRESH PARSLEY, CHOPPED

2 CUCUMBERS, PEELED, SEEDS REMOVED, DICED

2 TOMATOES, DICED

6 SCALLIONS, TRIMMED AND SLICED

1 CUP FRESH MINT LEAVES, CHOPPED

2 TABLESPOONS EXTRA-VIRGIN OLIVE OIL

BLACK PEPPER, TO TASTE

½ CUP CRUMBLED FETA CHEESE

1. Place the bulgur in a heatproof bowl and add the boiling water, salt, and half of the lemon juice. Cover and let sit for about 20 minutes, until the bulgur has absorbed the liquid and is tender. Drain excess liquid if necessary. Let the bulgur cool completely.

2. When the bulgur has cooled, add the parsley, cucumbers, tomatoes, scallions, mint, olive oil, pepper, and remaining lemon juice and stir to combine.

3. Top the tabbouleh with the feta and enjoy.

Pecan Muhammara

YIELD: 4 SERVINGS | **ACTIVE TIME:** 15 MINUTES | **TOTAL TIME:** 30 MINUTES

2 RED BELL PEPPERS

¼ CUP PECANS

1 TEASPOON KOSHER SALT

1 TEASPOON ALEPPO PEPPER

½ CUP EXTRA-VIRGIN OLIVE OIL

JUICE OF 1 LEMON

1 TABLESPOON POMEGRANATE MOLASSES

¼ CUP BREAD CRUMBS

1 TABLESPOON CHOPPED FRESH PARSLEY

1. Warm a cast-iron skillet over medium-high heat. Place the peppers in the pan and cook until they are charred all over, turning them as needed.

2. Place the peppers in a bowl, cover it with plastic wrap, and let them steam for 15 minutes.

3. Peel the peppers, remove the stems and seed pods, and place the peppers in a blender.

4. Add the pecans, salt, Aleppo pepper, olive oil, lemon juice, and molasses and puree until smooth.

5. Add the bread crumbs and fold to incorporate them. Sprinkle the parsley on top and enjoy.

Tabbouleh
SEE PAGE 174

Red Zhug

YIELD: 10 SERVINGS | **ACTIVE TIME:** 10 MINUTES | **TOTAL TIME:** 10 MINUTES

4 FRESNO CHILE PEPPERS, STEMS REMOVED, CHOPPED

2 CUPS FRESH PARSLEY LEAVES

1 ONION, CHOPPED

5 GARLIC CLOVES

JUICE OF 1 LEMON

1 TABLESPOON KOSHER SALT

1 TEASPOON CAYENNE PEPPER

1 TABLESPOON CUMIN

2 TABLESPOONS PAPRIKA

¾ CUP EXTRA-VIRGIN OLIVE OIL

¼ CUP WATER

1. Place the chiles, parsley, onion, garlic, and lemon juice in a food processor and pulse until the mixture is roughly chopped.

2. Add the salt, cayenne, cumin, and paprika, and, with the food processor running on high, add the olive oil in a slow stream. Add the water as needed until the mixture is smooth.

3. Taste, adjust the seasoning as necessary, and serve.

Pickled Applesauce

YIELD: 8 SERVINGS | **ACTIVE TIME:** 20 MINUTES | **TOTAL TIME:** 1 HOUR

3 LBS. GRANNY SMITH APPLES, PEELED AND SLICED

1 TEASPOON CINNAMON

PINCH OF GROUND CLOVES

½ CUP SUGAR

1½ CUPS WHITE VINEGAR

1. Place the ingredients in a large saucepan and bring to a boil over high heat.

2. Reduce the heat to medium-high and simmer until the liquid has reduced by one-third. Remove the pan from heat and let it cool to room temperature.

3. Place the mixture in a food processor and puree on high until smooth, about 2 minutes. Serve immediately or store in the refrigerator.

Cucumber, Tomato & Mango Relish

YIELD: 10 SERVINGS | **ACTIVE TIME:** 10 MINUTES | **TOTAL TIME:** 10 MINUTES

6 CUPS HALVED HEIRLOOM CHERRY TOMATOES

4 CUPS DESEEDED AND DICED PERSIAN CUCUMBERS

2 SMALL MANGOES, PITTED AND DICED

1 CUP DICED RED ONION

2 TABLESPOONS RED WINE VINEGAR

¼ CUP FRESH LEMON JUICE

2 TABLESPOONS ZA'ATAR SEASONING

1 TABLESPOON SUMAC

¼ CUP FINE SEA SALT, PLUS MORE TO TASTE

2 TABLESPOONS BLACK PEPPER

¼ CUP CHOPPED FRESH DILL

½ CUP EXTRA-VIRGIN OLIVE OIL

1. Place the ingredients in a large mixing bowl and stir until combined.

2. Taste, adjust the seasoning as necessary, and serve.

Baba Ghanoush

YIELD: 12 SERVINGS | **ACTIVE TIME:** 15 MINUTES | **TOTAL TIME:** 1 HOUR AND 15 MINUTES

2 LARGE EGGPLANTS, HALVED

4 GARLIC CLOVES, SMASHED

4 TEASPOONS FRESH LEMON JUICE, PLUS MORE TO TASTE

1½ TEASPOONS KOSHER SALT, PLUS MORE TO TASTE

½ CUP TAHINI PASTE

¼ CUP POMEGRANATE SEEDS

2 TEASPOONS FINELY CHOPPED FRESH PARSLEY

¼ CUP EXTRA-VIRGIN OLIVE OIL

PITA BREAD (SEE PAGE 102), FOR SERVING

1. Preheat the oven to 400°F. Place the eggplants on a baking sheet, cut side up, and roast until they have collapsed, about 50 minutes. Remove the eggplants from the oven and let them cool for 10 minutes.

2. Scoop the flesh of the eggplants into a food processor and discard the skins. Add the garlic, lemon juice, salt, and tahini and blitz until the mixture is smooth and creamy, about 1 minute. Taste and add more lemon juice and salt as necessary.

3. Transfer the mixture to a bowl, top with the pomegranate seeds, parsley, and olive oil, and serve with Pita Bread.

Baba Ghanoush
SEE PAGE 179

Cheesy Summer Vegetable Dip

YIELD: 6 SERVINGS | **ACTIVE TIME:** 20 MINUTES | **TOTAL TIME:** 1 HOUR AND 45 MINUTES

1 CUP QUARK CHEESE, SOFTENED

½ CUP SOUR CREAM

1 CUP SHREDDED MOZZARELLA CHEESE, PLUS MORE AS NEEDED

2 TABLESPOONS CHOPPED FRESH ROSEMARY

2 TABLESPOONS FRESH THYME

½ CUP DICED SUMMER SQUASH

1 CUP CHOPPED SWISS CHARD LEAVES

1 CUP SPINACH

6 GARLIC CLOVES, DICED

2 TEASPOONS KOSHER SALT

1 TEASPOON BLACK PEPPER

1. Place the quark, sour cream, and mozzarella in an oven-safe bowl and stir until well combined.

2. Add the remaining ingredients, stir to combine, and place in the refrigerator for at least 1 hour.

3. Approximately 30 minutes before you are ready to serve the dip, preheat the oven to 350°F. Top the dip with additional mozzarella and bake the dip until the cheese is melted and slightly brown, about 20 minutes. Remove the dip from the oven and let it cool briefly before serving.

Romesco Sauce

YIELD: 1 CUP | **ACTIVE TIME:** 5 MINUTES | **TOTAL TIME:** 5 MINUTES

2 LARGE ROASTED RED BELL PEPPERS

1 GARLIC CLOVE, SMASHED

½ CUP SLIVERED ALMONDS, TOASTED

¼ CUP TOMATO PUREE

2 TABLESPOONS FINELY CHOPPED FLAT-LEAF PARSLEY

2 TABLESPOONS SHERRY VINEGAR

1 TEASPOON SMOKED PAPRIKA

SALT AND PEPPER, TO TASTE

½ CUP EXTRA-VIRGIN OLIVE OIL

1. Place all of the ingredients, except for the olive oil, in a blender or food processor and pulse until the mixture is smooth.

2. Add the olive oil in a steady stream and blitz until emulsified. Season with salt and pepper and use immediately.

Labneh

YIELD: 8 SERVINGS | **ACTIVE TIME:** 10 MINUTES | **TOTAL TIME:** 2 DAYS

4 CUPS FULL-FAT GREEK
YOGURT

½ TEASPOON FINE SEA SALT

1 TABLESPOON EXTRA-
VIRGIN OLIVE OIL

2 TEASPOONS ZA'ATAR
SEASONING

1. Place the yogurt in a large bowl and season it with the salt; the salt helps pull out excess whey, giving you a creamier, thicker labneh.

2. Place a fine-mesh strainer on top of a medium-sized bowl. Line the strainer with cheesecloth or a linen towel, letting a few inches hang over the side of the strainer. Spoon the seasoned yogurt into the cheesecloth and gently wrap the sides over the top of the yogurt, protecting it from being exposed to air in the refrigerator.

3. Store everything in the refrigerator for 24 to 48 hours, discarding the whey halfway through if the bowl beneath the strainer becomes too full.

4. Remove the labneh from the cheesecloth and store it in an airtight container.

5. To serve, drizzle the olive oil over the labneh and sprinkle the za'atar on top.

Tapenade

YIELD: ½ CUP | **ACTIVE TIME:** 5 MINUTES | **TOTAL TIME:** 5 MINUTES

½ CUP FINELY CHOPPED
KALAMATA OLIVES

1 TEASPOON CAPERS,
DRAINED, RINSED, AND
FINELY CHOPPED

1 TEASPOON FINELY
CHOPPED SUNDRIED
TOMATOES IN OLIVE OIL

1 TEASPOON DRIED
OREGANO

1. Combine the ingredients in a mixing bowl and serve immediately.

Marinara Sauce

YIELD: 8 CUPS | **ACTIVE TIME:** 20 MINUTES | **TOTAL TIME:** 2 HOURS

4 LBS. TOMATOES, QUARTERED

1 LARGE YELLOW ONION, SLICED

15 GARLIC CLOVES, CRUSHED

2 TEASPOONS FINELY CHOPPED FRESH THYME

2 TEASPOONS FINELY CHOPPED FRESH OREGANO

2 TABLESPOONS EXTRA-VIRGIN OLIVE OIL

1½ TABLESPOONS KOSHER SALT

1 TEASPOON BLACK PEPPER

2 TABLESPOONS FINELY CHOPPED FRESH BASIL

1 TABLESPOON FINELY CHOPPED FRESH PARSLEY

1. Place all of the ingredients, except for the basil and parsley, in a Dutch oven and cook over medium heat, stirring constantly, until the tomatoes release their liquid and begin to collapse, about 10 minutes.

2. Reduce the heat to low and cook, stirring occasionally, for about 1½ hours, or until the flavor is to your liking.

3. Stir in the basil and parsley and season to taste. The sauce will be chunky. If you prefer a smoother texture, transfer the sauce to a blender and puree before serving.

Bacon Jam

YIELD: ½ CUP | **ACTIVE TIME:** 20 MINUTES | **TOTAL TIME:** 1 HOUR

½ LB. BACON

½ WHITE ONION, MINCED

1 GARLIC CLOVE, MINCED

2 TABLESPOONS APPLE CIDER VINEGAR

2 TABLESPOONS BROWN SUGAR

1 TABLESPOON MAPLE SYRUP

1. Preheat the oven to 350°F. Set a wire rack in a rimmed baking sheet, place the bacon on the rack, and place the sheet in the oven. Bake the bacon until it is crispy, about 10 minutes.

2. Remove the bacon from the oven and transfer it to a paper towel–lined plate to drain. Reserve the bacon fat. When the bacon is cool enough to handle, chop it into small pieces.

3. Place the reserved bacon fat in a large skillet and warm it over medium heat. Add the onion and cook, stirring frequently, until it has softened, about 5 minutes.

4. Stir in the bacon and the remaining ingredients, bring the mixture to a simmer, and cook until it has thickened slightly. Transfer the mixture to a bowl and let it chill in the refrigerator before serving.

Aioli

YIELD: 1 CUP | **ACTIVE TIME:** 5 MINUTES | **TOTAL TIME:** 5 MINUTES

2 LARGE EGG YOLKS

2 TEASPOONS DIJON MUSTARD

2 TEASPOONS FRESH LEMON JUICE

1 GARLIC CLOVE, MASHED

¾ CUP CANOLA OIL

¼ CUP EXTRA-VIRGIN OLIVE OIL

SALT AND PEPPER, TO TASTE

1. Place the egg yolks, mustard, lemon juice, and garlic in a food processor and blitz until combined.

2. With the food processor running on low, slowly drizzle in the oils until they are emulsified. If the aioli becomes too thick for your liking, stir in water 1 teaspoon at a time until it has thinned out.

3. Season the aioli with salt and pepper and use as desired.

Charred Scallion Sauce

YIELD: 1 CUP | **ACTIVE TIME:** 10 MINUTES | **TOTAL TIME:** 10 MINUTES

3 SCALLIONS

2 GARLIC CLOVES, MINCED

2 BIRD'S EYE CHILI PEPPERS, STEMS AND SEEDS REMOVED, MINCED

¼ CUP CHOPPED FRESH CILANTRO

1 TABLESPOON GRATED FRESH GINGER

1 TABLESPOON SESAME OIL

½ CUP SOY SAUCE

1 TABLESPOON SAMBAL OELEK

2 TABLESPOONS FRESH LIME JUICE

1 TEASPOON SUGAR

1 TABLESPOON SESAME SEEDS

SALT AND PEPPER, TO TASTE

1. On a grill or over an open flame on a gas stove, char the scallions all over. Remove the charred scallions from heat and let them cool.

2. Slice the charred scallions, place them in a mixing bowl, and add the remaining ingredients. Stir to combine, taste the sauce, and adjust the seasoning as necessary. Use immediately or store in the refrigerator until needed.

Lemony Yogurt Sauce

YIELD: 2½ CUPS | **ACTIVE TIME:** 5 MINUTES | **TOTAL TIME:** 5 MINUTES

6 TABLESPOONS FRESH LEMON JUICE

1 GARLIC CLOVE, GRATED

1 TEASPOON KOSHER SALT

1 TEASPOON BLACK PEPPER

2 CUPS FULL-FAT GREEK YOGURT

1. Place all of the ingredients in a mixing bowl and stir until thoroughly combined. Use immediately or store in the refrigerator.

Harissa Sauce

YIELD: 1 CUP | **ACTIVE TIME:** 10 MINUTES | **TOTAL TIME:** 1 HOUR

3 OZ. GUAJILLO CHILE PEPPERS, STEMS AND SEEDS REMOVED, TORN

1 OZ. DRIED CHIPOTLE CHILE PEPPERS, STEMS AND SEEDS REMOVED, TORN

1 TABLESPOON NIGELLA SEEDS

1 TEASPOON CORIANDER SEEDS

2 GARLIC CLOVES

1 TABLESPOON CUMIN

1 TEASPOON KOSHER SALT

½ TEASPOON ALEPPO PEPPER

½ CUP EXTRA-VIRGIN OLIVE OIL

2 TABLESPOONS WHITE WINE VINEGAR

1. Place the guajillo and chipotle chiles in a large heatproof bowl and cover them with boiling water. Let the chiles soak until they have softened, 40 to 45 minutes.

2. Drain the chiles and set them aside.

3. Grind the nigella seeds and coriander seeds into a powder, using a spice mill or a mortar and pestle. Transfer the powder to a food processor and add the garlic, cumin, salt, and Aleppo pepper. Pulse until the garlic is very finely chopped.

4. Add the chiles and pulse until they are chopped.

5. Add the oil and vinegar and pulse until the sauce is a chunky paste. Use immediately or store in the refrigerator until needed.

FOR THE
MEAT LOVERS

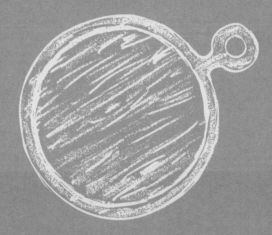

Empanadas

YIELD: 8 EMPANADAS | **ACTIVE TIME:** 30 MINUTES | **TOTAL TIME:** 1 HOUR AND 45 MINUTES

FOR THE DOUGH

¼ TEASPOON KOSHER SALT

6 TABLESPOONS WARM WATER (110ºF)

1½ CUPS ALL-PURPOSE FLOUR, PLUS MORE AS NEEDED

3 TABLESPOONS LARD OR UNSALTED BUTTER, CUT INTO SMALL PIECES

FOR THE FILLING

2 TEASPOONS EXTRA-VIRGIN OLIVE OIL

1 YELLOW ONION, MINCED

1 GARLIC CLOVE, MINCED

¾ LB. GROUND PORK

1 (14 OZ.) CAN OF CRUSHED TOMATOES

½ TEASPOON KOSHER SALT

¼ TEASPOON BLACK PEPPER

1 CINNAMON STICK, CHOPPED

2 WHOLE CLOVES

2 TABLESPOONS RAISINS

2 TEASPOONS APPLE CIDER VINEGAR

2 TABLESPOONS SLIVERED ALMONDS, TOASTED

CANOLA OIL, AS NEEDED

1. To prepare the dough, dissolve the salt in the warm water. Place the flour in a mixing bowl, add the lard or butter, and work the mixture with a pastry blender until it is coarse crumbs. Add the salted water and knead the mixture until a stiff dough forms. Cut the dough into eight pieces, cover them with plastic wrap, and chill in the refrigerator for 20 minutes.

2. To prepare the filling, place the olive oil in a skillet and warm over medium heat. When the oil starts to shimmer, add the onion and cook until it has softened, about 5 minutes. Add the garlic, cook for 2 minutes, and then add the ground pork. Cook, breaking it up, until it is light brown, about 5 minutes. Drain off any excess fat and add the tomatoes, salt, pepper, cinnamon stick, cloves, raisins, and vinegar. Simmer until the filling is thick, about 30 minutes. Remove from heat and let cool before folding in the toasted almonds.

3. Add canola oil to a Dutch oven until it is 2 inches deep and bring it to 350ºF. Preheat the oven to 200ºF and place a platter in the oven.

4. Place the pieces of dough on a flour-dusted work surface and roll each one into a 5-inch circle. Place 3 tablespoons of the filling in the center of one circle, brush the edge with water, and fold into a half-moon. Crimp the edge to seal the empanada tight, pressing down on the filling to remove as much air as possible. Repeat with the remaining filling and pieces of dough.

5. Working in two batches, place the empanadas in the hot oil and fry until golden brown, about 5 minutes. Drain the cooked empanadas on paper towels and place them in the warm oven while you cook the next batch.

Chicken Chorizo

YIELD: 4 SERVINGS | **ACTIVE TIME:** 45 MINUTES | **TOTAL TIME:** 24 HOURS

2 OZ. GUAJILLO CHILE PEPPERS

2 OZ. PASILLA CHILE PEPPERS

2 BONELESS, SKINLESS CHICKEN THIGHS

1 TABLESPOON ANNATTO SEASONING

2 GARLIC CLOVES, CHOPPED

1 TABLESPOON DRIED THYME

1 TABLESPOON DRIED MEXICAN OREGANO

1 TABLESPOON CUMIN

2 TABLESPOONS SMOKED PAPRIKA

1 TEASPOON CAYENNE PEPPER

1 TEASPOON GROUND CLOVES

1 TEASPOON ONION POWDER

SALT AND PEPPER, TO TASTE

1. Place the chiles in a heatproof bowl, pour boiling water over them, and let them sit for 30 minutes. Drain and let cool. When cool enough to handle, remove the stems and seeds from the peppers.

2. Grind the chicken thighs in a meat grinder or food processor. Place them in a large mixing bowl, add the chiles and remaining ingredients, and stir to combine. Cover with plastic wrap and let the mixture marinate in the refrigerator overnight.

3. You can either leave the chorizo as is, form it into patties, or stuff it into sausage casings. Cook it over medium heat in a large skillet until browned and cooked through, which will be about 8 minutes if left loose or formed into patties, and 12 to 15 minutes if stuffed into sausage casings.

Foie Gras Torchon

YIELD: 4 SERVINGS | **ACTIVE TIME:** 15 MINUTES | **TOTAL TIME:** 16 HOURS AND 15 MINUTES

1 LB. FOIE GRAS

2 CUPS WHOLE MILK

2 TEASPOONS KOSHER SALT

2 TEASPOONS SUGAR

⅛ TEASPOON PINK CURING SALT

1 TABLESPOON BOURBON

1. Place the foie gras in a baking pan, cover it with the milk, and let it soak in the refrigerator for at least 8 hours and up to 24.

2. Strain, and then pass the foie gras through a fine-mesh sieve into a mixing bowl. Stir in the kosher salt, sugar, curing salt, and bourbon and roll the mixture into a log. Wrap the log in cheesecloth and chill in the refrigerator for 8 hours.

3. Unwrap the torchon, slice it, and let the torchon come to room temperature before serving.

Prosciutto-Wrapped Figs

YIELD: 4 SERVINGS | **ACTIVE TIME:** 10 MINUTES | **TOTAL TIME:** 30 MINUTES

12 THIN SLICES OF PROSCIUTTO

6 RIPE FIGS, HALVED LENGTHWISE

AGED BALSAMIC VINEGAR, TO TASTE

1. Preheat your gas or charcoal grill to high heat (500ºF). Wrap the prosciutto tightly around the figs and place them on the grill, cut side down. Cook until browned and crispy all over, 2 to 3 minutes per side.

2. Transfer the figs to a platter, drizzle balsamic vinegar over the top, and serve.

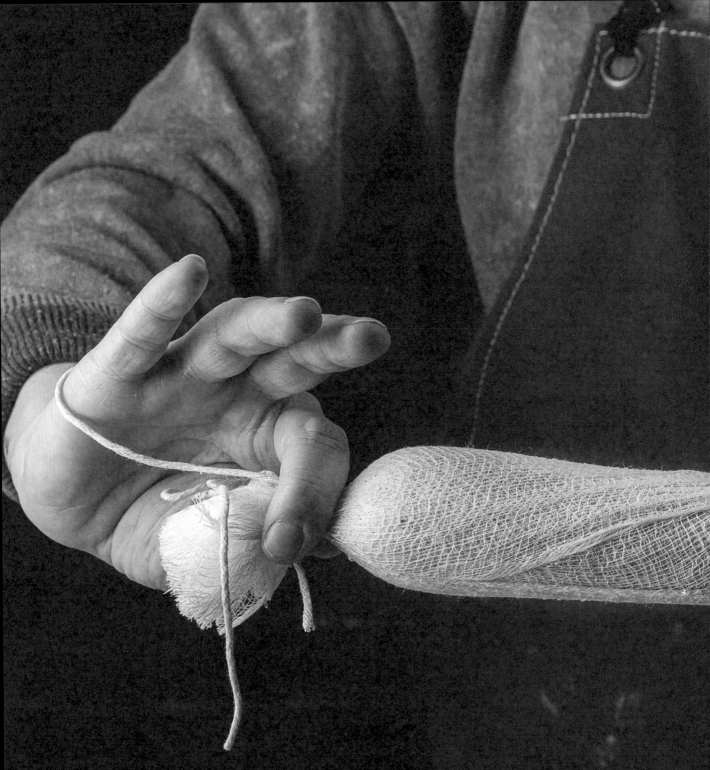

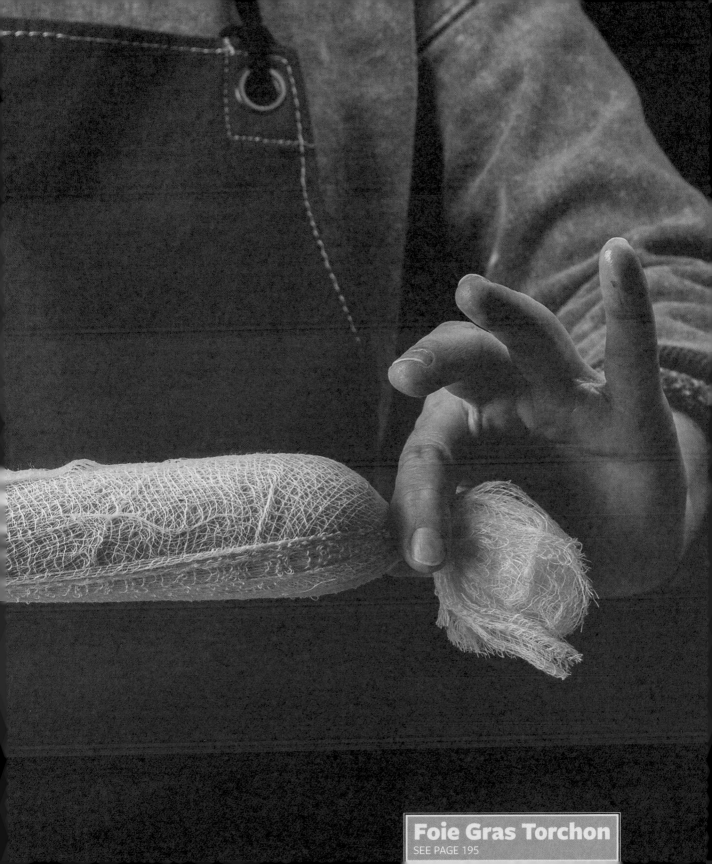

Foie Gras Torchon
SEE PAGE 195

Sicilian Meatballs

YIELD: 4 SERVINGS | **ACTIVE TIME:** 20 MINUTES | **TOTAL TIME:** 45 MINUTES

2 TABLESPOONS EXTRA-VIRGIN OLIVE OIL

½ SMALL RED ONION, CHOPPED

2 GARLIC CLOVES, MINCED

1 LARGE EGG

2 TABLESPOONS WHOLE MILK

½ CUP ITALIAN-SEASONED BREAD CRUMBS

¼ CUP FRESHLY GRATED PARMESAN CHEESE

¼ CUP PINE NUTS, TOASTED

3 TABLESPOONS MINCED DRIED CURRANTS

2 TEASPOONS DRIED OREGANO

2 TABLESPOONS CHOPPED FRESH PARSLEY

¾ LB. GROUND PORK

½ LB. SWEET OR SPICY GROUND ITALIAN SAUSAGE

SALT AND PEPPER, TO TASTE

1. Preheat the oven to 350ºF and line a rimmed baking sheet with aluminum foil.

2. Place the oil in a large skillet and warm it over medium-high heat. When it starts to shimmer, add the onion and garlic and cook, stirring frequently, until the onion is translucent, about 3 minutes. Remove the pan from heat and set it aside.

3. Place the egg, milk, bread crumbs, Parmesan, pine nuts, currants, oregano, and parsley in a mixing bowl and stir until combined. Add the pork, sausage, and onion mixture, season with salt and pepper, and stir until thoroughly combined. Working with wet hands, form the mixture into 1½-inch meatballs, arrange them on the baking sheet, and spray the tops with cooking spray.

4. Place the meatballs in the oven and bake until cooked through, about 15 minutes, turning them as necessary. Remove the meatballs from the oven and serve immediately.

Beef Carpaccio

YIELD: 2 SERVINGS | **ACTIVE TIME:** 20 MINUTES | **TOTAL TIME:** 1 HOUR AND 20 MINUTES

4 OZ. BEEF TENDERLOIN

SALT AND PEPPER, TO TASTE

1 TABLESPOON EXTRA-VIRGIN OLIVE OIL

1. Tie the tenderloin with kitchen twine so that it will maintain its shape while it sears. Season the beef with salt and pepper.

2. Coat a skillet with the olive oil and warm it over medium-high heat. Add the beef and cook, turning it as it browns, until it is seared all over. Remove the tenderloin from the pan and let it cool to room temperature.

3. Cover the tenderloin tightly with plastic wrap and freeze it for 1 hour.

4. To serve, slice the tenderloin as thin as possible and arrange the slices on a plate.

Chiles en Nogada

YIELD: 4 SERVINGS | **ACTIVE TIME:** 45 MINUTES | **TOTAL TIME:** 1 HOUR AND 15 MINUTES

4 POBLANO CHILE PEPPERS

1 CUP ALMONDS OR WALNUTS

¼ CUP CRUMBLED QUESO FRESCO

2 CUPS SOUR CREAM, PLUS MORE AS NEEDED

½ TABLESPOON SUGAR

SALT, TO TASTE

3 CUPS PICADILLO DE RES (SEE PAGE 555), AT ROOM TEMPERATURE

¼ CUP POMEGRANATE SEEDS, FOR GARNISH

FRESH CILANTRO, CHOPPED, FOR GARNISH

1. If you do not have a gas stove, preheat a grill or an oven to 400°F. Roast the poblanos over an open flame, on the grill, or in the oven until the skin is blackened and blistered all over, turning occasionally. Place the poblanos in a heatproof bowl, cover with plastic wrap, and let sit for 10 minutes.

2. Remove the charred skins from the poblanos. Make a small slit in the peppers and remove the seeds.

3. Place the nuts, queso fresco, sour cream, and sugar in a blender and puree until smooth. If the sauce seems too thick, incorporate more sour cream until the sauce is the desired texture. Season the sauce with salt and set it aside.

4. Stuff the peppers with the picadillo.

5. To serve, spoon the sauce over the peppers and garnish with the pomegranate seeds and cilantro.

Masala Short Rib Sandwiches

YIELD: 6 SERVINGS | **ACTIVE TIME:** 45 MINUTES | **TOTAL TIME:** 3 HOURS

3 LBS. BONE-IN SHORT RIBS

SALT AND PEPPER, TO TASTE

1 TABLESPOON EXTRA-VIRGIN OLIVE OIL

1 ONION, SLICED

5 GARLIC CLOVES, MINCED

1 TEASPOON GRATED FRESH GINGER

1 LB. TOMATOES, CHOPPED

1 TEASPOON CUMIN

1 TEASPOON CURRY POWDER

1 TEASPOON GARAM MASALA

½ TEASPOON CAYENNE PEPPER

1 TEASPOON CORIANDER

4 CUPS BEEF STOCK (SEE PAGE 553)

ROLLS, FOR SERVING

1. Season the short ribs generously with salt. Place the olive oil in a Dutch oven and warm it over medium-high heat. When the oil begins to shimmer, add the short ribs and cook until browned all over, about 2 to 3 minutes per side. Work in batches if necessary to avoid crowding the pan. Remove the browned short ribs and set them aside.

2. Add the onion to the pot and sauté until it begins to brown, about 4 minutes. Stir in the garlic, ginger, and tomatoes, cook for 1 minute, and then add the cumin, curry, garam masala, cayenne, and coriander.

3. Deglaze the pot with the stock, using a wooden spoon to scrape up the browned bits from the bottom. Cook until the stock has reduced by half.

4. Return the short ribs to the pot, cover it, and reduce the heat until the mixture simmers. Cook for about 2 hours, until the meat is extremely tender.

5. Remove the short ribs from the pot and let them rest for 20 minutes. Remove the bone and assemble the sandwiches using the rolls.

Chiles en Nogada
SEE PAGE 202

Chicken Souvlaki

YIELD: 4 SERVINGS | **ACTIVE TIME:** 20 MINUTES | **TOTAL TIME:** 2 HOURS AND 30 MINUTES

10 GARLIC CLOVES, CRUSHED

4 SPRIGS OF FRESH OREGANO

1 SPRIG OF FRESH ROSEMARY

1 TEASPOON PAPRIKA

1 TEASPOON KOSHER SALT

1 TEASPOON BLACK PEPPER

¼ CUP EXTRA-VIRGIN OLIVE OIL, PLUS MORE AS NEEDED

¼ CUP DRY WHITE WINE

2 TABLESPOONS FRESH LEMON JUICE

2½ LBS. BONELESS, SKINLESS CHICKEN BREASTS, CHOPPED

2 BAY LEAVES

PITA BREAD OR LAVASH (SEE PAGE 102 OR 32), FOR SERVING

1. Place the garlic, oregano, rosemary, paprika, salt, pepper, olive oil, wine, and lemon juice in a food processor and blitz to combine. Place the chicken and bay leaves in a bowl or a large resealable bag, pour the marinade over the chicken, and stir so that it gets evenly coated. Refrigerate for 2 hours, stirring or shaking occasionally.

2. Remove the chicken from the refrigerator, thread the pieces onto skewers, and allow them to come to room temperature. Prepare a gas or charcoal grill for medium-high heat (about 450°F).

3. Place the skewers on the grill and cook, turning frequently, until the chicken is cooked through, 6 to 8 minutes. Remove the skewers from the grill and let them rest for 10 minutes before serving with Pita Bread or Lavash and vegetables of your choice.

Swedish Meatballs

YIELD: 6 SERVINGS | **ACTIVE TIME:** 20 MINUTES | **TOTAL TIME:** 45 MINUTES

4 TABLESPOONS UNSALTED BUTTER

1 SMALL ONION, CHOPPED

¼ CUP MILK

1 LARGE EGG

1 LARGE EGG YOLK

3 SLICES OF WHITE BREAD

¼ TEASPOON ALLSPICE

¼ TEASPOON FRESHLY GRATED NUTMEG

PINCH OF GROUND GINGER

¾ LB. GROUND PORK

½ LB. GROUND BEEF

SALT AND PEPPER, TO TASTE

¼ CUP ALL-PURPOSE FLOUR

2½ CUPS CHICKEN STOCK (SEE PAGE 552)

½ CUP HEAVY CREAM

1. Preheat the broiler to high, position a rack so that the tops of the meatballs will be approximately 6 inches below the broiler, and line a rimmed baking sheet with aluminum foil.

2. Place 2 tablespoons of the butter in a large skillet and melt it over medium-high heat. Add the onion and sauté until it is translucent, about 3 minutes. Remove the pan from heat and set it aside.

3. Place the milk, egg, and egg yolk in a mixing bowl and stir to combine. Tear the bread into small pieces and add them to mixing bowl along with the allspice, nutmeg, and ginger. Stir in the pork, beef, and the onion, season the mixture with salt and pepper, and stir until thoroughly combined. Working with wet hands, form the mixture into 1½-inch meatballs, arrange them on the baking sheet, and spray the tops with nonstick cooking spray.

4. Place the meatballs in the oven and broil until browned all over, turning them as they cook. Remove the meatballs from the oven and set them aside.

5. Place the remaining butter in the skillet and melt it over low heat. Stir in the flour, cook for 2 minutes while stirring constantly, and then raise the heat to medium-high. Stir in the stock and cream and bring to a boil.

6. Add the meatballs to the sauce, reduce the heat to low, cover the pan, and simmer, turning the meatballs occasionally, until they are cooked through, about 15 minutes. Season with salt and pepper and serve.

Chicharron en Salsa Roja

YIELD: 6 SERVINGS | **ACTIVE TIME:** 25 MINUTES | **TOTAL TIME:** 1 HOUR AND 15 MINUTES

1 LB. PORK BELLY, CUT INTO 1-INCH-WIDE AND 6-INCH-LONG STRIPS

1½ TABLESPOONS KOSHER SALT

4 CUPS LARD OR CANOLA OIL

4 LARGE TOMATOES

3 SERRANO CHILE PEPPERS

3 GARLIC CLOVES

CORN TORTILLAS (SEE PAGE 26), WARMED, FOR SERVING

1. Set a wire rack in a rimmed baking sheet. Season the pork belly with the salt.

2. Place the lard in a Dutch oven (make sure it doesn't reach more than halfway up the sides of the pot) and warm it over medium-high heat. Add the pork belly and cook until golden brown and very crispy, about 1 hour.

3. Place the pork belly on the wire rack and let it drain. When the pork is cool enough to handle, chop it into ½-inch pieces.

4. Fill a medium saucepan with water and bring it to a boil. Add the tomatoes, serrano peppers, and garlic and cook until tender, about 10 minutes. Drain, transfer the vegetables to a blender, and puree until smooth.

5. Return the puree to the saucepan, add the pork belly, and simmer for about 20 minutes, so that the chicharron absorbs some of the sauce. Serve with tortillas and enjoy.

Chicken Satay

YIELD: 4 SERVINGS | **ACTIVE TIME:** 30 MINUTES | **TOTAL TIME:** 1 HOUR AND 30 MINUTES

¼ CUP KECAP MANIS

1 TABLESPOON KOSHER SALT

¼ CUP FINELY MINCED LEMONGRASS

2 TABLESPOONS FINELY MINCED SHALLOTS

4 TO 6 GARLIC CLOVES, MINCED

½ TABLESPOON CUMIN

1 TABLESPOON CORIANDER

1 TEASPOON FISH SAUCE

1½ LBS. BONELESS, SKINLESS CHICKEN BREASTS, SLICED INTO 1-INCH-LONG STRIPS

1. If using bamboo skewers, soak them in water for 30 minutes.

2. In a bowl, combine the kecap manis, salt, lemongrass, shallots, garlic, cumin, coriander, and fish sauce and stir until well combined. Add the chicken, place it in the refrigerator, and let it marinate for 1 hour.

3. Prepare a gas or charcoal grill for medium-high heat (about 450ºF). Thread the chicken onto the skewers.

4. Place the skewers on the grill and cook until the chicken is cooked through and seared on both sides, about 8 minutes, making sure to turn the skewers as little as possible.

5. Remove the skewers from the grill and enjoy immediately.

Tinga de Pollo

YIELD: 6 SERVINGS | **ACTIVE TIME:** 20 MINUTES | **TOTAL TIME:** 1 HOUR AND 20 MINUTES

2 BONE-IN, SKIN-ON CHICKEN LEGS

2 BONE-IN, SKIN-ON CHICKEN THIGHS

2 TABLESPOONS KOSHER SALT, PLUS MORE TO TASTE

2 BAY LEAVES

1 TABLESPOON EXTRA-VIRGIN OLIVE OIL

1 WHITE ONION, SLICED THIN

1 GARLIC CLOVE, SLICED THIN

3 LARGE TOMATOES, DICED

2 CHIPOTLE CHILE PEPPERS, STEMS AND SEEDS REMOVED

CORN TORTILLAS (SEE PAGE 26), WARMED, FOR SERVING

PICKLED RED ONION (SEE PAGE 399), FOR SERVING

QUESO FRESCO, FOR SERVING

1. Place the chicken in a large pot and cover with cold water by at least an inch. Add the salt and bay leaves and bring the water to a simmer. Cook the chicken until the meat pulls away from the bone, about 40 minutes.

2. While the chicken is simmering, place the olive oil in a large skillet and warm it over medium heat. Add the onion and garlic and cook, stirring frequently, until the onion is translucent, about 3 minutes. Reduce the heat to low and cook until the onion has softened.

3. Add the tomatoes and cook, stirring occasionally, for another 5 minutes.

4. Shred the chicken and reserve 2 cups of the cooking liquid. Place the chiles in a bowl with 1 cup of the cooking liquid and let them sit until tender, about 20 minutes.

5. Chop the chiles, add them to the skillet along with the shredded chicken, and cook, stirring occasionally, until the flavor has developed to your liking, about 8 minutes. Add the remaining cooking liquid to the pan if it becomes too dry.

6. Season with salt and serve with tortillas, pickled onion, and queso fresco.

Pig Ear Salad

YIELD: 4 SERVINGS | **ACTIVE TIME:** 30 MINUTES | **TOTAL TIME:** 1 HOUR AND 30 MINUTES

4 CUPS CHICKEN STOCK
(SEE PAGE 552)

2 CHIPOTLE MORITA CHILE
PEPPERS, STEMS AND SEEDS
REMOVED

½ WHITE ONION, SLICED

4 GARLIC CLOVES, 2 LEFT
WHOLE, 2 DICED

1 BAY LEAF

1½ LBS. PIG EARS, TRIMMED

CANOLA OIL, AS NEEDED

2 CUPS RICE FLOUR

SALT AND PEPPER, TO TASTE

¼ RED ONION, SLICED

2 TABLESPOONS TOASTED
RICE POWDER

15 CURRY LEAVES

10 CHERRY TOMATOES,
HALVED

JUICE OF 3 LIMES

2 TABLESPOONS EXTRA-
VIRGIN OLIVE OIL

1 TABLESPOON GINGER
JUICE

1 TABLESPOON EPAZOTE
POWDER

1. Place the stock in a medium saucepan and add the chiles, white onion, whole cloves of garlic, and bay leaf. Bring the stock to a simmer, add the pig ears, and gently simmer until they are very tender. You want to be able to pass a knife through the pig ears with ease. Drain the pig ears and let them cool. When cool, slice them into ½-inch-thick pieces.

2. Add canola oil to a Dutch oven until it is about 2 inches deep and warm it to 350°F.

3. Place the rice flour in a bowl, dredge the pig ears in the rice flour until coated, and then gently slip them into the hot oil. Fry until crispy on the outside, about 45 seconds. Transfer to a paper towel–lined plate to drain and season the pig ears with salt.

4. Place all of the remaining ingredients, except for the epazote powder, in a mixing bowl, add the fried pig ears, and toss to combine. Top with the epazote powder and enjoy.

Note: The toasted rice powder called for here is very easy to make at home—simply place a few tablespoons of jasmine rice in a dry skillet, toast it over medium heat, and then grind it into a fine powder with a mortar and pestle.

Tinga de Pollo
SEE PAGE 212

Bacon & Zucchini Frittata

YIELD: 6 SERVINGS | **ACTIVE TIME:** 10 MINUTES | **TOTAL TIME:** 45 MINUTES

¾ LB. THICK-CUT BACON, CHOPPED

1 SMALL ZUCCHINI, SLICED

1 GARLIC CLOVE, MINCED

4 OZ. GARLIC & HERB GOAT CHEESE

4 EGGS

½ LB. BABY SPINACH

1½ CUPS HALF-AND-HALF

½ TEASPOON KOSHER SALT

½ TEASPOON BLACK PEPPER

1. Preheat the oven to 350°F. Place the bacon in a 10-inch cast-iron skillet and cook it over medium heat, stirring occasionally, until crispy, about 10 minutes. Transfer the pieces to a paper towel–lined plate to drain.

2. Add the zucchini to the skillet and cook, stirring frequently, until the zucchini has softened, about 6 minutes. Add the garlic and goat cheese, return the pieces of bacon to the skillet, and stir until evenly distributed.

3. Whisk the eggs until they are scrambled. Add the spinach, half-and-half, salt, and pepper to the eggs and whisk to combine. Pour the egg mixture into the skillet and shake the pan evenly to distribute the mixture.

4. Put the skillet in the oven and bake until the frittata is puffy and golden brown and the eggs are set, about 30 minutes. Remove the frittata from the oven and let it sit for 5 minutes before slicing and serving.

Ham & Swiss Strata

YIELD: 4 SERVINGS | **ACTIVE TIME:** 20 MINUTES | **TOTAL TIME:** 1 HOUR

7 EGGS, BEATEN

2 CUPS WHOLE MILK

4 OZ. SWISS CHEESE, SHREDDED

PINCH OF FRESHLY GRATED NUTMEG

3 CUPS DAY-OLD BREAD PIECES

1 CUP DICED LEFTOVER HAM

1 YELLOW ONION, MINCED

2 CUPS CHOPPED FRESH SPINACH

SALT AND PEPPER, TO TASTE

2 TEASPOONS EXTRA-VIRGIN OLIVE OIL

1. Preheat the oven to 400°F. Place the eggs and milk in a large mixing bowl and whisk to combine. Add the cheese and nutmeg and stir to incorporate. Add the bread pieces and let the mixture sit for 10 minutes.

2. Add the ham, onion, and spinach to the egg-and-bread mixture and whisk until evenly distributed. Season with salt and pepper.

3. Coat a 10-inch cast-iron skillet with the olive oil. Pour in the strata, place the skillet in the oven, and bake until it is golden brown and set in the center, about 25 minutes. Remove the strata from the oven and let it cool for 10 minutes before cutting into wedges and serving.

THE ENCYCLOPEDIA OF TAPAS

Ham & Cheese Croissants

YIELD: 16 CROISSANTS | **ACTIVE TIME:** 15 MINUTES | **TOTAL TIME:** 45 MINUTES

1 SHEET OF FROZEN PUFF PASTRY, THAWED

⅔ CUP DIJON MUSTARD

16 SLICES OF SMOKED HAM

16 SLICES OF SWISS CHEESE

1 EGG, BEATEN

1. Preheat the oven to 400ºF and line two baking sheets with parchment paper. Roll out the sheet of puff pastry until it is very thin. Using a pizza cutter or a chef's knife, cut the puff pastry into rectangles, and then cut each rectangle diagonally, yielding 16 triangles. Gently roll out each triangle until it is 8 inches long.

2. Spread 2 teaspoons of the mustard toward the wide side of each triangle. Lay a slice of ham over the mustard and top it with a slice of cheese, making sure to leave 1 inch of dough uncovered at the tip of each croissant..

3. Roll the croissants up tight, moving from the wide side of the triangle to the tip. Tuck the tips under the croissants. Place 8 croissants on each of the baking sheets and brush them with the beaten egg.

4. Place the croissants in the oven and bake until they are golden brown, 20 to 22 minutes. Remove the croissants from the oven and place them on wire racks. Let the croissants cool slightly before enjoying.

Ham & Cheese Croissants
SEE PAGE 217

Sweet & Sour Meatballs

YIELD: 6 SERVINGS | **ACTIVE TIME:** 20 MINUTES | **TOTAL TIME:** 45 MINUTES

2 LBS. GROUND BEEF

½ SMALL ONION, DICED

½ CUP BREAD CRUMBS

2 EGGS

1 TEASPOON KOSHER SALT

1 TEASPOON BLACK PEPPER

1½ CUPS KETCHUP

¾ CUP CONCORD GRAPE JELLY

1. Preheat the oven to 350°F and line a baking sheet with aluminum foil. Place the beef, onion, bread crumbs, eggs, salt, and pepper in a mixing bowl and stir until combined. Working with wet hands, form the mixture into 1-inch meatballs and arrange them on the baking sheet.

2. Place the meatballs in the oven and bake until they are browned all over, 15 to 20 minutes, turning them as necessary.

3. Place the ketchup and jelly in a small saucepan and warm it over medium-low heat, stirring until the jelly has melted. Raise the heat to medium and bring the mixture to a boil.

4. Add the meatballs to the sauce, reduce the heat to low, and simmer the meatballs until they have the desired flavor and are cooked through, 15 to 20 minutes.

Classic Meatballs

YIELD: 4 SERVINGS | **ACTIVE TIME:** 20 MINUTES | **TOTAL TIME:** 40 MINUTES

1 LB. GROUND BEEF

1 WHITE ONION, GRATED

½ CUP BREAD CRUMBS

1 EGG

2 GARLIC CLOVES, MINCED

¼ CUP FRESH PARSLEY, CHOPPED

SALT AND PEPPER, TO TASTE

2 TABLESPOONS EXTRA-VIRGIN OLIVE OIL

MARINARA SAUCE (SEE PAGE 184), FOR SERVING

RICOTTA CHEESE, FOR SERVING

1. Place all the ingredients, except for the olive oil, in a mixing bowl and work the mixture with your hands until combined. Form the mixture into 1-inch meatballs and chill them in the freezer for 15 minutes.

2. Place the olive oil in a large skillet and warm it over medium heat. When the oil starts to shimmer, add the meatballs to the pan and cook, turning occasionally, until they are browned all over and cooked through, about 12 minutes. Let the meatballs cool slightly before serving with the Marinara Sauce and ricotta.

Pork Gyoza

YIELD: 10 SERVINGS | **ACTIVE TIME:** 10 MINUTES | **TOTAL TIME:** 40 MINUTES

½ LB. GROUND PORK

1 TEASPOON GRATED FRESH GINGER

1 LARGE GARLIC CLOVE, GRATED

2 TABLESPOONS FINELY CHOPPED SCALLIONS

½ TEASPOON SESAME OIL

1 TEASPOON LIGHT SOY SAUCE

½ TEASPOON SUGAR

½ TEASPOON WHITE PEPPER

½ TEASPOON KOSHER SALT

2 TABLESPOONS CANOLA OIL

22 ROUND WONTON WRAPPERS (SEE PAGE 560)

⅓ CUP WATER

1. Place the pork, ginger, garlic, scallions, sesame oil, soy sauce, sugar, pepper, and salt in a mixing bowl and stir until well combined.

2. Place half of the canola oil in a large skillet and warm it over medium heat. Add the ground pork mixture and cook, breaking it up with a wooden spoon, until browned and cooked through, about 8 minutes.

3. Fill a small dish with water and place it by the wrappers; this will be used to help seal the dumplings.

4. Place a wrapper in the palm of one hand. Use the index finger on your other hand to run a little water around the edges of the wrapper. Place a tablespoon of the pork mixture in the middle of the wrapper and fold it in half, bringing the edges almost together so it looks like a little taco shell. Press down on the edge to seal. Repeat until all of the dumplings have been filled.

5. Bring 2 inches of water to a simmer in a medium saucepan. Place the dumplings in a steaming tray, place the steaming tray over the simmering water, and steam for 5 minutes. Enjoy alongside your favorite dipping sauce.

Prosciutto & Cantaloupe Pops

YIELD: 4 SERVINGS | **ACTIVE TIME:** 10 MINUTES | **TOTAL TIME:** 10 MINUTES

2 CUPS CHOPPED
CANTALOUPE

4 OZ. PROSCIUTTO,
CHOPPED

1. Wrap each piece of cantaloupe in a piece of prosciutto and insert a toothpick or a wooden dowel in the bottom of the piece of cantaloupe. Repeat with the remaining cantaloupe and prosciutto and enjoy.

Sesame Chicken Wings

YIELD: 8 SERVINGS | **ACTIVE TIME:** 25 MINUTES | **TOTAL TIME:** 1 HOUR AND 15 MINUTES

½ CUP PACKED LIGHT BROWN SUGAR

3 TABLESPOONS FRESH LEMON JUICE

3 GARLIC CLOVES, SMASHED

2-INCH PIECE OF FRESH GINGER, PEELED AND GRATED

1 TEASPOON SALT, PLUS MORE TO TASTE

1 TABLESPOON SRIRACHA, PLUS MORE FOR SERVING

1 TABLESPOON SESAME SEEDS, TOASTED, PLUS MORE FOR GARNISH

3 LBS. CHICKEN WINGS

SCALLIONS, SLICED THIN, FOR GARNISH

FRESH CILANTRO, CHOPPED, FOR GARNISH

1. Preheat the oven to 475ºF. Place the brown sugar, lemon juice, garlic, ginger, and salt in a saucepan and stir to combine. Bring the mixture to a boil, reduce the heat so that everything simmers, and cook, stirring occasionally, until the mixture is syrupy, about 20 minutes.

2. Strain the glaze through a fine mesh sieve (you should have about ⅔ cup). Stir in the sriracha and toasted sesame seeds.

3. While the glaze is simmering, place the chicken wings in an even layer on a rimmed baking sheet and season them with salt. Place the chicken wings in the oven and bake until they are lightly golden brown, 20 to 25 minutes.

4. Remove the chicken wings from the oven and place them in a large bowl. Add half of the sauce and toss until the chicken wings are coated.

5. Place the chicken wings back on the baking sheet and return them to the oven. Bake until the glaze has caramelized, 5 to 7 minutes.

6. Remove the chicken wings from the oven, garnish with additional sesame seeds, scallions, and cilantro, and serve with the remaining sauce and additional sriracha.

THE ENCYCLOPEDIA OF TAPAS

Bacon Mac & Cheese

YIELD: 8 SERVINGS | **ACTIVE TIME:** 30 MINUTES | **TOTAL TIME:** 1 HOUR AND 15 MINUTES

1 TEASPOON KOSHER SALT, PLUS MORE TO TASTE

½ LB. MACARONI

3 SLICES OF THICK-CUT BACON

1 TABLESPOON UNSALTED BUTTER

1 SHALLOT, MINCED

2 GARLIC CLOVES, MINCED

1 TABLESPOON ALL-PURPOSE FLOUR

1 CUP MILK

½ LB. CHEDDAR CHEESE, GRATED

4 OZ. PARMESAN CHEESE, FRESHLY GRATED

¼ CUP BREAD CRUMBS

1. Preheat the oven to 350°F. Bring water to a boil in a large saucepan. Add salt and the macaroni to the boiling water and cook until the macaroni is al dente, 6 to 8 minutes. Drain the macaroni, place it back in the saucepan, and set it aside.

2. While the water is coming to a boil, place the bacon in a large skillet and cook until it is crispy and browned, 6 to 8 minutes, turning it as necessary. Transfer the cooked bacon to a paper towel–lined plate and let it drain. When the bacon is cool enough to handle, chop it into bite-size pieces.

3. Place the butter in a clean saucepan and melt it over medium heat. Add the shallot and garlic and cook, stirring frequently, until they have softened, about 5 minutes. Add the flour and salt and stir constantly until thoroughly incorporated.

4. While stirring continually, add the milk, half of the cheddar, and the Parmesan. Cook until the sauce is smooth and thick.

5. Add the sauce and chopped bacon to the macaroni and stir until combined. Transfer the mixture to a baking dish, smoothing the top so that it is even. Sprinkle the remaining cheddar over the top, top the cheese with the bread crumbs, and place the dish in the oven.

6. Bake until the top is golden brown and the mac & cheese is bubbling, 30 to 40 minutes. Remove the mac & cheese from the oven and let it cool slightly before serving.

Bourbon Smokies

YIELD: 6 SERVINGS | **ACTIVE TIME:** 25 MINUTES | **TOTAL TIME:** 40 MINUTES

¼ CUP BOURBON

½ CUP BARBECUE SAUCE

¼ CUP WATER

½ LB. HILLSHIRE FARM LIT'L SMOKIES SAUSAGES

2 (8 OZ.) CANS OF PILLSBURY CRESCENTS DOUGH

1. Preheat the oven to 375ºF. Place the bourbon, barbecue sauce, water, and sausages in a saucepan and warm over medium heat. Cook, stirring occasionally, until the sausages are glazed and the liquid has reduced by half.

2. Strain the sausages, reserving the liquid as a dipping sauce. Place the sausages on a baking sheet and let them cool completely.

3. Separate the dough into triangles. Cut each triangle evenly into three strips.

4. Line a baking sheet with parchment paper. Wrap each sausage in a strip of dough and place them on the parchment-lined baking sheet. Place the wrapped sausages in the oven and bake until the dough is cooked through and golden brown, about 5 minutes.

5. Serve the bourbon smokies alongside the dipping sauce.

Steamed Pork Buns

YIELD: 6 SERVINGS | **ACTIVE TIME:** 1 HOUR | **TOTAL TIME:** 24 HOURS

STEAMED BUNS (SEE PAGE 27)

6 CUPS WATER

1 TEASPOON FENNEL SEEDS

2 STAR ANISE PODS

1 CINNAMON STICK

1 TEASPOON PEPPERCORNS

6 WHOLE CLOVES

1 BAY LEAF

¼ CUP KOSHER SALT

1½ LBS. PORK BELLY, FAT SIDE SCORED ¼ INCH DEEP

PICKLED VEGETABLES, FOR SERVING

1. Start your preparations the night before making the Steamed Buns. Place the water, fennel seeds, star anise pods, cinnamon stick, peppercorns, whole cloves, bay leaf, and salt in a saucepan and bring to a boil. Turn off the heat and let the mixture cool completely. Place the pork belly in a roasting pan and pour the cooled liquid into the pan. Place the pan in the refrigerator overnight.

2. Preheat the oven to 450ºF and rinse the pork belly. Place the pork belly on a rimmed baking sheet, scored side up, place it in the oven, and roast for 30 minutes. Lower the temperature to 275ºF and roast the pork belly until it is tender, but not mushy, about 1 hour. While the pork belly is roasting, prepare the Steamed Buns.

3. When the pork belly is done, remove it from the oven and let it rest for 20 minutes. Place a few inches of water in a saucepan and bring it to a boil. Place a steaming basket above the water and, working in batches if necessary to avoid crowding the steaming basket, place the buns in the basket, making sure to leave them on the pieces of parchment paper. Steam the buns for 10 minutes.

4. Slice the pork belly thin, fill the buns with it, and serve with pickled vegetables.

Fig, Prosciutto & Camembert Tart

YIELD: 6 SERVINGS | **ACTIVE TIME:** 45 MINUTES | **TOTAL TIME:** 1 HOUR AND 30 MINUTES

2 TABLESPOONS EXTRA-VIRGIN OLIVE OIL

½ ONION, SLICED THIN

½ LB. PROSCIUTTO, TORN

1 PERFECT PIECRUST (SEE PAGE 562)

ALL-PURPOSE FLOUR, FOR DUSTING

1 TABLESPOON DIJON MUSTARD

1 ROUND OF CAMEMBERT CHEESE, SOFTENED

8 FRESH FIGS, STEMS REMOVED, HALVED

3 TABLESPOONS BALSAMIC VINEGAR

1 TABLESPOON HONEY

¼ CUP ARUGULA

1. Preheat the oven to 400ºF and line a baking sheet with parchment paper. Place the olive oil in a skillet and warm it over medium heat. Add the onion and cook, stirring occasionally, until it is lightly browned, about 6 minutes. Add the prosciutto to the skillet and cook, stirring continuously, for 1 minute. Remove the skillet from heat.

2. Place the crust on a flour-dusted work surface and roll it out to 12 inches. Place it on the baking sheet, spread the Dijon mustard evenly over the crust, and top it with the onion-and-prosciutto mixture. Cut the Camembert into wedges and place them on top. Then, arrange the figs on the tart. In a small bowl, whisk the balsamic vinegar and honey together and drizzle the mixture over the tart.

3. Place the baking sheet in the oven and bake the tart until the crust is golden brown and the figs are tender, about 25 minutes.

4. Remove the tart from the oven and let it cool slightly. Top the tart with the arugula and enjoy.

Steamed Pork Buns
SEE PAGE 228

Glazed Spam Musubi

YIELD: 6 SERVINGS | **ACTIVE TIME:** 30 MINUTES | **TOTAL TIME:** 30 MINUTES

2 TABLESPOONS SOY SAUCE

2 TABLESPOONS BROWN SUGAR

½ TEASPOON MIRIN

2 TEASPOONS AVOCADO OIL

1 CAN OF SPAM, SLICED HORIZONTALLY INTO 8 PIECES

6 CUPS COOKED SHORT-GRAIN WHITE RICE, AT ROOM TEMPERATURE

3 SHEETS OF ROASTED NORI, CUT INTO THIRDS

2 TEASPOONS FURIKAKE SEASONING

1. Place the soy sauce, brown sugar, and mirin in a bowl and whisk until the sugar has dissolved. Set the glaze aside.

2. Place the avocado oil in a large skillet and warm it over medium-high heat. Add the Spam and cook until it is browned and crispy on each side, 4 to 6 minutes.

3. Pour the glaze sauce over the Spam and turn off the heat. Let the Spam sit for 1 minute, then turn it in the glaze until it is evenly coated. Transfer the glazed Spam to a plate and set it aside.

4. Fill a musubi mold with some of the cooked rice and press down to pack it tightly. Remove the formed block of rice from the mold and repeat until all of the rice has been molded.

5. Place the nori on the counter, shiny side down. Place a piece of Spam in the center of each piece and sprinkle the furikake over the Spam. Place one of the molded rice blocks atop the Spam, carefully wrap the nori over the rice, and enjoy immediately.

Bacon-Wrapped Rice Cake Skewers

YIELD: 4 SERVINGS | **ACTIVE TIME:** 30 MINUTES | **TOTAL TIME:** 45 MINUTES

12 CYLINDRICAL RICE CAKES, HALVED

1 TABLESPOON SESAME OIL

12 SLICES OF BACON

PONZU SAUCE, TO TASTE

MALDON SEA SALT, FOR GARNISH

FRESH CHIVES, CHOPPED, FOR GARNISH

1 JALAPEÑO CHILE PEPPER, STEM AND SEEDS REMOVED, SLICED THIN, FOR GARNISH

1. Prepare a gas or charcoal grill for medium heat (about 400ºF). Place the rice cakes and sesame oil in a bowl and toss to coat. This both seasons the rice cakes and prevents them from sticking together.

2. Cut the slices of bacon in half and wrap each half around a rice cake. Thread 2 bacon-wrapped rice cakes onto skewers.

3. Place the skewers on the grill and cook until the bacon is crispy and the rice cakes are cooked through, 8 to 12 minutes, turning the skewers as necessary.

4. Transfer the skewers to a serving platter, drizzle the ponzu sauce over the top, and garnish with salt, chives, and jalapeño.

THE ENCYCLOPEDIA OF TAPAS

Beef Bulgogi Dumplings

YIELD: 4 TO 6 SERVINGS | **ACTIVE TIME:** 1 HOUR | **TOTAL TIME:** 13 HOURS

1 GARLIC CLOVE, MINCED

1 TABLESPOON SOY SAUCE

2 TEASPOONS GOCHUGARU

2 TEASPOONS CHOPPED FRESH GINGER

2 TEASPOONS LIGHT BROWN SUGAR

2 TEASPOONS SESAME OIL

½ LB. SIRLOIN STEAK, TRIMMED AND SLICED INTO THIN STRIPS

6 TABLESPOONS AVOCADO OIL

2 EGGS, BEATEN

24 BASIC DUMPLING WRAPPERS (SEE PAGE 559)

SCALLION GREENS, DICED, FOR GARNISH

PEANUTS, CRUSHED, FOR GARNISH

1. Place the garlic, soy sauce, gochugaru, ginger, brown sugar, sesame oil, and steak in a small bowl. Gently stir to combine, place the bowl in the refrigerator, and let the steak marinate for 12 hours.

2. Warm a large cast-iron skillet over medium-high heat until it starts to smoke. Add 1 tablespoon of the avocado oil and the marinated steak and cook for 1 minute. Turn the meat over and cook until it is just cooked through, about 2 minutes. Remove the steak from the pan, transfer it to a baking sheet, and let it cool. When cool enough to handle, chop the meat into small pieces.

3. Dip a finger into the beaten eggs and run it along the edge of a wrapper. Place a tablespoon of steak in the center, fold the circle over itself into a half-moon, and press down on the edge to seal it tightly. Repeat until all of the dumplings have been filled and sealed.

4. Fill a saucepan with 1 inch of water and bring it to a boil. Place a steaming basket over the water, place the dumplings in the basket, and steam until they are cooked through, about 6 minutes. Take care not to crowd the steaming basket, working in batches if necessary. Remove the steamed dumplings from the steaming basket and let them cool.

5. Place the remaining avocado oil in a large skillet and warm it over medium heat. Add the dumplings in batches and cook until golden brown on each side, about 2 minutes. Garnish with the scallion greens and peanuts and serve with your favorite dipping sauce.

Yukhoe

YIELD: 2 SERVINGS | **ACTIVE TIME:** 20 MINUTES | **TOTAL TIME:** 1 HOUR

½ LB. BEEF TENDERLOIN

1½ TABLESPOONS SOY SAUCE

1 TABLESPOON SUGAR

1 TEASPOON HONEY

2 TABLESPOONS SESAME OIL

1 TABLESPOON TOASTED SESAME SEEDS

5 GARLIC CLOVES, MINCED

½ SCALLION, TRIMMED AND MINCED

1 CUP WATER, CHILLED

½ KOREAN PEAR, PEELED AND CUT INTO MATCHSTICKS

8 PINE NUTS

1 TABLESPOON MINCED FRESH CHIVES

1 QUAIL EGG YOLK

1. Place the beef in the freezer for 45 minutes. This makes it easier to slice thin.

2. Using a sharp knife, slice the beef into thin matchsticks. Set the beef aside.

3. Place the soy sauce, half of the sugar, honey, sesame oil, sesame seeds, garlic, and scallion in a bowl and stir until well combined. Set the mixture aside.

4. Place the water and remaining sugar in a bowl and whisk until the sugar dissolves. Place the pear in the mixture and let it soak for 10 minutes. Drain the pear and set it aside.

5. Stir the beef into the sauce and let it marinate for 1 minute.

6. Arrange the marinated beef and pear on a serving plate and sprinkle the pine nuts and chives over the beef. Make a small well in the middle of the beef, place the egg yolk in the well, and enjoy.

Shengjian Baozi

YIELD: 4 SERVINGS | **ACTIVE TIME:** 1 HOUR | **TOTAL TIME:** 2 HOURS

10 OZ. GROUND PORK

1 TABLESPOON MINCED
FRESH GINGER

⅓ CUP CHOPPED SCALLIONS

¼ TEASPOON KOSHER SALT

⅛ TEASPOON WHITE
PEPPER

1 TEASPOON SUGAR

1 TABLESPOON PLUS 1
TEASPOON SOY SAUCE

2 TEASPOONS RICE VINEGAR

2 TEASPOONS SESAME OIL

1 TABLESPOON HOT WATER
(125°F), PLUS MORE AS
NEEDED

BAOZI WRAPPERS (SEE
PAGE 561)

¼ CUP AVOCADO OIL

1. Place the pork, ginger, and scallions in a mixing bowl and stir to combine. Place the remaining ingredients, except for the wrappers and avocado oil, in a separate bowl and stir until the salt and sugar have dissolved. Pour the liquid mixture over the pork mixture and stir to combine. Cover the mixing bowl and let the pork marinate for 30 minutes.

2. Place a wrapper in the palm of one hand and add about 1 tablespoon of the pork mixture. Cup the wrapper and close it over the filling. Squeeze it so that it is tightly sealed, and twist to remove any excess dough. Place the filled dumplings, seam side down, on a parchment-lined baking sheet and let them rise until doubled in size, about 30 minutes.

3. Place half of the avocado oil in a large skillet and warm it over medium heat. Working in two batches to ensure that the dumplings are at least ½ inch apart, add the baozi to the pan, seam side up, and cook until golden brown, 1 to 2 minutes.

4. Add hot water to the skillet until it is ¼ inch deep, holding the cover of the pan in front of you to prevent being harmed by any oil splattering. Cover the pan and cook the dumplings until the water has evaporated, about 6 minutes. Remove the lid and cook until the bottoms of the dumplings are crispy, about 2 minutes. Remove the dumplings from the pan, transfer them to a plate, and cover loosely with aluminum foil. Repeat with the remaining dumplings and avocado oil.

5. Serve immediately with your favorite dipping sauce.

Asian Meatballs

YIELD: 10 SERVINGS | **ACTIVE TIME:** 15 MINUTES | **TOTAL TIME:** 35 MINUTES

2 LBS. GROUND PORK

1 TABLESPOON SESAME OIL

¾ CUP PANKO

1½ TEASPOONS GRATED FRESH GINGER

2 EGGS

4 GARLIC CLOVES, MINCED

½ CUP THINLY SLICED SCALLIONS

⅔ CUP HOISIN SAUCE (SEE PAGE 127)

¼ CUP RICE VINEGAR

1½ TABLESPOONS SOY SAUCE

SESAME SEEDS, FOR GARNISH

1. Preheat the oven to 400°F. Coat a baking sheet with nonstick cooking spray. Place the pork, 2 teaspoons of sesame oil, panko, ½ teaspoon of ginger, eggs, 2 of the garlic cloves, and scallions in a mixing bowl and work the mixture with your hands until it is well combined.

2. Using your hands, form the mixture into balls and place them on the baking sheet. Place the meatballs in the oven and bake until the meatballs are golden brown and cooked through, 12 to 15 minutes.

3. While the meatballs are in the oven, place the remaining ingredients plus the remaining sesame oil, remaining ginger, and remaining garlic in a bowl and whisk until well combined.

4. Remove the meatballs from the oven and place them in a serving dish. Pour the sauce over the top, gently stir until the meatballs are coated, garnish with sesame seeds, and enjoy.

Chicken Katsu

YIELD: 2 SERVINGS | **ACTIVE TIME:** 30 MINUTES | **TOTAL TIME:** 30 MINUTES

1 LB. BONELESS, SKINLESS CHICKEN BREASTS, POUNDED ¼ INCH THICK

1 TEASPOON KOSHER SALT

½ TEASPOON BLACK PEPPER

¼ TEASPOON GRANULATED GARLIC

¼ CUP ALL-PURPOSE FLOUR

2 LARGE EGGS, BEATEN

2 CUPS PANKO

CANOLA OIL, AS NEEDED

1. Season both sides of the chicken with the salt, pepper, and granulated garlic.

2. Place the flour, eggs, and panko in 3 separate shallow bowls.

3. Dredge the chicken in the flour, shake it to remove any excess, dredge it in the eggs, and then dredge it in the panko. Repeat until the chicken is completely coated. Place the breaded chicken on a plate and set it aside.

4. Add canola oil to a large skillet until it is about ¼ inch deep and warm it over medium-high heat. Add the breaded chicken to the pan and cook until it is browned, crispy, and cooked through, 6 to 8 minutes. Transfer the chicken katsu to a paper towel–lined plate to drain.

5. Slice the chicken and serve with your favorite dipping sauce.

Char Siu

YIELD: 8 SERVINGS | **ACTIVE TIME:** 30 MINUTES | **TOTAL TIME:** 49 HOURS

¼ CUP HOISIN SAUCE (SEE PAGE 127)

1 TABLESPOON DARK SOY SAUCE

2 TABLESPOONS SHAOXING WINE

2 TABLESPOONS KETCHUP

1 TABLESPOON OYSTER SAUCE

¼ CUP SUGAR

2 TEASPOONS KOSHER SALT

3 PINCHES OF CURING SALT

1 TEASPOON FIVE-SPICE POWDER

1 TEASPOON RED FOOD COLORING (OPTIONAL)

4 LBS. PORK SHOULDER, CUT WITH THE GRAIN INTO 3 OR 4 LONG STRIPS

¼ CUP HONEY

1. Place all of the ingredients, except for the pork and honey, in a large bowl and stir until well combined. Add the pork and massage the marinade into the meat. Cover the bowl and marinate the pork in the refrigerator for 48 hours.

2. Preheat the oven to 375°F, placing a pan filled with water on the floor of the oven.

3. Place the pork on a baking sheet and reserve the marinade. Place the pork in the oven and roast for 25 to 30 minutes.

4. Place the reserved marinade in a bowl, stir in the honey, and set the mixture aside.

5. Turn the pork over, brush it with the marinade, and roast for another 20 minutes. Turn the pork over, brush with more of the marinade, and roast until the pork is cooked through, 15 to 20 minutes.

6. Remove the pork from the oven and let it rest for 20 minutes before slicing and serving.

Traditional Beef Jerky

YIELD: 12 SERVINGS | **ACTIVE TIME:** 20 MINUTES | **TOTAL TIME:** 10½ TO 24 HOURS

2 LBS. BEEF (TOP ROUND OR BOTTOM ROUND)

2 TABLESPOONS BROWN SUGAR

2 TABLESPOONS LIQUID SMOKE

¼ CUP GLUTEN-FREE TAMARI OR SOY SAUCE

1 TEASPOON MEAT TENDERIZER

2 TEASPOONS KOSHER SALT

1½ TEASPOONS BLACK PEPPER

2 TABLESPOONS WORCESTERSHIRE SAUCE

2 TEASPOONS PAPRIKA

1. Trim the meat to remove excess fat. Cut the meat into strips that are between ⅛ and ¼ inch thick, slicing with the grain for a chewier jerky or against the grain for a more tender jerky.

2. Place the remaining ingredients in a mixing bowl and whisk until the sugar has dissolved and the mixture is thoroughly combined.

3. Add the meat to the marinade and stir until the strips are evenly coated.

4. Cover the bowl with plastic wrap, place it in the refrigerator, and marinate for at least 6 hours. If time allows, let the meat marinate overnight.

5. Remove the meat from the refrigerator and give it a stir.

6. To prepare the jerky in a dehydrator, arrange the meat on the dehydrator trays, making sure to leave space between each piece. Place it in the dehydrator and dehydrate until the meat has dried out but is still flexible, 4 to 6 hours.

7. To prepare the jerky in an oven, preheat the oven to 175ºF. Line two rimmed baking sheets with aluminum foil and place wire racks over the foil. Arrange the strips of meat on the racks, making sure to leave space between each piece and to keep the meat in a single layer. Place the pans in the oven and bake for 1½ hours. Rotate the pans and then bake until the meat is dry to the touch, leathery, and slightly chewy, 1½ to 2½ hours.

8. Store the jerky at room temperature in an airtight container, where it will keep for a few weeks. If you are interested in a longer shelf life for your jerky, place it in a bag and vacuum seal it. Stored in a cool, dry place, the vacuum-sealed jerky will keep for 6 months to 2 years.

Teriyaki Beef Jerky

YIELD: 12 SERVINGS | **ACTIVE TIME:** 30 MINUTES | **TOTAL TIME:** 10½ TO 24 HOURS

2 LBS. BEEF (TOP ROUND, BOTTOM ROUND, OR TENDERLOIN)

2 TABLESPOONS BROWN SUGAR

2 TABLESPOONS LIQUID SMOKE

¼ CUP TAMARI OR SOY SAUCE

1 TEASPOON MEAT TENDERIZER

2 TEASPOONS KOSHER SALT

1½ TEASPOONS BLACK PEPPER

¼ CUP TERIYAKI SAUCE

1. Trim the meat to remove excess fat. Cut the meat into strips that are between ⅛ and ¼ inch thick, slicing with the grain for a chewier jerky or against the grain for a more tender jerky.

2. Place the remaining ingredients in a mixing bowl and whisk until the sugar has dissolved and the mixture is thoroughly combined.

3. Add the meat to the marinade and stir until the strips are evenly coated.

4. Cover the bowl with plastic wrap, place it in the refrigerator, and marinate for at least 6 hours. If time allows, let the meat marinate overnight.

5. Remove the meat from the refrigerator and give it a stir.

6. To prepare the jerky in a dehydrator, arrange the meat on the dehydrator trays, making sure to leave space between each piece. Place it in the dehydrator and dehydrate until the meat has dried out but is still flexible, 4 to 6 hours.

7. To prepare the jerky in an oven, preheat the oven to 175ºF. Line two rimmed baking sheets with aluminum foil and place wire racks over the foil. Arrange the strips of meat on the racks, making sure to leave space between each piece and to keep the meat in a single layer. Place the pans in the oven and bake for 1½ hours. Rotate the pans and then bake until the meat is dry to the touch, leathery, and slightly chewy, 1½ to 2½ hours.

8. Store the jerky at room temperature in an airtight container, where it will keep for a few weeks. If you are interested in a longer shelf life for your jerky, place it in a bag and vacuum seal it. Stored in a cool, dry place, the vacuum-sealed jerky will keep for 6 months to 2 years.

Honey & Jalapeño Pork Jerky

YIELD: 12 SERVINGS | **ACTIVE TIME:** 30 MINUTES | **TOTAL TIME:** 4½ TO 6½ HOURS

2 LBS. PORK TENDERLOIN

2 TABLESPOONS LIQUID SMOKE

1 TABLESPOON JALAPEÑO POWDER

2 TABLESPOONS BROWN SUGAR

1 TABLESPOON KOSHER SALT

1½ TEASPOONS BLACK PEPPER

2 TEASPOONS PAPRIKA

1. Trim the tenderloin to remove any excess fat and silvery skin. Cut the meat into strips that are between ⅛ and ¼ inch thick, slicing with the grain for a chewier jerky or against the grain for a more tender jerky.

2. Place the remaining ingredients in a mixing bowl and whisk until the mixture is thoroughly combined.

3. Add the meat to the rub and stir until the strips are evenly coated.

4. To prepare the jerky in a dehydrator, arrange the meat on the dehydrator trays, making sure to leave space between each piece. Place it in the dehydrator and dehydrate until the meat has dried out but is still flexible, 4 to 6 hours.

5. To prepare the jerky in an oven, preheat the oven to 175ºF. Line two rimmed baking sheets with aluminum foil and place wire racks over the foil. Arrange the strips of meat on the racks, making sure to leave space between each piece and to keep the meat in a single layer. Place the pans in the oven and bake for 1½ hours. Rotate the pans and then bake until the meat is dry to the touch, leathery, and slightly chewy, 1½ to 2½ hours.

6. Store the jerky at room temperature in an airtight container, where it will keep for a few weeks. If you are interested in a longer shelf life for your jerky, place it in a bag and vacuum seal it. Stored in a cool, dry place, the vacuum-sealed jerky will keep for 6 months to 2 years.

Turkey Jerky

YIELD: 10 SERVINGS | **ACTIVE TIME:** 30 MINUTES | **TOTAL TIME:** 24 HOURS

2 LBS. BONELESS, SKINLESS TURKEY BREASTS

2 TABLESPOONS BROWN SUGAR

2 TABLESPOONS LIQUID SMOKE

¼ CUP TAMARI OR SOY SAUCE

2 TEASPOONS KOSHER SALT

1½ TEASPOONS BLACK PEPPER

2 TABLESPOONS WORCESTERSHIRE SAUCE

2 TEASPOONS PAPRIKA

1. Slice the turkey breasts into ¼-inch-thick strips.

2. Place the remaining ingredients in a mixing bowl and whisk until the sugar has dissolved and the mixture is thoroughly combined.

3. Add the meat to the marinade and stir until the strips are evenly coated.

4. Cover the bowl with plastic wrap, place it in the refrigerator, and let it marinate overnight.

5. Remove the meat from the refrigerator and give it a stir.

6. To prepare the jerky in a dehydrator, arrange the meat on the dehydrator trays, making sure to leave space between each piece. Place it in the dehydrator and dehydrate until the meat has dried out but is still flexible, 6 to 8 hours.

7. To prepare the jerky in an oven, preheat the oven to 165°F. Line two rimmed baking sheets with aluminum foil and place wire racks over the foil. Arrange the strips of meat on the racks, making sure to leave space between each piece and to keep the meat in a single layer. Place the pans in the oven and bake for 3 hours. Rotate the pans and then bake until the meat is dry to the touch, leathery, and slightly chewy, 2½ to 3½ hours.

8. Store the jerky at room temperature in an airtight container, where it will keep for a few weeks. If you are interested in a longer shelf life for your jerky, place it in a bag and vacuum seal it. Stored in a cool, dry place, the vacuum-sealed jerky will keep for 6 months to 2 years.

Venison Jerky

YIELD: 4 SERVINGS | **ACTIVE TIME:** 15 MINUTES | **TOTAL TIME:** 7 TO 9 HOURS

½ LB. VENISON TRI-TIP, SLICED THIN

1 TABLESPOON SOY SAUCE

1 TEASPOON DISTILLED WHITE VINEGAR

1 TEASPOON SESAME OIL

½ TEASPOON HONEY

¼ TEASPOON ONION POWDER

¼ TEASPOON MINCED GARLIC

⅛ TEASPOON GRATED FRESH GINGER

1. Place all the ingredients in a mixing bowl and stir to combine. Let the venison marinate for 1 hour.

2. Place the venison on parchment-lined baking sheets, place them in a food dehydrator, and dehydrate at 140°F for 6 to 8 hours. When it is ready, the jerky should have lost about one-third of its weight and have a slightly bouncy texture.

Lemongrass Chicken Wings

YIELD: 4 SERVINGS | **ACTIVE TIME:** 30 MINUTES | **TOTAL TIME:** 12 HOURS

½ CUP SOY SAUCE

½ CUP FISH SAUCE

4 GARLIC CLOVES, MINCED

1 TABLESPOON MINCED FRESH GINGER

2 TABLESPOONS MINCED LEMONGRASS

¼ CUP HONEY

ZEST AND JUICE OF 3 LIMES

2 TABLESPOONS AVOCADO OIL

3 LBS. CHICKEN WINGS

1. Place all of the ingredients, except for the chicken wings, in a large bowl and stir until well combined. Place ¼ cup of the marinade in a separate bowl and store it in the refrigerator.

2. Add the chicken wings to the remaining marinade and to toss until they are coated. Marinate the chicken wings in the refrigerator for 12 hours.

3. Prepare a gas or charcoal grill for medium-high heat (about 450°F).

4. Place the wings on the grill and cook, basting them with the reserved marinade, until they are crispy and cooked through, 8 to 12 minutes, turning them just once.

5. Remove the chicken wings from the grill and let them cool briefly before enjoying.

Chickpea Poutine

YIELD: 4 SERVINGS | **ACTIVE TIME:** 45 MINUTES | **TOTAL TIME:** 2 HOURS

1 CUP CHICKPEA FLOUR

2 TEASPOONS KOSHER SALT

1 TEASPOON GARLIC POWDER

2 TABLESPOONS DRIED PARSLEY

PINCH OF CUMIN

2 CUPS BOILING WATER

CANOLA OIL, AS NEEDED

½ LB. LEFTOVER SHORT RIB OR BRISKET

½ CUP CRUMBLED FETA CHEESE

1. Place the flour, salt, garlic powder, parsley, and cumin in a mixing bowl and stir to combine. Add the boiling water and beat until the batter is smooth. Pour the batter into a small baking dish (small enough that the batter is about 1 inch deep), cover with plastic wrap, and refrigerate for 1 hour.

2. Turn the mixture out onto a cutting board and cut it into wide strips.

3. Add canola oil to a Dutch oven until it is about 3 inches deep and warm it to 350°F over medium heat. Add the chickpea fries and turn them as they cook until they are crispy and golden brown, 3 to 4 minutes. Place on a paper towel–lined plate to drain.

4. Place the short rib in a small saucepan, add about ½ cup of water, and bring it to a simmer. Cook until the liquid has reduced by half.

5. Arrange the fries on a platter and spoon the gravy from the short rib over them. Top with the short rib, sprinkle the feta over the fries, and serve.

Papas Rellenas

YIELD: 4 SERVINGS | **ACTIVE TIME:** 30 MINUTES | **TOTAL TIME:** 1 HOUR

3 LBS. POTATOES, PEELED AND CHOPPED

1 GARLIC CLOVE, MINCED

2 TEASPOONS KOSHER SALT

1 TEASPOON BLACK PEPPER

1 TABLESPOON EXTRA-VIRGIN OLIVE OIL

1 SMALL GREEN BELL PEPPER, STEM AND SEEDS REMOVED, MINCED

1 YELLOW ONION, MINCED

½ LB. GROUND BEEF

2 TABLESPOONS TOMATO PASTE

¼ CUP PITTED AND SLICED GREEN OLIVES

¼ CUP RAISINS

½ TEASPOON PAPRIKA

CANOLA OIL, AS NEEDED

2 EGGS, LIGHTLY BEATEN

½ CUP BREAD CRUMBS

1. Bring water to a boil in a large saucepan. Add the potatoes, cover the pan, and cook until the potatoes are fork-tender, about 20 minutes. Drain the potatoes, place them in a large bowl, and mash until smooth. Add the garlic and half of the salt and pepper and stir to incorporate.

2. Place the olive oil in a skillet and warm it over medium heat. When the oil starts to shimmer, add the bell pepper and onion and cook, stirring frequently, until the onion is translucent, about 3 minutes. Add the ground beef and cook, breaking it up with a fork, until it is browned, about 10 minutes. Stir in the tomato paste, olives, raisins, paprika, and the remaining salt and pepper and cook for 2 minutes. Transfer the mixture to a paper towel–lined baking sheet and let it drain.

3. Add canola oil to a Dutch oven until it is 2 inches deep and warm it to 375ºF. Place the eggs and bread crumbs in two separate bowls. Place 2 tablespoons of the potato mixture in one hand, pat it down until it is flat, and then place a tablespoon of the ground beef mixture in the center. Shape the potato around the filling to create a ball and dredge the ball in the egg. Roll the ball in the bread crumbs until coated and place it on a parchment–lined baking sheet. Repeat until all of the potato mixture and ground beef mixture have been used up.

4. Working in batches, slip the balls into the hot oil and deep-fry until they are golden brown, about 2 minutes. Remove with a slotted spoon and set them on a paper towel–lined plate to drain before enjoying.

Cornish Pasties

YIELD: 6 SERVINGS | **ACTIVE TIME:** 30 MINUTES | **TOTAL TIME:** 1 HOUR AND 15 MINUTES

FOR THE DOUGH

3 CUPS ALL-PURPOSE FLOUR, PLUS MORE AS NEEDED

¾ TEASPOON KOSHER SALT

½ CUP LARD OR UNSALTED BUTTER, CUT INTO SMALL PIECES

1 LARGE EGG, BEATEN

¼ CUP COLD WATER, PLUS MORE AS NEEDED

2 TEASPOONS DISTILLED WHITE VINEGAR

FOR THE FILLING

¾ LB. SKIRT STEAK, CUT INTO ½-INCH CUBES

¼ CUP PEELED AND CHOPPED PARSNIPS

¼ CUP PEELED AND CHOPPED TURNIPS

1 SMALL ONION, CHOPPED

1 CUP PEELED AND CHOPPED POTATO

1 TABLESPOON CHOPPED FRESH THYME

2 TABLESPOONS TOMATO PASTE

SALT AND PEPPER, TO TASTE

1 LARGE EGG, BEATEN

1 TABLESPOON WATER

1. To prepare the dough, place the flour and salt in a bowl, add the lard or butter, and use a pastry blender to work the mixture until it is coarse crumbs. Beat the egg, water, and vinegar together in a separate bowl and then drizzle this over the flour mixture. Use the pastry blender to work the mixture until it starts to hold together. Knead the dough with your hands, adding water in 1-teaspoon increments if it is too dry. Cut the dough into 6 pieces, cover them with plastic wrap, and chill in the refrigerator.

2. Preheat the oven to 400ºF. To prepare the filling, place all the ingredients, except for the egg and water, in a bowl and stir to combine. Place the egg and water in a separate bowl and beat to combine.

3. Place the pieces of dough on a flour-dusted work surface, roll each one into an 8-inch circle, and place ½ cup of the filling in the center of each circle. Brush the edge of each circle with water, fold into a half-moon, and crimp the edge to seal, gently pressing down on the filling to remove as much air as possible. Place the sealed handpies on a parchment-lined baking sheet.

4. Brush the handpies with the egg wash and use a paring knife to make a small incision in the side of each one. Bake in the oven for 15 minutes, reduce the temperature to 350ºF, and bake for another 25 minutes. Remove from the oven and let cool on a wire rack before serving.

Beef Tataki

YIELD: 4 SERVINGS | **ACTIVE TIME:** 20 MINUTES | **TOTAL TIME:** 1 HOUR AND 30 MINUTES

½ LB. BEEF TENDERLOIN

SALT AND PEPPER, TO TASTE

1 TABLESPOON EXTRA-VIRGIN OLIVE OIL, PLUS MORE AS NEEDED

JUICE OF 1 ORANGE

2 GARLIC CLOVES, MINCED

1 TEASPOON SUGAR

1 TEASPOON GRATED FRESH GINGER

1 TEASPOON DIJON MUSTARD

1. Cut the tenderloin in half and tie each piece with kitchen twine so that it will maintain its shape while being seared. Season the tenderloin with salt and pepper.

2. Coat the bottom of a large skillet with olive oil and warm it over medium-high heat. Place the tenderloin in the pan and cook, turning the pieces as they brown. Remove the beef from the pan and let it cool to room temperature.

3. Place the remaining ingredients in a bowl and stir to combine. Add the tenderloins and let them marinate for at least 1 hour before slicing and serving.

Chinese Spring Rolls

YIELD: 4 SERVINGS | **ACTIVE TIME:** 45 MINUTES | **TOTAL TIME:** 1 HOUR

4 OZ. PORK SHOULDER, SLICED THIN

1 TABLESPOON PLUS ½ TEASPOON CORNSTARCH

2 TABLESPOONS PLUS ½ TEASPOON SOY SAUCE

½ TEASPOON RICE WINE

1¼ TEASPOONS SESAME OIL

2 TABLESPOONS OYSTER SAUCE

PINCH OF FIVE-SPICE POWDER

8 DRIED SHIITAKE MUSHROOMS, SOAKED, DRAINED, STEMS REMOVED, FINELY DICED

¼ HEAD OF GREEN CABBAGE, SHREDDED

1 CARROT, PEELED AND GRATED

2 CELERY STALKS, FINELY DICED

1 CUP BEAN SPROUTS

3 SCALLIONS, TRIMMED AND SLICED THIN

1½ TEASPOONS WATER, PLUS MORE AS NEEDED

¼ CUP ALL-PURPOSE FLOUR

16 SPRING ROLL WRAPPERS

CANOLA OIL, AS NEEDED

PINEAPPLE & PLUM DIPPING SAUCE (SEE PAGE 119), FOR SERVING

1. Place the pork, ½ teaspoon of cornstarch, ½ teaspoon of soy sauce, rice wine, and ¼ teaspoon of sesame oil in a bowl and stir until well combined. Let the mixture marinate for 15 minutes.

2. Place the remaining soy sauce, the oyster sauce, five-spice powder, and remaining sesame oil in a separate bowl, stir until combined, and set the mixture aside.

3. Place the pork in a large skillet and stir-fry over medium-high heat until it is nearly cooked through, 4 to 5 minutes. Add the mushrooms, cook for 1 minute, and then stir in the add the remaining vegetables and cook, stirring frequently, for 3 minutes.

4. Place the remaining cornstarch and the water in a bowl and stir to combine. Stir the slurry and the soy sauce mixture into the pan and cook until the liquid has thickened. Transfer the mixture to a baking sheet and let it cool.

5. Place the flour in a bowl and add enough water until you have a paste. Divide the filling among the spring roll wrappers, roll them up, and seal each one with some of the flour paste. Place the spring rolls on a baking sheet and cover them with plastic.

6. Add canola oil to a Dutch oven until it is about 2 inches deep and warm it to 350°F. Working in batches to avoid crowding the pot, add the spring rolls and fry until they are crispy and golden brown. Transfer the fried spring rolls to a paper towel–lined plate to drain.

7. When all of the spring rolls have been cooked, serve with the Pineapple & Plum Dipping Sauce.

Lumpia

YIELD: 4 SERVINGS | **ACTIVE TIME:** 1 HOUR | **TOTAL TIME:** 1 HOUR

2 TABLESPOONS AVOCADO OIL

1 LB. GROUND PORK

2 TABLESPOONS MINCED FRESH GINGER

¼ CUP MINCED ONION

3 GARLIC CLOVES, MINCED

1½ CUPS MINCED CABBAGE

½ CUP MINCED CARROT

½ CUP MINCED CELERY

½ CUP MINCED JICAMA

6 DRIED SHIITAKE MUSHROOMS, SOAKED AND DRAINED, STEMS REMOVED, MINCED

1 TEASPOON BLACK PEPPER

1½ TEASPOONS KOSHER SALT

½ TEASPOON SUGAR

3 TABLESPOONS FISH SAUCE

¼ CUP ALL-PURPOSE FLOUR

8 LUMPIA WRAPPERS

CANOLA OIL, AS NEEDED

1. Place the avocado oil in a large skillet and warm it over medium-high heat. Add the pork, ginger, onion, and garlic and stir-fry until the meat is cooked through, 5 to 7 minutes.

2. Stir in the cabbage, carrot, celery, jicama, and mushrooms and stir-fry for 3 minutes. Add the pepper, salt, sugar, and fish sauce and stir to combine. Cook until the liquid has evaporated, remove the pan from heat, and let the mixture cool.

3. Place the flour in a bowl and add water until the mixture is a paste.

4. Cut a lumpia wrapper in half. Place some of the filling at a short end of the wrapper, roll it up tightly like a cigar, and use the flour paste to seal the lumpia. Repeat until all of the filling has been used.

5. Add canola oil to a Dutch oven until it is about 2 inches deep and warm it to 325°F. Working in batches to avoid crowding the pot, gently slip the lumpia into the hot oil and fry until they are golden brown. Transfer the fried lumpia to a paper towel–lined plate and let them drain and cool before enjoying with your favorite dipping sauce.

Croquetas

YIELD: 40 CROQUETAS | **ACTIVE TIME:** 1 HOUR | **TOTAL TIME:** 24 HOURS

2 TABLESPOONS EXTRA-VIRGIN OLIVE OIL, PLUS MORE AS NEEDED

1 ONION, CHOPPED

¼ CUP ALL-PURPOSE FLOUR

¾ LB. FINELY DICED LEFTOVER CHICKEN, PORK, OR BEEF

3 CUPS MILK

PINCH OF FRESHLY GRATED NUTMEG

SALT, TO TASTE

2 EGGS, BEATEN

BREAD CRUMBS, AS NEEDED

1. Place the olive oil in a medium skillet and warm it over medium heat. Add the onion and cook, stirring occasionally, until it starts to turn golden brown, about 6 minutes. Add the flour and cook, stirring continually, for 2 minutes.

2. Stir in the leftover meat and cook, stirring frequently, until it is warmed through, about 2 minutes. Add the milk in a slow stream, stirring until it is incorporated. Add the nutmeg, season the mixture with salt, and remove the pan from heat.

3. Cover a baking sheet with plastic wrap. Spread the mixture evenly over the baking sheet and cover it with a piece of parchment paper and more plastic wrap. Store the mixture in the refrigerator overnight.

4. Remove the baking sheet from the refrigerator. Add olive oil to a large, deep skillet until it is about 1 inch deep.

5. Place the beaten eggs in a bowl. Place bread crumbs in a separate bowl. Form the mixture into ovals, dredge them in the eggs, shake to remove excess, and dredge them in the bread crumbs until coated.

6. Working in batches to avoid crowding the pan, gently slip the croquetas into the hot oil and fry until golden brown, 4 to 5 minutes, turning them as necessary. Transfer the fried croquetas to a paper towel–lined plate to drain and season them with salt before serving.

Shepherd's Pie Bites

YIELD: 12 SERVINGS | **ACTIVE TIME:** 30 MINUTES | **TOTAL TIME:** 1 HOUR AND 45 MINUTES

3 LBS. RED POTATOES

½ LB. CHEDDAR CHEESE, SHREDDED

2 TABLESPOONS UNSALTED BUTTER

1 SMALL WHITE ONION, DICED

1 CARROT, PEELED AND DICED

1 GARLIC CLOVE, CRUSHED

1 LB. GROUND BEEF

SALT AND PEPPER, TO TASTE

3 OZ. BOURBON

¼ CUP PEAS

FRESH CHIVES, FINELY CHOPPED, FOR GARNISH

1. Preheat the oven to 375ºF. Place the potatoes in the oven and bake until they are fork-tender, about 1 hour. Remove the potatoes from the oven and let them cool.

2. When the potatoes are cool enough to handle, cut them in half lengthwise and scoop the flesh into a bowl, making sure to leave a ½-inch-thick wall around the edge of each half. Set the hollowed-out halves aside. Add the cheese to the potatoes in the bowl and mash until the mixture is smooth.

3. Warm a large skillet over medium heat. Add the butter and melt it. Add the onion, carrot, and garlic and cook, stirring continually, for 2 minutes.

4. Add the ground beef, season it with salt and pepper, and cook until it is browned and cooked through, 6 to 8 minutes, breaking the beef up with a wooden spoon as it cooks.

5. Deglaze the pan with the bourbon, scraping up any browned bits from the bottom. Bring the mixture to a simmer, stir in the peas, and cook, stirring occasionally, until the peas are cooked through, 3 to 4 minutes. Remove the pan from heat.

6. Fill the hollowed-out potato halves with the ground beef mixture. Top with the cheesy mashed potatoes, garnish with chives, and serve.

Chicken & Chestnut Sausages

YIELD: 4 SERVINGS | **ACTIVE TIME:** 25 MINUTES | **TOTAL TIME:** 1 HOUR

2 TABLESPOONS EXTRA-VIRGIN OLIVE OIL

1 CELERY STALK, FINELY DICED

1 WHITE ONION, FINELY DICED

½ CUP BLANCHED CHESTNUTS, FINELY DICED

1 LB. GROUND CHICKEN

2 SLICES OF BACON, FINELY DICED

1 CUP HEAVY CREAM

JUICE OF 1 LEMON

1 EGG

FRESH SAGE, CHOPPED, TO TASTE

FRESHLY GRATED NUTMEG, TO TASTE

FRESH THYME, TO TASTE

SALT AND PEPPER, TO TASTE

SAUSAGE CASINGS, RINSED WELL (OPTIONAL)

1. Place 1 tablespoon of the olive oil in a medium skillet and warm it over medium heat. Add the celery, onion, and chestnuts and cook, stirring frequently, until they have softened, about 4 minutes, making sure that they do not brown. Transfer the mixture to a mixing bowl and let it cool.

2. When the vegetable-and-chestnut mixture has cooled slightly, add the chicken, bacon, cream, lemon juice, and egg and stir to combine. Season the mixture with sage, nutmeg, thyme, salt, and pepper and stir to incorporate. Place a small piece of the mixture in a skillet and cook it until browned. Taste and adjust the seasoning as desired.

3. Form the sausage into patties or stuff it into casings. To cook the sausage patties, place them in a skillet with the remaining olive oil and cook them until browned on both sides and cooked through, 8 to 10 minutes. To cook the sausage links, place them in a skillet and cook until well browned all over and cooked through, 15 to 18 minutes.

Lamb Meatballs

YIELD: 4 SERVINGS | **ACTIVE TIME:** 20 MINUTES | **TOTAL TIME:** 40 MINUTES

1 LB. GROUND LAMB

1 WHITE ONION, GRATED

½ CUP BREAD CRUMBS

1 EGG

2 GARLIC CLOVES, MINCED

¼ CUP FRESH PARSLEY, CHOPPED

¼ CUP FRESH CILANTRO, CHOPPED

¾ TEASPOON CAYENNE PEPPER

¼ TEASPOON RED PEPPER FLAKES

SALT AND PEPPER, TO TASTE

2 TABLESPOONS EXTRA-VIRGIN OLIVE OIL

1. Place all the ingredients, except for the olive oil, in a mixing bowl and work the mixture with your hands until combined. Form the mixture into 1-inch meatballs and chill them in the freezer for 15 minutes.

2. Place the olive oil in a large skillet and warm it over medium heat. When the oil starts to shimmer, add the meatballs to the pan and cook, turning occasionally, until they are browned all over and cooked through, about 12 minutes. Let the meatballs cool slightly before serving.

Crispy Pancetta

YIELD: 4 SERVINGS | **ACTIVE TIME:** 10 MINUTES | **TOTAL TIME:** 40 MINUTES

3 OZ. PANCETTA, SLICED

1. Preheat the oven to 350ºF and line two baking sheets with Silpat mats. Divide the pancetta between the baking sheets.

2. Place the sheets in the oven and bake the pancetta until it is browned and crispy, about 20 minutes. Remove from the oven, transfer the pancetta to a piece of parchment paper, and let cool before serving.

Duck Rillette

YIELD: 4 SERVINGS | **ACTIVE TIME:** 15 MINUTES | **TOTAL TIME:** 3 HOURS

6 DUCK LEGS

SALT AND PEPPER, TO TASTE

2 TABLESPOONS EXTRA-VIRGIN OLIVE OIL

¾ CUP DUCK FAT

½ CUP FRESH PARSLEY, CHOPPED

6 TABLESPOONS UNSALTED BUTTER, MELTED AND COOLED SLIGHTLY

1. Pat the duck legs dry with paper towels and season them generously with salt. With the tip of a knife, gently poke the skin all around each leg. This will help release the fat as it renders. Let the legs rest at room temperature for at least 25 minutes.

2. Coat the bottom of a Dutch oven with the olive oil, add the duck legs, and set the oven to 285°F. Place the Dutch oven, uncovered, in the oven. You do not want to preheat the oven, as starting the duck at a low temperature allows its fat to render. After 1½ hours, check the duck. It should be under a layer of duck fat and the skin should be getting crisp. If the legs aren't browned and crispy, let the duck cook longer. When the skin is starting to crisp, raise the oven's temperature to 375°F and cook the duck for another 15 minutes.

3. Remove the pot from the oven, remove the duck legs from the fat, and let them rest for 10 minutes.

4. Remove the meat from the duck legs and finely chop it. Place the meat in a mixing bowl.

5. Add the duck fat and parsley, fold to combine, and season the mixture with salt and pepper.

6. Place the mixture in a jar, top it with the melted butter, and refrigerate until ready to serve. The rillette will keep in the refrigerator for 5 to 7 days.

Popcorn Chicken

YIELD: 4 SERVINGS | **ACTIVE TIME:** 25 MINUTES | **TOTAL TIME:** 1 HOUR AND 30 MINUTES

3 GARLIC CLOVES, SMASHED

1 EGG WHITE

1 TABLESPOON SOY SAUCE

1½ TABLESPOONS SESAME OIL

½ TEASPOON WHITE PEPPER

1 TABLESPOON CORNSTARCH

SALT, TO TASTE

1 LB. BONELESS, SKIN-ON CHICKEN BREAST, CUT INTO BITE-SIZE PIECES

7 TABLESPOONS TAPIOCA STARCH, PLUS MORE AS NEEDED

2 CUPS CANOLA OIL

1. Place the garlic, egg white, soy sauce, sesame oil, white pepper, cornstarch, and salt in a mixing bowl and stir to combine. Add the chicken, toss to coat, and cover the bowl. Chill in the refrigerator for 1 hour.

2. Dust a baking sheet with tapioca starch, add the chicken, and turn it in the starch until it is coated, adding more tapioca starch as necessary.

3. Place the canola oil in a Dutch oven and warm it to 350ºF over medium heat. Shake the chicken to remove any excess starch, add it to the pot in batches, and fry until golden brown. Make sure you do not overcrowd the pot.

4. Place the cooked chicken on a paper towel–lined plate to drain and briefly let it cool before serving.

Muffuletta

YIELD: 4 TO 6 SERVINGS | **ACTIVE TIME:** 45 MINUTES | **TOTAL TIME:** 24 HOURS

1 RED BELL PEPPER

1 CUP SUN-DRIED TOMATOES IN OLIVE OIL, DRAINED AND CHOPPED

1 CUP PITTED GREEN OLIVES, CHOPPED

1 CUP PITTED BLACK OLIVES, CHOPPED

¼ CUP EXTRA-VIRGIN OLIVE OIL

¼ CUP CHOPPED FRESH PARSLEY

2 TABLESPOONS FRESH LEMON JUICE

1 TEASPOON DRIED OREGANO

1 LOAF OF ITALIAN OR FRENCH BREAD, HALVED LENGTHWISE

2 CUPS TORN LETTUCE

4 OZ. MORTADELLA, SLICED THIN

4 OZ. PROVOLONE CHEESE, SLICED THIN

4 OZ. SOPPRESSATA, SLICED THIN

1. Preheat the oven to 400ºF. Place the bell pepper on a baking sheet, place it in the oven, and roast, turning it occasionally, until it is charred all over, about 25 minutes. Remove the pepper from the oven and let it cool. When cool enough to handle, remove the charred flesh, chop the pepper, and discard the seed pod and stem. Place the roasted pepper in a mixing bowl.

2. Add the tomatoes, olives, oil, parsley, lemon juice, and oregano to the bowl. Cover and refrigerate overnight.

3. Drain the olive mixture and reserve the liquid. Remove most of the crumb from one of the halves of the bread and generously brush the cut sides with the reserved liquid. Fill the piece of bread with the crumb removed with half of the olive mixture and top with half of the lettuce and all the mortadella, provolone, and soppressata.

4. Layer the remaining lettuce over the soppressata and top with the remaining olive mixture and the other piece of bread. Wrap the sandwich in plastic wrap and place it on a large plate. Place another plate on top and weigh it down with a good-sized cookbook or something similar. Refrigerate for at least 1 hour before slicing and serving.

Chicken 65

YIELD: 6 SERVINGS | **ACTIVE TIME:** 1 HOUR | **TOTAL TIME:** 2 HOURS

1 LB. BONELESS, SKINLESS CHICKEN THIGHS, CHOPPED

1 TEASPOON MASHED FRESH GINGER

1 GARLIC CLOVE, MINCED

½ TEASPOON CHILI POWDER, PLUS MORE TO TASTE

1 TEASPOON FRESH LEMON JUICE

½ TEASPOON BLACK PEPPER, PLUS MORE TO TASTE

⅛ TEASPOON TURMERIC

SALT, TO TASTE

2 TABLESPOONS CORNSTARCH

1 TABLESPOON RICE FLOUR

CANOLA OIL, AS NEEDED

½ TEASPOON SUGAR

2 TABLESPOONS PLAIN YOGURT

1 TABLESPOON UNSALTED BUTTER

3 TO 5 CURRY LEAVES

2 GREEN CHILE PEPPERS, STEMS AND SEEDS REMOVED, CHOPPED

½ TEASPOON CUMIN

1. Rinse the chicken and pat it dry. Place the ginger, one-third of the garlic, the chili powder, lemon juice, black pepper, turmeric, and salt in a mixing bowl and stir to combine. Add the chicken and stir to coat. Place it in the refrigerator and marinate for at least 1 hour.

2. When ready to cook the chicken, place the cornstarch and flour in a mixing bowl, stir to combine, and dredge the marinated chicken in the mixture.

3. Add canola oil to a Dutch oven until it is 2 inches deep and warm it to 350°F over medium heat.

4. Place the sugar, remaining garlic, and yogurt in a mixing bowl, season with chili powder and salt, and stir to combine. Set the mixture aside.

5. Working in batches if necessary to avoid crowding the pot, place the chicken in the oil and fry until golden brown and cooked through. Remove the cooked chicken from the pot and let it drain on a paper towel–lined plate.

6. Place the butter, curry leaves, chiles, and cumin in a small pan and sauté over medium heat until fragrant. Stir in the yogurt mixture and bring the sauce to a simmer. Add the fried chicken to the sauce and cook until the chicken has absorbed most of the liquid. Let cool briefly before serving.

Kefta

YIELD: 4 SERVINGS | **ACTIVE TIME:** 35 MINUTES | **TOTAL TIME:** 1 HOUR

1½ LBS. GROUND LAMB

½ LB. GROUND BEEF

½ WHITE ONION, MINCED

2 GARLIC CLOVES, ROASTED AND MASHED

ZEST OF 1 LEMON

1 CUP FRESH PARSLEY, CHOPPED

2 TABLESPOONS CHOPPED FRESH MINT

1 TEASPOON CINNAMON

2 TABLESPOONS CUMIN

1 TABLESPOON PAPRIKA

1 TEASPOON CORIANDER

SALT AND PEPPER, TO TASTE

¼ CUP EXTRA-VIRGIN OLIVE OIL

1. Place all the ingredients, except for the olive oil, in a mixing bowl and stir until well combined. Place a small bit of the mixture in a skillet and cook over medium heat until cooked through. Taste and adjust the seasoning in the remaining mixture as necessary. Working with wet hands, form the mixture into 18 ovals and place three meatballs on each skewer.

2. Place the olive oil in a Dutch oven and warm it over medium-high heat. Working in batches, add three skewers to the pot and sear the kefta until browned all over and nearly cooked through. Transfer the browned kefta to a paper towel–lined plate to drain.

3. When all the kefta have been browned, return all of the skewers to the pot, cover it, and remove from heat. Let stand for 10 minutes so the kefta get cooked through.

4. When the kefta are cooked through, remove them from the skewers and serve.

Curried Chicken Salad

YIELD: 6 SERVINGS | **ACTIVE TIME:** 10 MINUTES | **TOTAL TIME:** 10 MINUTES

4 CUPS DICED LEFTOVER CHICKEN

¼ CUP MAYONNAISE

3 TABLESPOONS FRESH LIME JUICE

¼ CUP MADRAS CURRY POWDER

1 TABLESPOON CUMIN

1 TABLESPOON GARLIC POWDER

½ TEASPOON CINNAMON

½ TEASPOON TURMERIC

SALT AND PEPPER, TO TASTE

3 CELERY STALKS, MINCED

2 GRANNY SMITH APPLES, MINCED

½ RED BELL PEPPER, STEMS AND SEEDS REMOVED, MINCED

¾ CUP PECANS, CHOPPED

3 OZ. ARUGULA

12 SLICES OF MARBLE RYE, TOASTED

1. Place the chicken, mayonnaise, lime juice, and the seasonings in a mixing bowl and stir to combine. Add the celery, apples, red pepper, and ½ cup of the pecans and stir to incorporate.

2. Add the arugula and toss to combine. Top with the remaining pecans and sandwich the chicken salad between the toasted slices of marble rye.

Corn Dogs

YIELD: 4 SERVINGS | **ACTIVE TIME:** 20 MINUTES | **TOTAL TIME:** 1 HOUR

1 CUP CORNMEAL

1 CUP ALL-PURPOSE FLOUR

2 TEASPOONS KOSHER SALT

¼ CUP SUGAR

4 TEASPOONS BAKING POWDER

1 EGG WHITE

1 CUP MILK

CANOLA OIL, AS NEEDED

4 HOT DOGS

1. Soak four bamboo skewers in water for 30 minutes. Place the cornmeal, flour, salt, sugar, and baking powder in a mixing bowl and stir to combine. Place the egg white and milk in a separate bowl and whisk to combine. Add the wet mixture to the dry mixture and stir until thoroughly combined.

2. Add oil to a Dutch oven until it is approximately 2 inches deep and warm it to 350°F over medium heat. Thread the hot dogs onto the skewers and roll them in the batter until well coated. When the oil is at the correct temperature, add the corn dogs and fry until golden brown, about 3 minutes.

Smoky & Spicy Chicken Wings

YIELD: 6 SERVINGS | **ACTIVE TIME:** 10 MINUTES | **TOTAL TIME:** 40 MINUTES

1½ TABLESPOONS SMOKED PAPRIKA

1½ TABLESPOONS BLACK PEPPER

2 TEASPOONS CHIPOTLE CHILE POWDER

1 TABLESPOON CHILI POWDER

1½ TEASPOONS CAYENNE PEPPER

½ TEASPOON CUMIN

½ TEASPOON DRIED OREGANO

SALT, TO TASTE

2 LBS. CHICKEN WINGS

CANOLA OIL, AS NEEDED

1. Preheat the oven to 400ºF. Place all the ingredients, except for the chicken wings and canola oil, in a mixing bowl and stir until combined.

2. Pat the chicken wings dry. Either toss the wings in the rub until they are evenly coated, or apply it by hand.

3. Place the wings on a baking sheet, arranging them so that they are not touching. Place them in the oven and roast until the internal temperature is 160ºF, about 20 minutes.

4. While the wings are in the oven, add canola oil to a Dutch oven until it is about 2 inches deep and warm it to 350ºF.

5. Remove the chicken wings from the oven, and, working in batches to avoid crowding the pot, gently slip the chicken wings into the oil and fry until crispy and golden brown, about 8 minutes. Drain the fried wings on a paper towel–lined plate and enjoy once all of the wings have been fried.

Southwestern Sliders

YIELD: 6 SERVINGS | **ACTIVE TIME:** 20 MINUTES | **TOTAL TIME:** 35 MINUTES

1 LARGE EGG

2 CHIPOTLES IN ADOBO

2 TABLESPOONS WHOLE MILK

½ CUP BREAD CRUMBS

½ CUP GRATED JALAPEÑO JACK CHEESE

3 TABLESPOONS FINELY CHOPPED FRESH CILANTRO

3 TABLESPOONS CANNED DICED GREEN CHILES, DRAINED

4 GARLIC CLOVES, MINCED

1 TABLESPOON DRIED OREGANO

1 TABLESPOON SMOKED PAPRIKA

2 TEASPOONS CUMIN

1¼ LBS. GROUND BEEF

SALT AND PEPPER, TO TASTE

SLIDER ROLLS, FOR SERVING

1. Preheat a gas or charcoal grill to medium-high heat (450°F). Place the egg, chipotles, milk, and bread crumbs in a food processor and puree until smooth. Place the mixture in a mixing bowl, add the cheese, cilantro, green chiles, garlic, oregano, paprika, and cumin, and stir until thoroughly combined.

2. Stir in the beef and season the mixture with salt and pepper. Working with wet hands, form the mixture into 3-inch patties. Place the sliders on the grill and cook until cooked through, about 10 minutes. Remove the sliders from the grill, transfer to a platter, and tent them loosely with aluminum foil.

3. Let the sliders rest for 10 minutes before serving with slider rolls and your favorite burger fixings.

FRUITS OF THE SEA

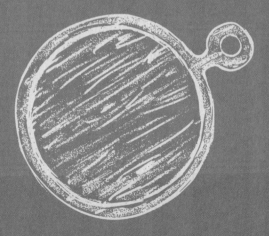

Shrimp Cocktail

YIELD: 4 SERVINGS | **ACTIVE TIME:** 20 MINUTES | **TOTAL TIME:** 1 HOUR

½ CUP KETCHUP

2 TABLESPOONS HORSERADISH

2 TABLESPOONS WORCESTERSHIRE SAUCE

JUICE OF ½ LEMON

1 TEASPOON OLD BAY SEASONING

½ LB. LARGE SHRIMP, SHELLS REMOVED, DEVEINED

1. Place the ketchup, horseradish, Worcestershire sauce, and lemon juice in a bowl, stir to combine, and chill in the refrigerator for 1 hour.

2. Prepare an ice bath. Place water in a medium saucepan and bring it to a boil. Add the Old Bay and the shrimp and poach the shrimp until cooked through, about 4 minutes.

3. Shock the shrimp in the ice water and chill in the refrigerator until ready to serve.

Smoked Trout Croquettes

YIELD: 8 SERVINGS | **ACTIVE TIME:** 40 MINUTES | **TOTAL TIME:** 3 HOURS

1 LB. RUSSET POTATOES

¾ LB. SMOKED TROUT, FLAKED

ZEST AND JUICE OF 1 LEMON

1 GARLIC CLOVE, GRATED

1 BUNCH OF FRESH CHIVES, MINCED

SALT, TO TASTE

CAYENNE PEPPER, TO TASTE

CANOLA OIL, AS NEEDED

ALL-PURPOSE FLOUR, AS NEEDED

¼ CUP MAYONNAISE

2 TEASPOONS DIJON MUSTARD

1. Preheat the oven to 400ºF. Line a baking sheet with parchment paper. Place the potatoes in the oven and bake until very tender, about 1 hour. Remove the potatoes from the oven, slice them in half, and let them cool.

2. Place the smoked trout in the work bowl of a stand mixer fitted with the paddle attachment. Add the lemon zest, garlic, and chives, season the mixture with salt and cayenne, and stir to combine. Remove the skin from the potatoes and use a potato ricer to press the flesh into the work bowl.

3. Beat the mixture until it is well combined and thick. Taste, adjust the seasoning as necessary, and form tablespoons of the mixture into balls. Place the balls on the parchment-lined baking sheet and chill them in the refrigerator for 1 hour.

4. Add canola oil to a Dutch oven until it is about 2 inches deep and warm it to 350ºF. Place some flour in a shallow bowl. Remove the croquettes from the refrigerator and dredge them in the flour until lightly coated. Working in batches to avoid crowding the pot, gently slip the croquettes into the hot oil and fry them until golden brown, 3 to 4 minutes, turning them as necessary. Transfer the cooked croquettes to a paper towel–lined plate to drain.

5. Place the mayonnaise, mustard, and lemon juice in a small bowl and stir to combine. Serve this dipping sauce alongside the croquettes.

Crab Rangoon

YIELD: 40 RANGOON | **ACTIVE TIME:** 25 MINUTES | **TOTAL TIME:** 45 MINUTES

1 LB. CREAM CHEESE, SOFTENED

6 OZ. FRESH CRABMEAT

2 TABLESPOONS CONFECTIONERS' SUGAR

¼ TEASPOON KOSHER SALT

40 SQUARE WONTON WRAPPERS (SEE PAGE 560)

CANOLA OIL, AS NEEDED

1. Place the cream cheese, crabmeat, sugar, and salt in a medium bowl and fold until the mixture is combined.

2. Place 1 tablespoon of the mixture in the middle of a wrapper. Rub the wrapper's edge with a wet finger, bring the corners together, pinch to seal tightly, and transfer the dumpling to a parchment-lined baking sheet. Repeat with the remaining wrappers and filling.

3. Add canola oil to a Dutch oven until it is 2 inches deep and warm it to 325°F over medium heat. Working in batches to avoid crowding the pot, gently slip the wontons into the hot oil and fry, while turning, until golden brown all over, about 3 minutes. Transfer the cooked dumplings to a paper towel–lined wire rack and let them cool briefly before serving.

Octopus with Whisky

YIELD: 6 SERVINGS | **ACTIVE TIME:** 30 MINUTES | **TOTAL TIME:** 2 HOURS AND 30 MINUTES

3½ LB. OCTOPUS

KOSHER SALT, AS NEEDED

SWEET PAPRIKA, TO TASTE

PINCH OF SZECHUAN PEPPER

PINCH OF ALLSPICE

PINCH OF BLACK PEPPER

SPLASH OF WHISKEY

EXTRA-VIRGIN OLIVE OIL, TO TASTE

1. Preheat the oven to 350°F. Place the octopus in a baking dish, season it generously with salt, and let it rest for 30 minutes.

2. Rinse the octopus, pat it dry, and place it in the baking dish. Season the octopus with paprika, sprinkle the Szechuan pepper, allspice, and black pepper over it, and splash the whisky on top. Cover the baking dish with aluminum foil, place it in the oven, and braise the octopus until it is al dente, about 1½ hours.

3. Remove the octopus from the oven, cut off the tentacles, and chop them.

4. Place the pan juices in a small saucepan and reduce them over medium heat until the consistency is to your liking. Season the dressing with a bit of olive oil and salt, drizzle it over the octopus tentacles, and enjoy.

Shrimp Toast

YIELD: 4 SERVINGS | **ACTIVE TIME:** 30 MINUTES | **TOTAL TIME:** 30 MINUTES

10 TO 12 SLICES OF WHITE SANDWICH BREAD

1 LB. SHRIMP, SHELLS REMOVED, DEVEINED, MINCED

2 GARLIC CLOVES, MINCED

¼ CUP WATER CHESTNUTS, MINCED

1 TABLESPOON MINCED LEMONGRASS

2 TABLESPOONS CORNSTARCH

2 TEASPOONS KOSHER SALT

2 TABLESPOONS RICE WINE

1 EGG, BEATEN

3 TABLESPOONS FINELY CHOPPED FRESH CHIVES, PLUS MORE FOR GARNISH

3 TABLESPOONS SESAME SEEDS

1 TABLESPOON PAPRIKA

2 TABLESPOONS AVOCADO OIL, PLUS MORE AS NEEDED

1. Trim the crusts from the bread and reserve them for another preparation. Place the bread on a plate and let it air-dry.

2. Place all of the remaining ingredients, except for the sesame seeds, paprika, and avocado oil, in a bowl and stir until well combined.

3. Cut each slice of bread into 3 or 4 pieces, in whatever shape you prefer. Spread the shrimp mixture on each piece of bread. Sprinkle the sesame seeds and paprika over the top.

4. Place the avocado oil in a large nonstick pan and warm it over medium heat. Working in batches to avoid crowding the pot, add the shrimp toasts to the pan, shrimp side down. Cook for 1 minute, flip the shrimp toasts over, and cook until the bread is golden brown, about 1 minutes. Transfer to a paper towel–lined plate. If the pan starts to look dry, add more avocado oil as needed.

5. When all of the shrimp toasts have been cooked, garnish them with additional chives and enjoy.

THE ENCYCLOPEDIA OF TAPAS

Fresh Spring Rolls with Shrimp

YIELD: 4 SERVINGS | **ACTIVE TIME:** 30 MINUTES | **TOTAL TIME:** 30 MINUTES

12 SHEETS OF RICE PAPER

12 LEAVES OF BUTTER LETTUCE

4 OZ. THIN RICE VERMICELLI NOODLES, COOKED

½ CUP JULIENNED CUCUMBER

½ CUP JULIENNED CARROTS

1 CUP BEAN SPROUTS

24 FRESH THAI BASIL LEAVES

24 FRESH MINT LEAVES

24 FRESH CHIVES, CHOPPED

12 SPRIGS OF FRESH CILANTRO, CHOPPED

18 SHRIMP, SHELLS REMOVED, DEVEINED, HALVED LENGTHWISE, AND POACHED

PEANUT HOISIN DIPPING SAUCE (SEE PAGE 127), FOR SERVING

1. Place a damp kitchen towel on a work surface. This will prevent the rice paper from sticking to the work surface.

2. Fill a bowl with lukewarm water. Quickly dip the rice paper in the water and lay it on the towel. The rice paper will continue to soften as it sits.

3. Lay a leaf of lettuce at the lower edge of the rice paper. On top of the lettuce, place the noodles, vegetables, and herbs. Place 3 pieces of halved shrimp in a line that is about 1½ inches from the top edge of the rice paper.

4. Place your thumbs at the lower edge of the rice paper and, using your fingers, roll the paper up until you reach the shrimp.

5. Fold both sides of the spring roll toward the center, and then roll it over itself, so the rice paper seals itself.

6. Repeat until all of the spring rolls are assembled and serve with the Peanut Hoisin Dipping Sauce.

Bacon-Wrapped Shrimp

YIELD: 4 TO 6 SERVINGS | **ACTIVE TIME:** 40 MINUTES | **TOTAL TIME:** 1 HOUR AND 15 MINUTES

8 SLICES OF BACON, HALVED CROSSWISE

16 LARGE SHRIMP, SHELLS REMOVED OTHER THAN TAILS, DEVEINED

1. Preheat the oven to 425°F. Place an oven-safe wire rack in a rimmed baking sheet. Place the bacon on the rack and cook the bacon until it is just about to become crispy, 5 to 10 minutes, depending on the thickness of the bacon. Remove the bacon from the oven and let it drain on a paper towel–lined plate.

2. When the bacon is cool enough to handle, wrap one piece around each shrimp, securing the bacon with a toothpick. Place the bacon-wrapped shrimp on the wire rack set in the baking sheet and place them in the oven.

3. Bake the shrimp until they are cooked through and the bacon is crispy, about 10 minutes. Remove the shrimp from the oven and enjoy.

Chili & Lime Shrimp

YIELD: 6 SERVINGS | **ACTIVE TIME:** 10 MINUTES | **TOTAL TIME:** 40 MINUTES

2 LIMES

6½ OZ. BROWN SUGAR

24 LARGE SHRIMP, SHELLS REMOVED, DEVEINED

2 TABLESPOONS CANOLA OIL

1 RED CHILE PEPPER, STEM AND SEEDS REMOVED, MINCED

1. Preheat the oven to 400°F. Grate one of the limes to remove the zest and set the lime zest aside. Squeeze the juice from the limes into a small saucepan, stir in the brown sugar, and warm the mixture over medium heat, stirring to dissolve the sugar. When the sugar has dissolved, raise the heat to high and bring the glaze to a boil. When the mixture has reduced, remove the pan from heat and stir in the lime zest. Set the glaze aside.

2. Place the shrimp in a baking dish in a single layer. Drizzle the canola oil over the shrimp and toss to coat. Brush the shrimp with the glaze and then sprinkle the chile pepper over them.

3. Place the shrimp in the oven and bake until they are cooked through and opaque, 10 to 15 minutes.

4. Remove the shrimp from the oven and let them cool slightly before serving.

Shrimp & Crab Cakes

YIELD: 4 SERVINGS | **ACTIVE TIME:** 30 MINUTES | **TOTAL TIME:** 30 MINUTES

1 LB. SHRIMP, SHELLS REMOVED, DEVEINED, CHOPPED

1 LB. CRABMEAT, PICKED OVER

2 GARLIC CLOVES, MINCED

1 TABLESPOON MINCED SHALLOT

1 TABLESPOON CHOPPED FRESH CILANTRO, PLUS MORE FOR GARNISH

1 TABLESPOON CHOPPED FRESH MINT, PLUS MORE FOR GARNISH

1 TABLESPOON MINCED LEMONGRASS

2 TEASPOONS KOSHER SALT

1 TEASPOON FISH SAUCE

¼ TEASPOON WHITE PEPPER

3 TABLESPOONS MAYONNAISE

1 EGG, BEATEN

2 CUPS PANKO

2 TABLESPOONS AVOCADO OIL, PLUS MORE AS NEEDED

6 LETTUCE LEAVES

1. Place all of the ingredients, except for the panko, avocado oil, and lettuce, in a large bowl and stir until well combined. Form the mixture into cakes that are each about 2 inches long and ½ inch high.

2. Place the panko in a shallow bowl. Dredge the cakes in the panko until they are completely coated on both sides.

3. Place the avocado oil in a large skillet and warm it over medium heat. Working in batches to avoid crowding the pan, add the cakes and cook until golden brown on both sides, 4 to 5 minutes. Transfer the cooked cakes to a wire rack. If the pan starts to look dry, add more avocado oil.

4. Arrange the lettuce on a plate and place the cakes on top. Garnish the cakes with the additional cilantro and mint and serve with your favorite dipping sauce.

Okonomiyaki

YIELD: 4 SERVINGS | **ACTIVE TIME:** 30 MINUTES | **TOTAL TIME:** 1 HOUR AND 30 MINUTES

3 TABLESPOONS WORCESTERSHIRE SAUCE

3½ TABLESPOONS KETCHUP

2 TABLESPOONS OYSTER SAUCE

1½ TABLESPOONS PLUS ¼ TEASPOON LIGHT BROWN SUGAR

1 CUP ALL-PURPOSE FLOUR

½ TEASPOON BAKING POWDER

½ TEASPOON SEA SALT

½ CUP PEELED AND GRATED MOUNTAIN YAM OR POTATO

1 CUP DASHI STOCK (SEE PAGE 553)

2 EGGS, BEATEN

⅓ NAPA CABBAGE, SHREDDED

1 TABLESPOON AVOCADO OIL, PLUS MORE AS NEEDED

½ CUP MINCED SHRIMP

2 TABLESPOONS OKONOMIYAKI SAUCE (SEE PAGE 136)

1 TABLESPOON KEWPIE MAYONNAISE

BONITO FLAKES, FOR GARNISH

TOASTED NORI POWDER, FOR GARNISH

1. Place the Worcestershire sauce, ketchup, oyster sauce, and 1½ tablespoons of brown sugar in a bowl and stir until well combined. Store the sauce in the refrigerator.

2. Place the flour, baking powder, salt, and remaining brown sugar in a mixing bowl and stir until well combined. Add the yam and dashi and stir until the mixture comes together as a batter. Chill the batter in the refrigerator for 1 hour.

3. Stir the eggs and cabbage into the chilled batter and set it aside.

4. Place the avocado oil in a nonstick skillet and warm it over medium-high heat. Ladle enough batter to make a 1-inch-thick pancake into the skillet, reduce the heat to medium, and cook until the bottom is set and golden brown, about 5 minutes.

5. Place the shrimp on the uncooked side of the pancake and carefully transfer the pancake to a plate, with the uncooked side facing up. Add more avocado oil to the pan if it looks dry. Invert the plate over the pan and flip the pancake over into the pan so that the uncooked side is now facing down. Cover the pan and cook until the pancake is cooked through and the edges are crispy, 3 to 4 minutes.

6. Transfer the cooked pancake to a plate and drizzle the sauce and mayonnaise over the top. Garnish the pancake with bonito flakes and toasted nori powder, slice it, and enjoy.

Turmeric & Ginger Shrimp Cocktail

YIELD: 6 SERVINGS | **ACTIVE TIME:** 30 MINUTES | **TOTAL TIME:** 2 HOURS AND 30 MINUTES

1½ LBS. SHRIMP

1 TABLESPOON GRATED FRESH GINGER

2 GARLIC CLOVES, MINCED

1 TABLESPOON GRATED FRESH TURMERIC

2 TABLESPOONS CHOPPED SCALLIONS

1 SHALLOT, MINCED

JUICE OF 1 LIME

JUICE OF 1 SCALLION

1 TABLESPOON KOSHER SALT

1 TEASPOON HONEY

1 TABLESPOON EXTRA-VIRGIN OLIVE OIL

1. Peel the shrimp, leaving only the tails, and devein them. Set them aside.

2. Place the remainder of the ingredients in a mixing bowl, stir until well combined, and then add the peeled shrimp. Cover the bowl with plastic wrap and chill in the refrigerator for at least 2, and no more than 6, hours.

3. Warm a large skillet over medium-high heat. Working in batches to avoid crowding the pan, add the shrimp and the marinating liquid to the pan and cook until the shrimp have turned pink, 3 to 5 minutes. Remove the cooked shrimp from the pan and let them cool.

4. Serve at room temperature or chilled.

Okonomiyaki
SEE PAGE 290

Shrimp & Crab Wontons

YIELD: 24 WONTONS | **ACTIVE TIME:** 35 MINUTES | **TOTAL TIME:** 45 MINUTES

4 OZ. SHRIMP, SHELLS REMOVED, DEVEINED, FINELY CHOPPED

4 OZ. CRABMEAT, PICKED OVER AND COOKED

1 TABLESPOON MINCED SCALLION

1 TABLESPOON CHOPPED FRESH CHIVES

1 TABLESPOON FISH SAUCE

2 TABLESPOONS MISO

1 TABLESPOON SHRIMP PASTE

2 TABLESPOONS CHOPPED RADISH

1 TABLESPOON SESAME SEEDS, TOASTED

1 TEASPOON SESAME OIL

1 TEASPOON SHERRY

24 SQUARE WONTON WRAPPERS (SEE PAGE 560)

1. Place a bowl of cold water near your work surface. Place all of the ingredients, except for the wrappers, in a mixing bowl and stir until well combined.

2. Place 2 teaspoons of the mixture in the center of a wrapper. Dip your finger into the cold water and rub it around the edge of the wrapper. Bring each corner of the wrapper together and press to seal the wonton. Repeat with the remaining wrappers and filling.

3. Place 2 inches of water in a large saucepan and bring it to a simmer. Place the wontons in a steaming basket, place the basket over the simmering water, and steam the wontons until they are cooked through, about 8 minutes. Remove the wontons from the steaming basket and let them cool slightly before enjoying.

Pork & Shrimp Wontons

YIELD: 24 WONTONS | **ACTIVE TIME:** 35 MINUTES | **TOTAL TIME:** 45 MINUTES

½ LB. GROUND PORK

4 OZ. SHRIMP, SHELLS REMOVED, DEVEINED, MINCED

1 TABLESPOON MINCED SHALLOT

1 TABLESPOON CHOPPED FRESH CHIVES

1 TABLESPOON FISH SAUCE

2 TABLESPOONS WHITE MISO

1 TABLESPOON SHRIMP PASTE

2 TABLESPOONS CHOPPED RADISH

1 TABLESPOON TOASTED SESAME SEEDS

1 TEASPOON SESAME OIL

1 TEASPOON SHERRY

24 SQUARE WONTON WRAPPERS (SEE PAGE 560)

1. Place the pork in a skillet and cook it over medium heat until it is browned all over and cooked through, about 8 minutes, breaking it up with a wooden spoon as it cooks. Remove the pan from heat and let the pork cool completely.

2. Place a bowl of cold water near your work surface. Place all of the remaining ingredients, except for the wrappers, in a mixing bowl and stir until well combined.

3. Place 2 teaspoons of the mixture in the center of a wrapper. Dip your finger into the cold water and rub it around the edge of the wrapper. Bring each corner of the wrapper together and press to seal the wonton. Repeat with the remaining wrappers and filling.

4. Place 2 inches of water in a large saucepan and bring it to a simmer. Place the wontons in a steaming basket, place the basket over the simmering water, and steam the wontons until they are cooked through, about 8 minutes. Remove the wontons from the steaming basket and let them cool slightly before enjoying.

Crispy Calamari

YIELD: 4 SERVINGS | **ACTIVE TIME:** 20 MINUTES | **TOTAL TIME:** 40 MINUTES

CANOLA OIL, AS NEEDED

12 SQUID TENTACLES

4 CALAMARI BODIES, SLICED INTO ¼-INCH RINGS

1 CUP BUTTERMILK

½ CUP ALL-PURPOSE FLOUR

½ CUP CORNMEAL

1 TEASPOON OLD BAY SEASONING

SALT AND PEPPER, TO TASTE

MARINARA SAUCE (SEE PAGE 184), FOR SERVING

1. Add canola oil to a Dutch oven until it is about 1 inch deep and warm it to 375°F.

2. Place the squid and buttermilk in a bowl, stir to combine, and let the squid marinate for 15 minutes.

3. Combine the flour, cornmeal, and Old Bay seasoning in a bowl. Dredge the squid in the mixture until evenly coated.

4. Gently slip the squid into the hot oil and cook until crispy, golden brown, and cooked through, about 2 minutes.

5. Transfer the squid to a paper towel–lined plate to drain, season them with salt and pepper, and serve with Marinara Sauce.

Crispy Calamari
SEE PAGE 297

Shrimp Crackers

YIELD: 6 SERVINGS | **ACTIVE TIME:** 40 MINUTES | **TOTAL TIME:** 24 HOURS

4 CUPS WATER

½ LB. RAW SHRIMP, SHELLS REMOVED, DEVEINED

1 TEASPOON KOSHER SALT, PLUS MORE TO TASTE

1 TEASPOON SUGAR

¼ TEASPOON GROUND BLACK PEPPER, PLUS MORE TO TASTE

½ TEASPOON BAKING POWDER

2 CUPS TAPIOCA STARCH

CANOLA OIL, AS NEEDED

PAPRIKA, TO TASTE

1. Place the water in a medium saucepan and bring it to a simmer. Place the shrimp in a food processor and blitz until pureed. Add the salt, sugar, pepper, and baking powder to the food processor and blitz the mixture for 2 minutes.

2. Add the tapioca starch and blitz until the mixture starts to come together as a ball of dough.

3. Place the dough on a work surface and knead it with your hands until it is smooth. Divide the dough in half, form each piece into a ball, and then roll the balls into 1-inch-thick logs. Cover each log tightly with plastic wrap and tie a knot at each end.

4. Prepare an ice bath. Gently slip the logs into the simmering water and reduce the heat to the lowest temperature. Cook for 20 minutes.

5. Remove the logs from the water and plunge them in the ice bath until cool. Remove the logs from the plastic wrap and place them on a paper towel–lined plate to drain. When they are dry, chill them in the refrigerator overnight.

6. Add canola oil to a Dutch oven until it is about 2 inches deep and warm it to 375°F. Cut the logs into ⅛-inch slices and gently slip them into the hot oil. Fry until crispy, 5 to 7 minutes.

7. Transfer the crackers to a paper towel–lined plate to drain, season them with salt, pepper, and paprika, and enjoy.

Confit Tuna

YIELD: 4 SERVINGS | **ACTIVE TIME:** 10 MINUTES | **TOTAL TIME:** 30 MINUTES

½ LB. YELLOW FIN TUNA

1 CUP EXTRA-VIRGIN OLIVE OIL, PLUS MORE AS NEEDED

ZEST OF 1 ORANGE

1 GARLIC CLOVE

1 BAY LEAF

5 BLACK PEPPERCORNS

1 BAGUETTE (SEE PAGE 66), SLICED AND TOASTED FOR SERVING

1. Place the tuna and olive oil in a small saucepan. The tuna needs to be completely covered by the olive oil; if it is not, add more olive oil as needed.

2. Add the orange zest, garlic, bay leaf, and peppercorns and warm the mixture over low heat. Cook until the internal temperature of the tuna is 135°F.

3. Remove the tuna from the oil and let it cool completely. Serve with toasted slices of Baguette or chill in the refrigerator.

Roasted Garlic & Chili Oysters

YIELD: 2 TO 4 SERVINGS | **ACTIVE TIME:** 15 MINUTES | **TOTAL TIME:** 25 MINUTES

18 OYSTERS, UNSHUCKED

¾ CUP UNSALTED BUTTER, SOFTENED

2 TABLESPOONS BROWN SUGAR

1 TEASPOON GARLIC POWDER

1 TEASPOON CHILI POWDER

1. Preheat the oven to 400ºF. Shuck the oysters, keeping them on the half shell.

2. Place the butter, brown sugar, garlic powder, and chili powder in a bowl and stir until well combined.

3. Top each oyster with a spoonful of the seasoned butter, place them in a cast-iron skillet, face up, and place them in the oven. Bake the oysters, keeping a close eye on them, until the liquid has been bubbling for a minute or two and/or the edges of the oysters are curling up, 4 to 6 minutes. Remove the oysters from the oven and enjoy.

Crab & Mango Salsa

YIELD: 4 SERVINGS | **ACTIVE TIME:** 15 MINUTES | **TOTAL TIME:** 45 MINUTES

½ CUP FINELY DICED
MANGO

½ CUP FINELY DICED RED
BELL PEPPER

3 TABLESPOONS MINCED
RED ONION

1 TEASPOON MINCED FRESH
CHIVES

1 TEASPOON RICE VINEGAR

2 TABLESPOONS EXTRA-
VIRGIN OLIVE OIL

SALT, TO TASTE

½ LB. PEEKYTOE CRABMEAT,
PICKED OVER AND COOKED

1. Place the mango, bell pepper, red onion, chives, rice vinegar, and olive oil in a mixing bowl and stir gently until combined. Season the salsa with salt and chill in refrigerator for 30 minutes.

2. Top the salsa with the crab and serve.

Taramasalata

YIELD: 4 SERVINGS | **ACTIVE TIME:** 15 MINUTES | **TOTAL TIME:** 45 MINUTES

10 OZ. PANKO, PLUS MORE
AS NEEDED

½ CUP WATER

10 OZ. TARAMA CARP ROE

½ RED ONION, CHOPPED

JUICE OF ½ LEMON

½ CUP EXTRA-VIRGIN OLIVE
OIL, PLUS MORE AS NEEDED

SALT AND PEPPER, TO TASTE

FRESH PARSLEY, CHOPPED,
FOR GARNISH

1. Place the panko and water in a mixing bowl. Let the panko soak for 5 minutes.

2. Place the soaked panko, roe, onion, and lemon juice in a food processor and blitz until smooth.

3. With the food processor running, slowly drizzle in the olive oil until it has been incorporated and the mixture is smooth. If the taramasalata is thinner than you'd like, incorporate more panko. If it is too thick, incorporate a little more olive oil.

4. Season the dip with salt and pepper and garnish with parsley.

Grilled Oysters with Blue Cheese

YIELD: 2 TO 4 SERVINGS | **ACTIVE TIME:** 15 MINUTES | **TOTAL TIME:** 25 MINUTES

1 TABLESPOON UNSALTED BUTTER

1 TABLESPOON CHOPPED FRESH TARRAGON

SALT AND PEPPER, TO TASTE

12 OYSTERS, UNSHUCKED

½ CUP CRUMBLED BLUE CHEESE

1. Prepare a gas or charcoal grill for medium heat (about 400ºF). Place the butter in a small skillet and cook it over medium heat until it starts to brown and give off a nutty fragrance. Remove the pan from heat and stir in the tarragon, salt, and pepper. Set the browned butter aside.

2. Place the oysters on the grill and cook them until they open slightly. Remove the oysters from the grill and pry them open with a sturdy knife. Remove the tops and place the oysters on the half shell back on the grill, face up. Top each oyster with a few drops of the browned butter and some of the blue cheese. Grill the oysters for another 5 minutes, remove them from the grill, and enjoy.

Salt Cod Beignets

YIELD: 4 SERVINGS | **ACTIVE TIME:** 45 MINUTES | **TOTAL TIME:** 3 HOURS

½ CUP MILK

3 TABLESPOONS UNSALTED BUTTER

¼ CUP ALL-PURPOSE FLOUR

1 EGG

4 OZ. SALT COD, CHOPPED

1 TABLESPOON CHOPPED FRESH CILANTRO

2 CUPS CANOLA OIL

SALT AND PEPPER, TO TASTE

1. Place the milk and butter in a small saucepan and bring the mixture to a boil.

2. Add the flour and cook, stirring continually, until the mixture comes together as a ball of dough. Remove the saucepan from heat and let the dough cool for 10 minutes.

3. Gradually add the egg and whisk until well combined. Add the salt cod and cilantro and stir until evenly distributed. Roll the dough into a log, cover it with plastic wrap, and place it in the freezer for 2 hours.

4. Add canola oil to a Dutch oven until it is about 2 inches deep and warm it to 375°F. Remove the dough from the freezer and cut it into ½-inch-thick slices.

5. Working in batches to avoid crowding the pot, gently slip the slices into the hot oil and fry them until puffy and golden brown. Transfer the beignets to a paper towel–lined plate to drain, season them with salt and pepper, and enjoy.

Caviar Crème Fraîche

YIELD: 1 CUP | **ACTIVE TIME:** 5 MINUTES | **TOTAL TIME:** 5 MINUTES

1 CUP CRÈME FRAÎCHE

2 TABLESPOONS CAVIAR

1 TEASPOON FRESH LEMON JUICE

SALT AND PEPPER, TO TASTE

CRACKERS OR CROSTINI, FOR SERVING

1. Place all of the ingredients in a mixing bowl and stir gently until well combined. Serve with crackers or crostini.

Grilled Oysters with Blue Cheese
SEE PAGE 304

Beet-Cured Salmon

YIELD: 4 SERVINGS | **ACTIVE TIME:** 30 MINUTES | **TOTAL TIME:** 17 HOURS

2 CUPS CHOPPED BEETS

1 CUP KOSHER SALT

½ CUP SUGAR

1 CUP WATER

1 LB. SALMON, SKIN REMOVED, DEBONED

1. Place the beets, salt, and sugar in a food processor and pulse until the beets are finely chopped. Add the water in a slow stream and pulse until the mixture is a smooth puree.

2. Place the salmon in a baking dish and pour the puree over it. Place the salmon in the refrigerator and let it cure for at least 12 hours.

3. Rinse the salmon under cold water. Place it on a wire rack set in a rimmed baking sheet and let it dry, uncovered, in the refrigerator for 4 hours before serving.

Ceviche de Pescado

YIELD: 6 SERVINGS | **ACTIVE TIME:** 25 MINUTES | **TOTAL TIME:** 2 HOURS

2 LBS. HALIBUT OR RED SNAPPER FILLETS, DEBONED AND DICED

SALT, TO TASTE

1 JALAPEÑO CHILE PEPPER, STEM AND SEEDS REMOVED, FINELY DICED

2 SERRANO CHILE PEPPERS, STEMS AND SEEDS REMOVED, FINELY DICED

½ BUNCH OF FRESH CILANTRO, FINELY CHOPPED, PLUS MORE FOR GARNISH

JUICE OF 6 LARGE LIMES

¼ RED ONION, SLICED THIN, FOR GARNISH

½ LB. CHERRY TOMATOES, PEELED AND DICED, FOR GARNISH

FLESH OF 1 AVOCADO, DICED, FOR GARNISH

1 CUCUMBER, PEELED AND FINELY DICED, FOR GARNISH

HOT SAUCE, FOR SERVING

TOSTADAS OR SALTINES, FOR SERVING

1. Place the fish in a bowl and season it with salt. Add the chile peppers, cilantro, and lime juice, stir to combine, and chill the ceviche in the refrigerator for 2 hours, allowing the fish to cure.

2. Garnish the ceviche with the red onion, tomatoes, avocado, cucumber, and additional cilantro and serve with hot sauce and tostadas or saltines.

Pub Sardines

YIELD: 1 SERVING | **ACTIVE TIME:** 10 MINUTES | **TOTAL TIME:** 10 MINUTES

1 TABLESPOON SAKE

1 TABLESPOON SOY SAUCE

1 CAN OF SARDINES IN OLIVE OIL, DRAINED

PINCH OF BLACK PEPPER

2 TEASPOONS SANSHO PEPPERCORNS

CRUSTY BREAD, FOR SERVING

1. Add the sake and soy sauce to the can of sardines.

2. Top with the black pepper and sansho peppercorns.

3. Place the can of sardines directly on a burner on your stove, cook over the lowest heat for 4 to 5 minutes, and serve with bread.

Beer-Battered Oysters

YIELD: 4 SERVINGS | **ACTIVE TIME:** 20 MINUTES | **TOTAL TIME:** 35 MINUTES

CANOLA OIL, AS NEEDED

¾ CUP ALL-PURPOSE FLOUR

¼ CUP CORNSTARCH

½ TEASPOON BAKING POWDER

½ CUP PLUS 2 TABLESPOONS ALE

12 OYSTERS, SHUCKED

SALT AND PEPPER, TO TASTE

1. Add canola oil to a Dutch oven until it is about 2 inches deep and warm it to 350°F.

2. Place ½ cup of the flour, the cornstarch, and baking powder in a bowl and stir until combined. Sift the mixture through a fine sieve.

3. Add the ale to the mixture and whisk until it comes together as a smooth batter.

4. Place the remaining flour and the oysters in a separate bowl and stir gently until the oysters are coated.

5. Dredge the oysters in the batter and then gently slip them into the hot oil. Fry the oysters until crispy, golden brown, and cooked through, 3 to 5 minutes.

6. Transfer the oysters to a paper towel–lined plate to drain, season them with salt and pepper, and enjoy.

Bagna Cauda

YIELD: 4 SERVINGS | **ACTIVE TIME:** 20 MINUTES | **TOTAL TIME:** 30 MINUTES

½ CUP QUALITY ANCHOVY FILLETS, RINSED, DEBONED, AND CHOPPED

⅔ CUP EXTRA-VIRGIN OLIVE OIL

2 TABLESPOONS UNSALTED BUTTER

4 GARLIC CLOVES, MASHED

SALT, TO TASTE

CRUDITÉS, FOR SERVING

1. Use a mortar and pestle to grind the anchovies into a paste. Set the anchovies aside.

2. Place 2 tablespoons of the olive oil and all of the butter in a small saucepan and warm the mixture over low heat. When the butter has melted, add the garlic, reduce the heat to the lowest possible setting, and cook, stirring continually to ensure that the garlic does not brown, for 5 minutes.

3. Add the anchovies and cook for 5 minutes, stirring occasionally. Cook until the mixture starts to darken, stir in the rest of the olive oil along with a pinch of salt, and cook at below a simmer for 15 to 20 minutes. If the mixture starts to sizzle, turn off the heat for a minute or so.

4. Serve warm with sliced raw vegetables for dipping. If the bagna cauda cools down, return it to the stove and warm it up again.

Shrimp in Adobo

YIELD: 4 SERVINGS | **ACTIVE TIME:** 30 MINUTES | **TOTAL TIME:** 45 MINUTES

4 GUAJILLO CHILE PEPPERS, STEMS AND SEEDS REMOVED

6 GARLIC CLOVES

2 SMALL ROMA TOMATOES

3 TABLESPOONS CHOPPED CHIPOTLES IN ADOBO

SALT, TO TASTE

1 LB. LARGE SHRIMP, SHELLS REMOVED, DEVEINED

¼ CUP LARD

1. Place the chiles in a dry skillet and toast them over medium heat until they darken and become fragrant and pliable. Submerge them in a bowl of hot water and let them soak for 15 to 20 minutes.

2. Drain the chiles and reserve the soaking liquid. Add the chiles to a blender along with the garlic, tomatoes, chipotles, and a small amount of the soaking liquid and puree until the mixture is a smooth paste. Season the marinade with salt and let it cool completely.

3. Place the shrimp in the adobo and marinate for at least 20 to 30 minutes.

4. Place some of the lard in a large skillet and warm it over medium-high heat. Working in batches if necessary to avoid crowding the pan, add the shrimp and cook until they are just firm and turn pink, 3 to 5 minutes. Add more lard to the pan if it starts to look dry. Enjoy immediately.

Cured Sardines

YIELD: 4 SERVINGS | **ACTIVE TIME:** 15 MINUTES | **TOTAL TIME:** 24 HOURS

1 LB. FRESH SARDINES

¾ CUP KOSHER SALT

¼ CUP SUGAR

EXTRA-VIRGIN OLIVE OIL, AS NEEDED

TOSTADAS OR SALTINES, FOR SERVING

1. Remove the spines from the sardines and butterfly them. Place them on a Silpat-lined baking sheet, skin side down.

2. Combine the salt and sugar in a mixing bowl and sprinkle some of the mixture over the sardines. Turn the sardines over and sprinkle this side with the salt-and-sugar mixture.

3. Cover the pan with plastic wrap and chill the sardines in the refrigerator for 1 day.

4. Transfer the sardines to a fresh Silpat-lined baking sheet and pat them dry with paper towels. Do not rinse the sardines, as this will wash away the flavor.

5. Place the sardines in a container, cover them with olive oil, and enjoy with tostadas or saltines.

Masa-Crusted Sardines

YIELD: 2 TO 4 SERVINGS | **ACTIVE TIME:** 10 MINUTES | **TOTAL TIME:** 30 MINUTES

½ LB. SARDINES, CLEANED, HEADS REMOVED

SALT, TO TASTE

1 CUP MASA HARINA

¼ CUP ALL-PURPOSE FLOUR

1 TEASPOON CUMIN

1 TEASPOON CORIANDER

½ TEASPOON GROUND CLOVES

1 TEASPOON ALLSPICE

1 TEASPOON GINGER

1 TEASPOON PAPRIKA

2 CUPS EXTRA-VIRGIN OLIVE OIL

1. Rinse the sardines and pat them dry with a paper towel. Season lightly with salt.

2. Place the masa harina, flour, and half of the seasonings in a mixing bowl and stir to combine.

3. Dredge the sardines in the masa mixture until completely coated. Set them on paper towels and let them rest for 5 minutes. The resting period allows the sardines to release a bit of moisture, which will help more of the masa stick to them, producing a lighter and crispier result.

4. After 5 minutes, dredge the sardines in the masa mixture again until coated.

5. Place the olive oil in a deep skillet and warm it to 325°F. Working in batches, gently slip the sardines into the oil and fry them until crispy and golden brown, about 4 minutes, turning them over once. Place the fried sardines on a paper towel–lined plate to drain, sprinkle the remaining seasonings over them, and enjoy.

Sea Bass Ceviche

YIELD: 4 SERVINGS | **ACTIVE TIME:** 1 HOUR AND 15 MINUTES | **TOTAL TIME:** 24 HOURS

5 OZ. TOMATILLOS, HUSKED AND RINSED

1 TABLESPOON COCONUT OIL

5-INCH PIECE OF FRESH GINGER, PEELED AND DICED

1 ONION, DICED

6 GARLIC CLOVES, DICED

5 TABLESPOONS SOY SAUCE

1½ TABLESPOONS FISH SAUCE

3½ CUPS COCONUT MILK

1 LEMONGRASS STALK, PEELED AND BRUISED

1 BUNCH OF SCALLIONS, TRIMMED AND SLICED

1 LARGE BUNCH OF FRESH CILANTRO, CHOPPED, PLUS MORE FOR GARNISH

7 TABLESPOONS FRESH LEMON JUICE

2 SERRANO CHILE PEPPERS, STEMS AND SEEDS REMOVED, SLICED, PLUS MORE FOR GARNISH

SALT, TO TASTE

FRESH LIME JUICE, TO TASTE

LIME ZEST, TO TASTE

4 OZ. SEA BASS, DEBONED AND SLICED

2 SHALLOTS, JULIENNED

2 TABLESPOONS SHAVED FRESH COCONUT

COCONUT DRESSING (SEE PAGE 554)

¼ CUP TOASTED PEANUTS

1. Prepare a gas or charcoal grill to medium-high heat (450°F). Place the tomatillos on the grill and grill until charred all over, about 6 minutes, turning occasionally. Remove the tomatillos from the grill and set them aside. When the tomatillos are cool enough to handle, chop them.

2. Place the coconut oil in a skillet and warm it over medium heat. Add the ginger, shallots, and garlic and cook until the onion is translucent, about 3 minutes, stirring frequently.

3. Add the tomatillos to the skillet and cook until all of the liquid in the pan has evaporated. Deglaze the pan with the soy sauce and fish sauce, scraping up any browned bits from the bottom of the pan.

4. Add the coconut milk and lemongrass and bring the mixture to a boil. Remove the pan from heat and let the mixture cool to room temperature. Store in the refrigerator overnight.

5. Remove the lemongrass from the mixture and stir in the scallions, cilantro, and lemon juice. Place the mixture in a blender and puree until smooth.

6. Place the serrano peppers in a mixing bowl and season with salt, lime juice, and lime zest. Strain the puree into the bowl, add the sea bass, and chill in the refrigerator for 40 to 50 minutes.

7. Drain the sea bass and season it with lime juice, lime zest, and salt.

8. Combine the shallots, coconut, and toasted peanuts in a mixing bowl and season with the Coconut Dressing. Arrange the salad as a line in the middle of a plate. Place the sea bass in a line beside the salad, garnish with additional cilantro and serrano, and enjoy.

Masa-Crusted Sardines
SEE PAGE 316

Takoyaki

YIELD: 20 TO 24 TAKOYAKI | **ACTIVE TIME:** 20 MINUTES | **TOTAL TIME:** 20 MINUTES

2 TEASPOONS SAKE

2 TEASPOONS MIRIN

2 TEASPOONS SOY SAUCE

2 TEASPOONS OYSTER SAUCE

2 TEASPOONS WORCESTERSHIRE SAUCE

1 TABLESPOON SUGAR

1 TABLESPOON KETCHUP

SALT AND WHITE PEPPER, TO TASTE

2 TABLESPOONS WATER, PLUS MORE AS NEEDED

1 LARGE EGG

1½ CUPS CHICKEN STOCK (SEE PAGE 552)

¾ CUP ALL-PURPOSE FLOUR

1 CUP MINCED COOKED OCTOPUS

2 SCALLION GREENS, SLICED THIN

¼ CUP MINCED PICKLED GINGER

OKONOMIYAKI SAUCE (SEE PAGE 136), FOR SERVING

1. Place the sake, mirin, soy sauce, oyster sauce, Worcestershire sauce, sugar, ketchup, salt, and white pepper in a mixing bowl and stir to combine. Set the mixture aside.

2. Place the water, egg, and stock in a bowl and stir until combined. Sprinkle the flour over the mixture and stir until all the flour has been incorporated and the mixture comes together as a thick batter. Add the sake-and-mirin mixture and stir to incorporate. Pour the batter into a measuring cup with a spout.

3. Coat the wells of an aebleskiver pan or a muffin pan with nonstick cooking spray and place it over medium heat. When the pan is hot, fill the wells of the pan halfway with the batter and add a pinch of octopus, scallion, and pickled ginger to each. Fill the wells the rest of the way with the batter, until they are almost overflowing.

4. Cook the dumplings for approximately 2 minutes and use a chopstick to flip each one over. Turn the takoyaki as needed until they are golden brown on both sides and piping hot. Transfer the takoyaki to a serving platter, drizzle the sauce over the top, and enjoy.

Oysters Rockefeller

YIELD: 2 TO 4 SERVINGS | **ACTIVE TIME:** 15 MINUTES | **TOTAL TIME:** 25 MINUTES

4 TABLESPOONS UNSALTED BUTTER

2 SHALLOTS, MINCED

4 OZ. SPINACH, TORN

JUICE OF ½ LEMON

½ CUP FRESHLY GRATED ROMANO CHEESE

SALT AND PEPPER, TO TASTE

18 OYSTERS, UNSHUCKED

1. Preheat the oven to 450ºF. Place the butter in a large skillet and melt it over medium heat. Add the shallots and cook, stirring occasionally, until they are translucent, about 3 minutes. Stir in the spinach and cook until it has wilted, about 2 minutes.

2. Remove the pan from heat, stir in the lemon juice and Romano cheese, and season the mixture with pepper.

3. Shuck the oysters, keeping them on the half shell. Season them with salt, unless they are especially briny, and top with some of the spinach mixture.

4. Place the oysters, face up, in a cast-iron skillet, place them in the oven, and bake for 6 to 8 minutes. Remove the oysters from the oven and enjoy.

Scallop Ceviche

YIELD: 2 SERVINGS | **ACTIVE TIME:** 15 MINUTES | **TOTAL TIME:** 30 MINUTES

1 TEASPOON HONEY

½ TEASPOON POMEGRANATE MOLASSES

JUICE OF 1 LIME

SPLASH OF WHITE VINEGAR

PINCH OF KOSHER SALT

½ SHALLOT, DICED

1 TABLESPOON SLICED SCALLIONS

2 FRESH MINT LEAVES, CHOPPED

1 TEASPOON CHOPPED JALAPEÑO CHILE PEPPER

6 LARGE SEA SCALLOPS, RINSED, FEET REMOVED

1. In a mixing bowl, combine the honey, pomegranate molasses, lime juice, and white vinegar. Add the salt, shallot, scallions, mint, and jalapeño to the bowl, mix well, and let the mixture rest for 15 minutes.

2. Using a sharp knife, cut the scallops into ⅛-inch-thick slices. Add the scallops to the marinade and gently stir to coat. In a minute or two, the scallops will cure and turn fully white. Enjoy immediately.

Mussels Escabeche

YIELD: 2 TO 4 SERVINGS | **ACTIVE TIME:** 30 MINUTES | **TOTAL TIME:** 1 HOUR

1 TABLESPOON EXTRA-VIRGIN OLIVE OIL

2 SHALLOTS, 1 CHOPPED; 1 SLICED INTO RINGS

2 GARLIC CLOVES, MINCED

½ CUP WHITE WINE

½ CUP WATER

ZEST AND JUICE OF 1 LEMON

2 SPRIGS OF FRESH THYME

1 TEASPOON DIJON MUSTARD

2 LBS. MUSSELS, SCRUBBED AND DEBEARDED

1 TEASPOON PAPRIKA

2 TABLESPOONS CHOPPED FRESH PARSLEY

SALT AND PEPPER, TO TASTE

1. Place the olive oil in a medium saucepan and warm it over medium heat. Add the chopped shallot and cook, stirring frequently, until it starts to soften, about 2 minutes.

2. Add the garlic and cook for 1 minute. Add the white wine and cook until the alcohol has been cooked off, about 2 minutes.

3. Add the water, lemon zest, lemon juice, thyme, and mustard and bring the mixture to a boil. Add the mussels and cover the pan. Cook until the majority of the mussels have opened, about 5 minutes. Discard any mussels that do not open.

4. Using a slotted spoon, remove the mussels from the liquid and place them in a bowl.

5. Boil the remaining liquid until about ¼ cup remains.

6. When the mussels are cool enough to handle, remove the meat from the shells. Discard the shells and place the mussels in a bowl.

7. Strain the reduction into a clean pan and bring to a simmer. Add the shallot rings and cook for 1 minute. Stir in the paprika and parsley and season with salt and pepper.

8. Remove the pan from heat and let it cool. Fold in the mussels and enjoy.

Shrimp Cocktail, Baja Style

YIELD: 4 SERVINGS | **ACTIVE TIME:** 15 MINUTES | **TOTAL TIME:** 15 MINUTES

1 LB. SHRIMP, SHELLS REMOVED AND RESERVED, DEVEINED

1 LEMON, HALVED

¼ CUP KOSHER SALT, PLUS MORE TO TASTE

1 TABLESPOON DRIED MEXICAN OREGANO

2 BAY LEAVES

7 TABLESPOONS FRESH LIME JUICE

1½ TABLESPOONS FRESH LEMON JUICE

5 TABLESPOONS ORANGE JUICE

1 TABLESPOON HORSERADISH

14 TABLESPOONS KETCHUP

1¼ TABLESPOONS FISH SAUCE

7 TABLESPOONS HOT SAUCE

7 TABLESPOONS SPICY CLAMATO

2⅔ TABLESPOONS WORCESTERSHIRE SAUCE

1 SMALL RED ONION, SLICED THIN

5 GARLIC CLOVES, GRATED

FLESH OF 1 AVOCADO, DICED

2 JALAPEÑO CHILE PEPPERS, STEMS AND SEEDS REMOVED, DICED

2 TOMATOES, DICED

FRESH CILANTRO, CHOPPED, FOR GARNISH

LIME WEDGES, FOR SERVING

TOSTADAS OR SALTINES, FOR SERVING

1. Place water in a medium saucepan, add the shrimp shells, lemon, salt, oregano, and bay leaves, and bring to a boil. Reduce the heat and simmer for 5 minutes.

2. While the broth is simmering, place the lime juice, lemon juice, orange juice, horseradish, ketchup, fish sauce, hot sauce, Clamato, and Worcestershire sauce in a mixing bowl and stir to combine.

3. Add the shrimp to the simmering broth and turn off the burner. Let the shrimp poach for 2 minutes, remove it, and let it cool slightly.

4. Add the onion, garlic, avocado, jalapeños, tomatoes, and shrimp to the dressing and fold to incorporate. Garnish with cilantro and serve with lime wedges and tostadas or saltines.

Roasted & Stuffed Sardines

YIELD: 2 SERVINGS | **ACTIVE TIME:** 20 MINUTES | **TOTAL TIME:** 45 MINUTES

5 WHOLE, FRESH SARDINES

3 TABLESPOONS EXTRA-VIRGIN OLIVE OIL

½ WHITE ONION, CHOPPED

¼ CUP CHOPPED CELERY

1 TEASPOON KOSHER SALT

1 TABLESPOON PAPRIKA

PINCH OF CUMIN

2 GARLIC CLOVES, MINCED

2 TABLESPOONS WATER

¼ CUP CHOPPED FRESH PARSLEY

1 CUP DAY-OLD BREAD PIECES

TAHINI & YOGURT SAUCE (SEE PAGE 116), FOR SERVING

1. Clean the sardines: make an incision in the belly of each one from head to tail. Remove the guts and carefully snap the spines at the neck and tail. This will leave the sardines intact enough to hold their shape when roasted. Rinse the sardines and set them aside.

2. Place 2 tablespoons of the olive oil in a medium skillet and warm it over medium-high heat. Add the onion, celery, salt, paprika, cumin, and garlic and cook, stirring frequently, until the onions are translucent, about 3 minutes.

3. Add the water and simmer for 3 or 4 minutes. Add the parsley and bread and cook, stirring frequently, allowing the bread to absorb the liquid and brown a bit. After 5 minutes, remove the pan from heat.

4. Preheat the oven to 450°F.

5. Place the sardines in a cast-iron skillet, keeping them nestled against each other so they hold their shape better. Fill the sardines' bellies with the stuffing, drizzle the remaining olive oil over them, and place the pan in the oven.

6. Roast the stuffed sardines until they reach an internal temperature of 145°F, 15 to 20 minutes.

7. Remove the sardines from the oven and serve with the sauce.

Tuna Kibbeh Nayeh

YIELD: 2 SERVINGS | **ACTIVE TIME:** 30 MINUTES | **TOTAL TIME:** 45 MINUTES

1 CUP BULGUR WHEAT

½ LB. SUSHI-GRADE TUNA

2 FRESH BASIL LEAVES, CHIFFONADE

2 FRESH MINT LEAVES, CHIFFONADE

JUICE OF 1 LIME

JUICE OF 1 LEMON

1 TEASPOON KOSHER SALT

PINCH OF BLACK PEPPER

¼ CUP RED ONION, FINELY DICED

2 TABLESPOONS SMOKED EGG AIOLI (SEE PAGE 149)

FLESH FROM 1 AVOCADO

PITA BREAD (SEE PAGE 102), TOASTED, FOR SERVING

1. Place the bulgur wheat in a small saucepan, cover it with water, and cook over medium heat until tender, 15 to 20 minutes. Drain and run the bulgur under cold water until it has cooled.

2. Using a sharp knife, cut the tuna into slices and then dice it into ¼-inch cubes.

3. Place the fresh herbs, lime and lemon juices, salt, and pepper in a mixing bowl and stir until well combined. Stir in the tuna, making sure to cover it with the liquid as much as possible. Let the mixture sit for 5 minutes.

4. Stir in the bulgur wheat, red onion, and the aioli.

5. Cut the avocado into ¼-inch cubes and gently fold these into the mixture, taking care to mash them up as little as possible. Serve with toasted pitas.

Tuna Kibbeh Nayeh
SEE PAGE 327

Oysters al Tapesco

YIELD: 4 SERVINGS | **ACTIVE TIME:** 30 MINUTES | **TOTAL TIME:** 45 MINUTES

1 BUNCH OF GREEN ALLSPICE LEAVES

12 OYSTERS, RINSED AND SCRUBBED

1 SMALL BUNCH OF BANANA LEAVES

7 TABLESPOONS EXTRA-VIRGIN OLIVE OIL

7 TABLESPOONS FRESH LIME JUICE

3 SERRANO CHILE PEPPERS, STEMS AND SEEDS REMOVED, MINCED

1 CUP FRESH CILANTRO, CHOPPED

SALTINES, FOR SERVING

1. Prepare a charcoal grill for medium-high heat (about 450°F). When the grill is hot and the coals are glowing and covered with a thin layer of ash, place a grill rack on top of the coals and cover it with the allspice leaves.

2. Place the closed oysters on top of the allspice leaves and cover them with the banana leaves. The leaves will begin to smolder and then catch fire. After 3 to 4 minutes, the oysters will begin to open and absorb the smoke. Using tongs, carefully remove the oysters and arrange them on a plate to serve.

3. Place the olive oil, lime juice, chiles, and cilantro in a bowl and stir until thoroughly combined. Serve this sauce and the saltines alongside the oysters.

Aguachile Verde

YIELD: 4 SERVINGS | **ACTIVE TIME:** 10 MINUTES | **TOTAL TIME:** 15 MINUTES

1¾ CUPS FRESH LIME JUICE

3 SERRANO CHILE PEPPERS, STEMS AND SEEDS REMOVED

1 CUP FRESH CILANTRO, CHOPPED, PLUS MORE FOR GARNISH

3 TABLESPOONS EXTRA-VIRGIN OLIVE OIL

2 TABLESPOONS APPLE JUICE

1 TEASPOON HONEY

SALT, TO TASTE

1 LB. SHRIMP, SHELLS REMOVED, DEVEINED

¼ RED ONION, SLICED

1 CUCUMBER, SLICED

FLESH OF 1 AVOCADO, DICED

TORTILLA CHIPS, FOR SERVING

1. Place the lime juice, serrano peppers, cilantro, olive oil, apple juice, and honey in a blender and puree until smooth. Season the aguachile with salt and set it aside.

2. Slice the shrimp in half lengthwise and place them in a shallow bowl. Cover with the red onion, cucumber, and avocado.

3. Pour the aguachile over the shrimp and let it cure for 5 to 7 minutes before garnishing with additional cilantro and serving with tortilla chips.

Swordfish Crudo

YIELD: 2 SERVINGS | **ACTIVE TIME:** 15 MINUTES | **TOTAL TIME:** 30 MINUTES

4 OZ. SUSHI-GRADE SWORDFISH

SALT, TO TASTE

1 TEASPOON BLACK PEPPER

JUICE OF ½ LEMON

1 TABLESPOON EXTRA-VIRGIN OLIVE OIL

1 TABLESPOON SLICED SCALLIONS

4 SLICES OF JALAPEÑO CHILE PEPPER

3 SLICES OF TOMATO

1. Chill a plate in the refrigerator for 10 minutes.

2. Slice the swordfish thin against the grain and arrange the slices on the chilled plate, making sure they do not overlap.

3. Season the fish generously with salt, then sprinkle the pepper and lemon juice over it. Drizzle the olive oil over the top and sprinkle the scallions over the fish.

4. Arrange the jalapeño and tomato on the side of the plate and chill in the refrigerator until ready to serve.

Shrimp Pot Stickers

YIELD: 24 POT STICKERS | **ACTIVE TIME:** 30 MINUTES | **TOTAL TIME:** 45 MINUTES

6 OZ. SHRIMP, FINELY DICED

½ CUP FINELY DICED CABBAGE

1 TABLESPOON GRATED FRESH GINGER

4 SCALLIONS, TRIMMED AND SLICED, WHITES AND GREENS SEPARATED

1 TABLESPOON SOY SAUCE

¼ CUP WATER

24 ROUND WONTON WRAPPERS (SEE PAGE 560)

1 EGG, BEATEN

2 TABLESPOONS CANOLA OIL

1. Place the shrimp, cabbage, ginger, scallion whites, soy sauce, and 2 tablespoons of the water in a bowl and stir until well combined.

2. Lay 6 wrappers on a clean, dry work surface. Dip a finger into the egg and rub it over the edge of each wrapper. Place a teaspoon of the filling in the middle of each wrapper. Fold over the wrapper and seal by pinching the edges together. Repeat with the remaining filling and wrappers.

3. Warm a large skillet over medium-high heat. Add the canola oil and warm it for 1 minute. Add the pot stickers and cook until browned on both sides, 2 to 4 minutes, turning them just once.

4. Add the remaining water to the pan, cover the pan, and cook until the wontons are cooked through, about 3 minutes. Enjoy immediately.

Lobster Wontons

YIELD: 24 WONTONS | **ACTIVE TIME:** 30 MINUTES | **TOTAL TIME:** 45 MINUTES

1½ CUPS MINCED LOBSTER MEAT

½ SHALLOT, MINCED

¼ TEASPOON MINCED GINGER

¼ TEASPOON MINCED GARLIC

1 TEASPOON FISH SAUCE

2 TABLESPOONS HEAVY CREAM

2 TABLESPOONS CHOPPED CHIVES

SALT AND PEPPER, TO TASTE

24 SQUARE WONTON WRAPPERS (SEE PAGE 560)

1 EGG, BEATEN

1. Place the lobster meat, shallot, ginger, garlic, fish sauce, heavy cream, chives, salt, and pepper in a mixing bowl and gently fold until the mixture is combined.

2. Place 1 tablespoon of the mixture in the center of a wrapper. Dip a finger into the beaten egg and rub it around the edge of the wrapper. Bring the corners together to make a purse and seal it closed. Repeat with the remaining filling and wrappers.

3. Bring water to a boil in a large saucepan. Working in batches to avoid crowding the pot, gently slip the wontons into the boiling water and cook for 3 minutes. Remove the wontons from the boiling water with a slotted spoon and enjoy immediately.

Swordfish Crudo
SEE PAGE 334

Crab Salad

YIELD: 2 SERVINGS | **ACTIVE TIME:** 10 MINUTES | **TOTAL TIME:** 10 MINUTES

½ LB. CRABMEAT, PICKED OVER AND COOKED

1 TABLESPOON CHOPPED SHALLOT

1 TABLESPOON CRÈME FRAÎCHE

1 TABLESPOON MAYONNAISE

¼ CUP CORN KERNELS

¼ TEASPOON FRESH LEMON JUICE

2 TABLESPOONS CHOPPED FRESH CHIVES

2 TABLESPOONS SALMON ROE

SALT AND PEPPER, TO TASTE

1. Place the crab, shallot, crème fraîche, mayonnaise, corn, and lemon juice in a bowl and gently stir to combine.

2. Add the chives and salmon roe and gently fold to incorporate. Season with salt and pepper and enjoy.

Brandade en Croute

YIELD: 4 SERVINGS | **ACTIVE TIME:** 1 HOUR | **TOTAL TIME:** 38 HOURS

¼ CUP SALT, PLUS MORE TO TASTE

4 OZ. COD FILLET, SKIN REMOVED, HALVED

1 SMALL POTATO

½ CUP MILK

1 GARLIC CLOVE, MINCED

½ ONION, CHOPPED

2 TEASPOONS UNSALTED BUTTER

2 TEASPOONS CAPERS, DRAINED AND RINSED

2 TEASPOONS CHOPPED FRESH DILL

2 TEASPOONS CHOPPED FRESH PARSLEY

1 TEASPOON FRESH LEMON JUICE

¼ TEASPOON TABASCO

SALT AND PEPPER, TO TASTE

SLICES OF BRIOCHE (SEE PAGE 20), TOASTED, FOR SERVING

1. Place half of the salt on a baking sheet. Lay the pieces of cod on top of the bed of salt. Sprinkle the remaining salt over the fish. Cover the baking sheet with plastic wrap, place it in the refrigerator, and chill for 12 hours.

2. Remove the baking sheet from the refrigerator and rinse the cod under cold water. Place the salt cod on a clean baking sheet, cover it with water, and cover the baking sheet with plastic wrap. Place the baking sheet in the refrigerator and chill for 24 hours, changing the water every 8 hours.

3. Preheat the oven to 375ºF. Drain the salt cod, pat it dry, and place it in the refrigerator.

4. Place the potato in the oven and bake for 45 minutes.

5. While the potato is baking in the oven, place the salt cod, milk, garlic, and onion in a small saucepan and bring the mixture to a simmer. Cook until the salt cod is flaky, about 10 minutes. Strain through a fine sieve, reserving both the salt cod and the cooking liquid.

6. Remove the potato from the oven, cut it in half, spoon the flesh into a small crock, and discard the skin. Add the salt cod, butter, capers, dill, parsley, lemon juice, and Tabasco to the bowl and mash the mixture until it is smooth. Add 2 to 3 tablespoons of the cooking liquid, just enough to make it creamy.

7. Season the brandade with salt and pepper and place it in a gratin dish. Set the oven's broiler to high and place the brandade under the broiler. Broil until the top is browned, remove the brandade from the oven, and serve on the toasted Brioche.

Chilled Calamari Salad

YIELD: 4 SERVINGS | **ACTIVE TIME:** 15 MINUTES | **TOTAL TIME:** 45 MINUTES

SALT AND PEPPER, TO TASTE

1½ LBS. SMALL SQUID, BODIES AND TENTACLES SEPARATED, RINSED WELL

3 TABLESPOONS RED WINE VINEGAR

2 TABLESPOONS HARISSA SAUCE (SEE PAGE 189)

1½ TEASPOONS DIJON MUSTARD

⅓ CUP EXTRA-VIRGIN OLIVE OIL

2 ORANGES, PEELED AND CUT INTO SEGMENTS

1 RED BELL PEPPER, STEM AND SEEDS REMOVED, CUT INTO STRIPS

2 CELERY STALKS, CHOPPED

¼ CUP HAZELNUTS, TOASTED

¼ CUP SHREDDED FRESH MINT

1. Bring approximately 8 cups of water to a boil in a large saucepan and prepare an ice bath. Season the boiling water generously with salt, add the tentacles of the squid, and cook for 1 minute. Add the bodies, cook for another minute, and use a slotted spoon to transfer the squid to the ice bath.

2. Drain the squid, pat it dry, and chill in the refrigerator.

3. Place the red wine vinegar, harissa, and mustard in a salad bowl and whisk to combine. While whisking, slowly drizzle in the olive oil until it has emulsified.

4. Add the chilled calamari, oranges, bell pepper, and celery and gently toss until combined.

5. Season the salad with salt and pepper, top with the hazelnuts and mint, and enjoy.

Lobster & Street Corn Salad

YIELD: 4 SERVINGS | **ACTIVE TIME:** 25 MINUTES | **TOTAL TIME:** 50 MINUTES

FOR THE SALAD

¼ CUP MAYONNAISE

¼ CUP CREMA OR SOUR CREAM

1 TEASPOON FRESH LIME JUICE

¼ TEASPOON TAPATIO HOT SAUCE

½ CUP GRATED QUESO ENCHILADO

SALT AND PEPPER, TO TASTE

KERNELS FROM 2 EARS OF CORN

2 TABLESPOONS UNSALTED BUTTER, MELTED

FOR THE LOBSTER

½ CUP UNSALTED BUTTER

6 OZ. LOBSTER TAIL (BAJA LOBSTER PREFERRED)

2 TABLESPOONS TAJÍN

FRESH CILANTRO, FINELY CHOPPED, FOR GARNISH

1. To begin preparations for the salad, preheat the oven to 375°F. Combine the mayonnaise, crema, lime juice, Tapatio, queso enchilado, salt, and pepper in a salad bowl, stir to combine, and set it aside.

2. Place the corn kernels in small mixing bowl along with the butter and toss to combine. Place the corn kernels in an even layer on a baking sheet, place them in the oven, and roast until the corn is golden brown, 15 to 20 minutes.

3. Stir the corn into the salad bowl and let it cool. Chill the salad in the refrigerator.

4. To begin preparations for the lobster, place the butter in a skillet and melt it over medium-low heat.

5. Remove the meat from the lobster tail using kitchen scissors. Add the meat to the pan and poach until it turns a reddish orange, 4 to 5 minutes. Remove the lobster meat from the pan with a slotted spoon and let it cool.

6. Slice the lobster into small medallions. To serve, spoon the corn salad onto each plate and arrange a few lobster medallions on top of each portion. Sprinkle the Tajín over the dishes and garnish with cilantro.

Spinach, Fennel & Apple Salad with Smoked Trout

YIELD: 4 SERVINGS | **ACTIVE TIME:** 15 MINUTES | **TOTAL TIME:** 30 MINUTES

2 TABLESPOONS WHITE WINE VINEGAR

1 TABLESPOON FRESH LEMON JUICE

1 TABLESPOON WHOLE GRAIN MUSTARD

1 TEASPOON HONEY

½ CUP EXTRA-VIRGIN OLIVE OIL

1 SHALLOT, MINCED

2 TEASPOONS CHOPPED FRESH TARRAGON

SALT AND PEPPER, TO TASTE

4 CUPS BABY SPINACH

2 GRANNY SMITH APPLES, HALVED, SEEDS REMOVED, SLICED THIN

1 FENNEL BULB, TRIMMED, CORED, AND SLICED THIN

½ LB. SMOKED TROUT, SKIN REMOVED, FLAKED

1. Place the vinegar, lemon juice, mustard, and honey in a salad bowl and whisk to combine. While whisking continually, slowly drizzle in the olive oil until it has emulsified. Stir in the shallot and tarragon and season the vinaigrette with salt and pepper.

2. Add the spinach, apples, and fennel to the salad bowl and toss to coat.

3. To serve, plate the salad, top each portion with some of the smoked trout, and enjoy.

Crab Roulade

YIELD: 10 SERVINGS | **ACTIVE TIME:** 25 MINUTES | **TOTAL TIME:** 40 MINUTES

1 LB. LUMP CRABMEAT

¼ CUP MINCED SHALLOTS

¼ CUP MAYONNAISE

¼ CUP CRÈME FRAÎCHE

¼ CUP CHOPPED FRESH CHIVES, PLUS MORE FOR GARNISH

SALT AND PEPPER, TO TASTE

5 AVOCADOS, HALVED, PITS REMOVED, SLICED THIN

PASSION FRUIT EMULSION (SEE PAGE 555), FOR GARNISH

1 FRESNO CHILE PEPPER, SLICED THIN, FOR GARNISH

¼ CUP SESAME SEEDS, TOASTED, FOR GARNISH

½ CUP MICROGREENS, FOR GARNISH

1. Place the crab, shallots, mayonnaise, crème fraîche, and chives in a mixing bowl, season the mixture with salt and pepper, and stir until well combined.

2. Place a piece of plastic wrap on a damp work surface. Place one-tenth of the crab salad on the plastic wrap and roll it up tightly into a cylinder, twisting the ends. Repeat until you have 10 cylinders of the crab salad. Place them in the refrigerator and chill for 15 minutes.

3. Remove the crab salad from the refrigerator and wrap each portion with the slices from half of an avocado.

4. Garnish the roulade with the Passion Fruit Emulsion, chile, sesame seeds, microgreens, and additional chives and enjoy.

Seared Shrimp Skewers

YIELD: 4 SERVINGS | **ACTIVE TIME:** 30 MINUTES | **TOTAL TIME:** 2 HOURS

⅓ CUP EXTRA-VIRGIN OLIVE OIL

5 GARLIC CLOVES, MINCED

ZEST AND JUICE OF 1 LIME

1 TEASPOON PAPRIKA

½ TEASPOON GROUND GINGER

½ TEASPOON CUMIN

½ TEASPOON KOSHER SALT

¼ TEASPOON CAYENNE PEPPER

1 LB. SHRIMP, SHELLS REMOVED, DEVEINED

FRESH CILANTRO, CHOPPED, FOR GARNISH

AIOLI (SEE PAGE 185), FOR SERVING

LIME WEDGES, FOR SERVING

1. Place the olive oil, garlic, lime zest, lime juice, paprika, ginger, cumin, salt, and cayenne in a mixing bowl and whisk to combine.

2. Thread the shrimp onto skewers. Place the skewers in a large resealable bag, add the marinade, and marinate in the refrigerator for 1 hour.

3. Warm a cast-iron skillet over medium-high heat. Place the shrimp skewers in the pan and cook until just browned on both sides, 3 to 4 minutes.

4. Divide the skewers among the serving plates, garnish with cilantro, and serve with the Aioli and lime wedges.

Smoked Trout Tostadas

YIELD: 4 SERVINGS | **ACTIVE TIME:** 15 MINUTES | TOTAL TIME: 15 MINUTES

½ CUP EXTRA-VIRGIN OLIVE OIL, PLUS MORE AS NEEDED

1 LARGE WHITE ONION, SLICED THIN

4 GARLIC CLOVES, SLICED

1 LB. SMOKED TROUT, SHREDDED

2 TEASPOONS ACHIOTE POWDER

½ LB. CARROTS, PEELED AND GRATED

½ CUP SHREDDED CABBAGE

2 TABLESPOONS CHOPPED CASTELVETRANO OLIVES

2 TABLESPOONS FRESH LEMON JUICE

2 TABLESPOONS KOSHER SALT

4 CORN TORTILLAS (SEE PAGE 26)

1. Place the olive oil in a large skillet and warm it over medium-high heat.

2. While the olive oil is warming up, coat another skillet with olive oil and warm it over medium heat. Add the onion and garlic and cook, stirring frequently, until the onion is translucent, about 3 minutes.

3. Stir the trout and achiote into the onion mixture and cook, stirring to break up the trout, until warmed through, about 3 minutes. Remove the pan from heat, stir in all of the remaining ingredients, except for the tortillas, and let the mixture sit.

4. Add the tortillas to the hot oil in the first pan and fry until they are crispy, 2 to 3 minutes. Transfer the tostadas to a paper towel–lined plate to drain.

5. Top each tostada with some of the smoked trout mixture and enjoy.

Cold Roast Salmon

YIELD: 10 SERVINGS | **ACTIVE TIME:** 20 MINUTES | **TOTAL TIME:** 1 HOUR AND 45 MINUTES

1 WHOLE SIDE OF SALMON (ABOUT 3½ LBS.)

7 TABLESPOONS AVOCADO OIL, PLUS MORE FOR SERVING

BLACK PEPPER, TO TASTE

4 TEASPOONS KOSHER SALT, PLUS MORE TO TASTE

½ TEASPOON RED PEPPER FLAKES, DIVIDED

¼ CUP FRESH LEMON JUICE

2 LBS. GREEN BEANS, TRIMMED

1 BUNCH OF RADISHES, TRIMMED

1 CUP SALTED AND ROASTED PISTACHIOS, SHELLED AND COARSELY CHOPPED

MALDON SEA SALT, TO TASTE

LEMON WEDGES, FOR SERVING

LEMONY YOGURT SAUCE (SEE PAGE 188), FOR SERVING

1. Preheat the oven to 300°F. Place the salmon on a rimmed baking sheet and rub 2 tablespoons of avocado oil over each side. Season the salmon all over with black pepper, 2 teaspoons of the salt, and ¼ teaspoon of the red pepper flakes.

2. Place the salmon skin side down on the baking sheet and place it in the oven. Roast until a paring knife inserted into the side of the salmon meets with no resistance, 20 to 25 minutes. The fish should be opaque throughout and you should just be able to flake it with a fork. Remove from the oven and let it cool completely.

3. While the salmon is roasting, place the lemon juice, remaining avocado oil, remaining salt, and remaining red pepper flakes in a large bowl and whisk to combine. Set the dressing aside.

4. Working in batches, place the green beans in a large resealable plastic bag. Seal the bag and whack the beans with a rolling pin to split their skins and soften their insides without completely pulverizing them. Place them in a bowl with the lemon dressing and massage the mixture with your hands to break down the beans further. Let the mixture sit at room temperature for at least 1 hour.

5. Slice the radishes thin lengthwise. Place them in a large bowl of ice water, cover, and chill until ready to serve; this will allow you to get the prep out of the way and keep the radishes crisp and firm.

6. Just before serving, drain the radishes and toss them with the green beans. Stir in the pistachios, taste, and adjust the seasoning as necessary. Transfer to a platter, drizzle avocado oil over the top, and sprinkle the Maldon sea salt on top.

7. Using two spatulas, carefully transfer the salmon to another platter, leaving the skin behind on the baking sheet. Drizzle avocado oil over it and squeeze a lemon wedge or two over the salmon. Sprinkle Maldon over the fish and serve with more lemon wedges and the Lemony Yogurt Sauce.

Oyster Sliders with Red Pepper Mayo

YIELD: 4 SERVINGS | **ACTIVE TIME:** 30 MINUTES | **TOTAL TIME:** 1 HOUR AND 15 MINUTES

3 RED BELL PEPPERS

CANOLA OIL, AS NEEDED

1 CUP CORNMEAL

SALT, TO TASTE

½ LB. OYSTER MEAT

2 EGGS, BEATEN

1 TABLESPOON UNSALTED BUTTER

4 KING'S HAWAIIAN ROLLS

½ CUP MAYONNAISE

1. Preheat the oven to 400°F. Place the red peppers on a baking sheet, place them in the oven, and roast, turning them occasionally, until the peppers are blistered all over, 35 to 40 minutes. Remove them from the oven and let them cool. When cool enough to handle, remove the skins and seeds from the peppers and set the roasted flesh aside.

2. Add canola oil to a Dutch oven until it is about 1 inch deep and warm it to 350°F.

3. Place the cornmeal and salt in a bowl and stir to combine. Dredge the oysters in the beaten eggs and then in the cornmeal-and-salt mixture. Repeat until the oysters are completely coated.

4. Gently slip the oysters into the hot oil and fry until crispy and golden brown, 3 to 5 minutes. Transfer the fried oysters to a paper towel–lined plate to drain.

5. Place the butter in a skillet and melt it over medium heat. Place the buns in the skillet and toast until lightly browned. Remove the buns from the pan and set them aside.

6. Place the roasted peppers and mayonnaise in a blender and puree until smooth. Spread the mayonnaise on the buns, sandwich the fried oysters between the buns, and enjoy.

Oysters with Juniper Cream

YIELD: 2 SERVINGS | **ACTIVE TIME:** 15 MINUTES | **TOTAL TIME:** 15 MINUTES

3 TABLESPOONS UNSALTED BUTTER, SOFTENED

2 OZ. GIN

1 TEASPOON BLACK PEPPER

¼ CUP HEAVY CREAM

2 SHALLOTS, MINCED

4 JUNIPER BERRIES

SALT, AS NEEDED

12 OYSTERS, SHUCKED, ON THE HALF SHELL

FRESH PARSLEY, CHOPPED, FOR GARNISH

1. Preheat your gas grill to high heat (about 500°F). Place the butter, gin, and black pepper in a bowl and whisk to combine. Set the mixture aside.

2. Place the cream, shallots, and juniper berries in a saucepan and warm over low heat for 2 minutes. Remove the pan from heat and let the mixture steep.

3. Fill a large cast-iron skillet with a bed of salt and nestle the oysters into the salt. Top each one with a spoonful of the butter mixture and a splash of the juniper cream.

4. Place the pan on the grill and cook until the oysters are caramelized and the liquid is bubbling, about 3 minutes.

5. Garnish with chopped parsley and serve immediately.

Mussels with Pickled Ramps

YIELD: 4 SERVINGS | **ACTIVE TIME:** 20 MINUTES | **TOTAL TIME:** 45 MINUTES

1 LB. PRINCE EDWARD ISLAND MUSSELS

⅓ CUP ALL-PURPOSE FLOUR

4 TABLESPOONS UNSALTED BUTTER

1 SMALL SHALLOT, CHOPPED

2 GARLIC CLOVES, CHOPPED

8 THIN SLICES OF FENNEL

½ CUP CHERRY TOMATOES

¼ CUP WHITE WINE

¼ CUP SLICED PICKLED RAMPS (SEE PAGE 363)

SALT AND PEPPER, TO TASTE

1 TABLESPOON EXTRA-VIRGIN OLIVE OIL

4 SLICES OF CRUSTY BREAD

FRESH PARSLEY, CHOPPED, FOR GARNISH

1. Place the mussels in a large bowl, cover them with water, and stir in the flour. Let the mussels soak for 30 minutes, then drain the mussels and debeard them.

2. Place half of the butter in a large skillet and melt it over high heat. Add the shallot, garlic, fennel, and tomatoes and cook, shaking the pan frequently, until the aromatics just start to brown, about 2 minutes.

3. Add the mussels and deglaze the pan with the wine, scraping up any browned bits from the bottom of the pan. Let the alcohol cook off (about 30 seconds) and stir in the remaining butter. Toss to coat the mussels, add the Pickled Ramps and a small pinch of salt and pepper, and cook until the majority of the mussels have opened.

4. Remove the pan from heat and discard any mussels that did not open.

5. Turn on the oven's broiler. Drizzle olive oil over the slices of bread and season them with salt and pepper. Place the bread under the broiler and toast until they just start to char. Remove the bread from the oven and set them aside.

6. Ladle the mussels and pan sauce into warmed bowls, garnish with parsley, and serve with the bread.

RETURN TO THE GARDEN

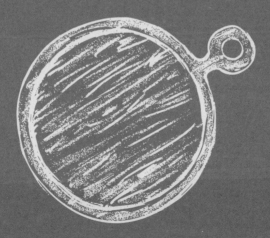

Spanakopita

YIELD: 8 SERVINGS | **ACTIVE TIME:** 1 HOUR | **TOTAL TIME:** 1 HOUR AND 30 MINUTES

½ LB. BABY SPINACH, STEMS REMOVED

1 CUP CRUMBLED FETA CHEESE

6 TABLESPOONS FULL-FAT GREEK YOGURT

2 SCALLIONS, TRIMMED AND CHOPPED

1 EGG, BEATEN

2 TABLESPOONS CHOPPED FRESH MINT

2 GARLIC CLOVES, MINCED

ZEST AND JUICE OF ½ LEMON

½ TEASPOON FRESHLY GRATED NUTMEG

PINCH OF CAYENNE PEPPER

SALT AND PEPPER, TO TASTE

½ LB. FROZEN PHYLLO DOUGH, THAWED

6 TABLESPOONS UNSALTED BUTTER, MELTED

1 CUP FRESHLY GRATED PECORINO ROMANO CHEESE

1 TABLESPOON SESAME SEEDS

1 TABLESPOON CHOPPED FRESH DILL

1. Prepare an ice bath. Fill a large saucepan three-quarters of the way with water and bring it to a boil. Add the spinach and boil for 2 minutes, making sure it is all submerged. Drain the spinach, plunge it in the ice bath, and let it cool.

2. Place the spinach in a linen towel and wring the towel to remove as much water from the spinach as possible. Chop the spinach, place it in a bowl, and add the feta, yogurt, scallions, egg, mint, garlic, lemon zest, lemon juice, nutmeg, and cayenne. Stir to combine, season the mixture with salt and pepper, and set the filling aside.

3. Preheat the oven to 425°F. Line a baking sheet with parchment paper. Place a piece of parchment paper on a work surface, place a sheet of phyllo on it, and brush it with some of the butter. Lay another sheet of phyllo on top, gently press down, and brush it with butter. Sprinkle a thin layer of the Pecorino over the second sheet. Repeat so that you have another layer of Pecorino sandwiched between two 2-sheet layers of phyllo. Make sure you keep any phyllo that you are not working with covered so that it does not dry out.

4. Working from the top of the rectangle, find the center point and cut down, as though you were cutting an open book in half. Cut these halves in two, so that you have four strips. Place 2 tablespoons of the filling on the bottom of each strip and shape the filling into a triangle.

5. Maintaining the triangle shape of the filling, roll the strips up into triangles, as if you were folding a flag. Crimp the pastries to seal, and place the spanakopita on the baking sheet, seam side down.

6. Repeat Steps 3, 4, and 5, giving you eight spanakopita. Sprinkle the sesame seeds over each spanakopita, place them in the oven, and bake until golden brown, about 20 minutes.

7. Remove the spanakopita from the oven, sprinkle the dill over them, and enjoy.

Marinated Artichokes

YIELD: 4 SERVINGS | **ACTIVE TIME:** 30 MINUTES | **TOTAL TIME:** 1 HOUR

2 CUPS EXTRA-VIRGIN OLIVE OIL, PLUS MORE AS NEEDED

4 TO 8 GLOBE ARTICHOKES, PEELED AND QUARTERED

JUICE OF 1 LEMON

6 GARLIC CLOVES

¼ TEASPOON RED PEPPER FLAKES

2 SPRIGS OF FRESH THYME

1 SHALLOT, SLICED THIN

FRESH BASIL, CHOPPED, FOR GARNISH

1. Place the olive oil and the artichokes in a medium saucepan. The artichokes need to be completely covered by the oil, as any contact with the air will make them turn brown. Add more oil to cover the artichokes, if necessary.

2. Add the remaining ingredients, except for the basil, and bring the mixture to a simmer over medium heat. Reduce the heat to the lowest setting and cook the artichokes until they are tender, about 30 minutes.

3. Remove the pan from heat and let the artichokes cool. Remove them from the oil, garnish with basil, and enjoy.

Vegetable Kebabs

YIELD: 4 SERVINGS | **ACTIVE TIME:** 30 MINUTES | **TOTAL TIME:** 1 HOUR AND 30 MINUTES

¼ CUP PLUS 1 TABLESPOON EXTRA-VIRGIN OLIVE OIL

2 TEASPOONS DIJON MUSTARD

2 GARLIC CLOVES, MINCED

2 TEASPOONS RED WINE VINEGAR

2 TEASPOONS HONEY

1 TEASPOON CHOPPED FRESH ROSEMARY

SALT AND PEPPER, TO TASTE

2 PORTOBELLO MUSHROOMS, STEMS REMOVED, CUT INTO 1-INCH CUBES

2 ZUCCHINI, CUT INTO 1-INCH CUBES

1 RED BELL PEPPER, STEM AND SEEDS REMOVED, CUT INTO 1-INCH CUBES

1 GREEN BELL PEPPER, STEM AND SEEDS REMOVED, CUT INTO 1-INCH CUBES

1. Place ¼ cup of the olive oil, the mustard, garlic, vinegar, honey, and rosemary in a mixing bowl and whisk to combine. Season the dressing with salt and pepper and set it aside.

2. Thread the vegetables onto skewers and place them on a baking sheet. Pour the dressing over the skewers, cover them with plastic wrap, and let them marinate at room temperature for 1 hour, stirring occasionally.

3. Place the remaining olive oil in a large skillet and warm it over medium-high heat. Remove the vegetable skewers from the dressing and reserve the dressing. Add the skewers to the pan and cook until golden brown all over and tender, about 8 minutes, turning them as necessary.

4. Place the skewers in a serving dish, pour the reserved dressing over them, and enjoy.

Spanakopita
SEE PAGE 358

Stuffed Grape Leaves

YIELD: 4 SERVINGS | **ACTIVE TIME:** 30 MINUTES | **TOTAL TIME:** 1 HOUR AND 30 MINUTES

1 (1 LB.) JAR OF GRAPE LEAVES

¼ CUP EXTRA-VIRGIN OLIVE OIL, PLUS MORE TO TASTE

1 RED ONION, CHOPPED

1 CUP LONG-GRAIN RICE, RINSED WELL

¼ CUP RAISINS, FINELY CHOPPED

¼ CUP CHOPPED FRESH MINT, PLUS MORE FOR GARNISH

¼ CUP CHOPPED FRESH DILL

ZEST OF 1 LEMON

PINCH OF CINNAMON

SALT AND PEPPER, TO TASTE

1 LEMON, SLICED, FOR SERVING

1. Remove the grape leaves from the jar and rinse off all of the brine. Pick out 16 of the largest leaves and lay them on a baking sheet. Cover them with plastic wrap and set them aside.

2. Place half of the olive oil in a medium saucepan and warm it over medium heat. Add the red onion and cook, stirring occasionally, until it has softened, about 5 minutes.

3. Add the rice and cook, stirring frequently, for 2 minutes. Add 1½ cups water and bring it to a boil. Reduce the heat to low, cover the pan, and simmer for about 15 minutes.

4. Remove the pan from heat, fluff the rice with a fork, and let it cool.

5. Add the raisins, mint, dill, lemon zest, and cinnamon to the rice and fold to combine. Season the mixture with salt and pepper and form it into 16 balls.

6. Lay down a grape leaf and remove the stem. Fold in the edges of the leaf. Place a ball of the rice mixture at the bottom of the leaf, fold the bottom of the leaf over the filling, and then roll the leaf up tightly. Place the stuffed grape leaf on a baking sheet, seam side down, and repeat with the remaining grape leaves and rice mixture.

7. Place the remaining olive oil in a large saucepan and warm it over medium-high heat. Add the stuffed grape leaves to the pan, seam side down, and cook for 1 minute.

8. Reduce the heat to the lowest setting and carefully add 1½ cups water to the pan. Cover the pan and cook for 30 minutes, adding more water if the pan starts to look dry. You should finish with very little water in the pan.

9. Drizzle more olive oil over the grape leaves, garnish with additional mint, and serve with the slices of lemon.

Pickled Ramps

YIELD: 2 SERVINGS | **ACTIVE TIME:** 5 MINUTES | **TOTAL TIME:** 2 HOURS

½ CUP CHAMPAGNE VINEGAR

½ CUP WATER

¼ CUP SUGAR

1½ TEASPOONS KOSHER SALT

¼ TEASPOON FENNEL SEEDS

¼ TEASPOON CORIANDER SEEDS

⅛ TEASPOON RED PEPPER FLAKES

10 SMALL RAMP BULBS

1. Place all of the ingredients, except for the ramps, in a small saucepan and bring the mixture to a boil over medium heat.

2. Add the ramps, reduce the heat, and simmer for 1 minute. Transfer the ramps and the brine to a mason jar, cover it with plastic wrap, and let the ramps cool completely before serving or storing in the refrigerator.

Gildas

YIELD: 6 SERVINGS | **ACTIVE TIME:** 10 MINUTES | **TOTAL TIME:** 10 MINUTES

4 OZ. ANCHOVIES IN OLIVE OIL, DRAINED AND OIL RESERVED

¼ CUP WATER

2 CUPS GORDAL OLIVES, PITS REMOVED, MARINATED IN OLIVE OIL AND GARLIC

2 RED CHILE PEPPERS, STEMS AND SEEDS REMOVED, CHOPPED

1. Place the anchovies, water, and reserved olive oil in a food processor and puree until the mixture has emulsified.

2. Fill the olives with the anchovy puree, close each one up with a piece of chile pepper, and enjoy.

Stuffed Grape Leaves
SEE PAGE 362

Eggplant with Miso

YIELD: 4 SERVINGS | **ACTIVE TIME:** 15 MINUTES | **TOTAL TIME:** 30 MINUTES

CANOLA OIL, AS NEEDED

1 LONG JAPANESE EGGPLANT, HALVED LENGTHWISE

10 TABLESPOONS SOY SAUCE

10 TABLESPOONS RED MISO

10 TABLESPOONS BROWN SUGAR

10 TABLESPOONS SCOTCH WHISKY

SESAME SEEDS, FOR GARNISH

FRESH CILANTRO, CHOPPED, FOR GARNISH

1. Add canola oil to a Dutch oven and warm it to 350°F. Cut each half of eggplant into four pieces, gently slip them into the canola oil, and fry until golden brown and cooked through, 6 to 8 minutes, turning them as necessary. Transfer the fried eggplant to a paper towel–lined plate to drain.

2. Place the soy sauce, red miso, brown sugar, and whisky in a mixing bowl and whisk until combined.

3. Add the fried eggplant to the sauce and toss until coated. Garnish with the sesame seeds and cilantro and enjoy.

Rustic Onion Galette

YIELD: 1 TART | **ACTIVE TIME:** 25 MINUTES | **TOTAL TIME:** 1 HOUR

1 PERFECT PIECRUST (SEE PAGE 562)

3 TABLESPOONS EXTRA-VIRGIN OLIVE OIL

3 ONIONS, SLICED THIN

1 TEASPOON FRESH THYME

1 PLUM TOMATO, SLICED

½ CUP CRUMBLED GORGONZOLA CHEESE

1 EGG, BEATEN

1. Line a baking sheet with parchment paper. Roll the piecrust out to 12 inches and place it on the baking sheet. Chill the crust in the refrigerator.

2. Place the olive oil in a large skillet and warm it over medium heat. Add the onions, thyme, and tomato and cook, stirring occasionally, until the onions are golden brown, about 15 minutes. Transfer the mixture to a plate and let it cool completely.

3. Remove the crust from the refrigerator and spread the cooled onions on top.

4. Preheat the oven to 350°F. Take the edge of the crust and fold it over about 1 inch of the onions. Place the sliced tomatoes in the center of the tart and top with the cheese.

5. Brush the top of the crust with the egg and place the galette in the oven. Bake the galette until the crust is golden brown and the cheese has melted, about 20 minutes.

6. Remove the tart from the oven and let it cool to room temperature before serving.

Tomato Pie

YIELD: 1 PIE | **ACTIVE TIME:** 40 MINUTES | **TOTAL TIME:** 1 HOUR AND 30 MINUTES

1½ LBS. HEIRLOOM TOMATOES

2 TEASPOONS KOSHER SALT

1½ CUPS GRATED SHARP CHEDDAR CHEESE

½ CUP GRATED PARMESAN CHEESE

½ CUP MAYONNAISE

1 LARGE EGG, LIGHTLY BEATEN

1 TABLESPOON CHOPPED FRESH CHIVES

1 TABLESPOON CHOPPED FRESH PARSLEY

1 TABLESPOON APPLE CIDER VINEGAR

1 SCALLION, SLICED THIN

2 TEASPOONS SUGAR

¼ TEASPOON BLACK PEPPER

1½ TABLESPOONS CORNMEAL

1 CREAM CHEESE PIECRUST (SEE PAGE 554)

1. Cut the tomatoes into ¼-inch-thick slices. Place tomatoes in a single layer on paper towels and sprinkle 1 teaspoon of salt over them. Let the tomatoes rest for 30 minutes.

2. Preheat the oven to 425°F. Place the cheeses, mayonnaise, beaten egg, chives, parsley, vinegar, scallion, sugar, pepper, and the remaining salt in a mixing bowl and stir until combined.

3. Pat the sliced tomatoes dry with a paper towel.

4. Sprinkle cornmeal over the bottom of the crust. Spread ½ cup of the cheese mixture over the crust and top it with half of the tomatoes, arranging the tomatoes in slightly overlapping rows. Spread ½ cup of the cheese mixture over the tomatoes and top it with the rest of the tomato slices.

5. Place the pie in the oven and bake until the crust is browned and the filling is bubbling, 40 to 45 minutes.

6. Remove the pie from the oven and let it cool for 2 hours before enjoying.

Pickled Fresno Peppers

YIELD: 3 CUPS | **ACTIVE TIME:** 30 MINUTES | **TOTAL TIME:** 2 HOURS

2 LBS. FRESNO CHILE PEPPERS, STEMS AND SEEDS REMOVED, SLICED THIN

¾ CUP RICE VINEGAR

⅔ CUP SUGAR

⅔ CUP WATER

1. Place the chiles in a bowl of cold water and let them soak for 15 minutes. Drain the chiles and place them in a mason jar.

2. Place the remaining ingredients in a saucepan and bring to a boil over medium-high heat, stirring to dissolve the sugar.

3. Pour the brine over the chiles and let them cool to room temperature. To can the pickled chiles, see page 396. Otherwise, the chiles will keep in the refrigerator for up to 1 month.

Pa Jun

YIELD: 4 SERVINGS | **ACTIVE TIME:** 30 MINUTES | **TOTAL TIME:** 30 MINUTES

2 CUPS ALL-PURPOSE FLOUR

2 TEASPOONS KOSHER SALT

½ TEASPOON BLACK PEPPER

2 EGGS

¼ CUP MIRIN

1 TEASPOON SOY SAUCE

1 CUP SODA WATER

CANOLA OIL, AS NEEDED

2 BUNCHES OF SCALLIONS, TRIMMED AND CHOPPED

1 RED BELL PEPPER, STEMS AND SEEDS REMOVED, SLICED THIN AND CHOPPED INTO 2-INCH PIECES

2 TABLESPOONS SESAME SEEDS

1. Place the flour, salt, pepper, eggs, mirin, soy sauce, and soda water in a bowl and stir until the mixture comes together as a smooth batter.

2. Place a tablespoon of canola oil in a nonstick skillet and warm it over medium heat. Ladle enough batter into the pan to form a thick, 3-inch pancake. Cook until the bottom starts to set.

3. Sprinkle the some of scallions, bell pepper, and sesame seeds over the top of the pancake and cook until the bottom is golden brown, 2 to 3 minutes. Flip the pancake over and cook until it is golden brown on that side. Transfer the pancake to a plate, cover it loosely with aluminum foil, and repeat Steps 2 and 3 until all of the batter has been used.

Asparagus & Goat Cheese Galette

YIELDS: 1 GALETTE | **ACTIVE TIME:** 10 MINUTES | **TOTAL TIME:** 1 HOUR

1⅓ CUPS WHOLE WHEAT FLOUR

PINCH OF FINE SEA SALT

½ CUP UNSALTED BUTTER, CUT INTO ½-INCH PIECES

1 EGG

1 EGG YOLK

1 CUP GOAT CHEESE, SOFTENED

2 TEASPOONS FRESH THYME

1½ TEASPOONS FRESH LEMON JUICE

1 LB. ASPARAGUS, TRIMMED

EXTRA-VIRGIN OLIVE OIL, AS NEEDED

SALT AND PEPPER, TO TASTE

1. Place the flour and the salt in a mixing bowl. Add half of the butter and work the mixture with a pastry blender until it is a coarse meal. Add the remaining butter and work the mixture until it is a collection of pea-sized pieces. Add the egg and egg yolk and work the mixture until it just comes together as a smooth dough, taking care not to overwork the mixture.

2. Place the dough on a flour-dusted work surface and knead it 2 or 3 times. Flatten the dough into a disk, cover it in plastic wrap, and chill it in the refrigerator for 30 minutes.

3. Preheat the oven to 375°F and line a baking sheet with parchment paper. In a small bowl, combine the goat cheese, thyme, and lemon juice.

4. Place the dough on a flour-dusted work surface and roll it out into a 12-inch circle. Place it on the parchment paper and then spread the goat cheese mixture over the dough, leaving a 2-inch border around the edge. Arrange the asparagus on top of the goat cheese mixture and fold up the edges of the dough over the filling.

5. Brush the top of the crust with olive oil. Sprinkle salt and pepper over the galette and place it in the oven. Bake the galette until it is golden brown, about 25 minutes.

6. Remove the galette from the oven and let it cool slightly before serving.

Punjabi Samosas

YIELD: 16 SAMOSAS | **ACTIVE TIME:** 45 MINUTES | **TOTAL TIME:** 1 HOUR AND 30 MINUTES

FOR THE WRAPPERS

2 CUPS MAIDA FLOUR, PLUS MORE AS NEEDED

¼ TEASPOON KOSHER SALT

2 TABLESPOONS EXTRA-VIRGIN OLIVE OIL

½ CUP WATER, PLUS MORE AS NEEDED

FOR THE FILLING

2 RUSSET POTATOES, PEELED AND CHOPPED

2 TABLESPOONS EXTRA-VIRGIN OLIVE OIL

1 TEASPOON CORIANDER SEEDS, CRUSHED

½ TEASPOON FENNEL SEEDS, CRUSHED

PINCH OF FENUGREEK SEEDS, CRUSHED

1-INCH PIECE OF FRESH GINGER, PEELED AND GRATED

1 GARLIC CLOVE, GRATED

1 TEASPOON MINCED JALAPEÑO CHILE PEPPER

2 TEASPOONS CHILI POWDER

¾ TEASPOON TURMERIC

1 TABLESPOON AMCHOOR POWDER

½ TEASPOON GARAM MASALA

SALT, TO TASTE

CANOLA OIL, AS NEEDED

1. To begin preparations for the wrappers, place the flour and salt in a mixing bowl and use your hands to combine. Add the oil and work the mixture with your hands until it is a coarse meal. Add the water and knead the mixture until a smooth, firm dough forms. If the dough is too dry, incorporate more water, adding 1 tablespoon at a time. Cover the bowl with a kitchen towel and set aside.

2. To begin preparations for the filling, place the potatoes in a saucepan and cover with water. Bring the water to a boil and cook until fork-tender, about 20 minutes. Transfer to a bowl, mash until smooth, and set aside.

3. Place the olive oil in a skillet and warm it over medium heat. Add the crushed seeds and toast until fragrant, about 2 minutes, shaking the pan frequently. Add the ginger, garlic, and jalapeño, stir-fry for 2 minutes, and then add the chili powder, turmeric, amchoor powder, and garam masala. Cook for another minute before adding the mashed potatoes. Stir to combine, season with salt, and taste the mixture. Adjust the seasoning as necessary, transfer the mixture to a bowl, and let it cool completely.

4. Divide the dough for the wrappers into eight pieces and roll each one out into a 6-inch circle on a flour-dusted work surface. Cut the circles in half and brush the flat edge of each piece with water. Fold one corner of the flat edge toward the other to make a cone and pinch to seal. Fill each cone one-third of the way with the filling, brush the opening with water, and pinch to seal. Place the sealed samosas on a parchment-lined baking sheet.

5. Add canola oil to a Dutch oven until it is 2 inches deep and warm it to 325ºF over medium heat. Working in batches, add the filled samosas to the hot oil and fry, turning them as they cook, until they are golden brown, about 5 minutes. Transfer the cooked samosas to a paper towel–lined plate and serve once they have all been cooked.

Perkedel Jagung

YIELD: 4 SERVINGS | **ACTIVE TIME:** 45 MINUTES | **TOTAL TIME:** 45 MINUTES

2 TABLESPOONS MINCED FRESH GALANGAL ROOT

½ CUP CHOPPED FRESH CILANTRO

4 SHALLOTS, MINCED

4 GARLIC CLOVES, MINCED

1 RED JALAPEÑO CHILE PEPPER, STEM AND SEEDS REMOVED, MINCED

4 MACADAMIA NUTS, SOAKED IN WATER FOR 10 MINUTES AND DRAINED

1½ TEASPOONS KOSHER SALT, PLUS MORE TO TASTE

2 TEASPOONS SUGAR

KERNELS FROM 4 EARS OF CORN

¼ CUP MINCED SCALLIONS

2 EGGS, BEATEN

¾ CUP ALL-PURPOSE FLOUR

1 TEASPOON BAKING POWDER

CANOLA OIL, AS NEEDED

1. Using a mortar and pestle, grind the galangal, cilantro, shallots, garlic, jalapeño, nuts, salt, and sugar into a paste. Set the paste aside.

2. Place the corn kernels in a bowl and roughly mash them. Add the scallions, eggs, flour, baking powder, and paste and stir until the mixture comes together as a smooth, thick batter.

3. Add canola oil to a Dutch oven until it is about 2 inches deep and warm it to 325°F. Add a small spoonful of batter to the oil and fry until it is until golden brown. Remove the fritter from the oil and let it cool slightly. Taste and adjust the seasoning of the remaining batter as necessary.

4. Working in batches to avoid crowding the pot, drop heaping spoonfuls of the batter into the hot oil and fry until golden brown and crispy, 4 to 6 minutes, turning them as needed. Transfer the fritters to a paper towel–lined plate to drain and season them with salt.

Kachori

YIELD: 20 DUMPLINGS | **ACTIVE TIME:** 45 MINUTES | **TOTAL TIME:** 1 HOUR

1 CUP ALL-PURPOSE FLOUR, PLUS MORE AS NEEDED

½ TEASPOON KOSHER SALT

1 TABLESPOON AVOCADO OIL, PLUS MORE AS NEEDED

2 TABLESPOONS SEMOLINA FLOUR

JUICE OF 1 LEMON

⅓ TO ½ CUP WATER

1 TABLESPOON EXTRA-VIRGIN OLIVE OIL

½ TEASPOON ASAFETIDA

2 CUPS FRESH GREEN PEAS OR DEFROSTED FROZEN PEAS

1 LARGE JALAPEÑO CHILE PEPPER, STEMS AND SEEDS REMOVED, MINCED

2 TABLESPOONS GRATED GINGER

1 TABLESPOON GARAM MASALA

1 TABLESPOON COARSELY GROUND FENNEL SEEDS

1 TEASPOON FINE SEA SALT

½ TEASPOON SUGAR

1. Place the all-purpose flour, kosher salt, avocado oil, semolina flour, and half of the lemon juice in a large bowl. Gradually add ⅓ cup of water, stirring with a wooden spoon until the mixture comes together as a dough. Knead the dough until it is smooth, about 3 to 5 minutes. If the dough feels too dry, add water 1 tablespoon at a time until the dough is stiff and not too sticky. Cover the dough with a towel and set aside.

2. Place the olive oil in a large skillet and warm it over medium heat. Add the asafetida and cook until it sizzles, 2 to 4 minutes. Add the peas and ¼ cup water, cover the pan, and cook until the peas are tender and the water has evaporated, about 5 minutes.

3. Add the jalapeño, ginger, garam masala, fennel seeds, sea salt, sugar, and remaining lemon juice and stir to combine. Cook the mixture until the jalapeño is tender, 10 to 15 minutes. Remove the pan from heat, coarsely mash the mixture with a potato masher, and let it cool for 15 minutes.

4. Add avocado oil to a Dutch oven until it is 2 inches deep and warm it to 350ºF.

5. Place the dough on a flour-dusted work surface. Roll out the dough until it is an approximately ¹⁄₁₆-inch-thick circle. Cut the dough into 2-inch circles and roll them out until they are about 4 inches. Place 1 tablespoon of the cooled filling in the center of each circle, bring the edges of the dough toward the center, and fold them over the filling to form little baskets. Crimp the edges of the dough to seal.

6. Working in batches, gently slip the dumplings into the oil and fry until they are golden brown, 4 to 5 minutes, turning them as necessary. Transfer the cooked dumplings to a paper towel–lined plate to drain before enjoying.

Vegetable Tempura

YIELD: 4 SERVINGS | **ACTIVE TIME:** 30 MINUTES | **TOTAL TIME:** 30 MINUTES

CANOLA OIL, AS NEEDED

2 CUPS ALL-PURPOSE FLOUR

1 TEASPOON BAKING POWDER

1 TEASPOON BAKING SODA

1 TEASPOON FINE SEA SALT

⅛ TEASPOON TURMERIC

2 EGG YOLKS

1¼ CUPS WATER OR SODA WATER, CHILLED

1¼ CUPS SAKE OR LIGHT BEER, CHILLED

4 OZ. GREEN BEANS, TRIMMED

4 OZ. CARROTS, PEELED AND SLICED

4 OZ. SWEET POTATOES, PEELED AND SLICED

4 OZ. ZUCCHINI, HALVED AND SLICED THIN LENGTHWISE

4 OZ. BROCCOLI FLORETS

1. Add canola oil to a Dutch oven until it is about 2 inches deep and warm it to 350°F.

2. Place the flour, baking powder, baking soda, salt, and turmeric in a mixing bowl and stir to combine. Set the mixture aside.

3. Place the egg yolks, water, and sake in a separate bowl and whisk to combine. Add this mixture to the dry mixture and stir until it comes together as a slightly lumpy, pancake-like batter, taking care not to overmix.

4. Working in batches to avoid crowding the pot, dip the vegetables into the batter, shake off any excess batter, and gently slip them into the hot oil. Fry until crispy, golden brown, and cooked through. Transfer the vegetable tempura to a wire rack and let it drain and cool before serving with your favorite dipping sauce.

Smashed Cucumber Salad

YIELD: 2 SERVINGS | **ACTIVE TIME:** 15 MINUTES | **TOTAL TIME:** 15 MINUTES

4 PERSIAN CUCUMBERS, CHOPPED INTO 3-INCH PIECES

1½ TABLESPOONS SOY SAUCE

1 TEASPOON SESAME OIL

1 TEASPOON RICE WINE VINEGAR

½ TEASPOON RED PEPPER FLAKES

SALT, TO TASTE

TOASTED SESAME SEEDS, FOR GARNISH

1. Place the cucumbers in a resealable plastic bag. Press as much air out of the bag as possible and use a rolling pin or the bottom of a cast-iron pan to smash the cucumbers.

2. Add the soy sauce, sesame oil, vinegar, and red pepper flakes to the bag and massage all of the ingredients together. Taste and season the salad with salt.

3. Transfer the cucumber salad to a serving plate, garnish with the sesame seeds, and enjoy immediately.

Green Papaya Salad

YIELD: 4 SERVINGS | **ACTIVE TIME:** 30 MINUTES | **TOTAL TIME:** 30 MINUTES

¼ CUP COCONUT OR PALM SUGAR

¼ CUP FISH SAUCE

3 GARLIC CLOVES

2 BIRD'S EYE CHILI PEPPERS, STEMS AND SEEDS REMOVED, CHOPPED

2 TABLESPOONS CHOPPED DRIED SHRIMP

3 CUPS GRATED GREEN PAPAYA

⅓ CUP GREEN BEANS, CHOPPED

⅓ CUP GRATED CARROTS

3 TABLESPOONS FRESH LIME JUICE

½ CUP CHOPPED ROASTED PEANUTS

⅓ CUP HALVED CHERRY TOMATOES

SALT, TO TASTE

FRESH THAI BASIL, TORN, FOR GARNISH

1. Place the sugar and the fish sauce and in a saucepan and cook, stirring occasionally, until the sugar has dissolved and the mixture has thickened slightly. Remove the pan from heat and set it aside.

2. Using a mortar and pestle, mash the garlic. Add the chilies and dried shrimp and mash them to release their oils.

3. Add the papaya, green beans, and carrots, and bruise gently with the pestle. Stir the mixture to combine.

4. Add the lime juice, fish sauce syrup, and peanuts and stir until well combined. Add the tomatoes, season the salad with salt, garnish with Thai basil, and enjoy.

Fried Green Beans

YIELD: 4 SERVINGS | **ACTIVE TIME:** 30 MINUTES | **TOTAL TIME:** 30 MINUTES

2 CUPS AVOCADO OIL

1 LB. GREEN BEANS, TRIMMED

4 GARLIC CLOVES, MINCED

4 OZ. GROUND PORK

1 TEASPOON SUGAR

1 TABLESPOON GOCHUJANG

1 TEASPOON CHINKIANG VINEGAR

SALT, TO TASTE

¼ TEASPOON WHITE PEPPER

½ TEASPOON GROUND SZECHUAN PEPPERCORNS

2 RED CHILE PEPPERS, STEMS AND SEEDS REMOVED, SLICED THIN

1. Place the avocado oil in a large skillet and warm it over medium-high heat. Working in batches to avoid crowding the pan, add the green beans and fry until the skin blisters, 1 to 3 minutes. Transfer the fried green beans to a paper towel–lined plate and let them drain.

2. When all of the green beans have been cooked, pour out all but 1 tablespoon of the avocado oil.

3. Raise the heat to high and add the garlic and pork. Stir-fry until the pork is cooked through, stir in the sugar, gochujang, vinegar, salt, white pepper, and Szechuan peppercorns, and return the green beans to the pan. Toss to combine.

4. Taste and adjust the seasoning as necessary. Top with the chiles and enjoy.

Spanish Tortilla

YIELD: 6 SERVINGS | **ACTIVE TIME:** 30 MINUTES | **TOTAL TIME:** 2 HOURS

5 LARGE RUSSET POTATOES, PEELED AND SLICED THIN

1 SPANISH ONION, SLICED

½ CUP CANOLA OIL, PLUS MORE AS NEEDED

½ CUP OLIVE OIL

10 EGGS, AT ROOM TEMPERATURE

LARGE PINCH OF KOSHER SALT

1. Place the potatoes, onion, canola oil, and olive oil in a 12-inch cast-iron skillet. The potatoes should be submerged. If not, add more canola oil as needed. Bring to a gentle simmer over low heat and cook until the potatoes are tender, about 30 minutes. Remove the pan from heat and let cool slightly.

2. Use a slotted spoon to remove the potatoes and onion from the oil. Reserve the oil. Place the eggs and salt in a large bowl and whisk to combine. Add the potatoes and onion to the eggs.

3. Warm the skillet over high heat. Add ¼ cup of the reserved oil and swirl to coat the bottom and sides of the pan. Pour the egg-and-potato mixture into the pan and stir vigorously to ensure that the mixture does not stick to the sides. Cook for 1 minute and remove from heat. Place the pan over low heat, cover, and cook for 3 minutes.

4. Carefully invert the tortilla onto a large plate. Return it to the skillet, cook for 3 minutes, and then invert it onto the plate. Return it to the skillet and cook for another 3 minutes. Remove the tortilla from the pan and let it rest at room temperature for 1 hour before serving.

Spanish Tortilla
SEE PAGE 383

Sweet Potato Börek

YIELD: 24 SERVINGS | **ACTIVE TIME:** 45 MINUTES | **TOTAL TIME:** 2 HOURS

1 SWEET POTATO, PEELED AND CUBED

1 TABLESPOON EXTRA-VIRGIN OLIVE OIL

1½ CUPS CHOPPED ONIONS

4 GARLIC CLOVES, MINCED

1 TEASPOON GRATED FRESH GINGER

1 CUP WHITE WINE

7 EGGS

1 TEASPOON KOSHER SALT

½ TEASPOON BLACK PEPPER

¾ LB. FONTINA CHEESE, GRATED

1 CUP FULL-FAT GREEK YOGURT

⅓ CUP HEAVY CREAM

½ CUP CHOPPED FRESH MINT

ZEST OF 1 LEMON

½ CUP MILK

1 LB. FROZEN PHYLLO DOUGH, THAWED

2 TEASPOONS POPPY SEEDS

1. Place the sweet potato in a small saucepan and cover it with water. Bring to a boil, reduce the heat, and simmer until the sweet potato is very tender, 15 to 20 minutes. Drain the sweet potato and let it cool.

2. Place the olive oil in a large skillet and warm it over medium heat. Add the onions and cook, stirring occasionally, until they have softened, about 5 minutes. Add the garlic and ginger and cook, stirring continually, for 1 minute. Add the white wine and cook until it has evaporated, about 8 minutes. Remove the pan from heat and let the mixture cool.

3. Preheat the oven to 400°F. In a food processor, combine the sweet potato, onion mixture, 6 of the eggs, the salt, and pepper and blitz until smooth.

4. Place the Fontina, yogurt, heavy cream, mint, and lemon zest in a bowl and stir to combine. Place the milk and the remaining egg in a separate bowl and whisk until combined.

5. In a deep 13 x 9–inch baking pan, spread ¾ cup of the sweet potato puree evenly over the bottom. Place 5 sheets of phyllo on top and press down gently on them. Brush the top sheet of phyllo with the egg wash.

6. Repeat with the puree, phyllo, and egg wash and then sprinkle half of the cheese mixture over the phyllo. Top with another 5-sheet layer of phyllo and press down gently on it.

7. Repeat Steps 5 and 6.

8. Brush the top sheet of phyllo with the egg wash. Sprinkle the poppy seeds over the börek and place it in the oven. Bake until the top is puffy and golden brown, about 45 minutes.

9. Remove the börek from the oven and let it cool slightly before cutting and enjoying.

Bourekas

YIELD: 12 SERVINGS | **ACTIVE TIME:** 1 HOUR | **TOTAL TIME:** 1 HOUR AND 50 MINUTES

3 YUKON GOLD POTATOES, PEELED AND CUT INTO 1-INCH CUBES

2 TABLESPOONS EXTRA-VIRGIN OLIVE OIL

1 SMALL ONION, CHOPPED

1 GARLIC CLOVE, MINCED

⅛ TEASPOON FRESHLY GRATED NUTMEG

1 CUP RICOTTA CHEESE

1 CUP GRATED KASHKAVAL CHEESE

SALT AND PEPPER, TO TASTE

2 LARGE EGGS

½ (1 LB.) PACKAGE OF FROZEN PUFF PASTRY, THAWED

TOASTED SESAME SEEDS, FOR TOPPING

1. Place the potatoes in a stockpot and cover them by 1 inch with cold water. Bring to a boil over medium-high heat and cook until the potatoes are fork-tender, 20 to 25 minutes. Drain the potatoes, place them in a bowl, and mash them. Let them cool.

2. Place the olive oil in a large skillet and warm it over medium-high heat. Add the onion and cook, stirring occasionally, until it is starting to brown, about 7 minutes. Add the garlic and cook, stirring frequently, until fragrant, about 1 minute. Remove the pan from heat and set it aside.

3. Place the nutmeg and cheeses in a bowl and stir until combined.

4. Add the onion mixture and the cheese mixture to the mashed potatoes and stir until well combined. Season the mixture with salt and pepper and set it aside.

5. In a bowl, beat one of the eggs. While stirring the cool potato mixture, slowly incorporate the beaten egg.

6. Preheat the oven to 375°F and line a large baking sheet with parchment paper. Fill a bowl with water and place it beside your work surface.

7. Cut the puff pastry into 5-inch squares. Place a heaping tablespoon of filling in the center of each square. Dip your fingers in the water and moisten the edges of the squares, then fold in half vertically to form triangles. Pinch the edges to seal the pockets.

8. Beat the second egg and brush it over the tops of the bourekas. Sprinkle the sesame seeds on top.

9. Place the bourekas in the oven and bake until puffy and golden brown, about 30 minutes.

10. Remove from the oven and let the bourekas cool slightly before enjoying.

Handrajo

YIELD: 16 SERVINGS | **ACTIVE TIME:** 1 HOUR | **TOTAL TIME:** 1 HOUR AND 45 MINUTES

¼ CUP SUNFLOWER OIL

2 TABLESPOONS EXTRA-VIRGIN OLIVE OIL

2 MEDIUM EGGPLANTS, PEELED AND CUT INTO ½-INCH CUBES

1 TEASPOON KOSHER SALT, PLUS MORE TO TASTE

1 GARLIC CLOVE

2 ONIONS, FINELY DICED

3 TOMATOES, HALVED, PEELED, AND GRATED

1½ TEASPOONS SUGAR

½ TEASPOON SWEET PAPRIKA

½ TEASPOON BLACK PEPPER

2 (28 OZ.) PACKAGES OF PUFF PASTRY, THAWED (PREFERABLY BUTTER BASED)

1 EGG, BEATEN

LABNEH (SEE PAGE 183), FOR SERVING

1. Place the oils in a large skillet and warm over high heat. Add the eggplants to the pan in an even layer, season with ½ teaspoon of the salt, and cook, undisturbed, until the eggplants start to brown, about 5 minutes.

2. Add the garlic and onions and stir to combine. Cover the pan with a lid, reduce the heat to medium, and cook until the vegetables are soft, about 10 minutes. Remove the lid and cook for 5 more minutes, until all of the liquid has evaporated.

3. Stir in the tomatoes, sugar, paprika, pepper, and the remaining salt and cook until the flavors have melded, 5 to 7 minutes. As the mixture cooks, break up any large chunks with a wooden spoon.

4. Remove the pan from heat, discard the garlic clove, and let the mixture cool completely.

5. Preheat the oven to 425°F and position a rack in the middle. Line a baking sheet with parchment paper. Spread the sheets of puff pastry on a clean work surface and cut each sheet in half lengthwise; you should end up with four 10 x 7–inch rectangles.

6. Divide the filling among the pieces of puff pastry, spreading it on one half of their length and leaving about 1 inch of pastry uncovered at the edge. Fold the other half of the dough over the filling, bringing the edges of the rectangles together. Using a fork, press down along each edge of the rectangles to seal the pastry together. Carefully transfer each pastry to the prepared baking sheet and brush them with the beaten egg.

7. Place them in the oven and bake the handrajo until they are golden brown and crispy, 20 to 25 minutes.

8. Remove from the oven, cut the handrajo diagonally, and serve with Labneh.

Grilled Cantaloupe

YIELD: 4 SERVINGS | **ACTIVE TIME:** 20 MINUTES | **TOTAL TIME:** 20 MINUTES

1 CANTALOUPE

1 TABLESPOON EXTRA-VIRGIN OLIVE OIL

4 OZ. FRESH MOZZARELLA CHEESE, TORN

1 TABLESPOON BALSAMIC GLAZE (SEE PAGE 562)

FRESH PARSLEY, CHOPPED, FOR GARNISH

1. Prepare a gas or charcoal grill for high heat (about 500°F). Remove the rind from the cantaloupe, halve it, remove the seeds, and then cut the cantaloupe into ½-inch-thick slices.

2. Place the cantaloupe in a mixing bowl, add the oil, and toss to coat.

3. Place the cantaloupe on the grill and cook until lightly charred on both sides and warmed through.

4. To serve, pile the warm cantaloupe, top with the mozzarella, and drizzle the Balsamic Glaze over the top. Garnish with parsley and enjoy.

Stuffed Avocados

YIELD: 2 SERVINGS | **ACTIVE TIME:** 45 MINUTES | **TOTAL TIME:** 1 HOUR AND 30 MINUTES

1 CUP FINELY DICED BUTTERNUT SQUASH

2 TABLESPOONS EXTRA-VIRGIN OLIVE OIL

1 TEASPOON KOSHER SALT

1 TEASPOON BLACK PEPPER

2 RIPE AVOCADOS

½ CUP CRUMBLED FETA CHEESE

2 TABLESPOONS SMOKED EGG AIOLI (SEE PAGE 149)

1. Preheat the oven to 450°F. In a bowl, combine the squash with 1 tablespoon of the olive oil, the salt, and pepper. Transfer the squash to a baking sheet, place it in the oven, and roast until lightly browned and soft enough to mash, 15 to 20 minutes. Remove the squash from the oven and set it aside.

2. Halve the avocados and remove their seeds, reserving the skins. Using a spoon, remove the avocado flesh and place it in a bowl. Add the feta and roasted squash and mash the mixture until it is smooth and well combined.

3. Fill the avocado skins with the mixture and lightly brush the top of each one with the remaining oil. Place them on a baking sheet and place them in the oven.

4. Roast until the tops of the avocados are browned, 10 to 15 minutes. Remove from the oven, drizzle the aioli over the tops, and enjoy.

Pomegranate-Glazed Figs & Cheese

YIELD: 4 SERVINGS | **ACTIVE TIME:** 35 MINUTES | **TOTAL TIME:** 1 HOUR

2 CUPS POMEGRANATE JUICE

1 TEASPOON FENNEL SEEDS

1 TEASPOON BLACK PEPPERCORNS

1 BAY LEAF

PINCH OF KOSHER SALT, PLUS MORE TO TASTE

½ CUP RICOTTA CHEESE

½ CUP MASCARPONE CHEESE

⅛ TEASPOON FRESHLY GROUND BLACK PEPPER

12 FRESH FIGS

1 TEASPOON CASTER SUGAR (SUPERFINE)

POMEGRANATE SEEDS, FOR GARNISH

1. Place the pomegranate juice, fennel seeds, peppercorns, bay leaf, and salt in a small saucepan and simmer the mixture over medium-high heat until it has been reduced to ⅓ cup.

2. Strain and let the glaze cool completely.

3. In a bowl, combine the cheeses. Add 1 tablespoon of the glaze and season the mixture with salt and the pepper. Place the mixture in a pastry bag that has been fitted with a plain ½-inch tip and set it aside.

4. Preheat the broiler in the oven. Cut the figs in half from tip to stem and place them in a heatproof dish, cut side up. Brush the cut sides with some of the glaze and dust with the caster sugar.

5. Pipe a ½-inch-wide and 6-inch-long strip of the cheese mixture on four plates.

6. Place the figs under the broiler until glazed and just warmed through, about 5 minutes.

7. To serve, arrange six fig halves on top of each strip of cheese, garnish with pomegranate seeds, and drizzle any remaining glaze over the top.

Kuku Sabzi

YIELD: 4 SERVINGS | **ACTIVE TIME:** 15 MINUTES | **TOTAL TIME:** 25 MINUTES

4 EGGS

1 TEASPOON CUMIN

1 TEASPOON BLACK PEPPER

1 TEASPOON KOSHER SALT

5 SCALLIONS, TRIMMED AND SLICED THIN

1 CUP CHOPPED FRESH PARSLEY

1 CUP CHOPPED FRESH CILANTRO

1 CUP CHOPPED FRESH DILL

2 TABLESPOONS AVOCADO OIL

1. In a large bowl, whisk the eggs until smooth. Add the remaining ingredients, except for the oil, and whisk until incorporated.

2. Place the avocado oil in a medium nonstick skillet and warm it over medium-low heat. Pour the egg mixture into the pan and let it cook for 1 minute.

3. Reduce the heat to low, cover the pan, and cook until the frittata begins to set and the bottom is lightly golden brown, about 6 minutes. Flip the frittata using a spatula (or slide it onto a plate and invert it back into the pan) and cook until it is completely set, about 2 minutes more.

4. Transfer the frittata to a platter, slice, and enjoy.

Roasted Tomato Caprese

YIELD: 2 SERVINGS | **ACTIVE TIME:** 25 MINUTES | **TOTAL TIME:** 45 MINUTES

½ CUP FRESH BASIL

½ CUP FRESH SPINACH

2 GARLIC CLOVES

½ CUP EXTRA-VIRGIN OLIVE OIL

½ CUP FRESHLY GRATED PARMESAN CHEESE

½ CUP BALSAMIC VINEGAR

2 TOMATOES

6 OZ. FRESH MOZZARELLA CHEESE, TORN

1. Preheat the oven to 450°F. Place the basil, spinach, garlic, 7 tablespoons of the olive oil, and Parmesan cheese in a food processor and blitz until smooth. Set the mixture aside.

2. Place the vinegar in a small saucepan and bring it to a simmer over medium-high heat. Reduce the heat to medium and cook the vinegar until it has been reduced by half, 6 to 8 minutes. Remove the pan from heat and let the reduction cool completely.

3. Cut the tomatoes into ⅛-inch-thick slices and place them on a baking sheet in a single layer. Drizzle the remaining olive oil over the top.

4. Distribute the mozzarella around the tomatoes, place the pan in the oven, and bake until the cheese and tomatoes start to brown, about 10 minutes. Remove the pan from the oven and let the tomatoes and mozzarella cool.

5. To serve, arrange the tomatoes and mozzarella on a plate, spoon the pesto over them, and drizzle the balsamic reduction over the top.

Roasted Pepper Salad

YIELD: 6 SERVINGS | **ACTIVE TIME:** 10 MINUTES | **TOTAL TIME:** 30 MINUTES

3 RED BELL PEPPERS

2 YELLOW BELL PEPPERS

1 GREEN BELL PEPPER

½ CUP PLUS 1 TABLESPOON AVOCADO OIL

½ ONION, SLICED THIN

1 TEASPOON WHITE VINEGAR

¼ TEASPOON KOSHER SALT

⅛ TEASPOON BLACK PEPPER

½ TEASPOON CUMIN

¼ BUNCH OF FRESH CILANTRO, CHOPPED

1. Roast the peppers on a grill or over the flame of a gas burner until they are charred all over and tender. Place the peppers in a baking dish, cover it with plastic wrap, and let the peppers steam for 10 minutes.

2. Remove the charred skins and the seed pods from the peppers. Slice the roasted peppers into strips and set them aside. Discard the charred skins and seed pods.

3. Place 1 tablespoon of the avocado oil in a saucepan and warm it over medium heat. Add the onion and cook, stirring occasionally, until it has softened, about 5 minutes. Remove the pan from heat and let the onion cool.

4. Place the peppers, onion, remaining avocado oil, vinegar, salt, pepper, cumin, and cilantro in a bowl, stir until combined, and enjoy.

Bread & Butter Pickles

YIELD: ½ CUP | **ACTIVE TIME:** 5 MINUTES | **TOTAL TIME:** 6 HOURS

2 PERSIAN CUCUMBERS, SLICED THIN

1 SMALL ONION, SLICED THIN

2 JALAPEÑO CHILE PEPPERS, SLICED THIN

4 SPRIGS OF FRESH DILL

2 TABLESPOONS CORIANDER SEEDS

2 TABLESPOONS MUSTARD SEEDS

2 TEASPOONS CELERY SALT

2 CUPS DISTILLED WHITE VINEGAR

1 CUP SUGAR

2 TABLESPOONS KOSHER SALT

1. Place the cucumbers, onion, jalapeños, dill, coriander seeds, mustard seeds, and celery salt in a mason jar.

2. Place the vinegar, sugar, and salt in a medium saucepan and bring it to a boil, stirring to dissolve the sugar and salt. Carefully pour the brine into the jar, filling it all the way to the top. If you want to can these pickles, see the sidebar on page 396. If you do not want to can the pickles, let the mixture cool completely before sealing and storing in the refrigerator, where they will keep for up to 1 week.

Pickled Pineapple

YIELD: 4 SERVINGS | **ACTIVE TIME:** 40 MINUTES | **TOTAL TIME:** 2 DAYS

2 STAR ANISE PODS

½ CINNAMON STICK

2 DRIED CHILES DE ARBOL

2¼ CUPS APPLE CIDER VINEGAR

7 TABLESPOONS WHITE VINEGAR

3 TABLESPOONS SUGAR

SALT, TO TASTE

1 PINEAPPLE, PEELED, CORED, AND SLICED

1. Preheat a gas or charcoal grill to medium heat (400°F).

2. Place the star anise, cinnamon stick, and chiles in a saucepan and toast until they are fragrant, about 2 minutes, shaking the pan frequently. Add the vinegars and sugar, generously season with salt, and bring to a boil, stirring to dissolve the sugar.

3. Pour the brine into a sterilized mason jar.

4. Place the pineapple on the grill and grill until charred on both sides, about 8 minutes. Add the pineapple to the brine while it is still warm and let the mixture cool to room temperature. Cover and refrigerate for 2 days before using.

Pickled Rhubarb

YIELD: 4 SERVINGS | **ACTIVE TIME:** 10 MINUTES | **TOTAL TIME:** 2 HOURS

½ CUP RED WINE

½ CUP RED WINE VINEGAR

½ CUP SUGAR

2 SPRIGS OF FRESH MINT

ZEST AND JUICE OF 1 ORANGE

1 CUP FINELY DICED RHUBARB

1. Place the red wine, red wine vinegar, and sugar in a medium saucepan and bring it to a boil.

2. Stir in the remaining ingredients and remove the pan from heat. Pour the mixture into a sterilized mason jar and let it cool to room temperature.

3. If canning, see page 396. If not, chill it in the refrigerator for 1 hour before serving.

Strawberry Chips

YIELD: 4 SERVINGS | **ACTIVE TIME:** 15 MINUTES | **TOTAL TIME:** 3 HOURS

½ CUP WATER

½ CUP SUGAR

1 TEASPOON PURE VANILLA EXTRACT

1 CUP HULLED AND THINLY SLICED STRAWBERRIES

1. Place the water and sugar in a small saucepan and bring to a boil, stirring to dissolve the sugar. Stir in the vanilla, remove the pan from heat, and let the syrup cool.

2. Dip the strawberries in the syrup and place them on a parchment-lined baking sheet. Place in a food dehydrator set at 140ºF and dehydrate for 1 hour.

3. Turn the strawberries over and dehydrate for another 1½ hours.

4. Remove the strawberries from the dehydrator and either serve immediately or store in an airtight container.

Canning 101

Bring a pot of water to a boil. Place your mason jars in the water for 15 to 20 minutes to sterilize them. Do not boil the mason jar lids, as this can prevent them from creating a proper seal when the time comes.

Bring water to a boil in the large canning pot. Fill the sterilized mason jars with whatever you are canning. Place the lids on the jars and secure the bands tightly. Place the jars in the boiling water for 40 minutes. Use a pair of canning tongs to remove the jars from the boiling water and let them cool. As they are cooling, you should hear the classic "ping and pop" sound of the lids creating a seal.

After 6 hours, check the lids. There should be no give in them and they should be suctioned onto the jars. Discard any lids and food that did not seal properly.

Pickled Avocado

YIELD: 4 SERVINGS | **ACTIVE TIME:** 15 MINUTES | **TOTAL TIME:** 4 HOURS AND 30 MINUTES

1 CUP WHITE WINE VINEGAR

1 CUP WATER

⅓ CUP SUGAR

1 TABLESPOON KOSHER SALT

1 TEASPOON RED PEPPER FLAKES

FLESH OF 2 FIRM AVOCADOS

1 GARLIC CLOVE, SMASHED

5 SPRIGS OF FRESH CILANTRO

1. Place the vinegar, water, sugar, salt, and red pepper flakes in a medium saucepan and bring to a boil, stirring to dissolve the sugar. Remove the pan from heat and let the brine cool completely.

2. Cut the avocados into wedges and place them in a sterilized mason jar along with the garlic and cilantro. Pour the cooled brine into the jar. If canning, see page 396. If not, place the jar in the refrigerator and let the avocado pickle for at least 4 hours before serving.

Fried Mustard Greens

YIELD: 4 SERVINGS | **ACTIVE TIME:** 20 MINUTES | **TOTAL TIME:** 30 MINUTES

1 BUNCH OF MUSTARD GREENS

4 CUPS CANOLA OIL

SALT, TO TASTE

1. Remove the mustard green leaves from their stems and rinse them well. Pat them dry with paper towels and set them aside.

2. Place the canola oil in a wide and deep cast-iron skillet and warm it to 300°F over medium heat. Add the greens and fry, turning them over once, until crispy, 1 to 2 minutes. Remove with a slotted spoon, place them on a paper towel–lined plate to drain, and season with salt. Serve once they have cooled slightly.

Duxelles

YIELD: 4 SERVINGS | **ACTIVE TIME:** 5 MINUTES | **TOTAL TIME:** 15 MINUTES

1 TABLESPOON EXTRA-VIRGIN OLIVE OIL

3 PORTOBELLO MUSHROOMS, FINELY DICED

½ SHALLOT, MINCED

2 TABLESPOONS FRESH THYME, CHOPPED

SALT AND PEPPER, TO TASTE

1. Place the olive oil in a large skillet and warm it over medium heat. When the oil starts to shimmer, add the mushrooms and cook, stirring frequently, until they have released all of their liquid and start to brown, about 8 minutes.

2. Stir in the shallot and thyme, cook, stirring occasionally, for 2 minutes, and transfer the mixture to a food processor. Pulse until the desired texture has been achieved.

3. Season with salt and pepper and serve with toasted bread.

Pickled Red Onion

YIELD: 4 SERVINGS | **ACTIVE TIME:** 15 MINUTES | **TOTAL TIME:** 4 HOURS AND 30 MINUTES

1 RED ONION, SLICED THIN

1 TABLESPOON BLACK PEPPERCORNS

PINCH OF KOSHER SALT

1 CUP RED WINE

1 CUP RED WINE VINEGAR

1 CUP SUGAR

1. Place the onion, peppercorns, and salt in a large mason jar.

2. Combine the wine, vinegar, and sugar in a saucepan and bring the mixture to a boil, stirring to dissolve the sugar.

3. Pour the brine into the mason jar and let it cool to room temperature. To can the pickled onion, see page 396. If not, chill in the refrigerator for at least 4 hours before serving.

Stuffed Prunes

YIELD: 4 SERVINGS | **ACTIVE TIME:** 10 MINUTES | **TOTAL TIME:** 10 MINUTES

15 DRIED PRUNES

3 OZ. BLUE CHEESE, CRUMBLED

1. Cut a slit in the top of each prune, stuff them with the blue cheese, and either serve immediately or chill in the refrigerator. If refrigerating, let the stuffed prunes come to room temperature before serving.

Eggplant Rings

YIELD: 4 SERVINGS | **ACTIVE TIME:** 40 MINUTES | **TOTAL TIME:** 1 HOUR

1 LARGE EGGPLANT, TRIMMED AND SLICED

2 EGGS, BEATEN

1 CUP ALL-PURPOSE FLOUR

1 CUP PANKO

1 TABLESPOON KOSHER SALT

1 TABLESPOON BLACK PEPPER

CANOLA OIL, AS NEEDED

¼ CUP RED ZHUG (SEE PAGE 178)

¼ CUP KETCHUP

1. Cut the centers out of the slices of eggplant, creating rings that have an about an inch of eggplant inside.

2. Place the eggs, flour, and panko in separate bowls. Add the salt and pepper to the bowl of panko and stir to combine. Dredge an eggplant ring in the flour, then the eggs, followed by the panko, until the ring is entirely coated. Place the coated rings on a baking sheet.

3. Add canola oil to a cast-iron skillet until it is about 1 inch deep and warm it to 375ºF over medium-high heat. Working in batches to avoid crowding the pan, gently slip the eggplant rings into the oil and fry until browned and crispy all over, about 4 minutes, turning as necessary. Place the cooked rings on a paper towel–lined plate to drain.

4. Place the zhug and ketchup in a small bowl, stir to combine, and serve alongside the eggplant rings.

Corn Fritters

YIELD: 4 SERVINGS | **ACTIVE TIME:** 20 MINUTES | **TOTAL TIME:** 40 MINUTES

1 EGG, BEATEN

1 TEASPOON SUGAR

½ TEASPOON KOSHER SALT

1 TABLESPOON UNSALTED BUTTER, MELTED

2 TEASPOONS BAKING POWDER

1 CUP ALL-PURPOSE FLOUR

⅔ CUP MILK

2 CUPS CORN KERNELS, AT ROOM TEMPERATURE

¼ CUP EXTRA-VIRGIN OLIVE OIL

1. Place the egg, sugar, salt, butter, baking powder, flour, and milk in a mixing bowl and stir until thoroughly combined. Add the corn and stir to incorporate.

2. Place the oil in a 12-inch cast-iron skillet and warm over medium-high heat. When the oil starts to shimmer, drop heaping tablespoons of batter into the skillet and gently press down to flatten them into disks. Work in batches to avoid crowding the pan. Cook until the fritters are browned on both sides, about 3 minutes per side. Transfer to a paper towel–lined plate and tent with aluminum foil to keep them warm while you cook the rest of the fritters. Serve once all the fritters have been cooked.

Stuffed Mushrooms

YIELD: 8 SERVINGS | **ACTIVE TIME:** 30 MINUTES | **TOTAL TIME:** 1 HOUR AND 30 MINUTES

10 OZ. BUTTON MUSHROOMS, STEMS REMOVED

¼ CUP EXTRA-VIRGIN OLIVE OIL, PLUS MORE AS NEEDED

3 TABLESPOONS BALSAMIC VINEGAR

SALT AND PEPPER, TO TASTE

½ LB. GROUND ITALIAN SAUSAGE

2 YELLOW ONIONS, GRATED

5 GARLIC CLOVES, GRATED

½ LB. CREAM CHEESE, SOFTENED

1 CUP SHREDDED ASIAGO CHEESE

1. Preheat the oven to 350ºF. Place the mushrooms, olive oil, and balsamic vinegar in a mixing bowl and toss to coat. Season the mixture with salt and pepper and then place it on a baking sheet. Place in the oven and bake until the mushrooms are just starting to brown, about 25 minutes. Remove from the oven and set them aside.

2. Coat the bottom of a large skillet with olive oil and warm it over medium heat. When the oil starts to shimmer, add the sausage and cook, breaking it up with a fork as it browns, until cooked through, about 8 minutes. Remove the sausage from the pan and place it in a mixing bowl.

3. Preheat the oven to 375ºF. Place the onions in the skillet, reduce the heat to medium-low, and cook until dark brown, about 15 minutes. Stir in the garlic, sauté for 1 minute, and then add the mixture to the bowl containing the sausage. Add the cheeses to the bowl containing the sausage and stir to combine.

4. Arrange the mushrooms on the baking sheet so that their cavities are facing up. Fill the cavities with the sausage mixture, place the mushrooms in the oven, and bake until the cheese has melted and is golden brown, about 25 minutes. Remove from the oven and let them cool slightly before serving.

Blistered Shishito Peppers

YIELD: 6 SERVINGS | **ACTIVE TIME:** 5 MINUTES | **TOTAL TIME:** 10 MINUTES

EXTRA-VIRGIN OLIVE OIL, AS NEEDED

2 LBS. SHISHITO PEPPERS

SALT, TO TASTE

1 LEMON, CUT INTO WEDGES

1. Add olive oil to a 12-inch cast-iron skillet until it is ¼ inch deep and warm it over medium heat.

2. When the oil is shimmering, add the peppers and cook, while turning once or twice, until they are blistered and golden brown, about 10 minutes. Take care not to crowd the pan with the peppers, working in batches if necessary.

3. Transfer the blistered peppers to a paper towel–lined plate. Season with salt and squeeze the lemon wedges over them before serving.

Asparagus Tart

YIELD: 8 SERVINGS | **ACTIVE TIME:** 15 MINUTES | **TOTAL TIME:** 45 MINUTES

½ TEASPOON KOSHER SALT, PLUS MORE TO TASTE

1 LB. ASPARAGUS, TRIMMED

1½ CUPS RICOTTA CHEESE

¼ CUP EXTRA-VIRGIN OLIVE OIL

2 TABLESPOONS HEAVY CREAM

2 EGG YOLKS

1 TEASPOON CHOPPED FRESH ROSEMARY

1 SAVORY TART SHELL (SEE PAGE 558)

1. Preheat the oven to 350°F. Bring water to a boil in a large saucepan. Add salt until the water tastes just shy of seawater, add the asparagus, and cook for 2 minutes. Drain the asparagus, pat it dry, and set it aside.

2. Place all of the remaining ingredients, aside from the tart shell, in a mixing bowl and stir to combine. Distribute the mixture evenly in the tart shell, arrange the asparagus on top, and place the tart in the oven. Bake until the custard is set and golden brown, about 25 minutes.

3. Remove the tart from the oven and serve warm or at room temperature.

Pickled Green Tomatoes

YIELD: 2 PINTS | **ACTIVE TIME:** 15 MINUTES | **TOTAL TIME:** 24 HOURS

1½ CUPS APPLE CIDER VINEGAR

¾ CUP WATER

2 TEASPOONS SUGAR

½ TEASPOON WHOLE BLACK PEPPERCORNS

½ TEASPOON CORIANDER SEEDS

½ TEASPOON CARAWAY SEEDS

½ TEASPOON CUMIN SEEDS

3 ALLSPICE BERRIES

2 BAY LEAVES

2 TABLESPOONS KOSHER SALT

1 LB. SMALL GREEN TOMATOES, SLICED

¼ WHITE ONION, SLICED THIN

1. Combine the vinegar, water, sugar, spices, and salt in a saucepan. Bring the mixture to a boil, stirring to dissolve the sugar.

2. Place the tomatoes and onion in a large mason jar and pour the brine over the vegetables. Let the mixture cool completely.

3. To can the tomatoes, see page 396. If not canning, cover and store in the refrigerator overnight before enjoying.

Marinated Olives

YIELD: 8 SERVINGS | **ACTIVE TIME:** 20 MINUTES | **TOTAL TIME:** 2 HOURS AND 30 MINUTES

1½ LBS. ASSORTED OLIVES

2 TEASPOONS LIGHTLY CRACKED CORIANDER SEEDS

1 TEASPOON LIGHTLY CRACKED FENNEL SEEDS

¾ CUP EXTRA-VIRGIN OLIVE OIL

2 TABLESPOONS RED WINE VINEGAR

4 GARLIC CLOVES, SLICED THIN

1½ TEASPOONS CHOPPED ROSEMARY

1½ TEASPOONS THYME

4 BAY LEAVES, TORN

1 SMALL DRIED RED CHILE PEPPER, STEM AND SEEDS REMOVED, CHOPPED

2 STRIPS OF LEMON ZEST

1. Rinse any dark olives under cold water so their juices don't discolor the other olives. Place all of the olives in a colander and drain them. Transfer the olives to a wide-mouthed jar and set them aside.

2. Warm a dry skillet over medium-high heat. Add the coriander and fennel seeds and toast until very fragrant, about 2 minutes, stirring occasionally. Add the olive oil and vinegar and cook for 1 minute.

3. Remove the pan from heat and add all the remaining ingredients. Stir to combine and let the mixture cool completely.

4. Pour the marinade over the olives, cover, and shake the jar to coat the olives.

5. Chill the olives in the refrigerator for 2 hours before serving. If preparing the olives a few days ahead of time, shake the jar daily to redistribute the seasonings.

Roasted Plums with Tahini Dressing

YIELD: 4 SERVINGS | **ACTIVE TIME:** 20 MINUTES | **TOTAL TIME:** 2 HOURS AND 30 MINUTES

2 LBS. PLUMS, HALVED AND PITTED

2 TABLESPOONS AVOCADO OIL

1½ TEASPOONS FINE SEA SALT, PLUS MORE TO TASTE

¼ TEASPOON BLACK PEPPER

1 TABLESPOON FRESH THYME OR OREGANO

3 TABLESPOONS FRESH LEMON JUICE, PLUS MORE TO TASTE

1 CUP TAHINI

1 ICE CUBE

MALDON SEA SALT, TO TASTE

1. Preheat the oven to 400°F and line a baking sheet with parchment paper. Arrange the plums, cut side up, on the baking sheet, drizzle the avocado oil over them, and sprinkle the fine sea salt, pepper, and herbs over them. Toss to coat.

2. Place the baking sheet in the oven and reduce the heat to 250°F. Roast until the plums are very soft and starting to caramelize, about 2 hours. Remove the plums from the oven and let them cool slightly.

3. Place the lemon juice, tahini, ¾ cup water, a few pinches of fine sea salt, and the ice cube in a mixing bowl and whisk vigorously until the dressing comes together. It should lighten in color and thicken enough that it holds an edge when the whisk is dragged through it. Remove the ice cube, if any of it remains, taste, and adjust the seasoning as necessary.

4. Arrange the plums on a plate, drizzle the dressing over the top, and sprinkle the Maldon sea salt over the top.

Okra & Lemons with Za'atar

YIELD: 4 SERVINGS | **ACTIVE TIME:** 20 MINUTES | **TOTAL TIME:** 20 MINUTES

2 TABLESPOONS AVOCADO OIL

1 LB. OKRA, TRIMMED

1 LEMON, CUT INTO WEDGES

SALT, TO TASTE

ZA'ATAR SEASONING, TO TASTE

FRESH PARSLEY, CHOPPED, FOR GARNISH

1. Place the avocado oil in a large skillet and warm it over high heat. Add the okra and lemon wedges, season with salt, and cook, stirring frequently, until the okra and lemon begin to char.

2. Remove the pan from heat and stir in the za'atar. Place the mixture in a serving bowl, garnish with parsley, and enjoy.

Falafel

YIELD: 4 SERVINGS | **ACTIVE TIME:** 30 MINUTES | **TOTAL TIME:** 2 HOURS

1 (14 OZ.) CAN OF CHICKPEAS, DRAINED AND RINSED

½ RED ONION, CHOPPED

1 CUP FRESH PARSLEY, CHOPPED

1 CUP FRESH CILANTRO, CHOPPED

3 BUNCHES OF SCALLIONS, TRIMMED AND CHOPPED

1 JALAPEÑO CHILE PEPPER, STEM AND SEEDS REMOVED, CHOPPED

3 GARLIC CLOVES

1 TEASPOON CUMIN

1 TEASPOON KOSHER SALT, PLUS MORE TO TASTE

½ TEASPOON CARDAMOM

¼ TEASPOON BLACK PEPPER

2 TABLESPOONS CHICKPEA FLOUR

½ TEASPOON BAKING SODA

CANOLA OIL, AS NEEDED

HUMMUS (SEE PAGE 112), FOR SERVING

1. Line a baking sheet with parchment paper. Place all of the ingredients, except for the canola oil, in a food processor and blitz until pureed.

2. Scoop ¼-cup portions of the puree onto the baking sheet and place it in the refrigerator for 1 hour.

3. Add canola oil to a Dutch oven until it is 2 inches deep and warm it to 320°F over medium heat.

4. Working in batches, add the falafel to the oil and fry, turning occasionally, until they are golden brown, about 6 minutes. Transfer the cooked falafel to a paper towel–lined plate to drain.

5. When all of the falafel have been cooked, serve with the Hummus.

Kale Chips

YIELD: 4 SERVINGS | **ACTIVE TIME:** 5 MINUTES | **TOTAL TIME:** 15 MINUTES

1 BUNCH OF KALE, STEMS REMOVED

1 TEASPOON KOSHER SALT

½ TEASPOON BLACK PEPPER

½ TEASPOON PAPRIKA

½ TEASPOON DRIED PARSLEY

½ TEASPOON DRIED BASIL

¼ TEASPOON DRIED THYME

¼ TEASPOON DRIED SAGE

2 TABLESPOONS EXTRA-VIRGIN OLIVE OIL

1. Preheat the oven to 400°F. Tear the kale leaves into small pieces and place them in a mixing bowl. Add the remaining ingredients and work the mixture with your hands until the kale pieces are evenly coated.

2. Divide the seasoned kale between two parchment-lined baking sheets so that it sits on each one in an even layer. Place them in the oven and bake until crispy, 6 to 8 minutes. Remove the kale chips and let them cool before serving.

Falafel
SEE PAGE 410

Fried Spring Rolls

YIELD: 4 TO 6 SERVINGS | **ACTIVE TIME:** 30 MINUTES | **TOTAL TIME:** 1 HOUR

2 OZ. GLASS NOODLES

2 CARROTS, PEELED AND GRATED

½ CUP MINCED WOOD EAR MUSHROOMS

3 TABLESPOONS MINCED SHALLOTS

2 GARLIC CLOVES, MINCED

1½ TEASPOONS GRATED GINGER

1 EGG WHITE

1½ TEASPOONS FISH SAUCE

2 TABLESPOONS CHOPPED FRESH CILANTRO

½ TEASPOON WHITE PEPPER

1 TEASPOON SUGAR

1½ TABLESPOONS SALT

¼ CUP WARM WATER

24 DRIED RICE PAPER WRAPPERS

CANOLA OIL, AS NEEDED

NUOC CHAM (SEE PAGE 135), FOR SERVING

1. Line a baking sheet with parchment paper. Place the glass noodles in a bowl of room-temperature water and soak them until pliable, 20 to 30 minutes. Drain the noodles and cut them into 3-inch lengths with kitchen scissors.

2. In a mixing bowl, combine the noodles with the carrots, mushrooms, shallots, garlic, ginger, egg white, fish sauce, cilantro, white pepper, sugar, and salt.

3. Place the warm water in a bowl and submerge a rice wrapper in the water. You want the wrapper to soften just slightly, taking care not to let it become too soft.

4. Form 3 tablespoons of the filling into a log in the middle of the wrapper. Roll the wrapper up tightly, pressing down to prevent any air pockets from forming. Lightly press down on each end of the filling to keep it tight. Fold both ends of the wrapper toward the middle. Place the spring roll on the baking sheet and repeat with the remaining wrappers and filling, making sure to leave enough space between the spring rolls on the baking sheet that they do not stick together.

5. When all of the spring rolls have been assembled, refrigerate them for 2 hours.

6. Add canola oil to a Dutch oven until it is about 2 inches deep and warm it to 350°F. Working in batches to avoid crowding the pot, gently slip the spring rolls into the oil and fry until they are crispy and golden brown, 4 to 6 minutes. Place the fried spring rolls on a paper towel–lined plate and let them drain before serving with Nuoc Cham.

Steamed Daikon Cake

YIELD: 4 SERVINGS | **ACTIVE TIME**: 30 MINUTES | **TOTAL TIME:** 1 HOUR AND 30 MINUTES

3 CUPS GRATED DAIKON

2 CUPS CHICKEN STOCK (SEE PAGE 552)

2 TABLESPOONS CANOLA OIL, PLUS MORE AS NEEDED

1 TABLESPOON DRIED SHRIMP, SOAKED UNTIL SOFT AND COARSELY CHOPPED

½ CUP FINELY CHOPPED LAP CHEONG

1 TABLESPOON DICED CHOAN CHOY (SALTED TURNIP)

1 TEASPOON KOSHER SALT

¼ CUP CHOPPED SCALLIONS

¼ CUP COARSELY CHOPPED CILANTRO

1½ CUPS RICE FLOUR

1. Place the daikon and stock in a medium saucepan and bring to a boil. Cook the daikon until it is tender and drain, reserving the cooking liquid.

2. Place the oil, shrimp, sausage, turnip, and salt in a large skillet and warm the mixture over medium heat. Add most of the scallions and cilantro and stir until well distributed. Remove the pan from heat and set the mixture aside.

3. Place the rice flour and some of reserved cooking liquid in a bowl and stir until well combined. Stir in the shrimp-and-sausage mixture and incorporate more of the reserved cooking liquid until the mixture comes together as a medium-thin batter.

4. Bring a few inches of water to a simmer in a large saucepan. Line an 8-inch cake pan with parchment paper and lightly coat it with canola oil. Pour the batter into the pan and place the pan in a steaming basket. Place the steaming basket over the simmering water and steam until it is set, 30 to 45 minutes. Check the water level occasionally to make sure it has not evaporated, adding more water as needed.

5. Remove the cake from the steaming basket and let it cool for 20 minutes.

6. Run a knife around the edge of the cake pan and invert the cake onto a piece of parchment paper. Remove the parchment that was at the bottom of the cake pan. Slice the cake, top with the remaining scallions and cilantro, and enjoy.

Shiitake Siu Mai

YIELD: 6 TO 8 SERVINGS | **ACTIVE TIME:** 45 MINUTES | **TOTAL TIME:** 1 HOUR AND 30 MINUTES

8 SHIITAKE MUSHROOM CAPS, MINCED

4 SCALLIONS, TRIMMED AND SLICED THIN

¼ RED BELL PEPPER, MINCED

¼ CUP RAISINS

¼ CUP PINE NUTS, TOASTED

¼ CUP CANNED CORN

1 TABLESPOON SOY SAUCE, PLUS MORE FOR SERVING

1 TABLESPOON SHAOXING RICE WINE OR DRY SHERRY

1 TEASPOON FISH SAUCE

1 TEASPOON TOASTED SESAME OIL

2 TEASPOONS CORNSTARCH

½ TEASPOON SUGAR

½ TEASPOON WHITE PEPPER

36 ROUND WONTON WRAPPERS (SEE PAGE 560)

CABBAGE LEAVES, AS NEEDED

CARROTS, PEELED AND MINCED, FOR GARNISH

1. Place all of the ingredients, except for the wrappers, cabbage leaves, and carrots, in a mixing bowl and stir until well combined.

2. Place a wrapper in a cupped hand and fill it with enough of the mixture to fill the wrapper to the top. Flatten the filling with a butter knife and gently tighten the wrapper around the filling, forming a rough cylindrical shape with a flat bottom. Place the filled dumplings on a parchment-lined baking sheet and repeat with the remaining wrappers and filling.

3. Place a few inches of water in a large saucepan and bring to a boil. Line a steaming basket with cabbage leaves and then add the siu mai, leaving ½ inch between each of the dumplings and also between the dumplings and the edge of the steaming basket. Place the steaming basket over the boiling water, cover, and steam until the dumplings are cooked through, tender, and still chewy, about 10 minutes.

4. Transfer the steamed dumplings to a warm platter, garnish with the carrots, and serve with additional soy sauce.

Shiitake Siu Mai
SEE PAGE 417

Peppers Stuffed with Tuna

YIELD: 6 SERVINGS | **ACTIVE TIME:** 15 MINUTES | **TOTAL TIME:** 45 MINUTES

1 LB. MINIATURE BELL PEPPERS

1 GARLIC CLOVE, PEELED

1 TABLESPOON CAPERS, DRAINED AND RINSED

1 (6 OZ.) CAN OF TUNA IN OLIVE OIL, DRAINED

1 TEASPOON DIJON MUSTARD

2 TABLESPOONS EXTRA-VIRGIN OLIVE OIL

2 TEASPOONS FRESH LEMON JUICE, PLUS MORE TO TASTE

1 TEASPOON CHOPPED FRESH ROSEMARY

2 TEASPOONS CHOPPED FRESH PARSLEY

1 ANCHOVY FILLET, RINSED, BONED, AND MINCED

1 TEASPOON APPLE CIDER VINEGAR

SALT AND PEPPER, TO TASTE

1. Preheat the oven to 425°F and line a baking sheet with aluminum foil. Place the peppers on the baking sheet, place them in the oven, and roast until soft and lightly charred, 10 to 15 minutes, turning them once or twice. As the peppers will be different sizes, there will be some variance between how quickly they cook, so make sure to keep an eye on them and remove them as they become ready. After removing the peppers from the oven, let them cool.

2. Use a mortar and pestle to grind the garlic and capers into a paste.

3. Place the tuna in a mixing bowl and incorporate the mustard, olive oil, lemon juice, rosemary, parsley, anchovy, vinegar, and garlic paste one at a time. Taste and season with salt and pepper.

4. When the peppers have cooled, slice off the tops, remove the seeds and stems, and discard them. Fill the peppers with the tuna mixture and either serve or store in the refrigerator, letting the peppers come to room temperature before serving.

Keftes de Espinaca

YIELD: 12 SERVINGS | **ACTIVE TIME:** 15 MINUTES | **TOTAL TIME:** 30 MINUTES

½ CUP PLUS 1 TABLESPOON AVOCADO OIL

1 ONION, MINCED

½ TEASPOON GRATED GARLIC

10 OZ. FRESH SPINACH

1 LARGE EGG

1 CUP MASHED POTATOES

½ CUP BREAD CRUMBS

1 TEASPOON KOSHER SALT

¼ TEASPOON BLACK PEPPER

PINCH OF CAYENNE PEPPER

1. Place the tablespoon of avocado oil in a large skillet and warm it over medium heat. Add the onion and cook, stirring frequently, until it starts to soften, about 5 minutes.

2. Add the garlic and cook until fragrant, about 1 minute. Add half of the spinach, cover the pan, and cook until the spinach has wilted. Add the remaining spinach, cover the pan again, and cook until all of the spinach has wilted.

3. Transfer the mixture to a fine-mesh strainer and gently press down on the mixture to remove excess moisture. Transfer the mixture to a cutting board and roughly chop it.

4. Place the mixture in a mixing bowl. Add the remaining ingredients and stir until thoroughly combined. Form ¼-cup portions of the mixture into patties and place them on a parchment-lined baking sheet.

5. Place the remaining avocado oil in the skillet and warm it to 365°F. Working in batches to avoid crowding the pan, slip the patties into the hot oil and fry until brown on both sides, about 8 minutes. Transfer the keftes to a paper towel–lined plate to drain before serving.

Zucchini Sott'olio

YIELD: 4 SERVINGS | **ACTIVE TIME:** 15 MINUTES | **TOTAL TIME:** 24 HOURS

¼ CUP KOSHER SALT, PLUS MORE AS NEEDED

2 ZUCCHINI, TRIMMED AND SLICED

4 ANCHOVY FILLETS, RINSED AND BONED

1 GARLIC CLOVE

EXTRA-VIRGIN OLIVE OIL, AS NEEDED

CRUSTY BREAD, FOR SERVING

1. Bring 8 cups of water to a boil in a medium saucepan. Add the salt and the zucchini and cook until the zucchini is just tender, about 4 minutes. Drain and let the zucchini cool.

2. Taste the zucchini. It should taste too salty, which is what you want. If not, season the zucchini with salt until it tastes too salty.

3. Place the zucchini in a jar, add the anchovies and garlic, and cover the mixture with olive oil. Place the mixture in the refrigerator and let it sit overnight before serving with crusty bread.

Crispy Lemon & Chickpea Cakes

YIELD: 4 SERVINGS | **ACTIVE TIME:** 15 MINUTES | **TOTAL TIME:** 45 MINUTES

3 TABLESPOONS EXTRA-VIRGIN OLIVE OIL

1 LEEK, TRIMMED, HALVED, RINSED WELL, AND SLICED THIN

2 GARLIC CLOVES, MINCED

½ CUP PINE NUTS, TOASTED

1 (14 OZ.) CAN OF CHICKPEAS, DRAINED AND RINSED

1 EGG

1 TABLESPOON FRESH LEMON JUICE

ZEST OF 1 LEMON

1 TABLESPOON DIJON MUSTARD

¼ CUP PANKO

SALT AND PEPPER, TO TASTE

¼ CUP ALL-PURPOSE FLOUR

LEMON WEDGES, FOR SERVING

1. Place 1 tablespoon of the olive oil in a medium saucepan and warm it over medium heat. Add the leek and cook, stirring occasionally, until it has softened, about 5 minutes. Add the garlic and cook, stirring continually, for 1 minute.

2. Remove the pan from heat, stir in the toasted pine nuts, and set the mixture aside.

3. Place the chickpeas in a food processor and pulse until they are minced. Add them to the leek mixture, fold in the egg, lemon juice, lemon zest, mustard, and panko, and season the mixture with salt and pepper.

4. Place the flour in a shallow bowl. Working with wet hands, form the chickpea mixture into eight patties. Dredge the patties in the flour until coated and gently brush off any excess.

5. Place the remaining olive oil in a skillet and warm it over medium heat. Working in batches, place the patties in the skillet and cook until crispy and golden brown on each side, 8 to 10 minutes.

6. Let the cakes cool briefly before serving with lemon wedges.

Caponata

YIELD: 6 SERVINGS | **ACTIVE TIME:** 1 HOUR | **TOTAL TIME:** 2 HOURS

1 LARGE EGGPLANT (ABOUT 1½ LBS.)

2 TABLESPOONS EXTRA-VIRGIN OLIVE OIL

1 ONION, CHOPPED

2 CELERY STALKS, PEELED AND CHOPPED

3 LARGE GARLIC CLOVES, MINCED

2 RED BELL PEPPERS, STEMS AND SEEDS REMOVED, CHOPPED

SALT AND PEPPER, TO TASTE

1 LB. RIPE ROMA TOMATOES, PEELED, SEEDS REMOVED, AND FINELY CHOPPED; OR 1 (14 OZ.) CAN OF CRUSHED TOMATOES, WITH THEIR LIQUID

2 TABLESPOONS PLUS 1 PINCH SUGAR

3 TABLESPOONS (HEAPING) CAPERS, RINSED AND DRAINED

3 TABLESPOONS CHOPPED GREEN OLIVES

3 TABLESPOONS RED WINE VINEGAR

1. Preheat the oven to 425°F. Place the eggplant on a baking sheet, place it in the oven, and roast until it has collapsed and is starting to char, about 25 minutes. Remove from the oven and let the eggplant cool. When cool enough to handle, roughly chop the eggplant.

2. Place 1 tablespoon of the olive oil in a large skillet and warm it over medium heat. Add the onion and celery and cook, stirring, until the onion starts to soften, about 5 minutes. Stir in the garlic, cook for 1 minute, and then add the peppers. Season with salt and cook, stirring frequently, until the peppers are tender, about 8 minutes.

3. Add the remaining olive oil and the eggplant and cook, stirring occasionally, until the eggplant begins to fall apart and the other vegetables are tender. Stir in the tomatoes and the pinch of sugar, season the mixture with salt, and cook, stirring frequently, until the tomatoes start to collapse and smell fragrant, about 7 minutes.

4. Stir in the capers, olives, remaining sugar, and vinegar. Reduce the heat to medium-low and cook, stirring often, until the mixture is quite thick, sweet, and fragrant, 20 to 30 minutes. Taste, season with salt and pepper, and remove the pan from heat.

5. Let the caponata cool to room temperature before serving. If time allows, chill in the refrigerator overnight and let it return to room temperature before serving.

Mushroom Barbacoa

YIELD: 4 SERVINGS | **ACTIVE TIME:** 1 HOUR | **TOTAL TIME:** 8 HOURS

1 TABLESPOON CORIANDER SEEDS

½ TEASPOON WHOLE CLOVES

½ TEASPOON ALLSPICE BERRIES

½ TEASPOON CUMIN SEEDS

1½ TABLESPOONS BLACK PEPPERCORNS

1 ANCHO CHILE PEPPER, STEM AND SEEDS REMOVED

1 GUAJILLO CHILE PEPPER, STEM AND SEEDS REMOVED

1 CHIPOTLE CHILE PEPPER, STEM AND SEEDS REMOVED

1 PASILLA CHILE PEPPER, STEM AND SEEDS REMOVED

2 SMALL ONIONS, SLICED, PLUS MORE FOR SERVING

1 CUP ORANGE JUICE

1 CUP FRESH LIME JUICE

SALT, TO TASTE

2¼ LBS. MUSHROOMS, JULIENNED

BANANA LEAVES, SPINES REMOVED, TOASTED, AS NEEDED

5 GARLIC CLOVES

2 BAY LEAVES

CORN TORTILLAS (SEE PAGE 26), FOR SERVING

SALSA VERDE (SEE PAGE 124), FOR SERVING

FRESH CILANTRO, CHOPPED, FOR SERVING

1. Place the coriander, cloves, allspice, cumin, and peppercorns in a dry skillet and toast until fragrant, shaking the pan frequently. Use a mortar and pestle or a spice grinder to grind the mixture into a powder.

2. Place the chiles in the skillet and toast until they are fragrant and pliable. Transfer the chiles to a bowl of hot water and soak for 20 minutes.

3. Drain the chiles and reserve the soaking liquid. Place the chiles, one of the onions and some of the soaking liquid in a blender and puree until smooth. Add the toasted spice powder, orange juice, and lime juice and pulse until incorporated.

4. Season the mixture with salt and place it in a mixing bowl. Add the mushrooms and let them marinate for at least 6 hours.

5. Preheat the oven to 420°F. Remove the mushrooms from the marinade and place them in the banana leaves. Layer the remaining onion, garlic, and bay leaves on top, fold the banana leaves over to form a packet, and tie it closed with kitchen twine.

6. Place the packet on a parchment-lined baking sheet, place it in the oven, and roast for 20 minutes.

7. Remove from the oven and open the packet. Return to the oven and roast for an additional 10 to 15 minutes to caramelize the mushrooms.

8. Remove the mushrooms from the oven and serve with tortillas, Salsa Verde, additional onion, and cilantro.

Stuffed Zucchini

YIELD: 4 SERVINGS | **ACTIVE TIME:** 25 MINUTES | **TOTAL TIME:** 45 MINUTES

4 ZUCCHINI, TRIMMED AND HALVED, SEEDS SCOOPED OUT WITH A SPOON

3 TABLESPOONS EXTRA-VIRGIN OLIVE OIL

SALT AND PEPPER, TO TASTE

½ LB. GROUND LAMB

4 SHALLOTS, MINCED

4 GARLIC CLOVES, MINCED

1 TABLESPOON RAS EL HANOUT

1 CUP CHICKEN STOCK (SEE PAGE 552)

½ CUP COUSCOUS

⅓ CUP DRIED APRICOTS, CHOPPED

3 TABLESPOONS PINE NUTS, TOASTED AND CHOPPED

2 TABLESPOONS CHOPPED FRESH PARSLEY

1. Preheat the oven to 400°F. Place the zucchini on a baking sheet, cut sides down, brush with 1 tablespoon of the olive oil, and season them with salt and pepper. Place the zucchini in the oven and roast until their skins start to wrinkle, about 7 minutes. Remove the zucchini from the oven and set them aside. Leave the oven on.

2. Place 1 tablespoon of the olive oil in a medium saucepan and warm it over medium-high heat. Add the lamb, season it with salt and pepper, and cook, breaking up the meat with a wooden spoon, until it is browned, about 5 minutes. Using a slotted spoon, transfer the lamb to a bowl and set it aside.

3. Drain the fat from the saucepan, add the remaining olive oil and the shallots and cook, stirring occasionally, until they are translucent, about 3 minutes. Add the garlic and ras el hanout and cook, stirring continually, for 1 minute.

4. Add the stock, couscous, and apricots and bring the mixture to a boil. Remove the pan from heat, cover it, and let it stand for 5 minutes.

5. Fluff the couscous mixture with a fork, stir in the pine nuts, parsley, and lamb, and season it with salt and pepper.

6. Turn the roasted zucchini over and distribute the filling between their cavities. Place them in the oven and roast until warmed through, about 5 minutes. Remove from the oven and let the stuffed zucchini cool slightly before enjoying.

Mushroom Barbacoa
SEE PAGE 424

Fried Artichokes

YIELD: 8 SERVINGS | **ACTIVE TIME:** 1 HOUR AND 15 MINUTES | **TOTAL TIME:** 2 HOURS

5 LEMONS, HALVED

4 LARGE ARTICHOKES

AVOCADO OIL, AS NEEDED

SALT AND PEPPER, TO TASTE

1. Prepare an ice bath in a large bowl. Squeeze two lemons into the ice bath, stir, and then throw the spent lemon halves into the ice bath. This lemon water will keep the artichokes fresh and green until you're ready to fry them. Keep a couple of fresh lemon halves on hand as you prep.

2. Rinse the artichokes under cold water. Pat them dry with a linen towel or paper towels. Using kitchen shears, remove the thorny tips from the leaves. For each artichoke, remove the bitter, fibrous end of the stem with a knife, leaving about 1½ inches of stem attached to each artichoke.

3. Using a serrated knife, peel the outer skin from the remaining stem. As the stem is more bitter than the rest of the artichoke, removing the skin tempers the bitterness. Rub the peeled stem with fresh lemon to keep it from browning.

4. Peel off 5 or 6 layers of external leaves from each artichoke, snapping off the leaves and setting them aside, until you reach inner leaves that are fresh looking and white at their base.

5. Using a serrated knife or sharp chef's knife, slice each artichoke horizontally, about ¾ inch above the base (aka the heart), and remove the pointy top of the artichoke, leaving a flat crown of leaves at the base of the artichoke while exposing the purple inner leaves.

6. Slice the artichokes in half lengthwise, splitting the stem and heart to reveal the fuzzy choke. Scoop out the white spines and purple leaves from each artichoke half with a melon baller, leaving two hollowed-out halves of the heart with a small crown of flat leaves.

7. Rub the artichokes with lemon and place them in the ice bath. Pour the artichokes and ice bath into a large saucepan and add the spent lemon halves. You will need about 1½ inches of water to steam the artichokes, so add more water if needed.

8. Place a steaming tray inside the pan and bring the water to a boil. Place the cleaned artichoke halves in the steaming tray and cover the pan. Reduce the heat to medium and steam the artichokes until the thickest part of the stem is just tender, 15 to 20 minutes. You want the artichokes to still be a bit firm—they should only be partially cooked.

9. Place the steamed artichokes on a paper towel–lined plate and let them dry completely.

10. Add avocado oil to a cast-iron skillet until it is 1 inch deep and warm it to 325°F. Season the artichokes with salt and pepper, making sure to season between the layers of leaves as well.

11. Gently slip the artichokes into the hot oil and fry them until the leaves are crispy and golden brown, about 15 minutes, turning the artichokes as needed. Remove the artichokes from the oil, transfer to a paper towel–lined plate, and let them drain before serving.

Couscous-Stuffed Tomatoes

YIELD: 4 SERVINGS | **ACTIVE TIME:** 30 MINUTES | **TOTAL TIME:** 1 HOUR AND 30 MINUTES

4 TOMATOES

2 TEASPOONS SUGAR

SALT AND PEPPER, TO TASTE

2 TABLESPOONS PLUS 1 TEASPOON EXTRA-VIRGIN OLIVE OIL

¼ CUP PANKO

1 CUP FRESHLY GRATED MANCHEGO CHEESE

1 ONION, CHOPPED

2 GARLIC CLOVES, MINCED

⅛ TEASPOON RED PEPPER FLAKES

4 CUPS BABY SPINACH

¾ CUP COUSCOUS

1½ CUPS CHICKEN STOCK (SEE PAGE 552)

2 TABLESPOONS CHOPPED KALAMATA OLIVES

2 TEASPOONS RED WINE VINEGAR

1. Preheat the oven to 350°F. Cut the top ½ inch off the tomatoes and scoop out their insides. Sprinkle the sugar and some salt into the tomatoes, turn them upside down, and place them on a wire rack. Let the tomatoes drain for 30 minutes.

2. Place 1 teaspoon of the olive oil in a large skillet and warm it over medium heat. Add the panko and cook, stirring continually, until golden brown, about 3 minutes. Remove the panko from the pan, place it in a bowl, and let it cool.

3. Stir half of the cheese into the cooled panko and set the mixture aside.

4. Place 1 tablespoon of the olive oil in a clean large skillet and warm it over medium-high heat. Add the onion and cook, stirring occasionally, until it has softened, about 5 minutes. Add the garlic and red pepper flakes and cook, stirring continually, for 1 minute.

5. Add the spinach and cook until it has wilted, about 2 minutes. Add the couscous and stock and bring the mixture to a simmer. Cover the pan, remove it from heat, and let it sit until the couscous is tender, about 7 minutes.

6. Fluff the couscous with a fork, add the olives, vinegar, and remaining cheese, and fold until incorporated. Season the stuffing with salt and pepper and set it aside.

7. Place the remaining olive oil in a baking dish. Add the tomatoes, cavities facing up, and fill them with the stuffing. Top with the toasted panko mixture and place the tomatoes in the oven. Roast until the tomatoes are tender, about 20 minutes.

8. Remove the tomatoes from the oven and let them cool slightly before enjoying.

Caprese Salad

YIELD: 4 SERVINGS | **ACTIVE TIME:** 15 MINUTES | **TOTAL TIME:** 15 MINUTES

1 LB. HEIRLOOM TOMATOES, SLICED (IN SEASON IS A MUST)

SALT AND PEPPER, TO TASTE

1 LB. FRESH MOZZARELLA CHEESE, SLICED

¼ CUP PESTO (SEE PAGE 162)

QUALITY EXTRA-VIRGIN OLIVE OIL, TO TASTE

1. Season the tomatoes with salt and pepper. While alternating, arrange them and the slices of mozzarella on a platter.

2. Drizzle the Pesto and olive oil over the tomatoes and mozzarella and serve.

Fried Squash Blossoms

YIELD: 4 SERVINGS | **ACTIVE TIME:** 20 MINUTES | **TOTAL TIME:** 50 MINUTES

10 SQUASH BLOSSOMS, STAMENS REMOVED

1 BUNCH OF FRESH SPEARMINT

2 CUPS CRUMBLED QUESO FRESCO

ZEST AND JUICE OF 1 LEMON

SALT, TO TASTE

1 CUP ALL-PURPOSE FLOUR

1 TEASPOON BAKING POWDER

2 EGG YOLKS

1 CUP SELTZER WATER

2 CUPS CANOLA OIL

1. Place the squash blossoms on a paper towel–lined baking sheet.

2. Finely chop the spearmint and combine it with the queso fresco. Add the lemon zest and juice, season the mixture with salt, and stir to combine.

3. Stuff the squash blossoms with the mixture, taking care not to tear the flowers.

4. In a small bowl, combine the flour, baking powder, egg yolks, and seltzer water and work the mixture with a whisk until it is a smooth batter. Let the batter rest for 20 minutes.

5. Place the canola oil in a deep skillet and warm it to 350°F over medium heat.

6. Fold the tips of the squash blossoms closed and dip them into the batter. Gently slip them into the oil and fry until crispy and golden brown all over, about 2 minutes, making sure you only turn the squash blossoms once.

7. Drain the fried squash blossoms on the baking sheet. Season them lightly with salt and enjoy.

Scallion Pancakes

YIELD: 6 SERVINGS | **ACTIVE TIME:** 40 MINUTES | **TOTAL TIME:** 1 HOUR AND 15 MINUTES

1½ CUPS ALL-PURPOSE FLOUR, PLUS MORE AS NEEDED

¾ CUP BOILING WATER

7 TABLESPOONS CANOLA OIL

1 TABLESPOON TOASTED SESAME OIL, PLUS MORE AS NEEDED

1 TEASPOON KOSHER SALT

4 SCALLIONS, TRIMMED AND SLICED THIN

1. Place the flour and water in a mixing bowl and work the mixture until it comes together as a rough dough. Transfer the dough to a flour-dusted work surface and knead it until it is a tacky, nearly smooth ball. Cover the dough with plastic wrap and let it rest for 30 minutes.

2. Place 1 tablespoon of the canola oil, the sesame oil, and 1 tablespoon of flour in a small bowl and stir to combine. Set the mixture aside.

3. Divide the dough in half, cover one piece with plastic wrap, and set it aside. Place the other piece on a flour-dusted work surface and roll it into a 12-inch disk. Drizzle approximately 1 tablespoon of the oil-and-flour mixture over the disk and use a pastry brush to spread the mixture evenly. Sprinkle half of the salt and scallions over the disk and roll it into a cylinder. Coil the cylinder into a spiral and flatten it with your palm. Cover with plastic wrap and repeat with the other piece of dough.

4. Warm a cast-iron skillet over low heat until it is warm. Roll one piece of dough into a 9-inch disk and make a slit, approximately ½ inch deep, in the center. Cover with plastic wrap and repeat with the other piece of dough.

5. Coat the bottom of the skillet with some of the remaining canola oil and raise the heat to medium-low. When the oil is warm, place 1 pancake in the pan, cover it, and cook until the pancake is golden brown, about 1 minute. Drizzle some sesame oil over the pancake, use a pastry brush to spread it evenly, and carefully flip the pancake over.

6. Cover the pan and cook until the pancake is browned on that side, about 1 minute. Remove the cover and cook the pancake until it is crisp and a deep golden brown, about 30 seconds. Flip and cook until crispy on that side, another 30 seconds. Remove the pancake from the pan, transfer it to a wire rack to cool, and cook the other pancake. When both pancakes have been cooked, slice each one into wedges and serve.

Ensalada de Nopales

YIELD: 4 SERVINGS | **ACTIVE TIME:** 30 MINUTES | **TOTAL TIME:** 45 MINUTES

3 LARGE NOPALES (CACTUS), SPINES REMOVED

1 TABLESPOON KOSHER SALT, PLUS MORE TO TASTE

½ WHITE ONION, FINELY DICED

2 LARGE TOMATOES, FINELY DICED

½ BUNCH OF FRESH CILANTRO, CHOPPED

JUICE OF 1 LEMON

QUESO FRESCO, CRUMBLED, FOR GARNISH (OPTIONAL)

COTIJA CHEESE, CRUMBLED, FOR GARNISH (OPTIONAL)

1. Place the nopales in a small bowl and sprinkle the salt over them. Let the nopales rest for 15 minutes.

2. Combine the onion, tomatoes, and cilantro in a separate bowl.

3. Place the nopales and 1 tablespoon of water in a large skillet, cover it, and cook over medium heat until the nopales are tender, about 12 minutes. Remove the nopales from the pan and let them cool. When cool enough to handle, cut the nopales into ¼-inch-thick strips.

4. Stir the nopales into the tomato mixture, add the lemon juice, and season the salad with salt. If desired, sprinkle queso fresco or cotija cheese over the top and enjoy.

Chili & Lime Taro Fries

YIELD: 4 SERVINGS | **ACTIVE TIME:** 15 MINUTES | **TOTAL TIME:** 20 MINUTES

CANOLA OIL, AS NEEDED

1 LARGE TARO ROOT, PEELED AND JULIENNED

SALT, TO TASTE

ANCHO CHILE POWDER, TO TASTE

2 TABLESPOONS FRESH LIME JUICE

1. Add canola oil to a Dutch oven until it is about 2 inches deep and warm it to 350°F over medium heat.

2. Add the strips of taro root and fry until golden brown and crispy, about 5 minutes. Make sure not to crowd the pot, working in batches if necessary.

3. Transfer the fries to a large bowl. Sprinkle immediately with the salt and chile powder and drizzle with lime juice. Toss until the seasonings are evenly distributed and enjoy.

Dudhi Kofta

YIELD: 6 SERVINGS | **ACTIVE TIME:** 30 MINUTES | **TOTAL TIME:** 1 HOUR AND 30 MINUTES

2 LBS. ZUCCHINI, TRIMMED AND GRATED

2 TEASPOONS KOSHER SALT

1 SMALL RED ONION, CHOPPED

¼ CUP RAW CASHEWS

2 GARLIC CLOVES, MINCED

1-INCH PIECE OF FRESH GINGER, PEELED AND MINCED

4 BIRD'S EYE CHILI PEPPERS, STEMS AND SEEDS REMOVED, MINCED

½ CUP CHICKPEA FLOUR

2 TABLESPOONS FINELY CHOPPED FRESH CILANTRO

CANOLA OIL, AS NEEDED

1. Place the grated zucchini in a bowl, add the salt, and stir to combine. Let the mixture rest for 20 minutes.

2. Place the onion, cashews, garlic, ginger, and chilies in a food processor and blitz until the mixture is a chunky paste.

3. Place the zucchini in a linen towel and wring the towel to remove as much liquid from the zucchini as possible. Place the zucchini in a mixing bowl and add the onion-and-cashew paste. Stir to combine, add the chickpea flour and cilantro, and fold to incorporate. The dough should be slightly wet.

4. Add canola oil to a Dutch oven until it is about 2 inches deep and warm it to 300°F over medium heat. As the oil warms, form tablespoons of the dough into balls and place them on a parchment-lined baking sheet. When the oil is ready, place the dumplings in the oil and fry until golden brown, about 5 minutes, turning the dumplings as necessary. Work in batches if necessary. Transfer the cooked dumplings to a paper towel–lined plate to drain.

Zucchini Fritters

YIELD: 4 SERVINGS | **ACTIVE TIME:** 15 MINUTES | **TOTAL TIME:** 1 HOUR AND 30 MINUTES

1½ LBS. ZUCCHINI

SALT AND PEPPER, TO TASTE

¼ CUP ALL-PURPOSE FLOUR

¼ CUP GRATED PARMESAN CHEESE

1 EGG, BEATEN

3 TABLESPOONS EXTRA-VIRGIN OLIVE OIL

1. Line a colander with cheesecloth and grate the zucchini into the colander. Generously sprinkle salt over the zucchini, stir to combine, and let it sit for 1 hour. After 1 hour, press down on the zucchini to remove as much liquid from it as you can.

2. Place the zucchini, flour, Parmesan, and egg in a mixing bowl and stir to combine. Use your hands to form handfuls of the mixture into balls and then gently press down on the balls to form them into patties.

3. Place the olive oil in a cast-iron skillet and warm it over medium-high heat. Working in batches, place the patties in the pan, taking care not to crowd the skillet.

4. Cook the fritters until golden brown, about 5 minutes. Flip them over and cook for another 5 minutes, until the fritters are also golden brown on that side. Remove from the skillet, transfer them to a paper towel–lined plate, and repeat with the remaining patties. When all of the fritters have been cooked, season them with salt and pepper and serve.

Crispy Spicy Potatoes

YIELD: 6 SERVINGS | **ACTIVE TIME:** 20 MINUTES | **TOTAL TIME:** 1 HOUR AND 30 MINUTES

1½ LBS. BABY POTATOES

2 TABLESPOONS CANOLA OIL

1 TEASPOON TOASTED SESAME SEEDS

1 TEASPOON CHILI POWDER

1 TEASPOON CUMIN

½ TEASPOON GROUND SZECHUAN PEPPERCORNS

1 TEASPOON LIGHT BROWN SUGAR

1 TEASPOON SMOKED PAPRIKA

½ TEASPOON KOSHER SALT

5 GARLIC CLOVES, MINCED

1-INCH PIECE OF FRESH GINGER, PEELED AND GRATED

½ RED ONION, SLICED THIN

2 SCALLIONS, TRIMMED AND SLICED THIN

1. Preheat the oven to 350°F. Place the potatoes on a baking sheet, drizzle 1 tablespoon of the canola oil over the top, and toss to coat. Place the potatoes in the oven and roast until they are golden brown, about 1 hour, rotating the pan halfway through.

2. Place the sesame seeds, chili powder, cumin, Szechuan peppercorns, brown sugar, paprika, and salt in a mixing bowl, stir until well combined, and set the mixture aside.

3. Add the remaining canola oil to a large skillet and warm it over medium-high heat. Add the garlic and ginger and stir-fry for 20 seconds. Add the onion and stir-fry for 30 seconds.

4. Reduce the heat to medium and add the spice mixture to the skillet. Cook, stirring continually, for 30 seconds.

5. Add the cooked potatoes to the skillet and toss to coat with the spice mixture.

6. Remove the pan from heat, sprinkle the scallions over the dish, and enjoy immediately.

Fried Brussels Sprouts with Tahini & Feta

YIELD: 4 SERVINGS | **ACTIVE TIME:** 15 MINUTES | **TOTAL TIME:** 15 MINUTES

CANOLA OIL, AS NEEDED

3 CUPS SMALL BRUSSELS SPROUTS, TRIMMED

2 TABLESPOONS TAHINI PASTE

1 TABLESPOON FRESH LEMON JUICE

½ CUP CRUMBLED FETA CHEESE

PINCH OF KOSHER SALT

1. Add canola oil to a Dutch oven until it is about 2 inches deep and warm it to 350°F.

2. Gently slip the Brussels sprouts into the hot oil, working in batches to avoid crowding the pot. Fry the Brussels sprouts until golden brown, about 4 minutes, turning them as necessary. Remove one Brussels sprout to test that it is done—let it cool briefly and see if the inside is tender enough. Transfer the fried Brussels sprouts to a paper towel–lined plate.

3. Place the Brussels sprouts, tahini, lemon juice, and feta in a mixing bowl and stir until combined. Sprinkle the salt over the dish and enjoy.

Seared Eggplant

YIELD: 4 SERVINGS | **ACTIVE TIME:** 10 MINUTES | **TOTAL TIME:** 30 MINUTES

1 CUP WOOD CHIPS

1 ONION, QUARTERED

2 TEASPOONS KOSHER SALT

¼ CUP AVOCADO OIL

1 SMALL EGGPLANT,
TRIMMED AND CUBED

1 RED BELL PEPPER, STEM
AND SEEDS REMOVED,
DICED

¼ CUP BALSAMIC VINEGAR

1. Place the wood chips in a small cast-iron skillet and light them on fire. Place the cast-iron pan into a roasting pan and place the onion beside the skillet. Cover the roasting pan with aluminum foil and smoke the onion for 20 minutes.

2. Transfer the onion to a food processor and puree until smooth. Add 1 teaspoon of the salt, stir to combine, and set the puree aside.

3. Place the avocado oil in a large skillet and warm it over high heat. Add the eggplant, season it with the remaining salt, and sear it for 1 minute. Turn the eggplant over, add the bell pepper, and cook for another minute.

4. Add the balsamic vinegar and toss to coat.

5. To serve, spoon the onion puree onto the serving plates and top with the vegetables.

Fried Brussels Sprouts with Tahini & Feta
SEE PAGE 436

Peperonata

YIELD: 6 SERVINGS | **ACTIVE TIME:** 30 MINUTES | **TOTAL TIME:** 2 HOURS

½ CUP EXTRA-VIRGIN OLIVE OIL

4 LARGE GARLIC CLOVES, SLICED THIN

1 RED ONION, HALVED AND SLICED

2 TEASPOONS KOSHER SALT, PLUS MORE TO TASTE

BLACK PEPPER, TO TASTE

4 RED BELL PEPPERS, STEMS AND SEEDS REMOVED, SLICED THIN

1 TABLESPOON SHERRY VINEGAR

1 TABLESPOON DRIED OREGANO

½ CUP BLACK OLIVES, PITS REMOVED

CAPER BERRIES, DRAINED, FOR GARNISH (OPTIONAL)

1. Position a rack in the center of the oven and preheat the oven to 400°F. Place the olive oil in a large skillet and warm it over medium-high heat. When the oil starts to shimmer, add the garlic and onion and cook, stirring continually, until they begin to soften, about 2 minutes.

2. Season with salt and pepper, add the bell peppers, and cook, stirring occasionally, until the peppers begin to soften, about 10 minutes.

3. Stir in the sherry vinegar and oregano and cook for another 2 minutes. Transfer the mixture to a large baking dish and use a wooden spoon to make sure it is distributed evenly.

4. Top the mixture with the olives, place the baking dish in the oven, and bake until the edges of the peperonata start to char, 1 to 1½ hours. Remove from the oven, top the peperonata with the caper berries (if desired), and serve.

Sautéed Sunchokes

YIELD: 4 TO 6 SERVINGS | **ACTIVE TIME:** 15 MINUTES | **TOTAL TIME:** 45 MINUTES

SALT AND PEPPER, TO TASTE

1½ LBS. SUNCHOKES, PEELED

¼ CUP EXTRA-VIRGIN OLIVE OIL

1 GARLIC CLOVE, MINCED

1 TABLESPOON CHOPPED FRESH PARSLEY

1. Bring water to a boil in a large saucepan. Add salt and the sunchokes and parboil for 30 seconds. Drain the sunchokes and let them cool. When the sunchokes are cool enough to handle, slice them thin and pat them dry with paper towels.

2. Place the olive oil in a large skillet and warm it over medium heat. Add the garlic and cook, stirring continually, for 1 minute. Add the sunchokes and parsley, season the mixture with salt and pepper, and cook, stirring occasionally, until the sunchokes are very tender, 10 to 15 minutes. Taste, adjust the seasoning as necessary, and enjoy.

Fava Beans, Roman Style

YIELD: 4 SERVINGS | **ACTIVE TIME:** 25 MINUTES | **TOTAL TIME:** 50 MINUTES

2 TABLESPOONS EXTRA-VIRGIN OLIVE OIL

2 TABLESPOONS MINCED ONION

4 OZ. PANCETTA OR BACON, CHOPPED

¾ LB. SHELLED AND PEELED FAVA BEANS

SALT AND PEPPER, TO TASTE

1. Place the olive oil in a large skillet and warm it over medium heat. Add the onion and cook, stirring occasionally, until it is translucent, about 3 minutes.

2. Add the bacon and cook, stirring occasionally, for 2 minutes. Add ⅓ cup of water and the fava beans, season the mixture with pepper, and bring it to a gentle simmer. Cover the pan and cook until the fava beans are tender, 10 to 15 minutes.

3. Season the mixture with salt, raise the heat to high, and cook until the water has evaporated. Serve immediately.

Spicy Bean Sprout Salad

YIELD: 4 SERVINGS | **ACTIVE TIME:** 10 MINUTES | **TOTAL TIME:** 15 MINUTES

2 TEASPOONS SOY SAUCE

2 TABLESPOONS SESAME OIL

1 TEASPOON TOGARASHI (SEE PAGE 561)

½ TEASPOON KOSHER SALT

¾ LB. BEAN SPROUTS

1 TABLESPOON TOASTED SESAME SEEDS

BLACK PEPPER, TO TASTE

1. In a bowl, combine the soy sauce, oil, Togarashi, and salt and whisk until well combined. Set the dressing aside.

2. Bring water to a boil in a large saucepan and prepare an ice bath. Add the bean sprouts to the boiling water and cook for 1 minute. Remove the bean sprouts, plunge them into the ice bath until cool, and then drain well.

3. Add the bean sprouts and the sesame seeds to the dressing and mix to combine. Season the salad with pepper, taste, adjust the seasoning as necessary, and enjoy.

Mujadara

YIELD: 4 SERVINGS | **ACTIVE TIME:** 20 MINUTES | **TOTAL TIME:** 1 HOUR

4 GARLIC CLOVES, MINCED

2 BAY LEAVES

1 TABLESPOON CUMIN

SALT AND PEPPER, TO TASTE

1 CUP BASMATI RICE

1 CUP BROWN OR GREEN LENTILS

⅓ CUP EXTRA-VIRGIN OLIVE OIL

2 ONIONS, HALVED AND SLICED THIN

½ CUP SLICED SCALLIONS

½ CUP CHOPPED FRESH CILANTRO

1. Place the garlic, bay leaves, cumin, and a few generous pinches of salt in a Dutch oven. Season with pepper, add 5 cups water, and bring to a boil over high heat.

2. Stir in the rice and reduce the heat to medium. Cover the pot and cook, stirring occasionally, for 10 minutes.

3. Add the lentils, return the mixture to a simmer, and cover the pot. Cook until the lentils are tender and the rice has absorbed all of the liquid, about 20 minutes.

4. Place the olive oil in a large skillet and warm it over medium-high heat. Add the onions and cook, stirring frequently, until they are deeply caramelized, about 20 minutes. Remove the onions from the pan with a slotted spoon and transfer them to a paper towel–lined plate. Season with salt and pepper and set the onions aside.

5. Uncover the Dutch oven, remove the bay leaves, and discard them. Stir half of the scallions and the cilantro into the rice mixture. Season with salt and pepper, transfer to a serving dish, top with the caramelized onions and the remaining scallions, and enjoy.

Escabeche

YIELD: 2 TO 4 SERVINGS | **ACTIVE TIME:** 15 MINUTES | **TOTAL TIME:** 4 HOURS AND 30 MINUTES

1 CARROT, PEELED AND SLICED THIN

1 CUP CAULIFLOWER FLORETS

1 RADISH, TRIMMED AND SLICED THIN

6 GREEN BEANS, CHOPPED

½ JALAPEÑO CHILE PEPPER, SLICED THIN

2 GARLIC CLOVES, SMASHED

1½ TEASPOONS SUGAR

½ TEASPOON FINE SEA SALT

½ TEASPOON PEPPERCORNS

½ CUP DISTILLED WHITE VINEGAR

1 CUP WATER

1. Layer the vegetables in a sterilized mason jar.

2. Place the remaining ingredients in a saucepan and bring to a boil over medium-high heat, stirring to dissolve the sugar. Pour the brine over the vegetables and let the escabeche cool to room temperature.

3. Cover the jar and chill it in the refrigerator for at least 4 hours before serving.

Stuffed Cucumber Kimchi

YIELD: 6 SERVINGS | **ACTIVE TIME:** 30 MINUTES | **TOTAL TIME:** 3 DAYS

10 PICKLING CUCUMBERS

3 TABLESPOONS KOSHER SALT

1 CUP FRESH ASIAN CHIVES, CHOPPED (½-INCH SLICES)

4 GARLIC CLOVES

1 TEASPOON MINCED FRESH GINGER

¾ CUP JULIENNED CARROTS

½ CUP THINLY SLICED YELLOW ONION

½ CUP GOCHUGARU (KOREAN CHILI FLAKES)

1 TABLESPOON SUGAR

¼ CUP WATER

1½ TABLESPOONS MINCED SAEUJOT (SALTED FERMENTED SHRIMP)

1½ TABLESPOONS FISH SAUCE

1 TABLESPOON TOASTED SESAME SEEDS

1. Quarter each cucumber lengthwise, leaving ¼ inch at one end intact and connected.

2. Season the cucumbers with the salt, being sure to get inside each one. Place the cucumbers in a bowl, cover the bowl, and let the cucumbers sit for 1 hour.

3. Rinse the cucumbers with cold water and gently pat them dry.

4. Place the remaining ingredients in a bowl and stir until well combined.

5. Stuff the mixture into the cucumbers and then place the stuffed cucumbers in an airtight jar. Let the jar sit at room temperature for 24 hours before refrigerating.

6. Store the jar in the refrigerator for 2 days before enjoying the cucumbers.

Shaved Snap Pea Salad

YIELD: 2 SERVINGS . | **ACTIVE TIME:** 20 MINUTES | **TOTAL TIME:** 50 MINUTES

1 LB. SNAP PEAS

1 TABLESPOON CHOPPED FRESH DILL

1 TABLESPOON CHOPPED FRESH BASIL

1 TABLESPOON CHOPPED FRESH MINT

2 TEASPOONS HONEY

¼ CUP WHITE VINEGAR

1 TEASPOON KOSHER SALT

1 TABLESPOON CRUSHED TOASTED WALNUTS

1. Using a sharp knife, stack 4 snap peas and cut them into thin slices on a bias. Transfer them to a bowl and repeat with the remaining snap peas.

2. Add the remaining ingredients and toss until well combined.

3. Let the salad rest for 30 minutes before serving.

Coconut & Cucumber Salad

YIELD: 4 SERVINGS | **ACTIVE TIME:** 30 MINUTES | **TOTAL TIME:** 40 MINUTES

5 LARGE CUCUMBERS, PEELED, HALVED LENGTHWISE, SEEDS REMOVED

½ CUP SHREDDED UNSWEETENED COCONUT

ZEST AND JUICE OF 2 LIMES

¼ CUP COCONUT MILK

1 TEASPOON CHILI GARLIC SAUCE, PLUS MORE TO TASTE

½-INCH PIECE OF FRESH GINGER, PEELED AND GRATED

1 TEASPOON SUGAR

1 TEASPOON CUMIN

1 TEASPOON KOSHER SALT, PLUS MORE TO TASTE

6 SCALLIONS, TRIMMED AND SLICED THIN, FOR SERVING

½ CUP ROASTED PEANUTS, CHOPPED, FOR SERVING

1. Quarter each cucumber half and then cut the quarters into long, ⅛-inch-wide strips. Set the strips on paper towels and let them drain.

2. Place the coconut, lime juice, coconut milk, chili garlic sauce, ginger, sugar, cumin, and salt in a small food processor or a blender and puree until smooth.

3. Place the cucumbers in a large serving bowl. Top with the coconut mixture and toss to coat.

4. Sprinkle the lime zest, scallions, and peanuts over the dressed "noodles," season to taste, and enjoy.

Spicy Carrots

YIELD: 2 SERVINGS | **ACTIVE TIME:** 15 MINUTES | **TOTAL TIME:** 15 MINUTES

2 LARGE CARROTS, PEELED

1 TABLESPOON AVOCADO OIL

1 TABLESPOON RAS EL HANOUT

2 TEASPOONS HONEY

2 TEASPOONS TAHINI PASTE

2 PINCHES OF WHITE SESAME SEEDS, FOR GARNISH

1. Cut the carrots into matchsticks that are approximately ½ inch wide and 3 inches long.

2. Place the avocado oil in a large skillet and warm it over high heat. Add the carrots to the pan, making sure to leave as much space between them as possible. Sprinkle the ras el hanout over the carrots and sear them until lightly charred all over, about 6 minutes, turning them as necessary.

3. Transfer the carrots to a paper towel–lined plate to drain.

4. Divide the carrots between the serving plates and drizzle the honey and tahini over each portion. Garnish with the sesame seeds and enjoy.

Minty Pickled Cucumbers

YIELD: 2 CUPS | **ACTIVE TIME:** 20 MINUTES | **TOTAL TIME:** 3 HOURS

½ CUP SUGAR

½ CUP WATER

½ CUP RICE VINEGAR

2 TABLESPOONS DRIED MINT

1 TABLESPOON CORIANDER SEEDS

1 TABLESPOON MUSTARD SEEDS

2 CUCUMBERS, SLICED

1. Place all of the ingredients, except for the cucumbers, in a small saucepan and bring to a boil, stirring to dissolve the sugar.

2. Place the cucumbers in a large mason jar. Remove the pan from heat and pour the brine over the cucumbers.

3. Let cool completely before using or storing in the refrigerator, where the pickles will keep for 1 week.

Spicy Carrots
SEE PAGE 449

Beets with Walnut Dukkah

YIELD: 2 SERVINGS | **ACTIVE TIME:** 30 MINUTES | **TOTAL TIME:** 1 HOUR AND 30 MINUTES

2 LARGE BEETS, UNPEELED

PINCH OF KOSHER SALT

1 TABLESPOON CHOPPED WALNUTS

1 TABLESPOON CHOPPED HAZELNUTS

1 TEASPOON BLACK PEPPER

1 TEASPOON POPPY SEEDS

1 TEASPOON BLACK SESAME SEEDS

1 TABLESPOON AVOCADO OIL

¼ CUP FULL-FAT GREEK YOGURT

1 CINNAMON STICK

1. Place the beets and salt in a saucepan with at least 5 cups of water and bring to a boil. Cook the beets until a knife can easily pass through them, 30 to 40 minutes.

2. Drain the beets, run them under cold water, and peel off the skin and stems; it is easiest to do this while the beets are still hot.

3. Cut the peeled beets into ¾-inch cubes and set them aside.

4. Place the nuts in a resealable bag and use a rolling pin to crush them. Transfer to a small bowl, add the black pepper and seeds, and stir to combine. Set the dukkah aside.

5. Place the avocado oil in a large skillet and warm it over high heat. Place the beets in the pan and sear until well browned all over, about 5 minutes, turning the cubes as necessary. Transfer the beets to a paper towel–lined plate to drain.

6. To serve, spread the yogurt across a shallow bowl, pile the beet cubes on top, and sprinkle the dukkah over the dish. Grate the cinnamon stick over the dish and enjoy.

Marinated Cauliflower & Chickpeas

YIELD: 4 SERVINGS | **ACTIVE TIME:** 20 MINUTES | **TOTAL TIME:** 45 MINUTES

SALT AND PEPPER, TO TASTE

1 HEAD OF CAULIFLOWER, TRIMMED AND CUT INTO FLORETS

½ CUP EXTRA-VIRGIN OLIVE OIL

4 GARLIC CLOVES, MINCED

1 TEASPOON SUGAR

1 TEASPOON PAPRIKA

2 TEASPOONS CHOPPED FRESH ROSEMARY

¼ TEASPOON SAFFRON

2 TABLESPOONS WHITE WINE VINEGAR

1 (14 OZ.) CAN OF CHICKPEAS, DRAINED AND RINSED

FRESH PARSLEY, CHOPPED, FOR GARNISH

LEMON WEDGES, FOR SERVING

1. Prepare an ice bath. Bring salted water to a boil in a medium saucepan. Add the cauliflower and cook until it has softened, about 4 minutes. Transfer the cauliflower to the ice bath, let it cool, and drain.

2. Place 1 tablespoon of the olive oil in a large, clean saucepan and warm it over medium heat. Add the garlic and cook, stirring continually, for 1 minute. Add the sugar, paprika, rosemary, and remaining olive oil and cook, stirring continually, for 1 minute.

3. Remove the pan from heat, stir in the saffron, and let the mixture cool.

4. Add the vinegar, chickpeas, and blanched cauliflower and stir to combine. Season the dish with salt and pepper, garnish with parsley, and serve with lemon wedges.

Beets with Walnut Dukkah
SEE PAGE 452

Warm Zucchini & Corn Salad

YIELD: 4 SERVINGS | **ACTIVE TIME:** 15 MINUTES | **TOTAL TIME:** 35 MINUTES

2 TABLESPOONS EXTRA-VIRGIN OLIVE OIL

3 DRIED CHILES DE ARBOL, STEMS AND SEEDS REMOVED

½ WHITE ONION, DICED

3 GARLIC CLOVES, SLICED THIN

KERNELS FROM 2 EARS OF CORN

2 LARGE TOMATOES, SEEDS REMOVED, DICED

4 ZUCCHINI, DICED

SALT, TO TASTE

3 SPRIGS OF FRESH EPAZOTE OR CILANTRO

1 CUP CRUMBLED QUESO FRESCO

1. Place the olive oil in a skillet and warm it over low heat. Add the chiles and toast lightly until fragrant, taking care not to burn them. Remove the chiles from the pan and set them aside. When cool enough to handle, chop the chiles.

2. Add the onion and garlic to the pan and cook until the onion is translucent, about 3 minutes, stirring frequently.

3. Add the corn and cook for 2 minutes, stirring occasionally. Add the tomatoes and cook until they begin to release their juices.

4. Add the zucchini, season the mixture with salt, and cook until the vegetables are tender, about 10 minutes.

5. Add the epazote to the pan and cook for 1 minute. Remove the epazote from the pan, add the chiles, and stir until evenly distributed.

6. To serve, top the salad with the crumbled queso fresco.

Romano Beans with Mustard Vinaigrette & Walnuts

YIELD: 8 SERVINGS | **ACTIVE TIME:** 15 MINUTES | **TOTAL TIME:** 30 MINUTES

1 CUP WALNUTS

SALT AND PEPPER, TO TASTE

3 LBS. ROMANO BEANS, TRIMMED

3 TABLESPOONS RED WINE VINEGAR

2 TABLESPOONS DIJON MUSTARD

1 GARLIC CLOVE, GRATED

2 TABLESPOONS EXTRA-VIRGIN OLIVE OIL, PLUS MORE TO TASTE

ZEST OF ½ LEMON

¾ CUP CHOPPED FRESH PARSLEY

1. Preheat the oven to 350°F. Place the walnuts on a rimmed baking sheet, place them in the oven, and toast until browned and fragrant, about 8 to 10 minutes, tossing halfway through.

2. Remove the walnuts from the oven and let them cool. When the walnuts have cooled slightly, chop them and set aside.

3. Bring salted water to a boil in a large saucepan and prepare an ice bath. Place the beans in the boiling water and cook until bright green and tender, 8 to 10 minutes. Using a slotted spoon, transfer them to the ice bath and let them cool. Drain, pat the beans dry, and set them aside.

4. Place the vinegar, mustard, garlic, and olive oil in a large mixing bowl and whisk until thoroughly combined. Let the dressing rest for 10 minutes.

5. Add the walnuts and beans to the dressing. Sprinkle the lemon zest and parsley over the beans, season with salt and pepper, and toss to coat. Transfer to a platter, drizzle more olive oil over the top, and enjoy.

Shaved Squash Salad with Herb Vinaigrette

YIELD: 6 SERVINGS | **ACTIVE TIME:** 15 MINUTES | **TOTAL TIME:** 1 HOUR

FOR THE SALAD

1 PINT OF CHERRY TOMATOES

1 TABLESPOON EXTRA-VIRGIN OLIVE OIL

5 GARLIC CLOVES, CRUSHED

LEAVES FROM 2 SPRIGS OF FRESH THYME

½ TEASPOON KOSHER SALT, PLUS MORE TO TASTE

¼ TEASPOON BLACK PEPPER, PLUS MORE TO TASTE

3 ZUCCHINI, SLICED THIN WITH A MANDOLINE

2 SUMMER SQUASH, SLICED THIN WITH A MANDOLINE

1 RED BELL PEPPER, STEMS AND SEEDS REMOVED, SLICED THIN WITH A MANDOLINE

FOR THE VINAIGRETTE

1 TABLESPOON SLICED FRESH CHIVES

1 TEASPOON FRESH THYME

1 TEASPOON CHOPPED FRESH OREGANO

1 TABLESPOON CHOPPED FRESH PARSLEY

3 TABLESPOONS APPLE CIDER VINEGAR

1 TABLESPOON HONEY

2 TEASPOONS DICED SHALLOT

1 TEASPOON KOSHER SALT

¼ TEASPOON BLACK PEPPER

¼ CUP EXTRA-VIRGIN OLIVE OIL

1. To begin preparations for the salad, preheat the oven's broiler to high. Place the cherry tomatoes, olive oil, garlic, thyme, salt, and pepper in a mixing bowl and toss until the tomatoes are evenly coated. Place the tomatoes on a baking sheet, place it in the oven, and broil until the tomatoes' skins begin to blister, 6 to 8 minutes. Remove the pan from the oven and let the mixture cool completely.

2. To prepare the vinaigrette, place all of the ingredients, except for the olive oil, in a mixing bowl and whisk to combine. Add the oil in a slow stream while whisking to incorporate. Season to taste and set aside.

3. Place the zucchini, squash, and pepper in a large mixing bowl, season with salt and pepper, and add the vinaigrette. Toss to evenly coat, plate the salad, and sprinkle the blistered tomatoes over the top.

Patatas Bravas

YIELD: 4 SERVINGS | **ACTIVE TIME:** 45 MINUTES | **TOTAL TIME:** 1 HOUR AND 15 MINUTES

4 POTATOES, CHOPPED

1 ONION, WITH SKIN AND ROOT, HALVED

3 TABLESPOONS EXTRA-VIRGIN OLIVE OIL

2 CUPS WOOD CHIPS

1 HEAD OF GARLIC, TOP ½ INCH REMOVED

1 (14 OZ.) CAN OF DICED TOMATOES, DRAINED

1 TABLESPOON SWEET PAPRIKA

1 TABLESPOON SHERRY VINEGAR

SALT, TO TASTE

SOUR CREAM, FOR SERVING

1. Bring water to a boil in a large saucepan. Add the potatoes and boil for 4 minutes. Drain the potatoes and run them under cold water.

2. Place the potatoes, onion, and 1 tablespoon of the olive oil in a mixing bowl and toss to coat.

3. Line a large wok with aluminum foil, making sure that the foil extends over the side of the pan. Add the wood chips and place the wok over medium heat.

4. When the wood chips are smoking heavily, place a wire rack above the wood chips and place the potatoes, onion, and garlic on top. Cover the wok with a lid, fold the foil over the lid to seal the wok as best you can, and smoke the vegetables for 20 minutes. After 20 minutes, remove the pan from heat and keep the wok covered for another 20 minutes.

5. Place the tomatoes, paprika, vinegar, and remaining olive oil in a blender and puree until smooth. Set the mixture aside.

6. Remove the garlic and onion from the smoker. Peel and roughly chop. Add to the mixture in the blender and puree until smooth. Season the salsa brava with salt and serve alongside the potatoes and sour cream.

Garlic & Chili Broccolini

YIELD: 4 SERVINGS | **ACTIVE TIME:** 10 MINUTES | **TOTAL TIME:** 30 MINUTES

SALT AND PEPPER, TO TASTE

½ LB. BROCCOLINI, ENDS TRIMMED

¼ CUP EXTRA-VIRGIN OLIVE OIL

2 GARLIC CLOVES, MINCED

1 TEASPOON RED PEPPER FLAKES

2 TABLESPOONS ALMONDS, TOASTED, FOR GARNISH

1. Bring a large saucepan of water to a boil. Add salt and the broccolini and cook for 30 seconds. Remove with a strainer, allow the majority of the water to drip off of the broccolini, and transfer it to a paper towel–lined plate.

2. Place the olive oil in a large skillet and warm it over medium-high heat.

3. When the oil starts to shimmer, add the broccolini and cook until it is well browned. Turn the broccolini over, add the garlic, season with salt and pepper, and toss to combine. When the broccolini is browned all over, add the red pepper flakes and toss to evenly distribute.

4. Transfer to a serving platter and garnish with the toasted almonds.

Butternut Squash Quiche

YIELD: 8 SERVINGS | **ACTIVE TIME:** 30 MINUTES | **TOTAL TIME:** 2 HOURS AND 30 MINUTES

8 EGGS

1 CUP HEAVY CREAM

1 TEASPOON KOSHER SALT

¼ TEASPOON BLACK PEPPER

1 TABLESPOON EXTRA-VIRGIN OLIVE OIL

2 CUPS DICED BUTTERNUT SQUASH (½-INCH CUBES)

2 GARLIC CLOVES, MINCED

1 CUP FRESH SPINACH

1 TEASPOON MINCED FRESH ROSEMARY

½ CUP CRUMBLED GOAT CHEESE

1 PERFECT PIECRUST (SEE PAGE 562), BLIND BAKED IN A 9-INCH PIE PLATE

1. Preheat the oven to 350°F. Place the eggs, heavy cream, salt, and pepper in a mixing bowl and whisk until combined. Set the mixture aside.

2. Place the olive oil in a large skillet and warm it over medium-high heat. Working in batches if necessary to avoid crowding the pan, add the butternut squash and cook, stirring occasionally, until it is nearly cooked through, about 10 minutes.

3. Add the garlic, spinach, and rosemary to the pan and cook, stirring frequently, until the spinach has wilted, about 2 minutes. Remove the pan from heat and let the vegetable mixture cool.

4. Sprinkle the goat cheese over the bottom of the baked crust and evenly distribute the vegetable mixture over the top. Pour the egg mixture into the crust, stopping when it reaches the top.

5. Place the quiche in the oven and bake until the center is set and the filling is lightly golden brown, 35 to 45 minutes.

6. Remove the quiche from the oven, transfer it to a cooling rack, and let it cool for 1 hour. The quiche will be enjoyable warm, at room temperature, or cold.

CHEESE, NUTS & OTHER DECADENT BITES

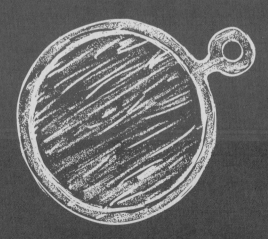

Baked Brie, Two Ways

YIELD: 4 TO 6 SERVINGS | **ACTIVE TIME:** 10 MINUTES | **TOTAL TIME:** 25 MINUTES

½ LB. ROUND OF
BRIE CHEESE

**FOR THE SAVORY
TOPPING**

¼ CUP CHOPPED ROASTED
TOMATOES

¼ CUP CHOPPED
ARTICHOKE HEARTS

2 TABLESPOONS PITTED
AND CHOPPED OLIVES

1 TABLESPOON CAPERS

PINCH OF BLACK PEPPER

FOR THE SWEET TOPPING

¼ CUP CHOPPED PECANS

¼ CUP CHOPPED DRIED
APRICOTS

⅓ CUP DIVINA FIG SPREAD

¼ CUP DRIED CHERRIES

PINCH OF CINNAMON

1. Preheat the oven to 350°F. Combine the ingredients for your chosen topping in a mixing bowl.

2. Place the Brie in a ceramic dish and top it with the chosen topping.

3. Place the dish in the oven and bake for 15 minutes, until the cheese is gooey.

4. Remove from the oven and serve.

Maple Walnuts

YIELD: 2 CUPS | **ACTIVE TIME:** 15 MINUTES | **TOTAL TIME:** 45 MINUTES

1 TABLESPOON UNSALTED BUTTER

⅓ CUP REAL MAPLE SYRUP

⅛ TEASPOON KOSHER SALT

2 CUPS WALNUT HALVES

1. Preheat the oven to 375°F and line a baking sheet with parchment paper.

2. Place the butter in a skillet and melt it over medium heat. Stir in the maple syrup and salt and simmer until the mixture is frothy, about 3 minutes.

3. Add the walnuts and stir to coat. Cook, stirring, for about 3 minutes.

4. Transfer the walnuts to the baking sheet, place them in the oven, and bake until caramelized, about 10 minutes. Remove, stir, and let cool until the maple glaze hardens, about 30 minutes.

Hard-Boiled Eggs

YIELD: 4 SERVINGS | **ACTIVE TIME:** 5 MINUTES | **TOTAL TIME:** 40 MINUTES

8 LARGE EGGS

1. Prepare an ice bath. Place the eggs in a saucepan large enough that they can sit on the bottom in a single layer. Cover with 1 inch of cold water and bring to a boil over high heat.

2. Remove the saucepan from heat, cover, and let the eggs stand for 12 minutes.

3. Drain the eggs and place them in the ice bath until they are completely chilled. Peel the eggs and enjoy.

Soft-Boiled Eggs

YIELD: 4 SERVINGS | **ACTIVE TIME:** 5 MINUTES | **TOTAL TIME:** 5 MINUTES

8 LARGE EGGS

1. Prepare an ice bath. Bring a medium saucepan of water to a boil. Reduce the heat so that the water simmers.

2. Working in two batches, slip the eggs into the simmering water. Simmer for 4 to 5 minutes and use a slotted spoon to remove the eggs and plunge them into the ice bath.

3. When the eggs have cooled completely, slice the tops off with a knife, place each one in a egg cup, and enjoy.

Curried Pistachios

YIELD: 4 SERVINGS | **ACTIVE TIME:** 10 MINUTES | **TOTAL TIME:** 30 MINUTES

1 CUP UNSHELLED ROASTED PISTACHIOS

½ CUP SHELLED ROASTED PISTACHIOS

½ TEASPOON CURRY POWDER

1 TABLESPOON EXTRA-VIRGIN OLIVE OIL

½ TEASPOON FINE SEA SALT

1. Preheat the oven to 350ºF. Place the pistachios in a mixing bowl, add the remaining ingredients, and toss until the nuts are coated.

2. Place the nuts on a baking sheet, place them in the oven, and roast until fragrant, about 12 minutes. Remove from the oven and let the pistachios cool before serving.

Soft-Boiled Eggs
SEE PAGE 473

Roasted Chestnuts

YIELD: 8 SERVINGS | **ACTIVE TIME:** 5 MINUTES | **TOTAL TIME:** 1 HOUR

1 LB. CHESTNUTS

½ TEASPOON KOSHER SALT

¼ TEASPOON BLACK PEPPER

2 TABLESPOONS UNSALTED BUTTER, MELTED

1 TABLESPOON EXTRA-VIRGIN OLIVE OIL

3 SPRIGS OF FRESH THYME

1 CINNAMON STICK

2 WHOLE CLOVES

1. Preheat the oven to 425°F. Carve an X on the rounded side of each chestnut and place them in a bowl of hot water. Soak for about 10 minutes.

2. Drain the chestnuts and create an aluminum foil pouch. Place the chestnuts in the pouch, sprinkle salt and pepper over them, drizzle the butter and olive oil over the top, and add the thyme, cinnamon stick, and cloves to the pouch. Close the pouch, leaving an opening so that steam can escape.

3. Place the chestnuts in the oven and roast until tender, 40 to 45 minutes. Remove the chestnuts from the oven and serve them warm.

Sicilian Bar Nuts

YIELD: 4 SERVINGS | **ACTIVE TIME:** 10 MINUTES | **TOTAL TIME:** 25 MINUTES

¾ CUP WALNUTS

¾ CUP CASHEWS

¾ CUP PECAN HALVES

2 TABLESPOONS UNSALTED BUTTER, MELTED

2 TABLESPOONS CHOPPED FRESH ROSEMARY

1 TEASPOON CAYENNE PEPPER

1 TABLESPOON BROWN SUGAR

1 TABLESPOON MALDON SEA SALT

1. Preheat the oven to 350ºF. Place the nuts on a baking sheet, place them in the oven, and toast until fragrant, about 12 minutes. Remove the nuts from the oven and transfer them to a mixing bowl.

2. Add the melted butter and toss until the nuts are evenly coated. Add the remaining ingredients, toss to coat, and enjoy.

Goat Cheese, Olive & Fennel Phyllo Triangles

YIELD: 16 SERVINGS | **ACTIVE TIME:** 30 MINUTES | **TOTAL TIME:** 1 HOUR AND 30 MINUTES

1 TABLESPOON EXTRA-VIRGIN OLIVE OIL

½ FENNEL BULB, TRIMMED, CORED, AND CHOPPED

2 GARLIC CLOVES, MINCED

6 TABLESPOONS WHITE WINE

1 TABLESPOON PERNOD

1 TABLESPOON MINCED RAISINS

6 GREEN OLIVES, PITS REMOVED, MINCED

1 CUP CRUMBLED GOAT CHEESE

1 TABLESPOON FINELY CHOPPED FRESH CHIVES

1 TEASPOON LEMON ZEST

1 TEASPOON FRESH LEMON JUICE

SALT AND PEPPER, TO TASTE

½ LB. FROZEN PHYLLO DOUGH, THAWED

6 TABLESPOONS UNSALTED BUTTER, MELTED

1 TABLESPOON BLACK SESAME SEEDS

1. Place the olive oil in a medium saucepan and warm it over medium heat. Add the fennel and cook, stirring occasionally, until it has softened and is starting to brown, about 8 minutes.

2. Add the garlic and cook, stirring continually, until fragrant, about 1 minute. Add the white wine, Pernod, and raisins and cook until the liquid has evaporated, about 5 minutes. Remove the pan from heat and let the mixture cool for 5 minutes.

3. Place the olives, goat cheese, chives, lemon zest, and lemon juice in a mixing bowl and stir to combine. Add the fennel mixture, fold to combine, and season the mixture with salt and pepper. Set the filling aside.

4. Preheat the oven to 425°F. Line a baking sheet with parchment paper. Place a piece of parchment paper on a work surface. Lay one sheet of phyllo on the parchment and brush it with some of the butter. Lay another sheet of phyllo on top and gently press down. Brush the phyllo with butter and then cut the rectangle into 2-inch-wide strips. Make sure to cover the rest of the phyllo dough so that it does not dry out.

5. Place 2 teaspoons of the filling at the bottom of each strip and shape the filling into a triangle. Taking care to maintain that triangle shape, roll up the strip, as if you were folding a flag. Crimp the folded-up pastries to seal them and place them, seam side down, on the baking sheet.

6. Repeat Steps 4 and 5 until you have 16 filled pastries.

7. Sprinkle the sesame seeds over the pastries, place them in the oven, and bake until golden brown, about 10 minutes.

8. Remove from the oven and let the pastries cool before serving.

Sicilian Bar Nuts
SEE PAGE 478

Granola

YIELD: 3 CUPS | **ACTIVE TIME:** 10 MINUTES | **TOTAL TIME:** 45 MINUTES

2 CUPS ROLLED OATS

¼ CUP REAL MAPLE SYRUP

1 CUP PECAN HALVES

2 TEASPOONS KOSHER SALT

1 TEASPOON CINNAMON

⅔ CUP DRIED CRANBERRIES

1. Preheat the oven to 350ºF and line a baking sheet with a Silpat mat. Place all of the ingredients in a mixing bowl and toss to combine.

2. Spread the mixture on the baking sheet in an even layer. Place it in the oven and bake until browned and fragrant, about 20 minutes. Remove from the oven and let the granola cool completely before serving.

Boiled Peanuts

YIELD: 8 SERVINGS | **ACTIVE TIME:** 30 MINUTES | **TOTAL TIME:** 24 HOURS

2 LBS. RAW PEANUTS, SHELLS ON

12 CUPS WATER

3 TABLESPOONS KOSHER SALT

2 STAR ANISE PODS

2 BAY LEAVES

½ TABLESPOON SZECHUAN PEPPERCORNS

1. Rinse the peanuts well and set them aside. Place the water, salt, star anise, bay leaves, and peppercorns in a large saucepan and stir to dissolve the salt.

2. Add the peanuts to the pan and place something heavy over the peanuts to keep them submerged. Let the pot sit at room temperature overnight.

3. Bring the peanuts to a boil, reduce the heat, and cover the pan. Simmer the peanuts until they are tender with a slight bite, 1 to 1½ hours.

4. Uncover the pan and remove it from heat. Let the peanuts cool in the cooking liquid for 1 hour.

5. Drain the peanuts and enjoy immediately or store in resealable bags in the refrigerator, where they will keep for 4 to 5 days.

Chilled Tofu With Gochugang

YIELD: 4 SERVINGS | **ACTIVE TIME:** 10 MINUTES | **TOTAL TIME:** 10 MINUTES

¾ LB. EXTRA-FIRM TOFU, CUT INTO RECTANGLES

3 TABLESPOONS GOCHUJANG & SCALLION SAUCE (SEE PAGE 188)

1 TABLESPOON SESAME OIL

SCALLIONS, SLICED THIN, FOR GARNISH

TOASTED SESAME SEEDS, FOR GARNISH

1. Arrange the pieces of tofu on a serving platter and top each piece with the sauce.

2. Drizzle sesame oil over the tofu, garnish with scallions and toasted sesame seeds, and enjoy.

Soy Sauce Eggs

YIELD: 8 SERVINGS | **ACTIVE TIME:** 15 MINUTES | **TOTAL TIME:** 10 HOURS

1½ CUPS SOY SAUCE

1 CUP SAKE

½ CUP MIRIN

1 CUP WATER

1½ TABLESPOONS SUGAR

2 TEASPOONS MINCED FRESH GINGER

12 SOFT-BOILED EGGS (SEE PAGE 473), PEELED

1. Combine all of the ingredients, except for the eggs, in a saucepan and bring the mixture to a boil. Reduce the heat and simmer for 3 to 4 minutes, stirring to dissolve the sugar.

2. Transfer the marinade to a container large enough to also accommodate the eggs and let it cool completely.

3. Add the eggs to the marinade, making sure they are submerged. Let the eggs steep for 8 to 10 hours. Do not let them marinate any longer than this, as they will become rubbery.

4. Remove the eggs from the marinade and enjoy.

Classic Fondue

YIELD: 6 SERVINGS | **ACTIVE TIME:** 10 MINUTES | **TOTAL TIME:** 20 MINUTES

1 LB. GRUYÈRE CHEESE, SHREDDED

½ LB. EMMENTAL CHEESE, SHREDDED

½ LB. GOUDA CHEESE, SHREDDED

2 TABLESPOONS CORNSTARCH

1 GARLIC CLOVE, HALVED

1 CUP WHITE WINE

1 TABLESPOON FRESH LEMON JUICE

SALT AND PEPPER, TO TASTE

FRESHLY GRATED NUTMEG, TO TASTE

1. Place the cheeses and the cornstarch in a bowl and toss until the cheeses are evenly coated.

2. Rub the inside of a caquelon (fondue pot) with the garlic and place the pot over the flame to warm it up.

3. Place the wine and lemon juice in a saucepan and bring the mixture to a simmer over low heat. Add the cheese mixture and cook, stirring constantly, until the cheeses have melted and the mixture is smooth. Season with salt, pepper, and nutmeg, transfer the mixture to the fondue pot, and enjoy.

Fondue Folklore

A fun fondue tradition is to leave a thin layer of fondue at the bottom of the caquelon (fondue pot). By carefully controlling the heat, you can form this layer into a crust known as *La Religieuse*—"The Religious One." Lift it out and distribute it among your guests. You'll soon see why it is considered a delicacy.

Marble Eggs

YIELD: 4 SERVINGS | **ACTIVE TIME:** 10 MINUTES | **TOTAL TIME:** 24 HOURS

1 TABLESPOON AVOCADO OIL

¼ CUP MINCED SCALLIONS, WHITE PART ONLY

4 GARLIC CLOVES, SMASHED

2-INCH PIECE OF FRESH GINGER, SLICED THIN AND SMASHED

1¾ CUPS SUGAR

½ CUP RICE WINE

1½ CUPS DARK SOY SAUCE

½ CUP LIGHT SOY SAUCE

2 STAR ANISE PODS

PEEL OF ½ ORANGE

½ CUP WATER

6 HARD-BOILED EGGS (SEE PAGE 472)

1. Place the avocado oil in a medium saucepan and warm it over medium heat. Add the scallion whites, garlic, and ginger and cook, stirring continually, for 2 minutes. Add the sugar and cook, stirring frequently, until the aromatics start to caramelize.

2. Stir in the wine, soy sauces, star anise, orange peel, and water and bring the mixture to a boil. Remove the pan from heat and let the sauce cool completely.

3. Lightly crack each hard-boiled egg all around with the back of a spoon. Slip the eggs into the sauce and let them steep for 12 to 24 hours, turning them often to ensure even coloring.

4. Peel the eggs, slice them, and enjoy.

Tamagoyaki

YIELD: 2 SERVINGS | **ACTIVE TIME:** 15 MINUTES | **TOTAL TIME:** 15 MINUTES

4 LARGE EGGS

¼ TEASPOON KOSHER SALT

1 TEASPOON SOY SAUCE

1 TABLESPOON MIRIN

1 TABLESPOON CANOLA OIL

1. Place the eggs, salt, soy sauce, and mirin in a bowl and whisk to combine.

2. Place the canola oil in a rectangular cast-iron pan and warm it over medium-high heat.

3. Pour a thin layer of the egg mixture into the pan, tilting and swirling to make sure the egg completely coats the bottom. When the bottom of the egg is just set and there is still liquid on top, use a chopstick to gently roll the egg up into a log. If you allow the egg to cook too much, it won't stick as you roll it.

4. When the first roll is at one end of the pan, pour another thin layer of the egg mixture into the pan. When the bottom of this layer is set, roll the log back onto it. Roll the layer up to the other end of the pan. Repeat until all of the egg mixture has been used up.

5. Remove the omelet from the pan and let it set for a few minutes before trimming the ends, slicing, and serving.

Fried Tofu

YIELD: 4 SERVINGS | **ACTIVE TIME:** 20 MINUTES | **TOTAL TIME:** 1 HOUR

5 OZ. TOFU, CUT INTO ¾-INCH CUBES

2 CUPS CANOLA OIL

2 EGGS, BEATEN

¼ CUP ALL-PURPOSE FLOUR

1½ CUPS PANKO, FINELY GROUND

SALT, TO TASTE

1. Place the tofu on paper towels and let it sit for 20 minutes.

2. Place the canola oil in a medium saucepan and warm it to 350°F.

3. Place the eggs, flour, and panko in 3 separate bowls.

4. Pat the tofu dry, dredge it in the flour, and shake to remove any excess. Dredge the tofu in the eggs, shake it to remove any excess, and then dredge the tofu in the panko until completely coated.

5. Gently slip the breaded tofu into the hot oil and fry until golden brown, about 4 minutes, turning it as necessary.

6. Transfer the fried tofu to a paper towel–lined plate to drain and cool slightly. Season it with salt and enjoy.

Candied Peanuts

YIELD: 4 SERVINGS | **ACTIVE TIME:** 10 MINUTES | **TOTAL TIME:** 1 HOUR

1 CUP ROASTED PEANUTS

1½ TABLESPOONS SUGAR

½ CUP WATER

1 TEASPOON TOGARASHI
(SEE PAGE 561)

1. Place the peanuts, sugar, and water in a nonstick pan and bring the mixture to a simmer over medium heat, stirring often.

2. Cook until all of the water has evaporated and the peanuts are glazed. Remove the pan from heat, sprinkle the Togarashi over the peanuts, and stir to coat.

3. Transfer the peanuts to a parchment-lined baking sheet and let them cool completely before enjoying.

Arancini

YIELD: 8 SERVINGS | **ACTIVE TIME:** 30 MINUTES | **TOTAL TIME:** 1 HOUR AND 30 MINUTES

5 CUPS CHICKEN STOCK
(SEE PAGE 552)

½ CUP UNSALTED BUTTER

2 CUPS ARBORIO RICE

1 SMALL WHITE ONION,
GRATED

1 CUP WHITE WINE

4 OZ. FONTINA CHEESE,
GRATED

SALT AND PEPPER, TO TASTE

CANOLA OIL, AS NEEDED

6 LARGE EGGS, BEATEN

5 CUPS PANKO

MARINARA SAUCE (SEE
PAGE 184), FOR SERVING

1. Bring the stock to a simmer in a large saucepan. In a large skillet, melt the butter over high heat. Add the rice and onion to the skillet and cook until the rice has a toasty fragrance, about 3 minutes. Deglaze the skillet with the white wine and cook until the rice has almost completely absorbed the wine.

2. Reduce the heat to medium-high and begin adding the stock ¼ cup at a time, stirring until it has been absorbed by the rice. Continue adding the stock until the rice is al dente.

3. Turn off the heat, stir in the cheese, and season the risotto with salt and pepper. Pour it onto a rimmed baking sheet and let it cool.

4. Add canola oil to a Dutch oven until it is 2 inches deep and warm it to 350°F. When the risotto is cool, form it into golf ball–sized spheres. Dredge them in the eggs and then the panko until completely coated.

5. Gently slip the arancini into the hot oil and fry until warmed through and golden brown, 3 to 5 minutes. Transfer the arancini to a paper towel–lined plate to drain and let them cool slightly.

6. To serve, garnish the arancini with additional Fontina and serve with Marinara Sauce.

Arancini
SEE PAGE 491

Couscous Arancini

YIELD: 2 SERVINGS | **ACTIVE TIME:** 40 MINUTES | **TOTAL TIME:** 1 HOUR AND 30 MINUTES

2 CUPS COUSCOUS

1 TABLESPOON PAPRIKA

1 TABLESPOON GARLIC POWDER

2 TEASPOONS KOSHER SALT

1 TEASPOON CUMIN

1 CUP CRUMBLED FETA CHEESE

CANOLA OIL, AS NEEDED

1. Place 2½ cups water in a saucepan and bring it to a boil.

2. Place the couscous and the seasonings in a mixing bowl and stir until well combined. Add the boiling water to the couscous and cover the bowl with plastic wrap. After 10 minutes, use a fork to fluff the couscous.

3. Add ½ cup of feta to the couscous and stir to incorporate it.

4. Add canola oil to a Dutch oven until it is about 2 inches deep and warm it to 350°F.

5. Using your hands, form 1-oz. portions of the couscous into balls. Press into each ball with your thumb and make a depression. Fill this with some of the remaining feta and then close the ball over it.

6. Working in batches of four to avoid crowding the pan, gently slip the balls into the hot oil and fry until golden brown, about 4 minutes. Transfer the fried arancini to a paper towel–lined plate to drain and cool, and enjoy once all of them have been cooked.

Hush Puppies

YIELD: 8 SERVINGS | **ACTIVE TIME:** 15 MINUTES | **TOTAL TIME:** 1 HOUR AND 15 MINUTES

1 CUP ALL-PURPOSE FLOUR

1½ CUPS CORNMEAL

2 TABLESPOONS BAKING POWDER

2 TABLESPOONS SUGAR

1 TABLESPOON BAKING SODA

2 TEASPOONS KOSHER SALT

½ TEASPOON CAYENNE PEPPER

1¼ CUPS BUTTERMILK

2 EGGS

1 LARGE YELLOW ONION, GRATED

CANOLA OIL, AS NEEDED

1. Place the flour, cornmeal, baking powder, sugar, baking soda, salt, and cayenne in a large bowl and stir to combine.

2. Place the buttermilk, eggs, and the grated onion (along with any juices that have collected) in a bowl and stir to combine. Add the wet mixture to the dry mixture, stir to combine, and let the batter sit for 1 hour.

3. Add canola oil to a large Dutch oven until it is 2 inches deep and warm it over medium heat until it is 350°F. Drop tablespoons of the batter into the oil, making sure to not crowd the Dutch oven. Cook, turning the hush puppies as they brown, until they are crispy and golden brown, about 3 to 4 minutes. Transfer the cooked hush puppies to a paper towel–lined plate to drain and let them cool briefly before enjoying.

Fried Feta

YIELD: 2 SERVINGS | **ACTIVE TIME:** 25 MINUTES | **TOTAL TIME:** 25 MINUTES

1 CUP ALL-PURPOSE FLOUR

1 TEASPOON KOSHER SALT

1 TEASPOON BAKING POWDER

1 CUP WATER

CANOLA OIL, AS NEEDED

1 BLOCK OF FETA CHEESE (½-INCH THICK)

1 TEASPOON EXTRA-VIRGIN OLIVE OIL

1 CUP GRAPE TOMATOES

LEAVES FROM ½ HEAD OF ROMAINE LETTUCE

1 TABLESPOON BALSAMIC GLAZE (SEE PAGE 562)

1. Place the flour, salt, baking powder, and water in a small bowl and whisk until the mixture is smooth.

2. Add canola oil to a small saucepan until it is about 1 inch deep and warm it over medium-high heat.

3. Carefully dip the block of feta in the batter until it is completely coated.

4. Submerge half of the feta in the canola oil for 5 seconds, then release it so that it floats. Fry for 1½ minutes on each side, while keeping a close eye on the feta; if the batter doesn't seal, the feta will ooze out and this won't work. Once the feta has browned, remove from the oil and set it on a cooling rack.

5. Place the olive oil in a medium skillet and warm it over high heat. Add the tomatoes and cook until they start to blister, 2 to 3 minutes. Add the lettuce leaves and brown them for about 1 minute. Remove the pan from heat.

6. To serve, place the lettuce in a shallow bowl, scatter the tomatoes on top, and nestle the fried block of feta on top. Drizzle the Balsamic Glaze over the cheese and enjoy.

Cheesy Poofs

YIELD: 4 SERVINGS | **ACTIVE TIME:** 15 MINUTES | **TOTAL TIME:** 35 MINUTES

CANOLA OIL, AS NEEDED

2 CUPS SWEET POTATO PUREE

1 EGG

½ CUP WHITE FLOUR

½ TEASPOON BAKING POWDER

¼ CUP GRATED ASIAGO CHEESE

¼ CUP GRATED PARMESAN CHEESE

⅓ CUP SHREDDED MOZZARELLA CHEESE

1. Add canola oil to a Dutch oven until it is 2 inches deep and warm it to 350ºF over medium heat. Place the sweet potato puree and egg in a mixing bowl. Add the flour and baking powder and stir until the mixture is smooth.

2. Add the cheeses one at a time and fold to incorporate. Form tablespoons of the mixture into balls and gently slip them into the hot oil. Fry until they are golden brown, 4 to 6 minutes, turning them as needed.

3. Remove the cheesy poofs from the hot oil and transfer them to a paper towel–lined plate to drain and cool slightly before serving.

Smoky & Spicy Almonds

YIELD: 2 CUPS | **ACTIVE TIME:** 10 MINUTES | **TOTAL TIME:** 45 MINUTES

4 TABLESPOONS UNSALTED BUTTER, MELTED

4 TEASPOONS WORCESTERSHIRE SAUCE

1 TEASPOON CUMIN

2 TEASPOONS CHILI POWDER

1 TEASPOON GARLIC POWDER

½ TEASPOON ONION POWDER

1 TEASPOON CAYENNE PEPPER

1 TEASPOON KOSHER SALT

2 CUPS WHOLE ALMONDS

1. Preheat the oven to 350°F and line a baking sheet with parchment paper. Place all the ingredients, except for the almonds, in a mixing bowl and stir until combined.

2. Add the almonds and toss to coat.

3. Transfer the almonds to the baking sheet, place it in the oven, and roast for about 15 minutes, until the almonds are fragrant and slightly darker. Turn the almonds occasionally as they roast.

4. Remove from the oven and let the almonds cool before serving.

Lemon Ricotta

YIELD: 2 CUPS | **ACTIVE TIME:** 10 MINUTES | **TOTAL TIME:** 3 HOURS

4 CUPS WHOLE MILK

JUICE OF 2 LEMONS

1 TABLESPOON KOSHER SALT

1. Place the milk in a saucepan and warm it over medium heat until it is just about to come to a boil (about 190°F). Remove the pan from heat, add the lemon juice, and stir for 1 minute. Cover the pan and let the mixture stand for 15 minutes. This will allow the curds to separate.

2. Ladle the curds into cheesecloth, tie it closed with kitchen twine, and let it drain at room temperature until almost all the liquid has been drained, about 2½ hours. Stir the salt into the ricotta and enjoy.

Parmesan Crisps

YIELD: 24 CRISPS | **ACTIVE TIME:** 10 MINUTES | **TOTAL TIME:** 25 MINUTES

2 CUPS FRESHLY GRATED PARMESAN CHEESE

2 TABLESPOONS EVERYTHING SEASONING (SEE PAGE 107)

2 TABLESPOONS ALL-PURPOSE FLOUR

1. Preheat the oven to 350ºF and line a baking sheet with a Silpat mat. Place all the ingredients in a food processor and blitz until combined.

2. Using a 2-inch ring mold, shape the mixture into rounds on the baking sheet. You want the rounds to be about ¼ inch thick.

3. Place the pan in the oven and bake until the rounds are brown and crispy, about 7 minutes. Remove from the oven and let cool before enjoying.

Parmesan Spheres

YIELD: 2 SERVINGS | **ACTIVE TIME:** 45 MINUTES | **TOTAL TIME:** 1 HOUR AND 45 MINUTES

4 CUPS FRESHLY GRATED PARMESAN CHEESE

1 CUP EGG WHITES

4 CUPS CANOLA OIL

1. Line a baking sheet with parchment paper. Place the cheese and egg whites in a food processor and blitz until pureed. Scoop ¼-cup portions of the puree onto the baking sheet and place it in the freezer for 45 minutes.

2. Add the canola oil to a Dutch oven and warm it to 350ºF over medium heat. Working in batches, add the spheres to the oil and fry, turning occasionally, until they are golden brown, about 4 minutes. Transfer the fried Parmesan spheres to a paper towel–lined plate to drain and cool slightly before enjoying.

Baked Camembert

YIELD: 4 SERVINGS | **ACTIVE TIME:** 5 MINUTES | **TOTAL TIME:** 25 MINUTES

½ LB. ROUND OF CAMEMBERT CHEESE

1 CUP GRANOLA (SEE PAGE 483)

½ CUP REAL MAPLE SYRUP

1. Preheat the oven to 350ºF. Place the Camembert in a small cast-iron skillet or a ceramic dish. Sprinkle the granola over the cheese and drizzle the maple syrup on top.

2. Place the skillet in the oven and bake until the cheese is gooey, about 15 minutes. Remove from the oven and serve immediately.

Cured Egg Yolks

YIELD: 4 SERVINGS | **ACTIVE TIME:** 30 MINUTES | **TOTAL TIME:** 3 DAYS

1½ CUPS KOSHER SALT
½ CUP SUGAR
4 EGG YOLKS

1. Combine the salt and sugar in wide bowl. Using a spoon, create four small wells in the mixture, one for each yolk.

2. Carefully place each yolk into its own well. Spoon the mixture over the yolks until they are covered completely.

3. Cover the bowl with plastic wrap, place it in the refrigerator, and let the egg yolks cure for 3 days.

4. Remove the yolks from the mixture, rinse under cold water, and slice before serving.

Marinated Feta

YIELD: 4 SERVINGS | **ACTIVE TIME:** 5 MINUTES | **TOTAL TIME:** 2 HOURS AND 5 MINUTES

½ LB. FETA CHEESE

1 SPRIG OF FRESH BASIL

¾ CUP EXTRA-VIRGIN OLIVE OIL

½ CUP WHITE WINE VINEGAR

2 TABLESPOONS BLACK PEPPER

1 TEASPOON KOSHER SALT

¾ TEASPOON RED PEPPER FLAKES

1. Cut the feta into bite-size chunks and place them in a mason jar.

2. Combine the remaining ingredients in a mixing bowl and then pour the marinade over the feta. Let the cheese marinate for at least 2 hours before enjoying.

Grilled Halloumi

YIELD: 4 SERVINGS | **ACTIVE TIME:** 5 MINUTES | **TOTAL TIME:** 20 MINUTES

½ LB. HALLOUMI CHEESE

EXTRA-VIRGIN OLIVE OIL, TO TASTE

1. Preheat a gas or charcoal grill to 350ºF. Cut the halloumi into pieces that are approximately ½ inch wide.

2. Drizzle olive oil over the cheese and place it on the grill. Grill until the cheese is warm and has grill marks on both sides, about 6 minutes. Remove from the grill and serve immediately.

Goat Cheese with Herbs

YIELD: 4 SERVINGS | **ACTIVE TIME:** 10 MINUTES | **TOTAL TIME:** 1 HOUR AND 10 MINUTES

½ LB. LOG OF GOAT CHEESE

2 TABLESPOONS CHOPPED FRESH TARRAGON

2 TABLESPOONS CHOPPED FRESH CHIVES

2 TABLESPOONS CHOPPED FRESH THYME

1 CUP EXTRA-VIRGIN OLIVE OIL

2 GARLIC CLOVES, CHOPPED

1 TEASPOON KOSHER SALT

1. Slice the goat cheese into rounds. Gently roll the rounds in the herbs and gently press down so that the herbs adhere to the cheese.

2. Layer the rounds in glass jars. Pour the olive oil over them until they are covered. Add the garlic and salt and let the mixture sit for an hour before serving.

Southern Deviled Eggs

YIELD: 6 EGGS | **ACTIVE TIME:** 15 MINUTES | **TOTAL TIME:** 30 MINUTES

6 HARD-BOILED EGGS (SEE PAGE 472)

2 TABLESPOONS YELLOW MUSTARD

2 TABLESPOONS MAYONNAISE

2 TEASPOONS WHOLE-GRAIN MUSTARD

2 CORNICHONS, DICED

2 TEASPOONS DICED PIMIENTO PEPPER

SALT AND PEPPER, TO TASTE

FRESH PARSLEY, CHOPPED, FOR GARNISH

FRESH DILL, CHOPPED, FOR GARNISH

1 SLICE OF SPAM, CUT INTO TRIANGLES AND FRIED, FOR GARNISH (OPTIONAL)

1. Cut the eggs in half, remove the yolks, and place them in a small bowl. Add the remaining ingredients, except for the garnishes, and stir until thoroughly combined.

2. Spoon the yolk mixture into the cavities in the egg whites. Garnish with parsley, dill, and, if desired, the Spam.

Marinated Mozzarella

YIELD: 4 SERVINGS | **ACTIVE TIME:** 5 MINUTES | **TOTAL TIME:** 5 MINUTES

1 (7 OZ.) CONTAINER OF MINIATURE BALLS OF MOZZARELLA CHEESE

PESTO (SEE PAGE 162)

1. Place the mozzarella and Pesto in a mixing bowl, toss until the cheese is coated, and serve immediately.

Almond Croissants

YIELD: 16 CROISSANTS | **ACTIVE TIME:** 45 MINUTES | **TOTAL TIME:** 17 HOURS

FOR THE DOUGH

28.4 OZ. ALL-PURPOSE FLOUR, PLUS MORE AS NEEDED

3½ OZ. SUGAR

1 TABLESPOON FINE SEA SALT

1¼ TEASPOONS INSTANT YEAST

1 CUP WHOLE MILK

1½ OZ. CULTURED BUTTER

POOLISH FOR CROISSANTS (SEE PAGE 565)

1 EGG YOLK

1 TEASPOON HEAVY CREAM

FOR THE LAMINATION LAYER

18 OZ. CULTURED BUTTER

FOR THE FILLING

FRANGIPANE (SEE PAGE 565)

1. To make the dough, combine the flour, sugar, salt, yeast, milk, and butter in the work bowl of a stand mixer fitted with the paddle attachment. Add the Poolish and beat on low speed until the mixture is just combined, about 2 minutes. Let the dough rest for 20 minutes and then mix for 2 minutes on low speed. Transfer the dough to a separate bowl, cover with plastic wrap, and let it stand at room temperature for 1 hour.

2. To prepare the lamination layer, place the cultured butter in a mixing bowl and beat until it is smooth and free of lumps. Place the butter on a piece of parchment paper and smash until it is a 6½ x 9–inch rectangle of uniform thickness. Place the butter in the refrigerator when the dough has 20 minutes left to stand.

3. Place the dough on a flour-dusted work surface and roll it out into a 13 x 9–inch rectangle. Remove the lamination layer butter from the refrigerator and place it on the right half of the dough. Fold the left side of the dough over the butter, making sure that the dough completely covers the butter. Essentially, you want to make a "butter sandwich."

4. Roll the dough out to a 12 x 27–inch rectangle, fold it in half, and then fold it in half again. Wrap the dough in plastic, place in the refrigerator, and chill for 1 hour.

5. Place the dough on a flour-dusted work surface and gently roll it out into a 12 x 30–inch rectangle. Cut the rectangle into 4-inch squares and then cut each square into two triangles. Spread some of the Frangipane in the center of each triangle.

6. Roll up the croissants, starting at the 90° angle and working toward the wide side (aka the hypotenuse). Place the croissants on parchment-lined baking sheets, making sure to leave enough space between them. Cover with a kitchen towel and let them stand at room temperature for 4 hours. The croissants can be refrigerated until the next day after this period of rest.

7. When you are ready to bake the croissants, preheat the oven to 425°F. Place the egg yolk and heavy cream in a mug and stir to combine. Brush the egg wash on the tops of the croissants, place them in the oven, and bake until golden brown, 20 to 25 minutes.

8. Remove the croissants from the oven and enjoy them immediately.

Pain Au Chocolat

YIELD: 16 CROISSANTS | **ACTIVE TIME:** 45 MINUTES | **TOTAL TIME:** 17 HOURS

FOR THE CROISSANTS

28.4 OZ. ALL-PURPOSE FLOUR, PLUS MORE AS NEEDED

3½ OZ. SUGAR

1 TABLESPOON FINE SEA SALT

1¼ TEASPOONS INSTANT YEAST

1 CUP WHOLE MILK

1½ OZ. CULTURED BUTTER

POOLISH FOR CROISSANTS (SEE PAGE 565)

16 PIECES OF PREFERRED CHOCOLATE

1 EGG YOLK

1 TEASPOON HEAVY CREAM

FOR THE LAMINATION LAYER

18 OZ. CULTURED BUTTER

1. To begin preparations for the croissants, combine the flour, sugar, salt, yeast, milk, and butter in the work bowl of a stand mixer fitted with the paddle attachment. Add the Poolish and beat on low speed until the mixture is just combined, about 2 minutes. Let the dough rest for 20 minutes and then mix for 2 minutes on low speed. Transfer the dough to a separate bowl, cover with plastic wrap, and let it stand at room temperature for 1 hour.

2. Place the butter for the lamination layer in a mixing bowl and beat until it is smooth and free of lumps. Place the butter on a piece of parchment paper and smash until it is a 6½ x 9–inch rectangle of uniform thickness. Place the butter in the refrigerator when the dough has 20 minutes left to stand.

3. Place the dough on a flour-dusted work surface and roll it out into a 13 x 9–inch rectangle. Remove the lamination layer butter from the refrigerator and place it on half of the dough. Fold the other half over the butter, making sure that the dough completely covers the butter.

4. Roll the dough out into a 12 x 27–inch rectangle, fold it in half, and then fold it in half again. Cover the dough completely with plastic wrap, place it in the refrigerator, and chill for 1 hour.

5. Place the dough on a flour-dusted work surface and gently roll it out into a 12 x 30–inch rectangle. Cut the rectangle in half and then cut each half every 3½ inches. Place a piece of chocolate in the center of each piece of dough. Fold the dough over the chocolate and place the croissants, seam side down, on parchment-lined baking sheets, making sure to leave enough space between them. Let them stand at room temperature for 4 hours or refrigerate until the next day.

6. When you are ready to bake the croissants, preheat the oven to 425°F. Place the egg yolk and heavy cream in a mug and stir to combine. Brush the tops of the croissants with the egg wash, place them in the oven, and bake until golden brown, 20 to 25 minutes.

7. Remove the croissants from the oven and enjoy immediately.

Almond Croissants
SEE PAGE 510

Apple Turnovers

YIELD: 4 SERVINGS | **ACTIVE TIME:** 25 MINUTES | **TOTAL TIME:** 1 HOUR AND 15 MINUTES

2 APPLES, PEELED, CORES REMOVED, CHOPPED

¾ CUP SUGAR

1 TABLESPOON FRESH LEMON JUICE

PINCH OF FINE SEA SALT

¼ CUP APPLESAUCE

1 SHEET OF FROZEN PUFF PASTRY, THAWED

ALL-PURPOSE FLOUR, AS NEEDED

1 TEASPOON CINNAMON

SANDING SUGAR, FOR TOPPING

1. Preheat the oven to 375°F and line a baking sheet with parchment paper. Place the apples, 10 tablespoons of the sugar, lemon juice, and salt in a food processor and pulse until the apples are minced. Strain the juice into a bowl through a fine sieve, reserve the juice, and place the solids in another small bowl. Stir in the applesauce and let the mixture sit for 5 minutes.

2. Place the sheet of puff pastry on a flour-dusted work surface and cut it into quarters. Place 2 tablespoons of the apple mixture in the middle of each quarter and brush the edges with some of the reserved liquid. Fold a bottom corner of each quarter to the opposing top corner and crimp to seal. Place the sealed pastries in the refrigerator for 10 minutes.

3. Place the remaining sugar and the cinnamon in a small bowl and stir to combine.

4. Place the turnovers on the baking sheet and brush the tops with some of the reserved liquid. Sprinkle the cinnamon-and-sugar mixture over the turnovers, place the sheet in the oven, and bake, rotating the baking sheet halfway through, until the turnovers are golden brown, about 25 minutes.

5. Remove the turnovers from the oven, transfer them to wire racks, sprinkle sanding sugar over the top, and let the turnovers cool before enjoying.

Apple Strudel

YIELD: 6 SERVINGS | **ACTIVE TIME:** 25 MINUTES | **TOTAL TIME:** 1 HOUR AND 30 MINUTES

¾ LB. APPLES, PEELED, CORES REMOVED, CHOPPED

¼ TEASPOON LEMON ZEST

1 TEASPOON FRESH LEMON JUICE

1½ TABLESPOONS SUGAR

DASH OF CINNAMON

¼ TEASPOON GROUND GINGER

2 PINCHES OF FINE SEA SALT

4 TABLESPOONS UNSALTED BUTTER, MELTED

7 SHEETS OF FROZEN PHYLLO DOUGH, THAWED

1 TABLESPOON CONFECTIONERS' SUGAR, PLUS MORE FOR DUSTING

1. Preheat the oven to 350°F and line a baking sheet with parchment paper. Place the apples, lemon zest, lemon juice, sugar, cinnamon, ginger, and a pinch of salt in a large mixing bowl and toss until the apples are evenly coated. Place the mixture in a skillet and cook over medium heat until the apples begin to release their liquid. Remove the pan from heat and let it cool for 10 minutes before draining the mixture.

2. Place the melted butter in a bowl and stir in the remaining salt.

3. Brush a sheet of phyllo dough with some of the salted butter and lightly dust it with some of the confectioners' sugar. Repeat with the remaining sheets of phyllo dough, stacking them on top of one another after they have been dressed.

4. Place the apple mixture in the center of the phyllo sheets, leaving a 2-inch border of dough on the sides. Fold the border over the filling so that they overlap and gently press down to seal.

5. Place the strudel on the baking sheet, place it in the oven, and bake, rotating the sheet halfway through, until the strudel is golden brown, 30 to 40 minutes. Remove the strudel from the oven, transfer it to a cutting board, and let it cool slightly. Slice the strudel into desired portions and dust with additional confectioners' sugar before serving.

Roasted Strawberry Handpies

YIELD: 8 SERVINGS | **ACTIVE TIME:** 40 MINUTES | **TOTAL TIME:** 2 HOURS

3 QUARTS OF FRESH STRAWBERRIES, HULLED AND SLICED

1 CUP SUGAR

2 TEASPOONS FRESH LEMON JUICE

1 TABLESPOON CORNSTARCH

1½ TEASPOONS WATER

1 BALL OF PERFECT PIECRUST DOUGH (SEE PAGE 562)

2 EGGS, BEATEN

1½ CUPS SIFTED CONFECTIONERS' SUGAR

3 TO 4 TABLESPOONS WHOLE MILK

1 TEASPOON CINNAMON

1. Preheat the oven to 400°F. Place the strawberries on a baking sheet, place them in the oven, and roast until they start to darken and release their juice, 20 to 30 minutes.

2. Remove the strawberries from the oven and place them in a saucepan with the sugar and lemon juice. Bring to a simmer over medium heat and cook for 20 minutes, until the mixture has thickened slightly.

3. Place the cornstarch and water in a small cup and stir until there are no lumps in the mixture. Add the slurry to the saucepan and stir until the mixture is syrupy. Remove the pan from heat.

4. Divide the ball of piecrust dough into two squares and then cut each square into quarters. Spoon some of the strawberry mixture into the center of each quarter.

5. Take a bottom corner of each pie and fold to the opposite top corner. Press down to ensure that none of the mixture leaks out and then use a fork to seal the edge. Place the handpies on a baking sheet and brush them with the beaten egg.

6. Place the handpies in the oven and bake until golden brown, about 20 to 30 minutes.

7. While the pies are cooking, place the confectioners' sugar, milk, and cinnamon in a bowl and whisk until well combined.

8. Remove the pies from the oven, brush them with the sugar-and-cinnamon glaze, and let cool before serving.

Squash Whoopie Pies

YIELD: 12 SERVINGS | **ACTIVE TIME:** 20 MINUTES | **TOTAL TIME:** 1 HOUR

1⅓ CUPS ALL-PURPOSE FLOUR

1 TEASPOON CINNAMON

1 TEASPOON GROUND GINGER

¼ TEASPOON GROUND CLOVES

½ TEASPOON FRESHLY GRATED NUTMEG

½ TEASPOON BAKING SODA

½ TEASPOON BAKING POWDER

1 TEASPOON KOSHER SALT

1 CUP PACKED LIGHT BROWN SUGAR

2 TABLESPOONS REAL MAPLE SYRUP

1 CUP PUREED BUTTERNUT OR ACORN SQUASH

1 EGG

1 CUP EXTRA-VIRGIN OLIVE OIL

1⅓ CUPS CONFECTIONERS' SUGAR

4 TABLESPOONS UNSALTED BUTTER

½ LB. CREAM CHEESE, AT ROOM TEMPERATURE

1-INCH PIECE OF FRESH GINGER, PEELED AND GRATED

½ TEASPOON PURE VANILLA EXTRACT

1. Preheat the oven to 350°F. Sift the flour, cinnamon, ground ginger, cloves, nutmeg, baking soda, baking powder, and salt into a mixing bowl.

2. Place the brown sugar, maple syrup, pureed squash, egg, and olive oil in a separate mixing bowl and stir until combined. Sift the dry mixture into the squash mixture and stir until it has been incorporated.

3. Use an ice cream scoop to place dollops of the batter onto parchment-lined baking sheets. Make sure to leave plenty of space between the scoops. Place the sheets in the oven and bake until the cakes are golden brown, about 10 to 15 minutes. Remove and let cool.

4. While the squash cakes are cooling, place the remaining ingredients in a bowl and beat with a handheld mixer until the mixture is fluffy.

5. When the cakes have cooled completely, spread the filling on one of the cakes. Top with another cake and repeat until all of the cakes and filling have been used.

Macarons

YIELD: 30 MACARONS | **ACTIVE TIME:** 1 HOUR | **TOTAL TIME:** 4 HOURS

11 OZ. FINE ALMOND FLOUR

11 OZ. CONFECTIONERS' SUGAR

8 EGG WHITES

PINCH OF FINE SEA SALT

11 OZ. SUGAR

½ CUP WATER

2 TO 3 DROPS OF GEL FOOD COLORING (OPTIONAL)

1. Place the almond flour and confectioners' sugar in a food processor and blitz for about 1 minute, until the mixture is thoroughly combined and has a fine texture. Place the mixture in a mixing bowl, add three of the egg whites and the salt, and stir with a rubber spatula until the mixture is almost a paste. Set the mixture aside.

2. Place the sugar and water in a small saucepan. Place a candy thermometer in the saucepan and cook the mixture over high heat.

3. While the syrup is coming to a boil, place the remaining egg whites in the work bowl of a stand mixer fitted with the whisk attachment, and whip on medium until they hold firm peaks.

4. Cook the syrup until it is 245°F. Remove the pan from heat and carefully add the syrup to the whipped egg whites, slowly pouring it down the side of the work bowl. When all of the syrup has been added, whip the mixture until it is glossy, holds stiff peaks, and has cooled slightly. If desired, stir in the food coloring.

5. Add half of the meringue to the almond flour mixture and fold to incorporate. Fold in the remaining meringue. When incorporated, the batter should be smooth, very glossy, and not too runny.

6. Fit a piping bag with a plain tip and fill it with the batter. Pipe evenly sized rounds onto baking sheets lined with Silpat baking mats, leaving an inch of space between each round. You want the rounds to be about the size of a silver dollar (approximately 2 inches wide) when you pipe them onto the sheet; they will spread slightly as they sit.

7. Gently tap each baking sheet to smooth the tops of the macarons.

8. Let the macarons sit at room temperature, uncovered, for 1 hour. This allows a skin to form on them.

9. Preheat the oven to 325°F.

10. Place the macarons in the oven and bake for 10 minutes. Rotate the baking sheet and let them bake for another 5 minutes. Turn off the oven, crack the oven door, and let the macarons sit in the oven for 5 minutes.

11. Remove from the oven and let the cookies sit on a cooling rack for 2 hours. When the macarons are completely cool, fill them as desired.

Whoopie Pies

YIELD: 20 WHOOPIE PIES | **ACTIVE TIME:** 30 MINUTES | **TOTAL TIME:** 1 HOUR

9 OZ. ALL-PURPOSE FLOUR

1.8 OZ. COCOA POWDER

1½ TEASPOONS BAKING SODA

½ TEASPOON KOSHER SALT

½ CUP UNSALTED BUTTER, SOFTENED

½ LB. SUGAR

1 EGG

1 TEASPOON PURE VANILLA EXTRACT

1 CUP BUTTERMILK

2 CUPS BUTTERFLUFF FILLING (SEE PAGE 563)

1. Preheat the oven to 350°F and line two baking sheets with parchment paper. Sift the all-purpose flour, cocoa powder, baking soda, and salt into a mixing bowl. Set the mixture aside.

2. In the work bowl of a stand mixer fitted with the paddle attachment, cream the butter and sugar on medium until the mixture is very light and fluffy, about 5 minutes. Scrape down the work bowl with a rubber spatula and then beat the mixture for another 5 minutes.

3. Reduce the speed to low, add the egg, and beat until incorporated. Scrape down the work bowl, raise the speed to medium, and beat the mixture for 1 minute.

4. Reduce the speed to low, add the vanilla and the dry mixture, and beat until it comes together as a smooth batter. Add the buttermilk in a slow stream and beat to incorporate.

5. Scoop 2-oz. portions of the batter onto the baking sheets, making sure to leave 2 inches between each portion. Tap the bottom of the baking sheets gently on the counter to remove any air bubbles and let the portions spread out slightly.

6. Place them in the oven and bake until a cake tester inserted at the centers of the whoopie pies comes out clean, 10 to 12 minutes.

7. Remove the whoopie pies from the oven and let them cool completely on the baking sheets.

8. Carefully remove the whoopie pies from the parchment paper. Scoop about 2 oz. of the Butterfluff Filling on half of the whoopie pies and then create sandwiches by topping with the remaining half.

Macarons
SEE PAGE 520

Madeleines

YIELD: 30 MADELEINES | **ACTIVE TIME:** 40 MINUTES | **TOTAL TIME:** 3 HOURS AND 30 MINUTES

½ LB. SUGAR

1 CUP EGG WHITES

ZEST OF 1 LEMON

3.2 OZ. FINE ALMOND FLOUR

3.2 OZ. ALL-PURPOSE FLOUR

7 OZ. UNSALTED BUTTER

1 TEASPOON PURE VANILLA EXTRACT

CONFECTIONERS' SUGAR, FOR DUSTING

1. In the work bowl of a stand mixer fitted with the paddle attachment, beat the sugar, egg whites, and lemon zest on medium until the mixture is light and fluffy. Add the flours and beat until incorporated. Set the mixture aside.

2. Place the butter in a small saucepan and melt it over low heat.

3. Set the mixer to low speed and slowly pour the melted butter into the mixer. When the butter has been incorporated, add the vanilla and beat until incorporated.

4. Place the madeleine batter into two piping bags. Place the bags in the refrigerator to set the batter, about 2 hours.

5. Coat your madeleine pans with nonstick cooking spray. Pipe about 1 tablespoon of batter into the center of each seashell mold.

6. Place the pans in the oven and bake until the edges of the madeleines turn golden brown, about 10 minutes. Remove the cookies from the oven, immediately remove the cookies from the pans, transfer them to a cooling rack, and let them cool completely.

7. Once cool, lightly dust the tops of the madeleines with confectioners' sugar.

Coconut Macaroons

YIELD: 12 MACAROONS | **ACTIVE TIME:** 45 MINUTES | **TOTAL TIME:** 3 HOURS

1 (14 OZ.) CAN OF SWEETENED CONDENSED MILK

7 OZ. SWEETENED SHREDDED COCONUT

7 OZ. UNSWEETENED SHREDDED COCONUT

¼ TEASPOON KOSHER SALT

½ TEASPOON PURE VANILLA EXTRACT

2 EGG WHITES

CHOCOLATE GANACHE (SEE PAGE 563), WARM

1. Line a baking sheet with parchment paper. In a mixing bowl, mix the sweetened condensed milk, shredded coconut, salt, and vanilla with a rubber spatula until combined. Set the mixture aside.

2. In the work bowl of a stand mixer fitted with the whisk attachment, whip the egg whites until they hold stiff peaks. Add the whipped egg whites to the coconut mixture and fold to incorporate.

3. Scoop 2-oz. portions of the mixture onto the lined baking sheet, making sure to leave enough space between them. Place the baking sheet in the refrigerator and let the dough firm up for 1 hour.

4. Preheat the oven to 350°F.

5. Place the cookies in the oven and bake until they are lightly golden brown, 20 to 25 minutes.

6. Remove from the oven, transfer the cookies to a cooling rack, and let them cool for 1 hour.

7. Dip the bottoms of the macaroons into the ganache and then place them back on the baking sheet. If desired, drizzle some of the ganache over the tops of the cookies. Refrigerate until the chocolate is set, about 5 minutes, before serving.

Kipferl Biscuits

YIELD: 12 COOKIES | **ACTIVE TIME:** 40 MINUTES | **TOTAL TIME:** 2 HOURS

6.7 OZ. ALL-PURPOSE FLOUR, PLUS MORE AS NEEDED

1½ OZ. COCOA POWDER

½ TEASPOON INSTANT ESPRESSO POWDER

¼ TEASPOON FINE SEA SALT

1 CUP UNSALTED BUTTER, SOFTENED AND DIVIDED INTO TABLESPOONS

3 OZ. CONFECTIONERS' SUGAR, SIFTED

2½ OZ. FINE ALMOND FLOUR

1 TEASPOON PURE VANILLA EXTRACT

½ CUP WHITE CHOCOLATE CHIPS

1. Place all of the ingredients, except for the white chocolate chips, in the work bowl of a stand mixer fitted with the paddle attachment and beat at medium speed until the mixture comes together as a soft dough. Flatten the dough into a disk, cover it completely with plastic wrap, and refrigerate for 1 hour.

2. Preheat the oven to 350°F and line two large baking sheets with parchment paper. Remove the dough from the refrigerator and let it stand at room temperature for 5 minutes. Roll the dough into a ¾-inch-thick log, cut it into 2-inch-long pieces, and roll the pieces into cylinders with your hands, while tapering and curling the ends to create crescent shapes. Place them on the baking sheets.

3. Place the cookies in the oven and bake for about 15 minutes, until set and firm. Remove from the oven and transfer the cookies to wire racks to cool.

4. Fill a small saucepan halfway with water and bring it to a gentle simmer. Place the white chocolate chips in a heatproof bowl, place it over the simmering water, and stir until melted. Drizzle the melted chocolate over the cooled biscuits and let it set before serving.

Rice Krispies Treats

YIELD: 12 BARS | **ACTIVE TIME:** 30 MINUTES | **TOTAL TIME:** 1 HOUR AND 30 MINUTES

1½ CUPS MARSHMALLOW CREME

4½ OZ. UNSALTED BUTTER

¾ TEASPOON FINE SEA SALT

9 CUPS CRISPY RICE CEREAL

¾ TEASPOON PURE VANILLA EXTRACT

2½ CUPS CHOCOLATE CHIPS OR M&M'S (OPTIONAL)

1. Line a 13 x 9–inch baking pan with parchment paper and coat it with nonstick cooking spray.

2. Fill a small saucepan halfway with water and bring it to a simmer. Place the marshmallow creme, butter, and salt in a heatproof mixing bowl over the simmering water and stir the mixture with a rubber spatula until the butter has melted and the mixture is thoroughly combined. Remove the bowl from heat, add the cereal and vanilla, and fold until combined. If desired, add the chocolate chips or M&M's and fold until evenly distributed.

3. Transfer the mixture to the baking pan and spread it with a rubber spatula. Place another piece of parchment over the mixture and pack it down with your hands until it is flat and even. Remove the top piece of parchment and refrigerate for 1 hour.

4. Run a knife along the edge of the pan, turn the mixture out onto a cutting board, and cut it into squares.

Gluten-Free Almond Torte

YIELD: 1 CAKE | **ACTIVE TIME:** 40 MINUTES | **TOTAL TIME:** 2 HOURS

2½ OZ. GLUTEN-FREE FLOUR

¼ TEASPOON XANTHAN GUM

¾ TEASPOON BAKING POWDER

¼ TEASPOON KOSHER SALT

4 OZ. ALMOND PASTE

½ CUP UNSALTED BUTTER, SOFTENED

4.7 OZ. SUGAR

¼ TEASPOON PURE VANILLA EXTRACT

¼ TEASPOON ALMOND EXTRACT

3 EGGS

½ CUP SLIVERED ALMONDS

ALMOND SYRUP (SEE PAGE 564)

CONFECTIONERS' SUGAR, FOR DUSTING

1. Preheat the oven to 375°F. Line a round 9-inch cake pan with parchment paper and coat it with nonstick cooking spray.

2. In a medium bowl, whisk together the flour, xanthan gum, baking powder, and salt. Set aside.

3. In the work bowl of a stand mixer fitted with the paddle attachment, cream the almond paste, butter, sugar, vanilla, and almond extract on high until the mixture is smooth and fluffy, about 10 minutes. Reduce the speed to low and incorporate the eggs one at a time. Scrape down the sides of the work bowl with a rubber spatula between each addition. Add the dry mixture, beat until combined, and raise the speed to high. Beat the mixture for 2 minutes to thicken it.

4. Pour the batter into the prepared cake pan. Bang the pan on the countertop to evenly distribute the batter and remove any air bubbles. Sprinkle the slivered almonds over the batter and place it in the oven.

5. Bake the cake until it is lightly golden brown and a cake tester comes out clean after being inserted, 20 to 25 minutes. Remove from the oven, transfer the cake to a cooling rack, and let it cool completely.

6. Gently brush the syrup over the torte and dust with confectioners' sugar before slicing and serving.

Chocolate Souffles

YIELD: 6 SOUFFLES | **ACTIVE TIME:** 30 MINUTES | **TOTAL TIME:** 1 HOUR

9 OZ. SUGAR, PLUS MORE
FOR COATING RAMEKINS

20 OZ. DARK CHOCOLATE
(55 TO 65 PERCENT)

½ CUP UNSALTED BUTTER

19 OZ. WATER, PLUS MORE
AS NEEDED

2 OZ. HEAVY CREAM

11 EGGS, SEPARATED

1½ OZ. SOUR CREAM

½ TEASPOON CREAM OF
TARTAR

1. Preheat the oven to 375°F. Coat the insides of six 8-oz. ramekins with nonstick cooking spray. Place 2 tablespoons of sugar in each ramekin and spread it to evenly coat the insides of the dishes. Knock out any excess sugar and set the ramekins aside.

2. Place the dark chocolate and butter in a large, heatproof bowl. Add 2 inches of water to a small saucepan and bring it to a simmer. Place the bowl on top and melt the butter and chocolate together.

3. In a medium saucepan, bring the water and heavy cream to a simmer and then whisk in the chocolate-and-butter mixture. Remove the saucepan from heat.

4. Place the egg yolks and sour cream in a mixing bowl and whisk until combined. Gradually incorporate the cream-and-chocolate mixture, while whisking constantly. Set aside.

5. In the work bowl of a stand mixer fitted with the whisk attachment, whip the egg whites and cream of tartar on high until the mixture holds stiff peaks. Reduce the speed to medium and gradually incorporate the 9 oz. of sugar. Once all of the sugar has been incorporated, raise the speed back to high and whip until it is a glossy, stiff meringue.

6. Working in three increments, add the meringue to the chocolate base, folding gently with a rubber spatula.

7. Spoon the souffle base to the rims of the ramekins. Gently tap the bottoms of the ramekins with the palm of your hand to remove any air bubbles, but not so hard as to deflate the meringue.

8. Place in the oven and bake until the souffles have risen significantly and have set on the outside, but are still jiggly at the center, 25 to 27 minutes. Remove from the oven and serve immediately.

Linzer Tart

YIELD: 1 TART | **ACTIVE TIME:** 30 MINUTES | **TOTAL TIME:** 2 HOURS AND 45 MINUTES

3.2 OZ. FINE ALMOND FLOUR

1 CUP SUGAR

¾ CUP UNSALTED BUTTER, SOFTENED

1 TEASPOON LEMON ZEST

3 EGGS

6¼ OZ. ALL-PURPOSE FLOUR, PLUS MORE AS NEEDED

½ TEASPOON CINNAMON

¼ TEASPOON GROUND CLOVES

1 TABLESPOON UNSWEETENED COCOA POWDER

¼ TEASPOON KOSHER SALT

1½ CUPS RASPBERRY JAM (SEE PAGE 133)

1. Preheat the oven to 250°F. Place the almond flour on a baking sheet, place it in the oven, and toast for 5 minutes. Remove from the oven and set aside.

2. In the work bowl of a stand mixer fitted with the paddle attachment, combine the sugar, butter, and lemon zest and beat on medium until the mixture is pale and fluffy.

3. Incorporate two of the eggs one at a time, scraping down the work bowl as needed.

4. Place the flour, almond flour, cinnamon, cloves, cocoa powder, and salt in a separate bowl and whisk to combine. Gradually add this mixture to the wet mixture and beat until the mixture comes together as a dough. Divide the dough in half, envelop each piece in plastic wrap, and refrigerate for 1 hour.

5. Preheat the oven to 350°F and coat a 9-inch tart pan with nonstick cooking spray. Place the pieces of dough on a flour-dusted work surface and roll them out to fit the tart pan. Place one piece of dough in the pan and then cut the other piece of dough into ¾-inch-wide strips.

6. Fill the crust in the pan with the jam. Lay some of the strips over the tart and trim any excess. To make a lattice crust, lift every other strip and fold back so you can place another strip across those strips that remain flat. Lay the folded strips back down over the cross strip. Fold back the strips that you laid the cross strip on top of and repeat until the lattice covers the surface of the tart. Beat the remaining egg until scrambled and brush the strips with it, taking care not to get any egg on the filling.

7. Place the tart in the oven and bake for about 45 minutes, until the lattice crust is golden brown. Remove from the oven and let it cool before serving.

Linzer Tart
SEE PAGE 533

Cannoli

YIELD: 10 CANNOLI | **ACTIVE TIME:** 45 MINUTES | **TOTAL TIME:** 4 HOURS

¾ LB. WHOLE MILK RICOTTA CHEESE

¾ LB. MASCARPONE CHEESE

4 OZ. CHOCOLATE, GRATED

¾ CUP CONFECTIONERS' SUGAR, PLUS MORE FOR DUSTING

1½ TEASPOONS PURE VANILLA EXTRACT

PINCH OF FINE SEA SALT

10 CANNOLI SHELLS

1. Line a colander with three pieces of cheesecloth and place it in sink. Place the ricotta in the colander, form the cheesecloth into a pouch, and twist to remove as much liquid as possible from the ricotta. Keep the pouch taut and twisted, place it in a baking dish, and place a cast-iron skillet on top. Weigh the skillet down with 2 large, heavy cans and place in the refrigerator for 1 hour.

2. Discard the drained liquid and transfer the ricotta to a mixing bowl. Add the mascarpone, half of the grated chocolate, the confectioners' sugar, vanilla, and salt and stir until well combined. Cover the bowl and refrigerate for at least 1 hour. The mixture will keep in the refrigerator for up to 24 hours.

3. Line an 18 x 13–inch baking sheet with parchment paper. Fill a small saucepan halfway with water and bring it to a gentle simmer. Place the remainder of the chocolate in a heatproof mixing bowl, place it over the simmering water, and stir until it is melted.

4. Dip the ends of the cannoli shells in the chocolate, let the excess drip off, and transfer them to the baking sheet. Let the shells sit until the chocolate is firm, about 1 hour.

5. Place the cannoli filling in a piping bag and cut a ½-inch slit in it. Pipe the filling into the shells, working from both ends in order to ensure they are filled evenly. When all of the cannoli have been filled, dust them with confectioners' sugar and enjoy.

Plum Galette

YIELD: 1 GALETTE | **ACTIVE TIME:** 20 MINUTES | **TOTAL TIME:** 1 HOUR

1 BALL OF PERFECT PIECRUST DOUGH (SEE PAGE 562)

ALL-PURPOSE FLOUR, AS NEEDED

5 PLUMS, PITS REMOVED, SLICED

½ CUP PLUS 1 TABLESPOON SUGAR

JUICE OF ½ LEMON

3 TABLESPOONS CORNSTARCH

PINCH OF FINE SEA SALT

2 TABLESPOONS BLACKBERRY JAM

1 EGG, BEATEN

1. Preheat the oven to 400°F. Place the ball of Perfect Piecrust dough on a flour-dusted work surface, roll it out to 9 inches, and place it on a parchment-lined baking sheet.

2. Place the plums, ½ cup of sugar, lemon juice, cornstarch, and salt in a mixing bowl and stir until the plums are evenly coated.

3. Spread the jam over the crust, making sure to leave a 1½-inch border. Distribute the plum mixture on top of the jam and fold the crust over it. Brush the folded-over crust with the beaten egg and sprinkle it with the remaining sugar.

4. Put the galette in the oven and bake until the crust is golden brown and the filling is bubbly, about 35 to 40 minutes. Remove from the oven and allow it to cool before serving.

Coconut Pudding Pancakes

YIELD: 30 PANCAKES | **ACTIVE TIME:** 20 MINUTES | **TOTAL TIME:** 50 MINUTES

1½ CUPS COCONUT MILK

1½ CUPS RICE FLOUR

½ CUP SWEETENED
SHREDDED COCONUT

5 TABLESPOONS CASTER
(SUPERFINE) SUGAR

½ TEASPOON FINE SEA SALT

1 CUP COCONUT CREAM

½ TABLESPOON TAPIOCA
STARCH OR CORNSTARCH

¼ CUP CORN KERNELS
(OPTIONAL)

1. Preheat the oven to 350°F and coat an aebleskiver pan with nonstick cooking spray.

2. Place the coconut milk, 1 cup of the rice flour, the coconut, 1 tablespoon of the sugar, and the salt in a bowl and whisk vigorously until the sugar has dissolved. Set the mixture aside.

3. Place the coconut cream, remaining rice flour, remaining sugar, and tapioca starch or cornstarch in another bowl and whisk until the starch has dissolved. Add this mixture to the coconut milk mixture and stir until combined.

4. Fill the wells of the aebleskiver pan with the batter and top with some of the corn, if using.

5. Place the pan in the oven and bake until the pancakes are firm, 15 to 20 minutes. Remove from the oven, transfer the cooked pancakes to a platter, and tent it with aluminum foil to keep them warm. Repeat Steps 4 and 5 with any remaining batter.

Meringue Kisses

YIELD: 50 KISSES | **ACTIVE TIME:** 30 MINUTES | **TOTAL TIME:** 1 HOUR AND 30 MINUTES

4 EGG WHITES

1 CUP SUGAR

PINCH OF KOSHER SALT

1 TO 2 DROPS OF GEL FOOD COLORING (OPTIONAL)

1 TEASPOON PURE VANILLA EXTRACT (OPTIONAL)

1. Preheat the oven to 200°F and line two baking sheets with parchment paper.

2. Fill a small saucepan halfway with water and bring it to a gentle simmer. In the work bowl of a stand mixer, combine the egg whites, sugar, and salt. Place the work bowl over the simmering water and whisk continually until the sugar has dissolved. Remove the bowl from heat and return it to the stand mixer.

3. Fit the mixer with the whisk attachment and whip the mixture on high until it holds stiff peaks. If using food coloring or vanilla, add it now and whisk to incorporate.

4. Transfer the meringue to a piping bag fit with a round tip.

5. Pipe the meringue onto the baking sheets, leaving about 1 inch between the meringues. Place the sheets in the oven and bake the meringues until they can be pulled off the parchment cleanly and are no longer sticky in the center, about 1 hour. If the meringues need a little longer, crack the oven door and continue cooking. This will prevent the meringues from browning.

6. Remove from the oven and enjoy immediately.

Churros

YIELD: 75 CHURROS | **ACTIVE TIME:** 25 MINUTES | **TOTAL TIME:** 30 MINUTES

CANOLA OIL, AS NEEDED

35.25 OZ. MILK

81.1 OZ. WATER

2.8 OZ. SUGAR, PLUS MORE TO TASTE

1.4 OZ. SALT

38.8 OZ. "00" FLOUR

38.8 OZ. ALL-PURPOSE FLOUR

32 EGGS

CINNAMON, TO TASTE

CHOCOLATE GANACHE (SEE PAGE 563), WARM, FOR SERVING

1. Add canola oil to a Dutch oven until it is about 2 inches deep and warm to 350°F. Place the milk, water, sugar, and salt in a large saucepan and bring it to a boil.

2. Gradually add the flours and cook, stirring constantly, until the mixture pulls away from the sides of the pan.

3. Place the mixture in the work bowl of a stand mixer fitted with the paddle attachment and beat until the dough is almost cool. Incorporate the eggs one at a time, scraping down the work bowl as needed.

4. Place the dough in a piping bag fitted with a star tip. Pipe 6-inch lengths of dough into the oil and fry until they are golden brown. Place them on paper towel–lined plates to drain and cool slightly. Toss in cinnamon and sugar and enjoy immediately, or store the churros in the freezer.

5. To serve frozen churros, preheat the oven to 450°F. Remove the churros from the freezer and toss them in cinnamon sugar until coated. Place them in the oven and bake for 5 minutes. Remove, toss them in cinnamon and sugar again, and serve with the ganache.

Note: This preparation is for a big batch, most of which you will have to freeze, but you can also enjoy a few straight out of the fryer.

Orange & Pistachio Biscotti

YIELD: 24 BISCOTTI | **ACTIVE TIME:** 1 HOUR | **TOTAL TIME:** 4 HOURS AND 30 MINUTES

½ CUP UNSALTED BUTTER, SOFTENED

ZEST OF 1 ORANGE

1 CUP SUGAR

¾ TEASPOON PURE VANILLA EXTRACT

2 EGGS

10 OZ. ALL-PURPOSE FLOUR

½ TEASPOON BAKING SODA

½ TEASPOON BAKING POWDER

½ TEASPOON FINE SEA SALT

4 OZ. SHELLED PISTACHIOS, TOASTED

1 CUP DRIED CRANBERRIES

1. Line a baking sheet with parchment paper. In the work bowl of a stand mixer fitted with the paddle attachment, cream the butter, orange zest, sugar, and vanilla on medium until the mixture is very light and fluffy, about 5 minutes. Scrape down the work bowl and then beat the mixture for another 5 minutes.

2. Add the eggs one at a time and beat on low until incorporated, again scraping down the work bowl as needed. When both eggs have been incorporated, scrape down the work bowl and beat on medium for 1 minute.

3. Add the remaining ingredients, reduce the speed to low, and beat until the mixture comes together as a dough.

4. Place the dough on the baking sheet and form it into a log that is the length of the pan and anywhere from 3 to 4 inches wide. Place the dough in the refrigerator for 1 hour.

5. Preheat the oven to 350°F.

6. Place the biscotti dough in the oven and bake until it is golden brown and a cake tester comes out clean when inserted into the center, 25 to 30 minutes. Remove from the oven, transfer the biscotti to a cooling rack, and let it cool completely before refrigerating for 2 hours.

7. Preheat the oven to 250°F. Cut the biscotti to the desired size, place the pieces on their sides, and bake for 10 minutes. Remove from the oven, turn them over, and bake for another 6 minutes. Remove the biscotti from the oven and let them cool completely before enjoying.

Churros
SEE PAGE 542

Eclairs

YIELD: 12 ECLAIRS | **ACTIVE TIME:** 40 MINUTES | **TOTAL TIME:** 1 HOUR AND 30 MINUTES

17 OZ. WATER

8½ OZ. UNSALTED BUTTER

1 TEASPOON FINE SEA SALT

2.4 OZ. SUGAR

12½ OZ. ALL-PURPOSE
FLOUR

6 EGGS

PASTRY CREAM (SEE PAGE
564)

CHOCOLATE GANACHE (SEE
PAGE 563), WARM

1. Preheat the oven to 425°F and line two baking sheets with parchment paper. In a medium saucepan, combine the water, butter, salt, and sugar and warm the mixture over medium heat until the butter is melted.

2. Add the flour to the pan and use a rubber spatula or wooden spoon to fold the mixture until it comes together as a thick, shiny dough, taking care not to let the dough burn.

3. Transfer the dough to the work bowl of a stand mixer fitted with the paddle attachment and beat on medium until the dough is no longer steaming and the bowl is just warm to the touch, at least 10 minutes.

4. Incorporate the eggs two at a time, scraping down the work bowl between each addition. Transfer the dough to a piping bag fit with a plain tip. Pipe 12 eclairs onto the baking sheets, leaving 1½ inches between them. They should be approximately 5 inches long.

5. Place the eclairs in the oven and bake for 10 minutes. Lower the oven's temperature to 325°F and bake until they are golden brown and a cake tester inserted into their centers comes out clean, 20 to 25 minutes. Remove from the oven and let them cool on wire racks.

6. Fill a piping bag fitted with a plain tip with the Pastry Cream.

7. Using a paring knife, cut 3 small slits on the undersides of the eclairs and fill them with the Pastry Cream.

8. Carefully dip the top halves of the eclairs in the ganache, or drizzle the ganache over the pastries. Allow the chocolate to set before serving.

Canelés

YIELD: 18 CANELÉS | **ACTIVE TIME:** 1 HOUR | **TOTAL TIME:** 2 DAYS

FOR THE PASTRIES

17.1 OZ. WHOLE MILK

1¾ OZ. CULTURED BUTTER, SOFTENED

1 VANILLA BEAN OR 1 TABLESPOON PURE VANILLA EXTRACT

3½ OZ. ALL-PURPOSE FLOUR

7 OZ. SUGAR

PINCH OF FINE SEA SALT

2 EGGS

2 EGG YOLKS

1¾ OZ. DARK RUM OR COGNAC

FOR THE MOLDS

1¾ OZ. BEESWAX

1¾ OZ. UNSALTED BUTTER

1. To begin preparations for the pastries, place the milk and butter in a saucepan. If using the vanilla bean, halve it, scrape the seeds into the saucepan, and add the pod as well. If using extract, stir it in. Place the pan over medium heat and bring the mixture to a simmer. Immediately remove the pan from heat and let it sit for 10 minutes.

2. In a large mixing bowl, whisk the flour, sugar, and salt together. Set the mixture aside. Place the eggs and egg yolks in a heatproof mixing bowl and whisk to combine, making sure not to add any air to the mixture.

3. While whisking the egg mixture, add the milk mixture in small increments. When all of the milk mixture has been thoroughly incorporated, whisk in the rum or Cognac.

4. Remove the vanilla bean pod and reserve. While whisking, add the tempered eggs to the dry mixture and whisk until just combined, taking care not to overwork the mixture. Strain the custard through a fine sieve. If the mixture is still warm, place the bowl in an ice bath until it has cooled.

5. Add the vanilla bean pod to the custard, cover it with plastic wrap, and refrigerate for at least 24 hours; however, 48 hours is strongly recommended.

6. Preheat the oven to 500°F. To prepare the molds, grate the beeswax into a mason jar and add the butter. Place the jar in a saucepan filled with a few inches of water and bring the water to a simmer. When the beeswax mixture is melted and combined, pour it into one mold, immediately pour it back into the jar, and set the mold, right side up, on a wire rack to drain. When all of the molds have been coated, place them in the freezer for 15 minutes. Remove the custard from the refrigerator and let it come to room temperature.

7. Pour the custard into the molds so that they are filled about 85 percent of the way. Place the filled molds, upside down, on a baking sheet, place them in the oven, and bake for 10 minutes. Reduce the oven's temperature to 375°F and bake until they are a deep brown, about 40 minutes. Turn the canelés out onto a wire rack and let them cool completely before enjoying. Reheat the beeswax mixture and let the molds cool before refilling them with the remaining batter.

APPENDIX

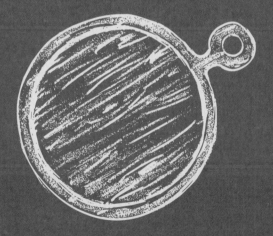

Vegetable Stock

YIELD: 6 CUPS | **ACTIVE TIME:** 20 MINUTES | **TOTAL TIME:** 3 HOURS

2 TABLESPOONS EXTRA-VIRGIN OLIVE OIL

2 LARGE LEEKS, TRIMMED AND RINSED WELL

2 LARGE CARROTS, PEELED AND SLICED

2 CELERY STALKS, SLICED

2 LARGE YELLOW ONIONS, SLICED

3 GARLIC CLOVES, UNPEELED BUT SMASHED

2 SPRIGS OF FRESH PARSLEY

2 SPRIGS OF FRESH THYME

1 BAY LEAF

8 CUPS WATER

½ TEASPOON BLACK PEPPERCORNS

SALT, TO TASTE

1. Place the olive oil and the vegetables in a large stockpot and cook over low heat until the liquid they release has evaporated. This will allow the flavor of the vegetables to become concentrated.

2. Add the garlic, parsley, thyme, bay leaf, water, peppercorns, and salt. Raise the heat to high and bring to a boil. Reduce the heat so that the stock simmers and cook for 2 hours, while skimming to remove any impurities that float to the surface.

3. Strain through a fine sieve, let the stock cool slightly, and place in the refrigerator, uncovered, to chill. Remove the fat layer and cover the stock. The stock will keep in the refrigerator for 3 to 5 days, and in the freezer for up to 3 months.

Chicken Stock

YIELD: 8 CUPS | **ACTIVE TIME:** 20 MINUTES | **TOTAL TIME:** 6 HOURS

7 LBS. CHICKEN BONES, RINSED

4 CUPS CHOPPED YELLOW ONIONS

2 CUPS CHOPPED CARROTS

2 CUPS CHOPPED CELERY

3 GARLIC CLOVES, CRUSHED

3 SPRIGS OF FRESH THYME

1 TEASPOON BLACK PEPPERCORNS

1 BAY LEAF

1. Place the chicken bones in a stockpot and cover them with cold water. Bring to a simmer over medium-high heat and use a ladle to skim off any impurities that rise to the surface.

2. Add the vegetables, thyme, peppercorns, and bay leaf, reduce the heat to low, and simmer for 5 hours, skimming the stock occasionally to remove any impurities that rise to the surface.

3. Strain the stock, let it cool slightly, and transfer it to the refrigerator. Leave the stock uncovered and let it cool completely. Remove the layer of fat and cover. The stock will keep in the refrigerator for 3 to 5 days, and in the freezer for up to 3 months.

Beef Stock

YIELD: 8 CUPS | **ACTIVE TIME:** 20 MINUTES | **TOTAL TIME:** 6 HOURS

7 LBS. BEEF BONES, RINSED

4 CUPS CHOPPED YELLOW ONIONS

2 CUPS CHOPPED CARROTS

2 CUPS CHOPPED CELERY

3 GARLIC CLOVES, CRUSHED

3 SPRIGS OF FRESH THYME

1 TEASPOON BLACK PEPPERCORNS

1 BAY LEAF

1. Place the beef bones in a stockpot and cover them with cold water. Bring to a simmer over medium-high heat and use a ladle to skim off any impurities that rise to the surface.

2. Add the vegetables, thyme, peppercorns, and bay leaf, reduce the heat to low, and simmer for 5 hours, occasionally skimming the stock to remove any impurities that rise to the surface.

3. Strain the stock, let it cool slightly, and transfer it to the refrigerator. Leave the stock uncovered and let it cool completely. Remove the layer of fat and cover. The stock will keep in the refrigerator for 3 to 5 days, and in the freezer for up to 3 months.

Dashi Stock

YIELD: 6 CUPS | **ACTIVE TIME:** 10 MINUTES | **TOTAL TIME:** 40 MINUTES

8 CUPS COLD WATER

2 OZ. KOMBU

1 CUP BONITO FLAKES

1. Place the water and the kombu in a medium saucepan. Soak the kombu for 20 minutes, remove it, and score it gently with a knife.

2. Return the kombu to the saucepan and bring to a boil. Remove the kombu as soon as the water boils, so that the stock doesn't become bitter.

3. Add the bonito flakes to the water and return it to a boil. Turn off the heat and let the mixture stand.

4. Strain the stock through a fine sieve. Use immediately or let it cool before using or storing.

Coconut Dressing

YIELD: 3 CUPS | **ACTIVE TIME:** 15 MINUTES | **TOTAL TIME:** 45 MINUTES

1 (14 OZ.) CAN OF COCONUT MILK

3½ OZ. GRATED FRESH GINGER

14 TABLESPOONS FRESH LEMON JUICE

1½ TEASPOONS KOSHER SALT

5 TEASPOONS CASTER (SUPERFINE) SUGAR

1½ CUPS CHOPPED FRESH CILANTRO

1½ TABLESPOONS CRACKED CORIANDER SEEDS

1. Place all of the ingredients in a mixing bowl, stir to combine, and chill in the refrigerator for 30 minutes.

2. Place the mixture in a blender and puree until emulsified, making sure the mixture does not get hot at all.

3. Strain the dressing through a fine-mesh sieve and use as desired.

Cream Cheese Piecrust

YIELD: 9-INCH PIECRUST | **ACTIVE TIME:** 20 MINUTES | **TOTAL TIME:** 45 MINUTES

1 TABLESPOON WATER, CHILLED

1 TEASPOON APPLE CIDER VINEGAR, CHILLED

1½ CUPS ALL-PURPOSE FLOUR

½ TEASPOON FINE SEA SALT

½ CUP UNSALTED BUTTER, CHILLED AND CUT INTO SMALL PIECES, PLUS MORE AS NEEDED

½ CUP CREAM CHEESE, CHILLED AND CUT INTO SMALL PIECES

1. Place the water and vinegar in a small bowl and stir to combine. In a separate bowl, combine the flour and salt.

2. Add the butter and cream cheese to the flour mixture and use a pastry cutter to work the mixture until it comes together as a crumbly dough.

3. Add the vinegar mixture to the dough and work the mixture until it holds together as a smooth dough. Cover the dough with plastic wrap and roll it out into a disk. Chill the dough in the refrigerator until it is firm.

4. Place the dough on a flour-dusted work surface and roll it out into a 12-inch circle. Coat a pie plate with butter, lay the dough in the pie plate, and trim away any excess, leaving a 1-inch overhang. Crimp the edge of the crust and place it in the refrigerator for another 15 minutes before filling and baking.

Passion Fruit Emulsion

YIELD: 1 CUP | **ACTIVE TIME:** 5 MINUTES | **TOTAL TIME:** 5 MINUTES

1 SHALLOT, CHOPPED

1 CUP PASSION FRUIT PUREE

1 CUP CANOLA OIL

1. Place the shallot and passion fruit puree in a blender and puree on medium until smooth.

2. Reduce the speed to low and slowly drizzle in the canola oil until it has emulsified.

Picadillo de Res

YIELD: 4 SERVINGS | **ACTIVE TIME:** 10 MINUTES | **TOTAL TIME:** 35 MINUTES

2 TABLESPOONS EXTRA-VIRGIN OLIVE OIL

2 LBS. GROUND BEEF

SALT, TO TASTE

1 TEASPOON CUMIN

1½ TEASPOONS DRIED MEXICAN OREGANO

1½ TEASPOONS CHILI POWDER

1 TABLESPOON TOMATO PASTE

1 ONION, FINELY DICED

2 SERRANO CHILE PEPPERS, STEMS AND SEEDS REMOVED, CHOPPED

2 BAY LEAVES

1 LB. YUKON GOLD POTATOES, PEELED AND DICED

½ LB. CARROTS, PEELED AND FINELY DICED

3 LARGE TOMATOES, FINELY DICED

½ CUP PEAS (OPTIONAL)

1. Place the olive oil in a large skillet and warm it over medium heat. Add the ground beef, season it with salt, and cook, breaking the meat up with a wooden spoon, until browned, about 6 minutes.

2. Stir in the cumin, oregano, and chili powder, cook for 1 minute, and then stir in the tomato paste, onion, and peppers. Cook, stirring occasionally, until the onion is tender, about 5 minutes.

3. Add the bay leaves, potatoes, carrots, and tomatoes and cook until the potatoes are tender and the flavors have developed to your liking, about 20 minutes. If using peas in the dish, add them during the last 5 minutes of cooking the potatoes.

4. Use as a filling for the Chiles en Nogada on page 202, empanadas, or enjoy on its own.

Savory Tart Shells

YIELD: 2 TART SHELLS | **ACTIVE TIME:** 30 MINUTES | **TOTAL TIME:** 2 HOURS

2½ CUPS ALL-PURPOSE FLOUR, PLUS MORE AS NEEDED

⅓ CUP EXTRA-VIRGIN OLIVE OIL

½ CUP ICE WATER

1 TEASPOON FINE SEA SALT

1. Place all of the ingredients in a bowl and work the mixture until it comes together as a dough. Divide the dough into two pieces, flatten them into disks, wrap them in plastic, and refrigerate for 1 hour.

2. Preheat the oven to 400°F. Coat two 9-inch pie plates with nonstick cooking spray. Place the pieces of dough on a flour-dusted work surface and roll them out into ¼-inch-thick rounds. Lay the crusts in the pie plates, trim away any excess, and prick the bottoms of the crusts with a fork. Cover the crusts with aluminum foil, fill the foil with uncooked rice, dried beans, or pie weights, and place them in the oven. Bake the crusts until they are firm and golden brown, about 20 minutes.

3. Remove the tart shells from the oven, remove the foil and weights, and fill the tart shells as desired.

Note: If not using right away, store in the refrigerator for up to 1 week or in the freezer for up to 6 months.

Basic Dumpling Wrappers

YIELD: 32 WRAPPERS | **ACTIVE TIME:** 1 HOUR | **TOTAL TIME:** 3 HOURS

2 CUPS ALL-PURPOSE FLOUR, PLUS MORE FOR DUSTING

¾ CUP JUST-BOILED WATER, PLUS MORE AS NEEDED

1. Place the flour in the work bowl of a stand mixer fitted with the paddle attachment. With the mixer running on low speed, add the water in a steady stream and beat the mixture until it just comes together as a dough, adding more water in 1-teaspoon increments if needed.

2. Place the dough on a flour-dusted work surface and knead it until it is smooth and elastic, about 5 minutes. Cover the dough tightly with plastic wrap and let it rest at room temperature for 2 hours.

3. Place the dough on a flour-dusted work surface and cut it in half. Cover one half with plastic wrap and roll the other into a 1-inch-thick log. Cut the log into 16 pieces. Dust each piece with flour, cover them with plastic wrap, and press down gently so that the rounds are about ¼ inch thick. Repeat with the other piece of dough.

4. You want to have your chosen filling prepared before starting on this step, as the dough sticks together better when it has not been exposed to the air for too long. Cut a resealable freezer bag at the seams so that you have two squares of plastic. Place the disks between the two squares of plastic and press down with a rolling pin until they are ⅛ inch thick. Transfer the wrappers to a flour-dusted work surface and fill them as desired or freeze, in layers that are separated by parchment paper, for up to 1 month.

Wonton Wrappers

YIELD: 48 WRAPPERS | **ACTIVE TIME:** 1 HOUR | **TOTAL TIME:** 3 HOURS

¼ CUP WATER, PLUS MORE AS NEEDED

1 LARGE EGG

¾ TEASPOON KOSHER SALT

1½ CUPS ALL-PURPOSE FLOUR, PLUS MORE AS NEEDED

CORNSTARCH, AS NEEDED

1. Place the water, egg, and salt in a measuring cup and whisk to combine. Place the flour in the work bowl of a stand mixer fitted with the paddle attachment. With the mixer running on low speed, add the egg mixture in a steady stream and beat until the mixture just comes together, adding water or flour in ½-teaspoon increments if the dough is too dry or too wet, respectively.

2. Fit the mixer with the dough hook and knead the dough at medium speed until it is soft, smooth, and springs back quickly when poked with a finger, about 10 minutes. Cover the bowl tightly with plastic wrap and let it rest for 2 hours.

3. Cut the dough into three pieces. Working with one piece at a time (cover the others tightly with plastic wrap), shape the dough into a ball. Place the dough on a flour-dusted work surface and roll it out into a rectangle that is about ½ inch thick. Feed the dough through a pasta maker, adjusting the setting to reduce the thickness with each pass, until the dough is a thin sheet, thin enough that you can see your hand through it (about 1/16 inch thick). Place the sheets on a parchment-lined baking sheet.

4. Dust a work surface with cornstarch and cut the sheets into as many 4-inch squares or 3-inch rounds as possible. Pile the cut wrappers on top of each other and fill as desired or cover in plastic wrap and store in the refrigerator for up to 3 days.

Baozi Wrappers

YIELD: 16 WRAPPERS | **ACTIVE TIME:** 45 MINUTES | **TOTAL TIME:** 1 HOUR AND 30 MINUTES

1 TABLESPOON ACTIVE DRY YEAST

1½ CUPS WATER, AT ROOM TEMPERATURE

¼ CUP CANOLA OIL, PLUS MORE AS NEEDED

¼ CUP PLUS 1 TEASPOON SUGAR

½ TEASPOON KOSHER SALT

4 TEASPOONS BAKING POWDER

2 CUPS ALL-PURPOSE FLOUR, PLUS MORE AS NEEDED

2 CUPS BREAD FLOUR

1. Place the yeast, water, and canola oil in a small bowl, gently stir, and let the mixture sit until it is foamy, about 10 minutes.

2. Place the sugar, salt, baking powder, and flours in a food processor and pulse for 15 seconds to combine. With the food processor running on low speed, add the yeast mixture and work the mixture until it comes together as a slightly tacky dough. Transfer the dough to a flour-dusted work surface and knead until it is smooth, about 3 minutes. Place the dough in a bowl coated with canola oil, cover the bowl with a kitchen towel, and let the dough rise in a naturally warm place until it has doubled in size, about 30 minutes.

3. Place the dough on a flour-dusted work surface, cut it in half, and roll each piece into a log. Cut each log into eight pieces. Roll each piece into a 4-inch circle and fill as desired. Cover the unrolled pieces of dough with a kitchen towel so that they do not dry out. To cook the filled baozi, follow the instructions on page 236.

Togarashi

YIELD: ¾ CUP | **ACTIVE TIME:** 5 MINUTES | **TOTAL TIME:** 2 MINUTES

¼ CUP CAYENNE PEPPER

2 TABLESPOONS GROUND DRIED ORANGE PEEL

2 TABLESPOONS SESAME SEEDS

2 TEASPOONS HEMP SEEDS

2 TEASPOONS GROUND SANSHO PEPPERCORNS

2 TEASPOONS MINCED NORI

1 TEASPOON GROUND GINGER

1. Place all of the ingredients in a mixing bowl and stir until well combined. Use immediately or store in an airtight container.

Balsamic Glaze

YIELD: ½ CUP | **ACTIVE TIME:** 10 MINUTES | **TOTAL TIME:** 25 MINUTES

1 CUP BALSAMIC VINEGAR

¼ CUP BROWN SUGAR

1. Place the vinegar and sugar in a small saucepan and bring the mixture to a boil.

2. Reduce the heat to medium-low and simmer for 8 to 10 minutes, stirring frequently, until the mixture has thickened.

3. Remove the pan from heat and let the glaze cool for 15 minutes before using.

Perfect Piecrusts

YIELD: 2 (9-INCH) PIECRUSTS | **ACTIVE TIME:** 15 MINUTES | **TOTAL TIME:** 2 HOURS AND 15 MINUTES

1 CUP UNSALTED BUTTER, CUBED

2½ CUPS ALL-PURPOSE FLOUR, PLUS MORE AS NEEDED

½ TEASPOON KOSHER SALT

4 TEASPOONS SUGAR

½ CUP ICE WATER

1. Transfer the butter to a small bowl and place it in the freezer.

2. Place the flour, salt, and sugar in a food processor and pulse a few times until combined.

3. Add the chilled butter and pulse until the mixture is crumbly, consisting of pea-sized clumps.

4. Add the water and pulse until the mixture comes together as a dough.

5. Place the dough on a flour-dusted work surface and fold it over itself until it is a ball. Divide the dough in two and flatten each piece into a 1-inch-thick disk. Cover each piece completely with plastic wrap and place the dough in the refrigerator for at least 2 hours before rolling it out to fit your pie plate.

Butterfluff Filling

YIELD: 4 CUPS | **ACTIVE TIME:** 10 MINUTES | **TOTAL TIME:** 10 MINUTES

1 CUP MARSHMALLOW CREME

10 OZ. UNSALTED BUTTER, SOFTENED

11 OZ. CONFECTIONERS' SUGAR

1½ TEASPOONS PURE VANILLA EXTRACT

¾ TEASPOON KOSHER SALT

1. In the work bowl of a stand mixer fitted with the paddle attachment, cream the marshmallow creme and butter on medium speed until the mixture is light and fluffy, about 5 minutes.

2. Add the confectioners' sugar, vanilla, and salt, reduce the speed to low, and beat for 2 minutes. Use immediately, or store in the refrigerator for up to 1 month.

Chocolate Ganache

YIELD: 1½ CUPS | **ACTIVE TIME:** 10 MINUTES | **TOTAL TIME:** 15 MINUTES

½ LB. CHOCOLATE, CHOPPED

1 CUP HEAVY CREAM

1. Place the chocolate in a heatproof mixing bowl and set it aside.

2. Place the heavy cream in a small saucepan and bring it to a simmer over medium heat.

3. Pour the cream over the chocolate and let the mixture rest for 1 minute.

4. Gently whisk the mixture until thoroughly combined. Use immediately if you are drizzling it over a dessert or serving with fruit. Let the ganache cool for 2 hours if you are piping it onto a dessert. The ganache will keep in the refrigerator for up to 5 days.

Almond Syrup

YIELD: ½ CUP | **ACTIVE TIME:** 10 MINUTES | **TOTAL TIME:** 1 HOUR

½ CUP WATER

½ CUP SUGAR

¼ TEASPOON ALMOND EXTRACT

1. Place the water and sugar in a small saucepan and bring to a boil over medium heat, stirring to dissolve the sugar.

2. Remove the saucepan from heat, stir in the almond extract, and let the syrup cool completely before using.

Pastry Cream

YIELD: 2½ CUPS | **ACTIVE TIME:** 20 MINUTES | **TOTAL TIME:** 2 HOURS AND 30 MINUTES

½ CUP SUGAR

6 EGG YOLKS

3 TABLESPOONS CORNSTARCH

2 CUPS MILK

¼ TEASPOON KOSHER SALT

1½ TEASPOONS PURE VANILLA EXTRACT

4 TABLESPOONS UNSALTED BUTTER, SOFTENED

1. Place the sugar, egg yolks, and cornstarch in a small bowl and whisk until the mixture is a pale yellow.

2. Place the milk in a medium saucepan and bring it to a boil over medium heat. Remove the pan from heat and gradually add the milk to the egg yolk mixture while whisking continually.

3. Place the tempered egg yolks in the saucepan and warm them over medium-low heat until they thicken and begin to bubble, whisking continually. Remove the pan from heat and whisk in the salt, vanilla, and butter.

4. Strain the custard through a fine mesh strainer into a small bowl.

5. Place plastic wrap directly on the custard to prevent a skin from forming.

6. Place the custard in the refrigerator and chill for at least 2 hours before using. The custard will keep in the refrigerator for up to 5 days.

Frangipane

YIELD: 4 CUPS | **ACTIVE TIME:** 10 MINUTES | **TOTAL TIME:** 10 MINUTES

¾ LB. ALMOND PASTE

½ CUP UNSALTED BUTTER, SOFTENED

¼ TEASPOON KOSHER SALT

4 EGGS

⅓ CUP ALL-PURPOSE FLOUR

1. In the work bowl of a stand mixer fitted with the paddle attachment, cream the almond paste, butter, and salt on medium speed until the mixture is light and fluffy, about 5 minutes.

2. Reduce the speed to low, add the eggs one at a time, and beat until incorporated, scraping the work bowl as needed. Add the flour and beat until incorporated. Use immediately or store in the refrigerator for up to 2 weeks.

Poolish for Croissants

YIELD: 4 CUPS | **ACTIVE TIME:** 10 MINUTES | **TOTAL TIME:** 10 MINUTES

1¾ CUPS ALL-PURPOSE FLOUR

1 TEASPOON INSTANT YEAST

1⅓ CUPS LUKEWARM WATER (90°F)

¾ CUP WHOLE WHEAT FLOUR

1. Place the all-purpose flour, ½ teaspoon of the yeast, and 1 cup of the water in a mixing bowl, stir to combine, and transfer the mixture to the refrigerator for 8 hours.

2. Place the whole wheat flour, remaining yeast, and remaining water in a separate bowl and stir to combine. Let stand at room temperature for 1 hour and then place in the refrigerator for 8 hours.

3. Combine the two mixtures and use the poolish as desired.

METRIC CONVERSION CHART

U.S. Measurement	Approximate Metric Liquid Measurement	Approximate Metric Dry Measurement
1 teaspoon	5 ml	—
1 tablespoon or ½ ounce	15 ml	14 g
1 ounce or ⅛ cup	30 ml	29 g
¼ cup or 2 ounces	60 ml	57 g
⅓ cup	80 ml	—
½ cup or 4 ounces	120 ml	113 g
⅔ cup	160 ml	—
¾ cup or 6 ounces	180 ml	—
1 cup or 8 ounces or ½ pint	240 ml	227 g
1½ cups or 12 ounces	350 ml	—
2 cups or 1 pint or 16 ounces	475 ml	454 g
3 cups or 1½ pints	700 ml	—
4 cups or 2 pints or 1 quart	950 ml	—

INDEX

About Cider Mill Press Book Publishers

Good ideas ripen with time. From seed to harvest, Cider Mill Press brings fine reading, information, and entertainment together between the covers of its creatively crafted books. Our Cider Mill bears fruit twice a year, publishing a new crop of titles each spring and fall.

"Where Good Books Are Ready for Press"

501 Nelson Place

Nashville, Tennessee 37214

cidermillpress.com